Fintech and Green Investment

Transforming Challenges into Opportunities

Transformations in Banking, Finance and Regulation

Print ISSN: 2752-5821
Online ISSN: 2752-583X

Presently, the banking and finance sectors evolve within a globalized and highly uncertain environment. Each business and financial decision requires careful consideration of country-specific and international factors due to high levels of shock transmission and volatility spillovers. Furthermore, it would be remiss to omit the COVID-19 health crisis, which caused harmful effects to all areas of the real economy and made profound changes in the way our firms, economies, and markets used to function.

Many other already well-known aspects, including the repercussions of quantitative easing policies, disruptive technologies in finance (e.g., FinTech, Big Data, Data Analytics, Artificial Intelligence, and Blockchains), as well as innovative financing instruments for startups (e.g., ICOs and crowdfunding) are currently revolutionizing banking and finance and posing numerous challenges to regulatory bodies and policymakers. Climate change emergencies also put pressure on governments and firms worldwide to improve policy on governance, corporate social responsibility, and sustainability practices.

This book series "Transformations in Banking, Finance and Regulation" attempts to address these issues by focusing on transformative perspectives in banking and finance. Accordingly, it provides evidence-based guidance, recommendations, and pathways to assist businesses and policy decision-makers through an interdisciplinary and in-depth understanding of ongoing changes in the behavior of economic agents.

Published

Vol. 14 *Fintech and Green Investment: Transforming Challenges into Opportunities*
edited by Cuong Nguyen, Khanh Hoang and Christopher Gan

Vol. 13 *Handbook of Banking and Finance in the MENA Region*
edited by Khaled Hussainey and Tamanna Dalwai

Vol. 12 *Green Finance and Sustainable Development Goals*
edited by Sabri Boubaker and Thai-Ha Le

Vol. 11 *Handbook of Environmental and Green Finance: Toward a Sustainable Future*
edited by Sabri Boubaker and Thai-Ha Le

For the complete list of volumes in this series, please visit
www.worldscientific.com/series/tbfr

Transformations in Banking, Finance and Regulation
Volume 14

Fintech and Green Investment

Transforming Challenges into Opportunities

Edited by

Cuong Nguyen
Lincoln University, New Zealand

Khanh Hoang
Lincoln University, New Zealand

Christopher Gan
Lincoln University, New Zealand

World Scientific

NEW JERSEY • LONDON • SINGAPORE • BEIJING • SHANGHAI • HONG KONG • TAIPEI • CHENNAI • TOKYO

Published by

World Scientific Publishing Europe Ltd.

57 Shelton Street, Covent Garden, London WC2H 9HE

Head office: 5 Toh Tuck Link, Singapore 596224

USA office: 27 Warren Street, Suite 401-402, Hackensack, NJ 07601

Library of Congress Cataloging-in-Publication Data

Names: Nguyen, Cuong (College teacher), editor. | Hoang, Khanh (College teacher), editor. | Gan, Christopher, editor.

Title: Fintech and green investment : transforming challenges into opportunities / Cuong Nguyen, Lincoln University, New Zealand, Khanh Hoang, Lincoln University, New Zealand, Christopher Gan, Lincoln University, New Zealand.

Description: New Jersey : World Scientific, [2024] | Series: Transformations in banking, finance and regulation, 2752-5821 ; volume 14 | Includes bibliographical references and index.

Identifiers: LCCN 2023028688 | ISBN 9781800614598 (hardcover) | ISBN 9781800614604 (ebook) | ISBN 9781800614611 (ebook other)

Subjects: LCSH: Sustainable development. | Finance--Technological innovations. | Clean energy investment.

Classification: LCC HC79.E5 F65 2024 | DDC 338.9/27--dc23/eng/20230727

LC record available at https://lccn.loc.gov/2023028688

British Library Cataloguing-in-Publication Data

A catalogue record for this book is available from the British Library.

For any available supplementary material, please visit
https://www.worldscientific.com/worldscibooks/10.1142/Q0431#t=suppl

Desk Editors: Nimal Koliyat/Shi Ying Koe

Typeset by Stallion Press
Email: enquiries@stallionpress.com

https://doi.org/10.1142/9781800614604_fmatter

Preface

In recent decades, a remarkable shift towards sustainable and green finance has unfolded, spurred by the pressing imperative to confront the complex challenges posed by climate change and environmental degradation. This paradigm shift has been further catalysed by the advent of financial technologies, commonly known as fintech, which has fundamentally reshaped our perception of both sustainable finance and traditional finance. The convergence of sustainability paradigms and technological innovation has created an environment rich with potential and exciting opportunities for green investment inspired by fintech.

Fintech stands at the forefront of transforming the landscape of green investments, offering tremendous potential for positive changes. With its ability to harness technological advancements, fintech holds the key to unlocking greater transparency, traceability, efficiency, and accessibility in the realm of sustainable finance. By leveraging digital solutions, fintech platforms can streamline the investment process, making it easier for individuals and institutions to direct their investments towards environmentally conscious projects. This, in turn, fosters the growth of impact investing, where financial decisions are driven by both financial returns and positive environmental outcomes. Furthermore, fintech introduces innovative financial products specifically designed to cater to the needs of green initiatives, allowing for more tailored and sustainable investment options.

Amidst these promising prospects, challenges emerge that necessitate careful consideration. These challenges range from regulatory complexities and ensuring data accuracy to addressing the risks associated with emerging technologies and maintaining investor confidence. Effectively navigating these challenges is vital to harnessing the full potential of fintech in revolutionising green investments. However, despite the tremendous potential and growing interest in both fintech and green investment, little is known about the intersection of these two domains. As a result, there is a knowledge gap surrounding the specific ways in which fintech can effectively support and accelerate the transition to a more sustainable and environmentally conscious financial ecosystem. In order to fully leverage the transformative power of fintech in driving green investment, it is imperative to delve deeper into this integration, uncovering insights and best practices that can guide stakeholders towards informed decision-making and sustainability. Therefore, our book aims to explore the complex challenges facing the intersection of **fintech and green investment** and provides valuable insights into how to turn these challenges into opportunities. By exploring the evolving landscape of fintech and its potential to drive positive environmental change, our book offers a comprehensive analysis of how the two domains can intersect effectively and contribute to the transition towards a more sustainable future.

This book is a collection of chapters written by experts in the fields of fintech and sustainable finance. The chapters cover a wide range of topics, including the role of fintech in facilitating green investment, the far-fetched impact of digital currencies on the environment, and the potential of blockchain technology to enhance transparency and traceability. The first part of the book introduces the readers to blockchain, fintech, and contemporary green matters. In particular, modern concepts and empirical findings about blockchain, digital currencies, green banking, and green finance are presented in the second part by emphasising the roles of green cryptocurrencies, central bank digital currency, green banking regulation, and gender equality in the current era of financial innovations. The last part of the book closes with case studies representing the intersection of fintech and sustainable finance.

Chapter 1 introduces the intricate relationship between the **food, energy, and water trilemma** and examines the impact of neoliberalism on the transitions from industrial to financial capitalism, highlighting the need for a new institutional framework grounded in fintech and distributed ledger technology to address the problem of trust and promote international cooperation for mitigating climate change and preventing catastrophic consequences for humanity. Chapter 2 comprehensively explores the concept of **sustainability in the blockchain ecosystem**, providing an overview of what already exists in the literature, as this new technology is rapidly gaining interest in different sectors as the global economy is moving towards sustainable development of financial markets and businesses. Considering the dominant uses of this technology for the green economy narrative, this chapter expands our knowledge on the topic of blockchain, which could also allow effective ecological regeneration, facilitating degrowth objectives, socially equitable outcomes, and sustainable investments. Chapter 3 emphasises the importance of accurate **measurement and traceability in food waste minimisation**, highlighting the potential of material flow analysis and blockchain technology for end-to-end traceability, transparent data storage, and collaborative efforts to reduce food loss and waste in the food system while promoting circular economy principles. Chapter 4 investigates **fintech and green digital finance in sustainable development** in China. It shows that green finance should promote high-quality economic development through its positive impact on the ecology, generating economic efficiencies and achieving solid economic structures. It indicates that a cautious and slow approach to changes and transformation will be appropriate in China so as to avoid destabilising the country's economy when progressing towards China's 2060 "carbon-neutral" agenda.

Chapter 5 inaugurates the second part of the book by examining the **environmental impact of blockchains and Bitcoin**, suggesting that while the energy consumption of Bitcoin is significant, its carbon footprint is comparatively smaller than that of the mining sector in the US. However, the chapter records the alarming rate of increase in Bitcoin's energy consumption since 2017 and raises concerns that its carbon footprint may eventually exceed that of all industries in a foreseeable future. Chapter 6 reveals a two-way relationship between **cryptocurrency returns and investor attention**, then suggests the interconnectedness between investor sentiment and the financial performance of cryptocurrencies. Chapter 7 addresses the current trends in the financial sector, focusing on the **emergence of fintech** and the challenges faced by traditional financial systems in meeting societal demands and sustainability criteria. The main takeaway of this chapter is its investigation of the factors driving the rise of decentralised finance and its analysis of whether the measures adopted by the banking system are adequate to adapt to a new model of innovative development characterised by closer stakeholder–company relationships, diverging from the traditional banking–company paradigm. From a green banking regulation perspective, Chapter 8 investigates the **impact of green banking regulation** on cross-border lending using country-level data from 1995 to 2019. It distinguishes between de jure and de facto regulations, with the former capturing explicit sustainability objectives and support for government policies, and the latter reflecting central bank engagement in green activities. Chapter 9 underscores the **pivotal role of technology** in building inclusive, environmentally friendly digital societies post pandemic, with women at the forefront of adopting digital and green financial solutions to advance economic and social goals. Set against the backdrop of escalating economic inequality, Chapter 10 explores the potential of **Central Bank Digital Currencies** in reducing disparities and identifies three legal obstacles that may arise during their implementation.

Chapter 11 provides a discussion of the development and trends of **Digital Youth Banking**. The chapter explores challenges and opportunities from accessibility, practicability, and sustainability perspectives, showcasing exemplary cases from traditional banks, neobanks, and fintech companies. The chapter concludes with recommendations to enhance financial inclusion efforts for young people and society. Chapter 12 explores the intersection between sustainability and digital transformation in business, focusing on the **Energy Efficiency Sector** and the role of Green Investments and Energy Service Companies. It further illustrates how fintech and blockchain innovations are pushing the boundaries of energy efficiency and supporting green investment initiatives. Chapter 13 concludes the book with a case study of the collaboration between a **digital platform**

and Savills to digitise financing solutions in the property industry to offer competitive financing options and promote sustainability through accredited green financing.

Cuong Nguyen, Khanh Hoang, and Christopher Gan
Lincoln University, New Zealand
February 2024

https://doi.org/10.1142/9781800614604_fmatter

About the Editors

Cuong Nguyen is an Associate Professor in Finance and Fintech at Lincoln University, New Zealand, and a recipient of the Australian Leadership Awards. He is also a Research Fellow on "Stochastics with Emphasis on Finance" at the Austrian Academy of Sciences (OAW) and Johann Radon Institute for Computational and Applied Mathematics (RICAM), Austria. He was a Research Fellow on "Risk Theory and Related Topics" at the European Mathematical Society and Institute of Mathematics Polish Academy of Sciences (IMPAN), Poland, in 2008. He is a Certified Practicing Accountant (with CPA Australia) and a Chartered Accountant in Australia and New Zealand (with CA ANZ). His research interests include financial econometrics and financial markets. Dr. Nguyen's work has appeared in the *Journal of International Financial Markets, Institutions, and Money*, *International Journal of Economics and Finance*, *Economic Modelling*, *International Review of Economics and Finance*, *Quality & Quantity: International Journal of Methodology*, *Emerging Market Finance and Trade*, the *Journal of Statistical Theory and Applications*, and *Financial Research Letters*.

Khanh Hoang is a Senior Lecturer in Finance at Lincoln University, New Zealand. He obtained his Ph.D. in Finance from Lincoln University in May 2021. Khanh has been active in research and academia. His research interests lie primarily in corporate finance, climate finance, corporate social responsibility, economic uncertainty, and financial economics. His current research projects aim to investigate how international climate policy influences corporate decision-making. Dr. Hoang has published his research works in prestigious international academic journals, such as *International Review of Economics and Finance*, *Finance Research Letters, Journal of Behavioral and Experimental Finance*, *International Journal of Emerging Markets*, *Applied Economics Letters*, and *Managerial and Decision Economics*. He also served as a Guest Editor of the special issue "A New Era of Financial Risk" for *Research in International Business and Finance* (Elsevier). He has been a member of organising committees at national and international academic conferences in Vietnam. Besides academic experience, he also has industry experience in financial consulting and investment analysis at different institutions in Vietnam.

Christopher Gan is Head of Department, Department of Financial and Business System, Faculty of Agribusiness and Commerce, Lincoln University, Christchurch, New Zealand. He is recognised internationally for research leadership in banking, microfinance, stock markets, and Asian financial economics. His approach is quantitative in nature with a focus on application. He aims to expand existing knowledge and develop recommendations for relevant agencies, government, and businesses. This includes studies of the Asian financial markets, the banking system in China, and rural credit and microfinance in Asia. Professor Gan actively collaborates with academics from other universities (mainly from Asia) and inspires the next generation of scholars through postgraduate supervision. He has an extensive publication record in well-ranked peer-reviewed journals and is regularly cited by other researchers. He serves on the editorial boards of several distinguished international journals and is the Chief Editor of the *Review of Applied Economics*. He has also won several awards for excellence in teaching, including the National Teaching Excellence Award in 2003. Professor Gan is a Minjiang Scholar and Distinguished Professor at the College of Economics and Finance in Fujian Agriculture and Forestry University (awarded by the Education Department of Fujian Province government). He is also an Adjunct Professor, Finance and Economics, at the Faculty of Economics and Business, Universitas Airlangga, Surabaya, Indonesia, and a Visiting Professor of the International Department, Chonnam National University, Gwangju, South Korea.

https://doi.org/10.1142/9781800614604_fmatter

About the Contributors

Adalberto Rangone has a double Ph.D. in Management and Business Administration at the Gabriele d'Annunzio University of Chieti and Pescara, Italy, and in Economics at the National University of Oradea, Romania. Adalberto is an Assistant Professor (tenure track) at the Department of Law at the University of Perugia, Italy, for the classes of Business Administration, Economics and Accounting Processes of Innovation, Administration and Control of the Sustainable Enterprise. Before this position, Adalberto was an Adjunct Professor at the Department of Business Administration at the University of Pavia, Italy, teaching international corporate governance and strategic management. Then, was an Assistant Professor (non-tenure track) at the Department of Management and Business Administration at the Gabriele d'Annunzio University of Chieti and Pescara, Italy (course on corporate finance). In 2019, Adalberto was nominated as an "Innovation Manager" and included in the public register of the Italian Ministry for Economic Development. In 2021, he received the Italian ASN qualification as Associate Professor. Adalberto has specialised in strategic management, performance management, corporate innovation, and governance. These topics have been analysed in his monographs published by prestigious international and national publishers (Springer and Rirea) and in works published in journals indexed on prestigious international databases (Scopus and Web of Science).

Annie Koh is Professor Emeritus of Finance (Practice) at Lee Kong Chian School of Business, Singapore Management University (SMU). She is a renowned conference speaker, panel moderator, and commentator. In addition, Professor Koh is a member of the World Economic Forum Global Future Council on New Agenda for Work, Wages, and Job Creation. She also chairs the Asian Bond Fund 2 supervisory committee for the Monetary Authority of Singapore and is a committee member of Singapore's Customs Advisory Council and HR Transformation Advisory Panel. Professor Koh was appointed as chairperson of Prime US REIT and is currently an independent director of AMTD IDEA Group, Prudential Assurance Company Singapore Pte Ltd, and Yoma Strategic Holdings Ltd. She has been an investment committee member of iGlobe Partners since July 2010. She has also been an advisor to CUBE3 Ventures since October 2021 and Asia Food Sustainability Fund since February 2022. Professor Koh received her Ph.D. in International Finance as a Fulbright scholar from Stern School of Business, New York University, USA, in 1988. In recognition of her contribution to education and the public sector, she was awarded the bronze and silver Singapore Public Administration medal in 2010 and 2016, respectively, and the Adult Education Prism Award in 2017.

Bernadette Andreosso-O'Callaghan is Jean Monnet Professor of Economics at the University of Limerick (Ireland) where she co-founded the first research centre dealing with contemporary Asian studies in Ireland (in 1997). She is also an International Research Fellow at the Fakultät für Wirtschaftswissenschaft, Ruhr Universität Bochum (Germany), and she has taught in several Asian universities, including Seoul National University, Chulalongkorn University (Bangkok), and Tsuda University (Tokyo). She has served as a consultant for the European Commission, the Irish Government, and the International Trade Center in Geneva. She has also been the coordinator of an Erasmus Mundus project with Australia and New Zealand. She has published extensively in the areas of comparative Europe–Asia economic integration, as well as economic growth models and structural change, with a focus on East Asian countries. Her latest publication is *Economic Policy and the COVID-19 Crisis: The Macroeconomic Response in the US, Europe* *and East Asia*, editors: Bernadette Andreosso-O'Callaghan, Woosik Moon, and Wook Sohn (Routledge: London, 2022).

Christian Bux has a Ph.D. in Economics and Management with Doctor Europaeus certification. He is a Research Fellow at the University of Bari Aldo Moro, Department of Economics, Management and Business Law, Italy and has obtained the National Scientific Habilitation for Associate Professor in Commodity Science. His main field of interest is the relationship between natural resources, commodity production and consumption (e.g., agri-food commodities, textile products), and sustainable environmental management systems. He is also interested in environmental accountancy, with reference to empirical and theoretical applications of material flow analysis, material flow cost accounting, and life cycle assessment. He has authored more than 30 papers published in scientific journals and academic volumes, and is a reviewer for international peer-reviewed journals for Elsevier, Springer, Emerald, MDPI, and SAGE. He has been an oral presenter and discussant in several scientific international conferences and has been a member of the organising committee of the XXX National Congress of Commodity Science (AISME2022).

Doan Ngoc Thang received his Ph.D. in Policy Analysis from the National Graduate Institute for Policy Studies, Japan. He is Dean of the Faculty of International Economics, Vietnam Banking Academy. His main research areas are digitalisation, government issues, international economics, macroeconomic analysis, international economics, financial stability, and corporate performance analysis. He is an expert in the fields of finance, green finance, and financial governance issue. He has many publications in the finance and monetary issue journals.

Gang Nathan Dong is Assistant Professor of Practice in Finance at the Carroll School of Management in Boston College. His teaching and research interests include corporate finance, financial intermediation, fintech, cryptocurrency investment, international capital market, and financial management of non-profit and healthcare organisations. Earning his graduate degrees from Rutgers University, Columbia University, Indiana University, and Illinois Institute of Technology, Dr. Dong has previously taught in Columbia

University's MHA and MPH Executive programs and Rutgers Business School's MBA program. Prior to his academic career, he was a certified Financial Risk Manager (FRM) and held a variety of analyst and consulting positions in the finance industry, working at Bank of New York, Bear Stearns, Credit Suisse, Reuters, and Capgemini. Dr. Dong has written over 20 research articles and chapters in business and finance publications including *Review of Corporate Finance Studies*, *Journal of International Business Studies*, *Journal of Corporate Finance*, *Journal of Banking & Finance*, *Journal of Empirical Finance*, and *The Oxford Handbook of IPOs*.

Gao Phoebe (Fei) is Assistant Professor of Accounting at Singapore Institute of Technology. She received a B.Sc. and an M.Phil. in Risk Management Science (with full scholarship) from the Chinese University of Hong Kong and received her Ph.D. in Business (Finance) from Singapore Management University. Phoebe specialises in quantitative analysis, investment and risk management, and derivatives pricing as she has strong research interests and academic training in statistics, risk management, asset pricing, and mathematical modelling. Her research and publications include the topics of loan loss provisions and return predictability (*China Journal of Accounting Research*), the journey of exchange traded funds (*International Finance Review*), and risk dynamics with option term structures (Asia FA 2021 and 14th Annual Risk Management Conference). She received a research grant for MIDFID II and analyst forecast, and served as a reviewer for the *European Financial Management Journal*. Phoebe was appointed as an advisor for derivatives pricing for PKF. She teaches for the CFA program, as well as an artificial intelligence workshop for accountants and finance professionals. Prior to her academic journey, Phoebe worked in the insurance industry and specialised in director and officers' liability insurance.

Ge (Luna) Zhang is currently a Doctor of Juridical Science (J.S.D.) candidate at Washington University in St. Louis School of Law, United States. Her research interests lie in the fields of comparative commercial law, financial regulation, and information privacy law, with particular interests in fintech law, securities regulation, data governance and compliance, and other cutting-edge areas of financial regulation. Before entering the JSD programme, she obtained her Bachelor of Laws (LL.B.) and Bachelor of Administration degrees from China University of Political Science and Law, China, and her Master of Laws (LL.M.) and Master of Legal Studies (M.L.S.) degrees from Washington University in St. Louis School of Law, United States.

Giulia Napolitano is enrolled as a Ph.D. student at the University of Naples Federico II and works with a permanent employment contract as an Administrative Officer at the University of Campania Luigi Vanvitelli, where she deals with the teaching planning of two degree courses. Her research and teaching interests include blockchain, cybersecurity applied to governance, and ethical finance. After graduating cum laude from both her bachelor's and master's degrees, and finishing both a Master of Public Administration (MPA) and a postgraduate course in "Tax Procedural Law", her master's degree thesis was awarded two national prizes: Manlio Resta 2021 (sponsored by Manlio Resta Foundation, Ecosistemi Foundation, and Compraverde Buygreen) and Giovanni Marra 2021 (assigned by the mayor of the city of Milan). She recently delivered two keynote presentations (Leadership and Blockchain Summit, held by the University of South Florida Muma College of Business M3 Center for Hospitality Technology and Innovation) and attended various conferences all over Europe presenting her articles, such as the 12th and 13th editions of the Workshop on Cooperative and Responsible Finance for Development (promoted by Euricse), the 4th Alternative Accounts Europe Conference (promoted by the Birmingham Business School), and the Joint Annual Conference (organised by the British Accounting and Finance Association Corporate Finance and Asset Pricing SIG and the Northern Area Group in 2022).

Giulio Ferrigno is a Senior Assistant Professor at Sant'Anna School of Advanced Studies of Pisa. He has held visiting positions at the University of Cambridge, Tilburg University, and the University of Umea. His main research themes include strategic alliances, big data, and Industry 4.0. His works have been published in *Small Business Economics, Technological Forecasting and Social Change, International Journal of Management Reviews, R&D Management, Technology Analysis & Strategic Management, Review of Managerial Science, European Journal of Innovation Management*, and *International Journal of Entrepreneurial Behavior & Research*. He is an Associate Editor of *Technology Analysis & Strategic Management*.

Ivan Muck is Co-Founder and CEO at ff.next, a fintech design and development agency that has been helping financial services innovators introduce mobile and web applications for banks and fintechs from Singapore through the DACH region to the UK by combining "off-the-shelf" banking modules and unmatched domain expertise to create tailored solutions. Before co-founding his fintech start-up, Ivan had been working as a fintech analyst at a global management consulting firm. As a former CEMS MIM student, he studied in Hungary, Germany, and Austria and gained experience in the fields of education as well as special needs for Gen Z while volunteering at a Hungarian NGO for 5 years. Ivan, together with a team of youth banking experts, has co-founded Strive, which helps parents teach kids financial literacy in a fun and engaging way.

Kevin Ow Yong is Associate Professor of Accounting at Singapore Institute of Technology. He holds a First Class Honours Degree (with University Medal) in Accounting from Nanyang Technological University and received his Ph.D. from Duke University. He has previously worked at Peking University and Singapore Management University as an Assistant Professor, and at Singapore Airlines as a regional accountant and financial analyst. He currently sits on the *IS Chartered Accountant Journal* Editorial Advisory Panel. He is also a member of the UAFRS Advisory Council with Valens Research. He has previously served on the Candidate Programmes Committee with the CFA Society (Singapore) and was on the advisory board with Brahm Centre, a non-profit charity organisation, as their Finance Advisor. His work has been published in numerous accounting research journals including the *Review of Accounting Studies, Contemporary Accounting Research, Journal of Business Finance and Accounting, Journal of Accounting and Public Policy, European Accounting Review, Advances in Accounting*, and *China Journal of Accounting Research.*

Le Thanh Ha received his Ph.D. in Policy Analysis from National Graduate Institute for Policy Studies. He is currently a Lecturer at the Faculty of Economics, National Economics University. His main research areas are digitalisation, government issues, international economics, macroeconomic analysis, international economics, financial stability, and corporate performance analysis. Le Thanh Ha has recently focussed more on digital finance, green finance, environmental economics, energy economics, and international economics. He has many publications in prestigious journals.

Lucía Morales is an Academic Innovator and Active Researcher at Technological University Dublin (Ireland) where she coordinates a group of doctoral students in the fields of Economics and Finance that integrate a broad dimension to the significance of our global economic and financial system. Lucía has taught at several European Universities where she is a visiting scholar and researcher. She is part of the European University of Technology (EUt+) where she collaborates in the development of education and the significance of pedagogy to bring together STEM and the Social Sciences. She has published her work in international journals and as book chapters in the fields of international economics, financial economics, time series, Asian studies, economic and financial integration, data analytics, and education. She is passionate about education and its role to promote economic development, social integration, and inclusion.

Nigel Bassett-Jones is a currently a Senior Lecturer at Oxford Brookes University. His research interests lie at the intersection of human resource management, innovation, and systems theory. He is the author of a book on human resource management from a systems perspective, several book chapters, and various journal articles and conference contributions. He has worked as a consultant specialising in organisation and management development, serving both public and private sector organisations. He has taught on MA, MBA, and M.Sc. programmes in various institutions in the UK and has contributed as a visiting lecturer on MBA programmes in Finland, France, and South Africa.

Nimisha Tailor is a competition and regulation specialist with international experience. She is the founder of E-nomics, a boutique economics consultancy, helping organisations compete and innovate in an inclusive and sustainable manner. Her research interests include digital economy, digital finance, and digital trade, and she has advised large tech companies, central banks, think tanks, and international organisations (The World Bank, OECD) in the Asia-Pacific, United States, and Latin America. Previously, she was Deputy Director at the Competition and Consumer Commission of

Singapore and has worked at competition authorities in United Kingdom, New Zealand, and Australia (secondment). Nimisha frequently writes and presents to academics, industry associations, and government agencies. She is the author of "Competition in the New ASEAN Economy", and is an online guest lecturer for a New York University marketing class (Prague campus). Nimisha is a mentor on global and university mentoring programmes and is passionate about supporting young female professionals. Nimisha served in the UK Government Economic Service and has an M.Sc. degree in Economics from the London School of Economics and Political Science.

Ricky Celenta is a Ph.D. student in Big Data Management at the University of Salerno. His research and teaching interests include entrepreneurship and innovation management. He is a member of LisaLab, the Research Centre on Innovative Entrepreneurship and Academic Spin-Off, at the University of Salerno. He was a visiting Ph.D. student at Uppsala University (Sweden).

Ruilin Zhu is Lecturer (Assistant Professor) in Information Systems and Director of M.Sc. in Management at Lancaster University Management School. His research focuses on digital innovation and digital transformation and their implications on industry and societal development. Specifically, he leverages the traditional technical view by integrating behavioural, economic, and policy perspectives in order to understand these digital phenomena, such as fintech, insurtech, smart tourism, and mobile healthcare. His academic work builds on previous expertise gained from working for leading financial and banking institutions and international organisations and being a visiting scholar at a number of prominent academic institutions in the UK, the USA, and Australia. He is a Fellow of the Higher Education Academy.

Sarmad Ali is currently a Postdoctoral Researcher at Bocconi University in Milan. He received his Ph.D. in Accounting, Management, and Business Economics (AMBE) from Gabriele d'Annunzio University of Chieti and Pescara in Italy. He was recently a Visiting Researcher at Complutense University of Madrid in Spain. His research interests span interdisciplinary topics such as capital structure, debt financing, private equity, sustainable finance, fintech, strategic management, and corporate governance. His publications include articles in international and national peer-reviewed academic journals such as the *Journal of Risk and Financial Management, Managerial Finance*, and *Economia Aziendale Online*. Prior to joining his Ph.D. programme, he earned his Master of Business Administration degree with a specialisation in Corporate Finance and a Bachelor of Commerce with "Distinction". He also has three years of professional experience in the areas of financial planning, budgeting, and corporate taxation.

Smita Paul is currently a research consultant and has held previous academic posts in Management and International Business. She holds a Ph.D. from the University of Auckland in International Business. As an organisational sociologist, her research interests include the intersection of digital innovation and vulnerable groups, and methodological perspectives for examining strategic organisational relationships. Her work has received awards such as the AIB 2018 Best Research Methods Paper and has been published in *The SAGE Handbook of Contemporary Cross-Cultural Management* and *Advances in International Management*. She has chaired and delivered a number of streams/presentations at highly ranked conferences in International Business and is a repeat invited reviewer for ECIS and PACIS.

Valentina Cucino is an Assistant Professor of Innovation Management at Scuola Superiore Sant'Anna, Pisa. She received her Ph.D. in Management Innovation, Sustainability, and Healthcare from Scuola Superiore Sant'Anna, Pisa. She has published in *Technological Forecasting and Social Change, R&D Management, Total Quality Management, Journal of Knowledge Management, European Journal of Innovation Management*, and *Studies in Higher Education*. Her research interest deals with technology transfer process, innovation management, and hybrid organisations.

Vera Amicarelli has a Ph.D. in Commodity Science and is Associate Professor (Full Professor, national qualifications) at the University of Bari Aldo Moro, Italy. She teaches industrial ecology, quality environment and sustainability, and resource and waste management in bachelor and master's degree courses. She is the author of more than 80 papers published in scientific journals and academic volumes. Her current research interests focus on material flow analysis, environmental indicators such as water and carbon footprint, food and textile waste minimisation, and circular economy. Her main academic activities are related to the Erasmus+ exchange programme. She is a member of the Ph.D. Professor Committee and advisor of Ph.D. projects. She is also a member of the Italian Commodity Science Academy (AISME), the IGWT (International Society of Commodity Science and Technology), and the Italian Circular Economy Stakeholders Platform (ICESP). She is in the CREA (Council for Agricultural Research and Analysis of the Agricultural Economy) expert register. She is a reviewer for several international scientific journals and a member of international research groups.

Zeliha Can Ergün is an Assistant Professor at the Aydın Adnan Menderes University, Faculty of Business, Turkey. She received her Ph.D. in Business Administration with a specialisation in Finance from Dokuz Eylul University, Turkey. Her master's thesis and Ph.D. dissertation were on the topics of herd behaviour and investor sentiment, respectively. Her areas of research expertise are behavioural finance, international finance, and financial markets. She is the author of a book on investor sentiment and has written book chapters about the effects of financial innovation on financial markets, the effect of herd behaviour during financial crisis periods, and the estimation of carbon dioxide emissions with macroeconomic variables using machine learning techniques. She has academic publications in numerous highly qualified international journals and has made presentations at several international conferences.

https://doi.org/10.1142/9781800614604_fmatter

Acknowledgements

Many thanks to Tu Nguyen, HR Analyst, Office of Human Resources, United Nations Development Programme, New York, for her excellent assistance during the initial preparation of this book.

https://doi.org/10.1142/9781800614604_fmatter

Contents

https://doi.org/10.1142/9781800614604_0001

Chapter 1

Can Fintech Enable the World to Avoid the Tragedy of the Commons?

Nigel Bassett-Jones
Oxford Brookes University, Oxford, England
nbassett-jones@brookes.ac.uk

This chapter begins by addressing the food, energy, and water trilemma. A critique of the impact of neoliberalism that traces the transition from industrial to financial capitalism follows. The trade-off arising from improvements in living standards and environmental impact is then explored. In a context where socioeconomic and cultural differences result in conflicting views of what is virtuous, there is a problem of trust. The central proposition is that a new frame grounded in New Institutional Economics (NIE) is required. Fintech and distributed ledger technology (DLT) offer a unique way of building the essential institutional infrastructure required to overcome the problem of trust. Examples showing how fintech can address climate change follow. Whilst these initiatives are to be applauded, new international institutional infrastructure is required to enable fintech to realise its potential. Examples of future possibilities are presented. The chapter concludes by making the case for a new paradigm that prioritises international cooperation because unrestrained competition will lead to rising temperatures, mass migrations, and the collapse of civilisation as we know it.

Keywords: Fintech; system; new institutional economics; climate change; commons; financialisation; distributed ledger technology; neoliberalism; trilemma; securitisation; blockchain

1. Introduction

The tragedy of the commons as expounded by Hardin (1968) is an ancient economic problem that pits the interests of the individual against the general good. In its original formulation, the problem arose in contexts where nature's bounty was freely available to all. The question posed was the following: "What happens to land held in common if shepherds graze sheep freely?" The answer is that it results in overgrazing because there is no incentive for individuals to plant new seed. The consequence is underinvestment. There is excess demand and no new supply. Anthropologists suggest this was the problem that resulted in the demise of the society on Easter Island. Today, commons take different forms. Obvious examples include the rainforests of the Amazon and Borneo, the ocean fisheries that sit outside national territorial waters, and glaciers that encase millions of tons of freshwater that once melted feed the great rivers of the world. Less obvious are knowledge commons that take the form of human artefacts such as open-source software.

The most significant example of competition to create and preserve a knowledge common was that which emerged between Craig Venter's Celera Genomics Corporation and global public sector effort to sequence the human genome. Venter's ambition to patent human genes would have enabled him to appropriate the human genome, thereby making it more costly and challenging for medical research to advance. Whilst the competition between the public and private sectors accelerated the rate of discovery, it is fortunate that the human genome was consigned to a knowledge common.

Since industrialisation, it is true to say that humankind has to a considerable extent imposed its will on the environment. The result has been economic and population growth, accompanied by reductions in hunger and poverty, and a general improvement in human well-being. The price has been an increasing frequency of drought, extreme weather events, coastal erosion, and environmental degradation. The world is, therefore, becoming more chaotic and unstable. This observation not only applies to natural systems but also applies to human activity systems because of the rate of technological advance and the fact that human activity systems and natural systems interact. Today, we face a trilemma. Competition between the requirements for food, water, and energy is intensifying and whilst it would be wrong to assert that these resources have always been available in abundance, they have not, until recently, been recognised as being in head-to-head competition. In the future, this threat will become increasingly intense.

During the next 200 years, it is the natural environment that will shape the pattern of human existence. If human survival and prosperity are to be assured, then an understanding of systems and systemic interactions that impact decision-making will be an essential precondition, if we are to avoid the tragedy of the commons. It is this issue and the role that fintech can play that provide the focus for the present chapter.

Scholars like Brummer and Yadav (2018) and Odinet (2020) opined that fintech is a disruptive phenomenon that disintermediates because of the way in which it uses qualitatively different forms of data and self-learning operational systems that change the way financial transactions are conducted. In the context of this chapter, the term fintech is applied more broadly to also include products and services that rely upon distributed ledger technologies (blockchains) that culminate in financial and other forms of transaction that in international contexts may include countertrading.

People are fundamentally cooperative. The human predisposition to create systems, and to function within the boundaries defined by the systems they have created, demands cooperation. Systems are themselves predicated on a set of assumptions about what is virtuous and valuable. Once established, they pursue purposes dictated by their founding logic. They shape and can also undermine the institutions of governance created for their control, especially in contexts where societal agendas are redefining what is virtuous and valuable. Neoliberal capitalism is such a system. It is predicated on the furtherance of the short-term interest of the individual, the maximisation of profit, and the accumulation of capital. It is buttressed by the tradition of positive and normative economics that functions tautologically within the neoliberal frame. Its legacy persists in a world in which the long-term dynamic of climate change is creating a positive feedback loop with the potential to lead human society to enact the tragedy of the commons. If the tragedy is to be averted, what is required is a change in thinking in favour of New Institutional Economics (NIE). NIE emphasises the importance of effective governance and regulatory systems and the role of transaction cost economics.

Whilst distributed ledger technology (DLT) overcomes the problems associated with trust and creates vital opportunities to establish new patterns of institutional cooperation across international boundaries, such cooperation will require new regulatory frameworks that must operate in a multipolar world where differences in perception of what is virtuous and valuable create major impediments to both trust and understanding.

For those readers that may not be conversant with systems theory, the context is set by defining what a system is and how systems interact. A review of the literature on the systemic relationship between climate change, human activity systems, the emergent tensions between water, food, and energy, and the financialisation of resource inputs follows. A polemic is presented that argues that the neoliberal rules-based system that evolved after the ending of the Bretton Woods agreement, resulted in the emergence of a dominant socioeconomic cultural paradigm that has shaped the world order. This paradigm is embedded in Hobbesian assumptions about human nature that drive both commercial activity and international relations. Fintech with its decentralised ledger technology helps to address the problem of trust. In so doing, it presents the potential for the evolution of a new paradigm that can serve to build bridges between the four socioeconomic systems that shape the modern world. To succeed, however, new governance structures that facilitate the trade and exchange of carbon, energy, food, and water must be created as a matter of urgency. Fintech offers significant opportunities to address the challenges posed. The chapter concludes with an argument that to realise the possibilities that fintech offers, new definitions of virtue and value must be created within the frame of NIE from which the four dominant socioeconomic paradigms can draw.

1.1. *What is a system?*

A system is an arbitrary construct obtained by imposing a boundary that differentiates the system from that which surrounds it. A system can either be closed or open. A closed system can draw energy from the supra system of which it is a part but cannot exchange matter. An example would be a waterborne central heating system. An open system can exchange both matter and energy with the surrounding supra system from which it extracts resources, and into which it excretes two types of output, product and waste. Both natural and human activity systems are open. They are, therefore, capable of interaction. The process of interaction with other systems within the supra system results in the generation of positive and negative feedback loops. Positive feedback has an amplifying effect that, if not contained, will result in the system's self-destruction. Negative feedback has a dampening effect. It brings the system back under control. Open systems, therefore, constantly strive to achieve homeostasis with their external environment which is often characterised by perturbation. To do this, an open system must be endowed with a sufficient requisite variety of responses to meet the complexity presented by the dynamics of the external environment. Feedback loops facilitate this process of adjustment. The pattern of constant adjustment reflects the law of requisite variety or "Ashby's law" (after Ross Ashby, the British cybernetician). A system that lacks sufficient requisite variety will become overwhelmed and will collapse.

1.2. *The systemic relationship between climate change and human activity systems*

Historically, human activity systems, whether they be government, public, private, or not-for-profit entities, evolve in contexts where climate is conducive to food production and human settlement. In addition to the supply of food, settlements require both water and energy. Changes in climate can put these resources under stress. When environmental change overwhelms the requisite variety with which a human community is endowed, it results in migration.

2. The Climate Change Discourse

2.1. *Climate change advocacy and the rise of the climate change counter movement*

Controversy around global warming began when an engineer by the name of Guy Callendar published a paper asserting that increased atmospheric CO_2 from the combustion of fossil fuels was causing global warming in 1938 (Callendar, 1938). Callendar's thesis was dismissed. Debate revived in 1958 and again in 1977 when Christopher Keeling reported rising atmospheric CO_2 in the journal *Energy and Climate* (Keeling, 1977; Keeling and Whorf, 1958). In 1988, NASA published the Charney report. This was a landmark study. The results have remained the benchmark that has underpinned the work of the International Panel on Climate Change since its foundation in 1988.

Public concern triggered alarm amongst fossil fuel companies. They organised a climate denial network. Their activity was covert. The network modelled its efforts on the strategy deployed by "Big Tobacco". The bankruptcy of the Peabody Corporation, a major coal producer, however, resulted in confidential documentation falling into the public domain. Brulle (2014) undertook an exhaustive study of the documentation submitted to the US Internal Revenue Service. The study revealed for the first time the magnitude of the investment made in deceiving the US public and the world. The analysis contained financial information on the annual payment made to foundations for the period 2003–2010. Brulle showed that 140 foundations provided 91 climate change counter movement (CCCM) organisations with over US$900 million per annum. Over the seven years, the CCCM had invested more than US$6 billion in climate change denial.

2.2. *The interaction between human and natural systems*

Malthus's gloomy prognosis failed to materialise during the 20th century, largely because of the large-scale expansion of land under cultivation and innovations in chemistry that provided farmers with fertilisers and pesticides (Erisman *et al.*, 2008). Whilst dousing the soil with chemicals brought environmental and sustainability problems, it boosted agricultural productivity dramatically, staving off the Malthusian dystopian prediction.

Global warming and the attendant problem of climate change are impacting rainfall patterns adversely across the world, including in Australia, California, Northwestern China, and Brazil. Desertification and water stress (DeMeo, 1989; Liu and Xue, 2020) are the result. Unprecedented flooding is now a persistent feature in news reporting on India, Bangladesh, China, Ghana, and Nigeria (Bermúdez *et al.*, 2021; Brouwer *et al.*, 2007; Douglas *et al.*, 2008).

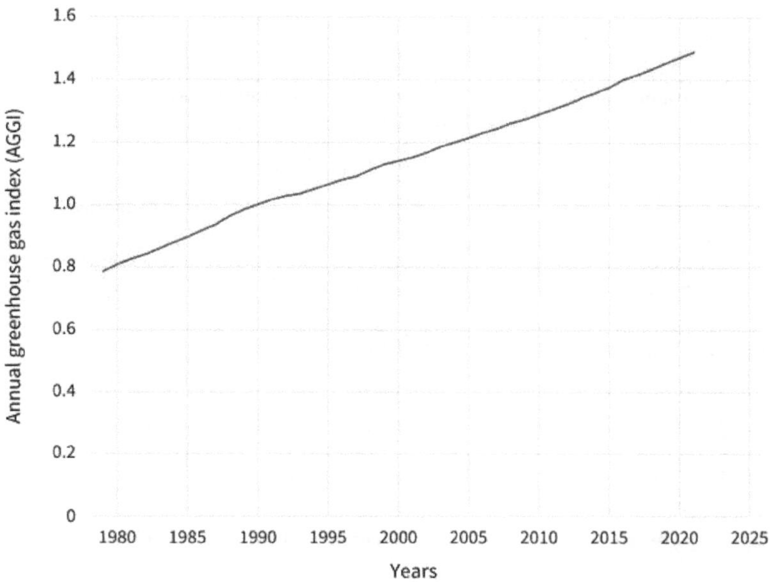

Fig. 1. Annual Greenhouse Gas Index of long-lived GHGs. (Image courtesy of NOAA.)

Whilst flood waters recede, precipitating a gradual but painful return to an apparent normality, rising sea levels change coastlines permanently. Figure 1 shows a graph of the growing rate of greenhouse gas (GHG) emissions between 1980 and 2020. The trend is unambiguous and 2021 and 2022 were two of the hottest years ever. Each year delivered increasingly dramatic extreme weather events.

The Annual Greenhouse Gas Index (AGGI) reports the combined warming influence of all long-lived GHGs as a fraction of their influence in 1990. NOAA Climate.gov graph, based on data from NOAA Global Monitoring Lab.

3. The Food, Energy, and Water (FEW) Trilemma

3.1. *The relationship between natural and human activity systems*

Water is a critical resource in the production of both food and energy (Biggs *et al.*, 2015; Cai *et al.*, 2018; de Grenade *et al.*, 2016;

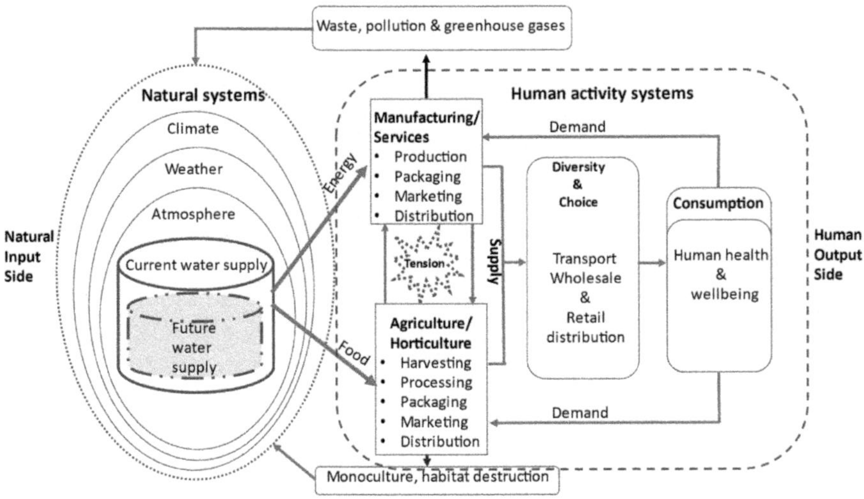

Fig. 2. The relationship between natural and human activity systems.

Scanlon *et al.*, 2017; Wichelns, 2017). The trilemma received prominence at the World Economic Forum in 2008 (D'Odorico *et al.*, 2018). Competition for each of the three resources demands trade-offs. The challenge, therefore, is to manage the inherent tensions by optimising social benefits whilst minimising social costs. Human activity systems can survive and prosper in perpetuity, so long as natural systems remain benign.

Human settlements are typically a product of an abundance of natural resources that attracts businesses and workers to an area. When the climate changes, positive feedback loops are entrained that bring the demand for water into direct conflict with the demand for food and energy. Sustainability is compromised. Rising costs hit employers and workers alike. Companies struggle and ultimately both employers and employees migrate. The tensions are illustrated in Fig. 2.

The natural system is shown in the ellipse on the left and the human activity system on the right. The availability of clean water is a function of climate, weather, and atmosphere. Water is essential to supply energy for manufacturing and for agriculture and horticulture. When the supply of water contracts, both manufacturing and agriculture come under stress. Lack of water supply results in reductions in the diversity and choice of food, products, and services.

Declining food supply impacts nutrition and human health. Reductions in products and services hit human well-being. High consumption improves well-being but results in increases in waste, pollution, and GHGs. These adversely impact climate, weather, and the atmosphere, promoting drought and desertification.

3.2. *The literatures that have shaped the FEW discourse*

Zhang *et al.* (2018) grouped the studies addressing the (FEW) discourse into two categories. The first evaluates the interactions between the various subsystems. Energy production, for example, is dependent on the availability of water and the nexus can be defined as the interplay between water and energy systems. The system boundaries, however, are malleable and can be extended to incorporate food systems and subsystems.

The second category approaches the nexus by establishing and quantifying the links between the different nodes within the food, energy, and water supra system. The discourse began with a focus on resource recovery but soon evolved into a dynamic approach that addresses the nature of the interactions between the different nodes. For example, the airline industry wants to reduce its reliance on fossil fuels. It requires energy in the form of ethylene from agriculture. The US Department of Energy estimates that global demand for ethanol — safe aerospace fuel (SAF) — will reach 230 billion gallons by 2050. To produce one gallon today requires three gallons of water. It is hoped that over time this can be reduced to a ratio of 2:1, if genetically modified grain can be developed that requires less water. Assuming that degree of efficiency is achieved, 460 billion gallons of water will be abstracted to support SAF production.

Between 2002 and 2012, there were 293 reported land grabs by companies around the world, securing over 17 million hectares for biofuel production. This is the equivalent of over 66,000 square miles — a land mass over twice the size of Belgium. An inevitable consequence of these land grabs is that many small farmers are forced into destitution (*Sources*: ILC Land Matrix, Biofuels Digest, GRAIN). Mechanisms will have to be found to mediate between the interests of disparate communities and the companies seeking to maximise profits by supporting aviation consumed by non-essential leisure tourism. Such patterns of appropriation create a tension between holidays for the rich and the price of hunger or starvation for the poor in less developed economies. The current food crises arising from the stand-off between Russia and NATO over Ukraine may be the catalyst for such a large-scale tragedy to emerge.

4. Neoliberalism and the Evolution of Privatisation, Financialisation, and Securitisation in Human Activity Systems

4.1. *The neoliberal dynamic*

The most powerful dynamic that has shaped human activity systems for more than 50 years is neoliberal ideology. Monbiot (2016) defined the phenomenon as follows:

> Neoliberalism *sees competition as the defining characteristic of human relations. It redefines citizens as consumers, whose democratic choices are best exercised by buying and selling, a process that rewards merit and punishes inefficiency. It maintains that "the market" delivers benefits that could never be achieved by planning.*
>
> *Attempts to limit competition are treated as inimical to liberty. Tax and regulation should be minimised, public services should be privatised. The organisation of labour and collective bargaining by trade unions are portrayed as market distortions that impede the formation of a natural hierarchy of winners and losers. Inequality is recast as virtuous: a reward for utility and a generator of wealth, which trickles down to enrich everyone. Efforts to create a more equal society are both counterproductive and morally corrosive. The market ensures that everyone gets what they deserve.*

Neoliberalism has functioned as a catalyst that has progressively unleashed three powerful phenomena in the form of privatisation, financialisation, and securitisation.

4.2. *Privatisation*

Privatisation is a transmission mechanism through which state-owned assets are sold and transferred into private hands. Since the 1970s, encouraged by the IMF and The World Bank, this transfer of wealth globally has been enormous.

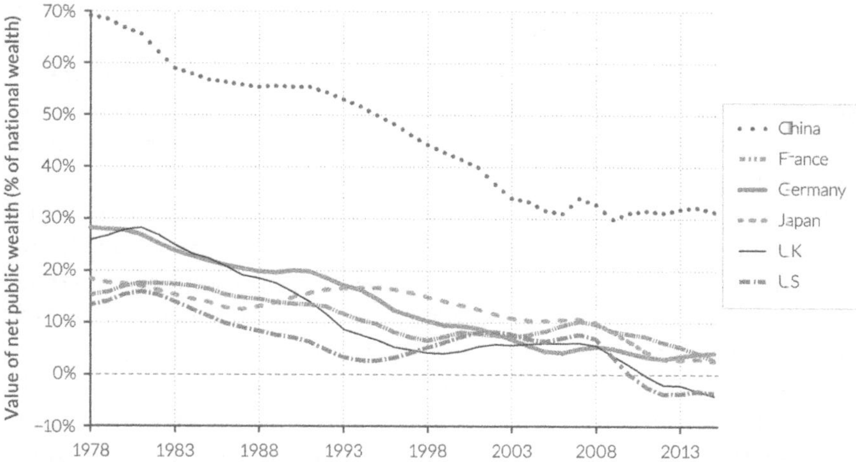

Fig. 3. The redistribution of public and private wealth. (Graph courtesy of World Inequality Database.)

Source: WID.world (2017). See wir2018.wid.world/methodology.html for data series and notes. In 2015, the share of public wealth in national wealth in France was 3%, compared to 17% in 1980.

Figure 3 captures the magnitude of the redistribution of public and private wealth over the period 1978–2017.

4.3. *Financialisation*

The ending of the fixed exchange rate for the dollar in 1971 and the impact of the oil shock of 1974 ushered in a new phase of financial liberalisation and a gradual shift to shareholder capitalism. It propelled a transition in hegemonic control from productive to financial capital.

Palley (2007) described financialisation in the following terms:

> A *process whereby financial markets, financial institutions, and financial elites gain greater influence over economic policy and economic outcomes. Financialisation transforms the functioning of economic systems at both the macro and micro levels. Its principal impacts are to (1) elevate the significance of the financial sector relative to the real sector, (2) transfer income from the real sector to the financial sector, and (3) increase income inequality and contribute to wage stagnation.*

The process can be studied through a macro lens that addresses issues of state and corporate governance, and the consequences that flow therefrom. At the meso level, interactions between financial and non-financial agencies are the focus, and at the micro level, household and individual engagement with the corporate sector is evaluated.

The discourses on the consequences of financialisation conflict. On the one hand, conventional macroeconomic theory argues that financialisation enhances efficiency in the allocation of resources (Epstein, 2005; Perissich, 1996; Whalley, 2004). At the meso level, increased engagement on the part of corporate traders promotes growth in trade volumes and market liquidity. It also enhances market stability whilst speculation is regarded as stabilising because economic fundamentals determine prices. When discrepancies arise, arbitrage re-establishes pricing fundamentals (Friedman, 1953). At the micro level, people across the world are better off because of global free trade.

Critics of conventional economic theory assert that when the US came off the gold standard, and the Bretton Woods agreement unravelled, financialisation dramatically increased its traction. In a bid to avert losses, financial institutions sought growth and stability through the advancement of shareholder interest and ownership of productive enterprise, thereby subjecting the latter to the exigencies of short-term accumulation at the expense of longer-term resilience. According to Demir (2007, p. 352), at the macro level, over the period 1973–2004, there was an exponential growth in the value of financial assets globally. In the early 1970s, the value of global trade expressed as a ratio of foreign exchanges was 2:1. Thirty years later, the ratio was 90:1. Branch banking morphed into retail banking; commercial banking ballooned. Contrary to the claims made by conventional economic theory that comparative advantage benefits all who participate, research has shown that wealth flowed north from the global south (Eich, 2022).

At the mesolevel, a shadow banking system emerged composed of institutional investors including pension, hedge, and mutual funds, investment banks, and insurance companies. As they were not banks, these institutions could escape banking regulations whilst extending lines of credit to the corporate sector. In 1990, institutional cash pools stood at US$100 billion. By 2007, they had grown to over

US$2.2 trillion (Pozsar, 2013). In the early 2000s, between them, US and UK institutional investors owned 70% of their stock markets (Wong, 2010). What also becomes apparent is that the profit rate of productive capital fell significantly, whilst that of financial capital improved markedly (Duménil and Lévy, 2004a, 2004b).

At the micro level, Montgomerie, (2009), Odinet (2020), and Plank (2003) have argued that the Anglo-American world functions on debt. Economies in other parts of the world, whilst similarly afflicted, are so far less impacted. Households have been subtly drawn into the financial services net through pensions tied to stock market performance, by the exponential growth of online credit, and by advances in securitisation. According to Maloney and Tempkin (2019), between 2009 and 2019, American household incomes rose by 15% whilst housing costs shot up 26%, medical expenses by 33%, and college fees by a massive 45%. Online instalment loans moved dramatically to meet customer need for credit to the point where payday bridging loans became a thing of the past with credit terms extending to months and years, further impoverishing house-holds.

4.4. *Securitisation*

Securitisation is an alchemy that transforms receivables into securities that can be packaged and then traded on the capital markets. Nothing of value is immune. Securitising mortgages, credit cards, cars, and student loan debts has made consumer indebtedness extremely profitable. It was the securitisation of mortgages and their salami slicing into packages containing good and bad debt rated AAA by the credit rating agencies that triggered a loss of confidence in 2007. This prompted capital markets to dry up. The financial crash of 2008 followed. It comes as no surprise, therefore, that whilst corporate financial executive reward packages grew dramatically in line with Palley's 2007 definition, the profit rate on productive capital declined and wage levels fell (Gerstle, 2022). Working people in the developed world have become poorer, spawning a search for security. This has resulted in Trumpism in the US, Brexitism in the UK, and right-wing revivalism in Germany, France, Hungary, Italy, Argentina, and Israel. With household debt rising, the gap between rich and poor has grown substantially (Barba and Pivetti, 2009: De Vita and Luo, 2021). In short, until 2008, the world had seen substantial corporate wealth accumulation, accompanied by a redistribution of income and wealth in favour of the corporate sector, along with improvements in human diet, health, and well-being, fuelled by nature's bounty, especially in the developing world.

5. The Financialisation of Food, Energy, and Water and Its Consequences

5.1. *The rise of financial capital's hegemony*

There is substantial discourse on the financialisation of the three key resources that sustain humanity (Boyd *et al.*, 2018; Cheng and Xiong, 2014; Ouma, 2014; Rudebeck, 2022). Neoliberalism brought the world what Moore (2010) described as the "four cheaps", cheap food, energy, raw materials, and labour. He along with Fuglie (2008) also persuasively argued that the rate of global food productivity declined during the two decades leading to the financial crash in 2008. The fall was offset by increases in the global hectarage under the plough.

In the early decades following the collapse of Bretton Woods, financialisation and securitisation brought a dramatic increase in agricultural factor inputs. The result was greater investment in research and development in both production and agrochemical technologies along with genomics and land management. Agricultural productivity rose and human calorific intake improved, whilst prices fell. The hegemony of financial capital, perpetually driven by the short-term need to deliver improvements to the bottom line, remorselessly incentivised by practices associated with the new discipline of human resource management, was unfortunately blind to critical considerations that could not be captured in balance sheets and P&L statements (Sommerville and Magnan, 2015).

Improved productivity was underpinned by a rising dependence of food producers on lines of credit advanced by financial capital. Farmers experienced declining margins on increased output. The industrialisation of production through factory farming and the use of hormones to accelerate the growth of livestock contributed to a rise in GHGs, whilst the extensive use of pesticides, herbicides, and fertilisers resulted in the degradation of both the soil and the water supply (Gomiero, 2016: Keesstra *et al.*, 2018: Singh, 2000).

5.2. *Legitimating the private appropriation of water*

Climate change combined with the competing demands of both agriculture and energy is rendering water a scarce and valuable resource in many regions of the world. As such, it has increasingly become the target of financialisation. Water is accepted to be a gift of nature and a necessity of life. The fourth principle of the Dublin Statement on Water and Sustainable Development, 1992, asserted that it should be managed as an economic good, thereby legitimating the private appropriation of water. In the 1980s, privatisation of water was accompanied by new patterns of licencing and concession in many countries. It stripped away the rights of traditional interests and reallocated them to financial capital in its various guises. Citing developments in California, Chile, Spain, and Australia, the UN special rapporteur Arrojo-Agudo (2021) argued that "although the water trading markets have developed in different historical and political contexts, the four countries share common features:

1. Separation of water from land to allow water commodification.
2. Deregulation of water rights trading between users and between different kinds of use.
3. Transition from public regulated tariffs, usually for non-profit cost recovery, to market water pricing.
4. Increasing de facto private appropriation of water, marginalisation of vulnerable users and disregard for affected third parties and non-productive values."

The countries cited in the report are in the vanguard of regions experiencing increasing water stress. However, the four attributes of the water trading market Arrojo-Agudo identified are now a characteristic of countries that are behind the curve in terms of water stress.

In short, neoliberal ideology, sponsored by the Anglo-American world, has provided the motive power to shift the locus of control away from managerial capitalism characteristic of the early post-World War II years to shareholder capitalism which appropriates a disproportionate amount of added value to shareholders, corporate executives, and financial services (Duminel and Levy, 2004). The 2008 financial crisis, however, has seriously weakened western capitalism, potentially raising the possibility of an alternative socioeconomic doctrine achieving dominance or at least influencing the future evolution of the capitalist frame.

6. Contemporary Socioeconomic Ideologies and the Inherent Paradoxes Within Them

6.1. *The four dominant socioeconomic ideologies*

There are four major transnational socioeconomic ideologies currently shaping human activity systems. Their influence determines the ways in which transnational institutions evolve and interact. They are Anglo-American Capitalism, State Capitalism, Social Market Capitalism, and Islamic Capitalism.

6.1.1. *Anglo-American capitalism*

The US enthusiasm for innovation and its hegemony within the anglophonic world are likely to create the most positive climate for the advance of fintech. A cross-party senatorial group headed by Cynthia Lummis, the Senator for Wyoming, is proposing that whilst other cryptocurrencies should undergo the "Howey test", both Bitcoin and Ethereum should be classed as commodities. This will place the two most important cryptocurrencies under the aegis of the CFTC (US commodities regulator) which has shown itself to be sympathetic to DLT, more so than the SEC (US securities regulator). The legislative proposals also include a requirement that energy consumption by miners should be studied to determine their environmental impact. Most US miners are sourcing their energy from renewables. This is likely to accelerate the adoption of DLT more generally. Given the enormous power wielded by financial capital to define what is virtuous by funding the election of legislators, a fundamental repositioning of the climate change agenda in favour of environmental resilience is unlikely.

6.1.2. *State capitalism*

Whilst the US dominates the anglophonic world, China dominates in the world of state capitalism characteristic of Southeast Asia. China is the world's leading investor in green energy and is the first major nation to launch a digital currency. It also has the most advanced system of social credit, designed to reward citizens whose behaviours conform to the priorities of the Chinese Communist Party (CCP). Bitcoin and other established cryptocurrencies, however, are banned. Whilst these characteristics may be potentially favourable to the evolution of Chinese fintech, its integration with the rest of the world may be problematic. The danger that DLT and fintech will become servants of narrow elites in state capitalist contexts is high. The largest emitters in China are state-owned and their record in embracing innovation is not outstanding; however, a determined CCP position, if held unwaveringly, could result in rapid policy advances. According to Net Zero 2022, China, together with India, accounts for 55% of world emissions. It is one of only 10 countries to set its net-zero targets beyond 2050. Only 4% of Chinese companies had made any form of net-zero pledge by June 2022.

6.1.3. *Social market capitalism*

Of the four systems, social market capitalism (SMC) has advanced furthest in terms of a climate change commitment. It also nurtures a rapidly developing fintech ecosystem. Civil society within this socioeconomic system is also arguably amongst the most climate aware in the world. As in the US and the UK, consideration is being given to a digital euro, but with a central bank that lacks powers equivalent to the US Federal Reserve, progress is likely to be slow, both in terms of a digital currency and fintech regulation. The EU's willingness, however, to impose regulatory constraints on large US social media and retail platforms is worthy of note and may be an advance indicator of progressive fintech and climate change regulation.

6.1.4. *Islamic capitalism*

Islamic finance has evolved under the hegemony of the neoliberal order. It is the least developed of the four systems. It is, however, of growing importance. Its basic tenets are as follows:

> *Society should be structured in such a way that social, political, and economic institutions function within Islamic ideals "the dynamic interplay especially between the economic and the moral, ensures that values such as human equality, liberty, social and economic justice, and social welfare are the main derivatives of this structure.*
>
> Elshurafa (2012, p. 340)

Islamic capitalism is also the least well institutionally developed and the most poorly codified of the four ideologies. Whilst Islamic countries like Egypt possess a civil code that embraces western legal frameworks, many rely upon Sharia as the main source of law. According to Elshurafa (2012, p. 347), financial transactions under Islam tend to be approved on a case-by-case basis and lack a clearly defined body of law. Sharia standards such as those promulgated by the Accounting and Auditing Organisation of Islamic Financial Institutions constitute best practice. They are not binding or codified into national legislation. Transactions costs, therefore, are high because Islamic scholars must decide on whether a contract accords with Sharia.

6.2. *Value creation or value extraction?*

Following the financial crises of 2008, various scholars have declared an end to neoliberal hegemony (Appel and Orenstein, 2016; Duménil and Lévy, 2011; Gerstle, 2022; Stiglitz, 2019). They point to the failure of the western dominated rule-based framework and the emergence of various patterns of autocratic leadership that have emerged and that refuse to acquiesce to the former established order. The truth is, however, old systems like old trees die slowly and the question that remains unanswered is as follows: *What will replace it?* The fact is that the shareholder capitalism that took hold in the 1980s was hailed by its champions as a vehicle of value creation that promoted the efficient allocation of capital to productive sectors of an economy. It has in fact presided over western deindustrialisation, a systemically driven transfer of wealth, and a dramatic decline in corporate investment.

Since 2008, the rate of decline has increased, and yet the egregious behaviours described by Lazonick (2019) as value extraction persist. Investment in R&D gave way to financial engineering on a monstrous scale. Share buybacks by public corporations enabled executives to achieve improvements in the share price performance that triggered entitlement to executive share distributions. According to Asker and Ljungqvist (2011), whilst private companies in the US were investing 10% of total assets each year between 2001 and 2007, their publicly owned counterparts of the same size and in the same sector were investing 4%. This pattern of executive avarice has persisted ever since.

Whilst most research on investment by public companies has been done in the US, the situation in the UK suggests a similar pattern of value extraction, especially in the context of water supply. Between 1981 and 2019, the nine privatised water companies paid out £51 billion in dividends to shareholders. When the companies were first privatised, most debt was eliminated and yet at the end of the period, the water companies had built up a debt mountain of £46 billion, only 16% less than that paid out in dividends. In 2020, there were more than 200,000 incidents of significant environmental pollution in England. These point to the prioritisation of shareholder interest over that of the commons.

In summation, the last 70 years has been a long cycle during which neoliberalism evolved, characterised by a gradual but persistent transfer of wealth from the public sector into private hands, driven by the dynamics of privatisation, financialisation, and securitisation. It has resulted in the relative impoverishment of large swathes of the population in both the developed and underdeveloped worlds, arising from the fact that both income and wealth have been redistributed to favour the ultrarich — a situation exacerbated since 2008 by high levels of borrowing on the part of western governments combined with low-interest rates. Because government borrowing was injected into the economy initially to provide liquidity and subsequently to prevent recession, these funds found their way into financial assets, inflating their value. Inflation and financial repression eroded both the wages and the savings of those in the lower echelons of social hierarchy whilst driving savings into financial assets, thereby further inflating their value along with the bonuses of senior executives. It must also be acknowledged, however, that there has been a relative improvement in dietary and nutritional values, leading to improvement in life expectancy amongst poorer people in emerging economies, especially those working under the aegis of state capitalism. Whether the redistributive pendulum will swing the other way in coming decades is the question to which we turn next.

7. Fintech as a Challenger to the Determinism of the Tragedy of the Commons

7.1. *Fintech and trust*

Fintech sits in the vanguard of the development and application of DLT. It is certainly a highly disruptive technology. It enables fractionation of financial instruments, accelerates the speed of exchange exponentially, removes transaction costs associated with layers of intermediation, and eliminates barriers associated with traditional finance (Tradfi) by substituting five working days for 24/7 service. Most significantly, fintech can dispense with the need for trust, especially in the context of short-term routine contractual obligations because of the transparency of blockchains and the self-executing nature of smart contracts (algorithms of code that trigger automated responses as each step in a contract is executed).

In invoking the tragedy of the commons, Hardin (1968) sought to present a deterministic argument that exploited game theory and the Nash equilibrium to show the futility of commons and the imperative to advance the cause of private ownership.

> *Ruin is the destination toward which all men rush, each pursuing his own best interest in a society that believes in the freedom of the commons. Freedom in a commons, brings ruin to all.*
>
> Hardin (1968)

Fintech, whilst not a panacea, can at least help address the free-rider problem. Ostrom (1998) persuasively challenged Hardin's conception of a Hobbesian world devoted to the ruthless pursuit of self-interest by highlighting that commons are subject to rules to which communities of commoners voluntarily comply. Unlike the prisoners' dilemma in which the prisoners were unable to communicate, upon which Hardin's thesis was grounded, individuals and communities can communicate and build consensus around optimum solutions. Ostrom went on to argue that there are multiple alternatives to the public–private dichotomy advanced by Samuelson upon which an entire generation of economists was schooled (Wall, 2014).

Fintech has been spearheaded by start-ups keen to exploit the opportunities that DLT, AI, 5G, and IOT afford. Frequently, they have been funded or acquired by "Tradfi", once their technology is perceived to be viable. Fintech can be divided into two categories: fintech that serves the broader financial services industry of which there are already thousands of established companies and fintech that serves the real economy.

Contemporary examples of fintech services and projects that address the needs of the real economy are detailed in Table 1. The table highlights examples of existing businesses together with their mission in serving the needs in the energy, oceanic, and food sectors, together with web links.

7.2. *Fintech evolution*

Fintech Board is a financial services company that has identified 10 leading domains of fintech innovation:

- Alternative credit scoring
- Alternative insurance underwriting
- Transaction delivery
- Peer-to-peer lending
- Small ticket loans
- Payment gateways
- Digital wallets
- Asset management
- Digital/open banking
- Digital insurance

7.3. *Fintech as a disruptive force addressing the FEW dilemmas*

In his paper, "Don't Automate Obliterate", Hammer (1990) made an important observation. New innovations are initially typically used to speed up existing processes. This is as true of fintech as of other historic patterns of innovation. The above-identified applications primarily focus on services to existing markets and serving those excluded from those markets. The potential for fintech to address the FEW challenges in the real economy are enormous. They go far beyond the present pattern of pioneering effort that largely functions within national economies.

Table 1. Examples of innovative Fintech projects offering services to newly emergent markets.

Sector	Fintech Initiative	Nature of Project Mission
Energy	Energy Web	The Energy Web Decentralised Operating System (EW-DOS) has three layers that work together to enable development and deployment of decentralised applications for the energy sector and beyond. The platform supports a Relay Chain Consortium and a series of sector- and geography-specific para chains using Substrate technology. https://www.energyweb.org/; https://www.youtube.com/channel/UC3y_C3oZnzVO3KF_yn6m45w
	Nextra	A trading and portfolio management platform for easy access to power markets for various participants. NEXTRA enables utilities, balancing responsible parties or consumers (commercial & industrial) to manage their assets themselves. The possibilities range from trading excess or shortfall quantities, balancing a portfolio, or directly procuring the energy needed for consumption. https://www.nexteraenergyresources.com/
	Share&Charge	Share&Charge has just launched the Open Charging Network (OCN). The aim is to create a charging roaming network that will make digital communication between charging point operators, eMobility service providers, and other market participants easier, safer, and more cost effective. The OCN is based on the Open Charge Point Interface (OCPI) and other tools such as blockchain technology. https://shareandcharge.atlassian.net/wiki/spaces/OCN/overview?homepageId=265257095
	European Energy Exchange	Is a leading energy exchange which builds secure, successful, and sustainable commodity markets worldwide. https://www.eex.com/en/

Table 1. (*Continued*)

Sector	Fintech Initiative	Nature of Project Mission
Oceanic	Fishcoin	There are millions of small-scale seafood producers — fishers and farmers especially in developing nations. Whilst they almost all have mobile phones, they generally cannot afford even the most basic electronic Catch Documentation & Traceability (eCDT) technologies. In short, 90% of the world's seafood comes from developing nations (plus other important agricultural products). There are no mechanisms to collect data from the source. No data = no management = questionable sustainability. https://fishcoin.co/
	Xpertsea	XpertSea leverages AI technology, machine learning, and computer vision to help farmers modernise their operations and boost profits by providing access to valuable production insights. https://agfundernews.com/xpertsea-changes-course-following-20m-series-b-raise
	Rooser Seafood Trading	On Rooser's marketplace, processing plants upload the fish they have available daily along with the price they want to sell it at. WhatsApp messages are sent to each plant's customers with a link to their online marketplace. Rooser takes a 3% commission for each transaction. https://sifted.eu/articles/rooser-seafood-trading-marketplace/
Agriculture	OriginClear	A water company deploying fintech to improve its quality and delivery of water supplies to municipalities. https://www.originclear.com/ceo/fintech-for-clean-water

(*Continued*)

Table 1. (*Continued*)

Sector	Fintech Initiative	Nature of Project Mission
	FarmDrive	FarmDrive is a technology company that applies data science and machine learning to build software that increases access to meaningful financial services — loans, digital payments, insurance, and savings. FarmDrive's mission is to drive capital to underserved rural clients and transform them into sustainable and profitable businesses. https://cr.linkedin.com/company/farmdrive
	Producepay	Aims to increase the velocity of cash flow for suppliers across the US, Mexico, and Latin America. Farmers gain access to invoice finance before their buyers pay. https://producepay.com/about-us/

7.3.1. *Alternative credit scoring*

This service presently uses AI to identify key characteristics in targets groups like the self-employed who are excluded from current scoring services because they are characterised as high risk. Many have excellent records of probity that AI can learn to discern, thereby enabling rating agencies to distinguish those who are a good risk from those who are not. Water companies could score heavy users against a set of criteria, deliver a score for usage efficiency, and impose differential pricing strategies that reflect efficiency scores. Farmers who prioritise crops that produce ethanol might be charged differently from farmers producing wheat for human consumption at scale.

To prevent conflict over water resources, countries that share the same rivers could elect to create a single water authority with an executive board composed of senior executives experienced in water management from each country. The board would set standard tariffs calculated and based upon seasonal or monthly rainfall volumes. Tributaries would collect data on water volumes per hour and data on herbicide and fertiliser contamination. The data would be fed back digitally to the International Water Agency which would set tariffs for the next quarter accordingly. The national water agencies that abstract and distribute water would then have to settle by charging corporate and private consumers standard local tariffs. All charges would be transparent and open to scrutiny by all local water agencies.

7.3.2. *Asset management*

Fintech companies such as Robinhood Markets, Inc. are offering free access to investment services in return for user data. The data are forwarded to high-frequency traders who can influence the price of an equity. The investor may pay a slightly higher price, but it is less than the commission normally pays whilst traders are able to aggregate data ahead of the market to achieve a margin.

A regulator might require water companies to provide access to data generated when contaminated water is discharged. Volumes of measured discharge would incur penal levies to be settled by smart contracts. A regulatory role will also be required to balance water consumption for energy as opposed to food, with differential pricing imposed to reflect local conditions and priorities. In regions where water is a scarce resource, regional water regulators would need to be established to enable equitable water abstraction from rivers flowing through different countries. The individual countries would then have to determine local priorities and establish appropriate governance mechanisms. Failure to seek collaborative solutions is likely to result in wars.

As renewable energy systems develop, DLT is increasingly able to facilitate decentralised peer-to-peer trading as projects in Australia, US, and Norway are already demonstrating. The trade and exchange of carbon credits is also advancing at pace along with innovation in Green Finance such as the Green Asset Wallet initiative that addresses problems of transparency (Nassiry, 2018).

7.3.3. *Payment gateways*

Payment gateways are currently used to enable consumers to pay suppliers using multiple alternative methods. Similar technology could be created to enable farmers in emerging economies to band together and bargain to improve the price that Western confectionary producers pay for cocoa or any other primary good. By using smart contracts and with the benefit of AI, it will become possible to calculate parities between different currencies in real time and disburse funds to the growers in proportion to their individual contributions to the quantum sold, with payment disbursed to the farmers' digital wallets via smart contracts.

These examples illustrate the possibilities that fintech innovation can deliver. It must not be forgotten, however, that the internet's potential for democratisation was hijacked by corporate finance. Fintech and blockchains will follow the same pathway if allowed to do so. New technology is often perceived to be neutral, promulgated as beneficial, and exploited by those in positions to do so. It is the sociopolitical contexts within which adoption occurs and the robustness of the institutional frameworks created within those contexts that determine the extent to which technological innovations are benign or malign in respect of the public good.

8. The Challenges Ahead

8.1. *Fintech in a multipolar world*

The steady unravelling of the post-World War II rules-based system alluded to earlier, and the rise of autocracy, makes consensus building around climate change and fintech regulation more challenging. In general, democracies search for win-win solutions. Autocracies tend to seek win-lose outcomes. Following COP 26, corporate commitment to address the challenges of climate change in the Anglo-American world appeared to be rising. Institutional investors had begun to switch from investment in carbon-sourced energy and put pressure on oil companies to reduce their carbon footprint. Indeed, some experts were predicting a catastrophic decline in investment in oil exploration that would result in oil supplies falling off a cliff at a time when carbon energy was most needed to fuel the energy transition. After the invasion of Ukraine, oil moved from being shunned to becoming one of the best-in-class investments within a new commodity supercycle. Rising inflation, oil and food prices placed short-term cost-of-living concerns above climate change in the minds of both populations and political elites. Systemic inertia is the consequence.

8.2. *The preconditions for maximum fintech impact*

A report produced by the Oxford-based research group Net Zero (Hans *et al.*, 2022) concluded that of the world's two thousand largest companies, around half with net-zero targets have an interim GHG emission reduction target of some kind — a poor result given the need to halve global emissions by 2030 to have any chance of holding global warming to 1.5°C. The authors concluded, *It is clear that regulation will ultimately be needed to ensure near-term targets are put in place and procedural criteria satisfied across the whole global economy.* This is an enormous regulatory challenge in and of itself. Postures on fintech regulation vary. For fintech to achieve a high impact on climate change, three vital conditions must be met. Firstly, environmental awareness and a desire to tackle it must be present in civil society. Secondly, political vision, commitment, and leadership are essential. Finally, political and institutional leaders must create institutional infrastructures that promote DL and AI innovation, and create regulatory frameworks to reign in the pursuit of short-term private interest at the cost of long-term environmental resilience.

Figure 4 shows the percentage of the Forbes Global 2000 companies in the G7 nations that meet all or some of the criteria for a

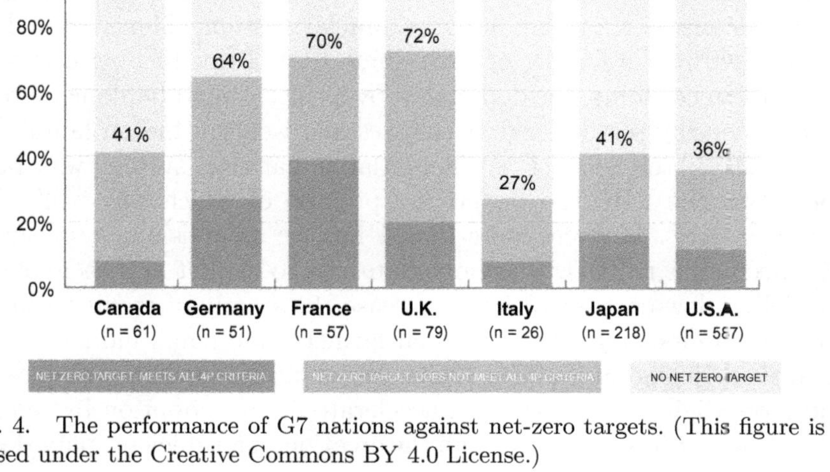

Fig. 4. The performance of G7 nations against net-zero targets. (This figure is reused under the Creative Commons BY 4.0 License.)

net-zero (or other) target. France and Germany in particular stand out. The anglophonic world lags. The UK's commitment to voluntarism may prove an impediment to progress. However, voluntarism can sometimes deliver better results than regulation.

9. Fintech as the Catalyst for Greater Liberty

9.1. *Self-identification*

Seven years ago, India launched Aadhaar numbers, a government-sponsored initiative lead by Nandan Nilekani, Chairman of Infosys. It enabled Indian citizens to register and create a personal identity. Since its launch, 99% of Indians have registered. This has given them access via mobile phones to the world wide web, enabling them to register for bank accounts, own property, use merchants, access cash and credit to support small business activity, pay for goods, and transact in cryptocurrency, many for the first time. This single innovation makes it possible for Indians of all castes to become active participants in socioeconomic activities and to embrace fintech.

9.2. *Promoting financial inclusion*

According to Rajeshwar Rao (2022), Deputy Governor of the Reserve Bank of India (RBI), since independence, the RBI has presided over the liberalisation of the Indian financial system. The system has grown 320% at a CAGR of 4.5% since 1951. Prior to liberalisation, the Indian economy was dominated by a state-owned banking system that primarily served large businesses and wealthy Indian families.

In 2013, the idea of a differentiated banking system was proposed by the RBI, the underlying premise of which was "differentiated reach". Licences were issued for the establishment of small finance banks (SFBs). Their mandate was to exploit new technology to deliver low-cost operations, increase the supply of credit to small business units, small and marginal farmers, and small industries. In addition, 75 Digital Banking Units were established. Their role was to promote digital awareness and accelerate digital adoption by reducing customer hesitation through the creation of an efficient, paperless, safe, and secure digital environment. Payment banks were also created. Rajeshwar Rao described them as "truly the first-generation new age differentiated banks designed on activity-based functional differentiation."

9.3. *Controlling the rate of fintech expansion*

In June 2022, the RBI caused a furore amongst Indian fintech start-ups when it announced that it was barring the practice of loading non-bank prepaid payment instruments with credit lines. The decision was perceived as likely to have a major impact on the whole financial services ecosystem, especially fintech. Indeed, some fintechs argued that the policy shift posed an existential threat, asserting that the established banks had successfully lobbied the RBI to slow down the rate of progress the challengers were making. It was a policy move that was redolent of China's suppression of fintech in 2021 (Singh, 2022). This judgement is ill-informed given the exponential rate of growth in "buy now, pay later" and other forms of credit growth.

Rajeshwar Rao, in his Talwar Memorial Lecture in June 2022, highlighted that there were 11.4 million mobile banking transactions with a value of 11.5 billion rupees in June 2020. In the month of August 2022, this had risen to 47.3 million transactions with a value of 46.3 billion rupees. The RBI's intervention appears to be an attempt to contain the rate of growth in securitisation and the problems that are apparent in western economies that have resulted in unsustainable household indebtedness and accompanying economic fragility.

10. Striking a Balance

10.1. *Reconciling the libertarian paradox*

Human activity systems are grounded in institutional arrangements that evolve over time into grand paradigms. At the most basic level, a paradigm is a framework for solving problems. Neoliberalism is such a paradigm and the problem it evolved to solve was the freedom of individuals to persist in the accumulation of capital. It is predicated on what Isiah Berlin (2017) defined as negative liberty, a deterministic position that advocates freedom from external constraint and an acceptance that those with power should wield it in their own self-interest. To do otherwise erodes the power of the elite and with it the capacity to maintain social stability, inviting one elite to be replaced by another. Positive freedom in contrast enables individuals and groups in democratic societies to realise their full potential through social, political, and economic engagement.

10.2. *An emergent paradigm*

A paradigm becomes a lens through which both individuals and societies view and interpret the world around them. They become blind to alternative possibilities. If we look back into history, feudalism was predicated on the Ptolemaic conception of the universe. It was believed that in creating the universe, God placed the earth at its centre around which the sun and the stars revolved. It took Copernicus who exploited the new technology of the telescope to disprove the Ptolemaic thesis that had prevailed for over a millennium. In doing so, his discovery challenged the authority of the church, which through its power and authority legitimated the divine right of kings. The feudal order imposed a rigid and unyielding social hierarchy. For serfs, the social system operated like the bars of a cage from which it was impossible to escape. Enlightenment followed, culminating in regicides, first in England and then France, opening the door first to mercantilism and then capitalism. In the same way, neoliberalism has forged the bars to a new cultural cage from which the world must now escape. It has entrained positive feedback loops that are enormous and accelerating so fast that they are rapidly eroding the planet's life support systems. The oceans, the rainforests, and the great glaciers of the Himalayas, Alps, Andes, and the Rocky Mountains, along with the rainforests and oceans are the contemporary commons. They drive global climatic conditions that underpin our socioeconomic ecosystems. Blockchains, with their devolved and decentralised architecture, not only serve as a technology that affords the opportunity to address the fundamental issue of trust in data but also serve as a metaphor for an alternative pluralistic approach to social organisation that, in terms of potential, is analogous to the Copernican telescope. It opens the door to an alternative world view. It allows humankind living within any of the four socioeconomic and cultural frameworks cited earlier to achieve a better balance between Isiah Berlin's negative and positive liberty. It can do this by enabling individuals and groups to engage freely with others to create rules through which enlightened self-interest can overcome the free-rider dilemma, with the potential to deliver consensus-based optimum solutions to problems previously dogged by sub-optimal Nash equilibrium outcomes.

10.3. *COP 26, a study of myopia*

It is worthy of note that at COP 26, it was leaders of states with more autocratic systems of governance and/or populist leadership that triggered the collapse of a consensus outcome. A key area of shortfall was the failure of leaders and their advisers to grasp the nettle afforded by fintech to achieve a better balance between communal obligations and individual freedom at all levels of recursion, be it the individual, the corporation, or the state. Bolsonaro, President of Brazil, failed to show up, and when the environmentalist and journalist Dom Phillips and his expert guide Bruno Pereira were murdered in the Amazon rainforest, he shrugged off the killings, implying that it was their ill judgement in being in the rainforest that led to their fate. The leaders of India and China opted for exceptional status. It enabled them to avoid a commitment to carbon neutrality by 2050. Whilst it is arguable that late development mitigates the charge of free riding, if global warming is not halted, these two states face a potential mutual catastrophe from which neither will escape. The great flood plains of China, India, and Pakistan are fed by ice melt from Himalayan and Tibetan glaciers. Richard Holbrook, former US Ambassador to the UN, expressed the view that contention between India and China over the water resources that feed their flood plains is a potential catalyst for World War III. The glaciers are not just suffering from rising temperatures, pollution is also eroding their whiteness and their ability to reflect sunlight rather than absorb it. As the glaciers melt, glacial lakes expand and burst, creating catastrophic flooding.

When rivers dry up, the land around estuaries becomes salinised, ground water becomes undrinkable, and land becomes uncultivable. Combine glacial melt in mountains with glacial melt at the polls and the result is gradual desertification inland and rising sea levels that render coastal strips uninhabitable. Given that 40% of the world population lives within one hundred kilometres of a coastline, displaced populations will create enormous social and economic upheaval initially within nation-states and ultimately across them.

10.4. *NIE, A new frame for economics*

NIE as articulated by Elinor and Vincent Olsen and fellow institutional advocates is perceived to be driven by pragmatism. It is, however, both an economic and philosophic paradigm. Like cyberneticians, advocates of NIE recognise that responsibility should be devolved to the lowest level capable of dealing with the problems at hand (Klein, 1998). They recognise two types of knowledge, scientific empiricism and local insights and understanding often accumulated over generations. Overcentralisation is to be avoided because it snuffs out localism and a sense of ownership at the local interface. Typically, local expertise informed by scientific insight is the best combination. China's Great Green Wall is today seen as a success; however, billions of inappropriate saplings were planted and died during the early days of the project because scientists ignored local knowledge, opted for monoculture, and introduced varieties that local people knew would fail. Institutional economists recognise both the value and the importance of diversity in property rights, arguing that private and public ownership plays a key role as a system of governance. However, there are contexts where alternative forms of property right and approaches to governance will be more beneficial, for individuals, communities, and for society at large. Optimum solutions must be determined by redefining utility to reflect the importance not just of socioeconomic considerations but also of geophysical considerations. It is easy to cut down a rainforest in the interest of short-term profit. Having done so, it is impossible to replace the forest because the act of clearing alters the soil's biome, eliminating the conditions to support regrowth. Moreover, the soil that supports the grasslands that replace rainforests becomes vulnerable to erosion as the soil dries out.

Given the diversity of the four great socioeconomic and cultural paradigms previously discussed, and the diversity of their underpinning values, it is apparent that human activity systems, like their natural counterparts, are complex and diverse. Both leaders and policymakers need new frameworks for defining and solving problems within and between the human activity systems that embraces knowledge of how human and natural systems interact. NIE offers the promise of such a framework and the DLT embedded in fintech creates the avenue through which distrust born of the free-rider dilemma can for the first time be overcome.

11. Conclusion

In the opening to this chapter, the following question was posed: "Can the world escape the tragedy of the commons?" It has been argued that people are fundamentally cooperative when they design systems to deliver solutions that address some form of virtuous end. Definitions of what constitutes virtue differ between cultures and change over time. As institutional arrangements evolve, so does the paradigm upon which socioeconomic relationships are grounded. Neoliberalism is such a paradigm. Whilst some allege that in the wake of the 2008 financial crisis and the aftermath of COVID-19, it is slowly dying, it leaves a toxic legacy that is poisoning the wells of the commons from which all of humankind must drink. DLT and fintech are the potential catalysts for the emergence of a new paradigm on a scale of international institutional development even greater than that which followed World War II. It must be grounded in a paradigm of NIE.

References

Appel, H. and Orenstein, M. A. (2016). Why did neoliberalism triumph and endure in the post-communist world? *Comparative Politics*, 48(3), pp. 313–331. Available at: http://www.jstor.org/stable/24886207.

Arrojo-Agudo (2021). Risks and impacts of the commodification and financialisation of water on the human rights to safe drinking water and sanitation, Report presented to the *76th UN General Assembly by the Special Rapporteur on the Human Rights to Safe Drinking Water and Sanitation*, A/76/159.

Asker, J. F.-M. and Ljungqvist, J. (2011). Comparing the investment behaviour of public and private firms, NBER Working Paper No. 17394.

Barba, A. and Pivetti, M. (2009). Rising household debt: Its causes and macroeconomic implications — A long-period analysis, *Cambridge Journal of Economics*, 33(1), pp. 113–137.

Bermúdez, M., Farfán, J. F., Willems, P., and Cea, L. (2021). Assessing the effects of climate change on compound flooding in coastal river areas, *Journal of Water Resources Research*, 57(10), p. e2020WR029321.

Berlin, I. (2017). Two concepts of liberty. In Liberty Reader (pp. 33–57). Routledge.

Biggs, E. M., Bruce, E., Boruff, B., Duncan, J. M., Horsley, J., Pauli, N., McNeill, K., Neef, A., Van Ogtrop, F., Curnow, J., and Haworth, B. (2015). Sustainable development and the water–energy–food nexus: A perspective on livelihoods, *Journal of Environmental Science & Policy*, 54, pp. 389–397.

Boyd, N. E., Harris, J. H., and Li, B. (2018). An update on speculation and financialisation in commodity markets, *Journal of Commodity Markets*, 10, pp. 91–104.

Brouwer, R., Akter, S., Brander, L., and Haque, E. (2007). Socioeconomic vulnerability and adaptation to environmental risk: A case study of climate change and flooding in Bangladesh, *Risk Analysis: An International Journal*, 27(2), pp. 313–326.

Brulle, R. J. (2014). Institutionalising delay: Foundation funding and the creation of US climate change counter-movement organisations, *Climatic Change*, 122(4), pp. 681–694.

Brummer, C. and Yadav, Y. (2018). Fintech and the innovation trilemma. *Georgetown Law Journal*, 107, p. 235.

Cai, X., Wallington, K., Shafiee-Jood, M. and Marston, L. (2018). Understanding and managing the food-energy-water nexus-opportunities for water resources research. *Advances in Water Resources*, 111, pp. 259–273.

Callendar, G. S. (1938). The artificial production of carbon dioxide and its influence on temperature. *Quarterly Journal of the Royal Meteorological Society*, 64(275), pp. 223–240.

Cheng, I. H., and Xiong, W. (2014). Financialisation of commodity markets. *Annual Review of Finance Economics*, 6(1), pp. 419–441.

De Grenade, R., House-Peters, L., Scott, C. A., Thapa, B., Mills-Novoa, M., Gerlak, A., and Verbist, K. (2016). The nexus: Reconsidering environmental security and adaptive capacity. *Current Opinion in Environmental Sustainability*, 21, pp. 15–21.

De Vita, G. and Luo, Y. (2021). Financialisation, household debt and income inequality: Empirical evidence, *International Journal of Finance & Economics*, 26(2), pp. 1917–1937.

DeMeo, J. (1989). Desert expansion and drought: environmental crisis, Part I. *Journal of Agronomy*, 23(1), pp. 15–26.

Demir, F. (2007). The rise of rentier capitalism and the financialisation of real sectors in developing countries. *Review of Radical Political Economics*, 39(3), pp. 351–359.

D'Odorico, P., Davis, K. F., Rosa, L., Carr, J. A., Chiarelli, D., Dell'Angelo, J., Gephart, J., MacDonald, G. K., Seekell, D. A., Suweis, S., and Rulli, M. C. (2018). The global food-energy-water nexus. *Reviews of Geophysics*, 56(3), pp. 456–531.

Douglas, I., Alam, K., Maghenda, M., Mcdonnell, Y., McLean, L., and Campbell, J. (2008). Unjust waters: Climate change, flooding, and the urban poor in Africa. *Environment and Urbanisation*, 20(1), pp. 187–205.

Duménil G. and Lévy D. (2004a). The real and financial components of profitability (United States, 1952–2000). *Review of Radical Political Economics* 36(1), pp. 82–110. doi:10.1177/0486613403261127.

Duménil, G. and Lévy, D. (2004b). *Capital Resurgent: Roots of the Neoliberal Revolution* (Harvard University Press, London).

Duménil, G. and Lévy, D. (2011). *The Crisis of Neoliberalism* (Cambridge, MA and London, England: Harvard University Press).

Eich, S. (2022). *The Currency of Politics: The Political Theory of Money from Aristotle to Keynes*. Available at: https:press.princeton.edu/books/hardcover/9780691191072/the-currency-of-politics.

Elshurafa, D. (2012). Islamic capitalism — An imminent reality or a hopeful possibility for Islamic finance? *Arab Law Quarterly*, 26(3), pp. 339–360. Available at: http://www.jstor.org/stable/23235576.

Epstein, G. A. (ed.) (2005). *Financialisation and the World Economy* (Edward Elgar Publishing).

Erisman, J. W., Sutton, M. A., Galloway, J., Klimont, Z., and Winiwarter, W. (2008). How a century of ammonia synthesis changed the world. *Nature Geoscience*, 1(10), 636. Available at: https://doi.org/10.1038/ngeo325.

Freed, J. (2022). UPDATE 1-Qantas, Airbus invests as much as $200 million to develop Australia's sustainable aviation fuels trade. *Popular New*. Available at: https://popularnews.us/update-1-qantas-airbus-invests-as-much-as-200-million-to-develop-australias-sustainable-aviation-fuels-trade/, accessed 21/06/22.

Friedman, M. (1953). Essays in positive economics. University of Chicago Press.

Fuglie, K. O. (2008). Is a slowdown in agricultural productivity growth contributing to the rise in commodity prices? *Agricultural Economics*, 39, pp. 431–441.

Gerstle, G. (2022). *The Rise and Fall of the Neoliberal Order: America and the World in the Free Market Era.* Oxford University Press, New York, NY.

Gomiero, T. (2016). Soil degradation, land scarcity and food security: Reviewing a complex challenge. *Sustainability*, 8(3), p. 281.

Hammer, M. (1990). Reengineering work: Don't automate, obliterate. *Harvard Business Review*, 68(4), pp. 104–112.

Hans, F., Kuramochi, T., Black, T., Hale, T., and Lang, J. (2022). Net Zero Stocktake 2022. Available at: https://newclimate.org/resources/publications/net-zero-stocktake-2022, accessed 15/6/22.

Hardin, G. (1968). The tragedy of the commons: The population problem has no technical solution; it requires a fundamental extension in morality. Science, 162(3859), pp. 1243–1248.

Keeling, C. D. (1977). Impact of industrial gases on climate. *Energy and Climate*, pp. 72–95.

Keeling, C. D. and Whorf, T. P. (1958). Atmospheric CO_2 from continuous air samples at Mauna Loa Observatory, Hawaii, USA. *Methods*, 2001.

Keesstra, S., Mol, G., De Leeuw, J., Okx, J., Molenaar, C., De Cleen, M., and Visser, S. (2018). Soil-related sustainable development goals: Four concepts to make land degradation neutrality and restoration work. *Land*, 7(4), p. 133.

Klein, P. G. (2000). *New Institutional Economics* (Edward Elgar Publishing: Northampton, MA).

Kuhn, T. S. (1970). *The Structure of Scientific Revolutions* (Vol. 111) (University of Chicago Press: Chicago).

Lazonick, W. and Shin, J. S., (2019). Predatory value extraction: How the looting of the business corporation became the US norm and how sustainable prosperity can be restored. Oxford University Press.

Liu, Y. and Xue, Y. (2020). Expansion of the Sahara Desert and shrinking of frozen land of the Arctic. *Scientific Reports*, 10(1), pp. 1–9.

Maloney, C. and Tempkin, A. (2019). America's middle class is addicted to a new kind of credit, *Bloomberg*. Available at: https://perma.cc/B9Q4-PPBK.

Monbiot, G. (2016). Neoliberalism–the ideology at the root of all our problems. *The Guardian*, 15(04).

Moore, J. (2010). Cheap Food & Bad Money: Food, Frontiers, and Financialization in the Rise and Demise of Neoliberalism. *Review*, 33. 225–261. 10.2307/23346883.

Montgomerie, J. (2009). The pursuit of (past) happiness? Middle-class indebtedness and American financialisation. *New Political Economy*, 14(1), pp. 1–24.

Nassiry, D. (2018). The role of fintech in unlocking green finance: Policy insights for developing countries, ADBI Working Paper Series No. 883.

National Research Council (1977). *Energy and Climate: Studies in Geophysics.* (The National Academies Press: Washington, DC) https://doi.org/10.17226/12024.

Odinet, C. K. (2020). Securitising digital debts, *Arizona State Law Journal,* 52, p. 477.

Olsen, H. P. (2009). February. Law in the light of global threats. In *IOP Conference Series — Earth and Environmental Science* (Vol. 6, No. 22). (IOP Publishing).

Ostrom, E. (1998). A behavioural approach to the rational choice theory of collective action: Presidential address, American Political Science Association, 1997, *American Political Science Review*, 92(1), pp. 1–22.

Ouma, S. (2014). Situating global finance in the land rush debate: A critical review. *Geoforum*, 57, pp. 162–166.

Palley, T. I. (2007). *Financialization, What It Is and Why It Matters.* Working Paper No. 525. Annandaleon-Hudson, NY: The Levy Economics Institute.

Perissich, R. (1996). The costs and benefits of international liberalisation and deregulation: An Italian view, *The International Spectator*, 31(2), 51–59. doi:10.1080/03932729608456738.

Plank, T. E. (2004). The security of securitization and the future of security. *Cardozo Law Review*, 25(5), pp. 1655–1742. University of Tennessee Legal Studies Research Paper No. 55. Available at SSRN: https://ssrn.com/abstract=1334831.

Polites, G. L., and Karahanna, E. (2012). Shackled to the status quo: The inhibiting effects of incumbent system habit, switching costs, and inertia on new system acceptance, *MIS Quarterly*, pp. 21–42.

Pozsar, Z. (2013). Institutional cash pools and the triffin dilemma of the US Banking system, *Financial Markets, Institutions & Instruments*, 22(5), pp. 283–318.

Rajeshwar Rao, M. (2022). *Reflections on Policy Choices in the Indian Financial System*, 12th R.K. Talwar Memorial Lecture (delivered by Shri M. Rajeshwar Rao, Deputy Governor, Reserve Bank of India, October 21, 2022, Mumbai).

Rudebeck, T. (2022). Framing water as a financial risk: Reviewing the processes shaping a narrative. *Wiley Interdisciplinary Reviews: Water*, p. e1596.

Scanlon, B. R., Ruddell, B. L., Reed, P. M., Hook, R. I., Zheng, C., Tidwell, V. C., and Siebert, S. (2017). The food-energy-water nexus: Transforming science for society. *Water Resources Research*, 53(5), pp. 3550–3556.

Shapiro, A. L. (1999). The internet. *Foreign Policy*, 115, pp. 14–27. Available at: https://doi.org/10.2307/1149490, accessed 06/06/22.

Singh, M. (2022). *India's Central Bank Cracks Down on Fintech Start-ups*, Tech Crunch, June 24.

Singh, R. B. (2000). Environmental consequences of agricultural development: A case study from the Green Revolution state of Haryana, India, *Agriculture, Ecosystems & Environment*, 82(1–3), pp. 97–103.

Soederberg, S. (2014). Student loans, debt fare and the commodification of debt: The politics of securitisation and the displacement of risk, *Critical Sociology*, 40(5), pp. 689–709.

Sommerville, M. and Magnan, A. (2015). 'Pinstripes on the prairies': Examining the financialisation of farming systems in the Canadian prairie provinces, *Journal of Peasant Studies*, 42(1), pp. 119–144.

Stiglitz, J. (2019). *The End of Neoliberalism, and the Rebirth of History*. Project Syndicate. Available at: https://www.dailymaverick.co.za/opinionista/2019-11-05-the-end-of-neoliberalism-and-the-rebirth-of-history/, accessed 13/06/22.

Wall, D. (2014). *The Sustainable Economics of Elinor Ostrom: Commons Contestation and Craft* (Abingdon Oxon: Routledge).

Whalley, J. (2004). Assessing the benefits to developing countries of liberalisation in services trade, *World Economy*, 27(8), pp. 1223–1253.

Wichelns, D. (2017). The water-energy-food nexus: Is the increasing attention warranted, from either a research or policy perspective? *Environmental Science & Policy*, 69, pp. 113–123.

Wong, S. (2010). *How Institutional Investors Should Step Up as Owner* (McKinsey & Company Insights and Publications).

Zhang, C., Chen, X., Li, Y., Ding, W., and Fu, G. (2018). Water-energy-food nexus: Concepts, questions, and methodologies. *Journal of Cleaner Production*, 195, pp. 625–639.

https://doi.org/10.1142/9781800614604_0002

Chapter 2

Sustainability in the Blockchain Trilemma: Time for a "Deficracy"

Giulia Napolitano
Department of Economics, Management, Institutions, University of Naples Federico II, Naples, Italy
studiogiulianapolitano@gmail.com

This chapter intends to explore the concept of sustainability in the blockchain ecosystem, providing an overview of what already exists in the literature, as this new technology is rapidly gaining interest in different sectors and nowadays the global economy is moving towards sustainable development of financial markets and businesses. Considering the dominant uses of this technology for the green economy narrative, the purpose of this chapter is to expand knowledge on the topic of blockchain that could also allow effective ecological regeneration, facilitating degrowth objectives (Balaguer Rasillo, 2020) and socially equitable outcomes, through institutional reforms that disrupt debt-based economic systems, inspired by alternative currencies. In fact, after the COVID-19 lockdowns, there is a real need for a green, inclusive economy to build a stronger financial system, and blockchain could enable sustainable investments, mainly through collectively owned energy systems for a reduction in total energy use.

Keywords: Blockchain; sustainability; innovation; circular economy; implementation; governance; challenge; security; decentralisation digital currencies

1. Introduction

Currently, information and communications technology, artificial intelligence (AI), big data, innovation, digitisation, industry 4.0, and sustainability appear to be among the most recurring research themes, with blockchain being the second-highest priority in this field (Talafidaryani *et al.*, 2021).

Distributed ledger technology (DLT) and AI are interesting applications for the sustainable finance sector, as the former enables the creation of electronic databases shared and distributed across a number of different participants, with an exact copy stored and accessible from each location.

AI, along with big data, can also be used for more efficient pricing (and risk weighting) in lending activity; those algorithms have also been employed by firms for a more cost-efficient compliance with financial regulation (RegTech) and by supervisors to facilitate the examination of the considerable flow of data and documentation coming from supervised entities to detect violations in documents and risks for the market (SupTech).

Blockchain adoption is also positively associated with environmental efficiency and the relationship appears to be stronger for financial and technological firms; through this empirical evidence, policy-makers could be incentivised to adopt innovative technologies, such as blockchain, to reach environmental sustainability (Tawiah *et al.*, 2022).

Thus, digital technologies (DTs), such as big data, Internet of Things (IoT), AI, and blockchain, are considered enablers for more sustainable and circular business models, but extant literature on these topics mostly focused on specific DTs and subareas of sustainable product management (SPM) (Rusch *et al.*, 2022).

Additionally, there is scarce application of DTs' radical forms of improvement, the majority being incremental, such as increased efficiency of existing processes (Rusch *et al.*, 2022).

In this sense, Rusch *et al.* (2022) provide a comprehensive overview of current and potential examples of DT applications in SPM (such as business models) through a systematic literature review, using quantitative and qualitative content analysis.

Deductive and inductive analyses revealed the potential of DTs in terms of their usability along the product life cycle and their role as enablers for Circular Economy strategies, suggesting that greater adoption and optimisation of DTs, in various areas of SPM, can help to accelerate the transition towards sustainability.

Therefore, in this research, the huge topic of blockchain technology is confined to the field of sustainability, while also considering implementation challenges and solving the trilemma of security, scalability, and decentralisation.

The interest in the topic is validated by the fact that fintech applications, such as crowdfunding, tokens and DLT systems, data analytics, AI, and machine learning, could fill some of the gaps in the sustainable finance framework, especially in terms of transparency, verification, availability, and reliability of disclosures, data, and ratings.

In fact, those technologies could help resolve the lack of standardisation of Environmental, Social and Governance reporting and rating, while allowing customisation that is increasingly requested by investors.

Unfortunately, many blockchain projects are merely using environmental credentials to enable new forms of "green grabbing" (Howson *et al.*, 2019), and fast, scalable, and energy-efficient applications of blockchain technology require alternative validation models.

This underlines the need to find solutions that combine energy efficiency, scalability, speed, and security, without significant trade-offs, as blockchain consensus protocols have different energy intensities: for example, "Proof of Stake" (PoS) requires less than 1% of the energy consumption needed for "Proof of Work" (PoW).

Finally, attention must be paid to the paradox that Gunderson *et al.* (2018) describe as an "energy boomerang effect", where an increase in resource efficiency and decarbonised energy production could result in increased energy usage and unsustainable material consumption throughout the economy.

2. Statement of the Problem

As the title suggests, "DeFicracy" is a concept similar to that of blockocracies and is linked to bureaucracies (Weber's rational-legal ideal type of domination), which are multi-layered, polycentric forms of organising, based on a rational-legal authority linked to permissionless, public, coin-based blockchains.

In this field, there are a range of potentially fruitful and interesting inquiries to explore, such as what are the new governance structures and practices, how can a decentralised governance platform power green finance, how can blockchain technology be integrated into existing platforms to enable decentralised decisions, and what are real-use cases, thus exploring the potential of tangible applications.

The discussion will outline how blockchain is a particular form of DLT database, where entries are recorded subsequently in a "chain" of blocks and cryptographically validated by a network of independent participants through a consensus method, becoming immutable, more transparent, and less prone to attacks than central-based systems.

Before legitimising and spreading the use of smart contracts, blockchain, and AI in the financial sector, the need to provide clear and internationally coordinated answers about the legal validity and effects of smart contracts is discussed, along with the principles for blockchain governance (e.g., distribution of responsibilities and decisional power across the network, formal processes for shared decisions, and processes to respond to threats and errors).

An irony to outline is that stability, immutability, and permanence are the characteristics of blockchain (considering that like bureaucracies are designed to create order), but it is described as a disruptive technology.

It is also commonly promoted as an open, public, and transparent platform, when in reality it ensures privacy and anonymity using cryptography.

In fact, the rules for how the software runs are coded in a programming language, which makes them inscrutable to almost everyone (Introna, 2016), and the combination of cryptography and other algorithms such as multi-party secure computing can assure information integrity and privacy of the source.

In a shared distributed ledger, integrity is validated and secured by cryptography and time stamping: These accounting practices aim to keep the correct record of each financial transaction without a central intermediary.

This hybrid organisational form is favourable for peer-to-peer exchanges and open innovation networks, where all miners in the network share continually expanding and identical copies of the blockchain through the consensus protocol.

Finally, some relevant obstacles of this technology to examine are related to technical shortcomings.

For instance, its decentralised nature creates operational risk because of the difficulty in ensuring the functioning of the system where no one has exclusive and total control (e.g., core developers need the consent of 51% of miners to revert a fork or anyway maintain the updated system), many developers are voluntary workers, the governance of the blockchain is not clear (with unclear distribution/concentration of power and responsibility), and errors are immutable.

Nonetheless, the blockchain so far deployed in the sustainable finance sector has been permission-based, therefore not presenting the above-mentioned risks but entailing lower resilience because of the higher level of centralisation.

As explained in Fig. 1, a blockchain is a decentralised ledger that stores transactions across a peer-to-peer network, without the need for a central clearing authority. In this context, a cryptocurrency is a digital medium of exchange that enables the transfer of funds and the creation of monetary units, through its protocol and cryptographic techniques.

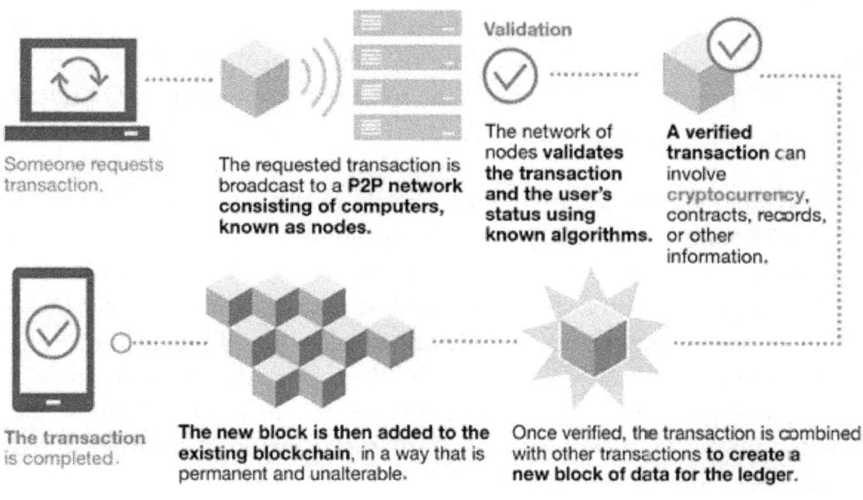

Fig. 1. How blockchain works.

Source: PricewaterhouseCoopers. (2022). Making Sense of Bitcoin, Cryptocurrency and Blockchain. Available at: https://www.pwc.com/us/en/industries/financial-services/fintech/bitcoin-blockchain-cryptocurrency.html.

3. Theoretical Framework

Currently, there is scant scientific discourse about the role of blockchain in non-financial and sustainability reporting and the need to reform assurance in non-financial reporting practices (Pizzi *et al.*, 2022).

In fact, even considering the relevance of the application of blockchain technology in this sector, to date, researchers mostly focused on the technological and industrial view, organisational and managerial view, and global and social view (Talafidaryani *et al.*, 2021).

In particular, what is lacking is the development of a theoretical model on blockchain's role as an enabler of the transition to a CE, as this technology appears to play a moderating role, being an infrastructural resource (Böhmecke-Schwafert, 2022).

As this subject is especially relevant in the current context of the pandemic, and academics and professionals need to be assisted in identifying the application focus of the blockchain and informed on its main opportunities and challenges (Botene *et al.*, 2021), this chapter will investigate the topic through a qualitative method using a review of the most recent literature.

In fact, through current performance measurement tools, it is difficult to measure the benefits of CE, a concept that gained increased importance during the recovery from the COVID-19 pandemic, specifically with regard to sustainability (Nandi *et al.*, 2021).

A systematic literature review is the approach used, for example, by Botene *et al.* (2021): These authors aim to study how this technology can help in the struggle against the COVID-19 pandemic.

Although the study was performed at a time when the crisis was still in progress, the results show that the adoption of blockchain, considered as an enabling technology, could support the implementation of various applications and practical use cases, as it was useful in the effective planning of the operation, the distribution of resources, and in counteracting misinformation.

Nandi *et al.* (2021) provide a CE performance measurement model and also create seven COVID-19 disruption scenarios to provide insights that can be addressed through CE practices.

The authors argue that organisations can evaluate their CE performance using non-market-based environmental valuation methods, and they find that an ecosystem of multi-stakeholder DTs such as blockchain can enhance the effectiveness of the CE performance measurement model to support supply chain sustainability and resilience.

Then, Böhmecke-Schwafert (2022) interviews experts implementing blockchain innovations across Europe and the US for the CE, and proposes a theoretical model through a thematic analysis exploring drivers and barriers of the transition to a circular economy, along with the related blockchain innovation and technical challenges.

Massaro *et al.* (2020) investigate how the blockchain can foster financial and social sustainability, along with the creation of sustainable business models (SBMs), considering its ability to promote inclusivity even in traditional sectors, creating long-term benefits for stakeholders.

This study has been conducted through real business case evidence (a case study methodology) to explore the state-of-the-art literature on the application of emerging technologies to organisational sustainability, underlining the need to merge the sustainability perspective into business models (Massaro *et al.*, 2020).

This need requires one to investigate how digitalisation may enhance, hinder, or change the concept of sustainability, as the design and subsequent implementation of DLT may support the application of sustainable development initiatives and a more centralised or networked governance (Schulz *et al.*, 2020).

In fact, considering the main areas of public administration and governance which will adopt DLT over the next two decades, such as digital identity, social service provision, and climate finance, it is useful to compare use cases (Schulz *et al.*, 2020) and there is a need to produce interdisciplinary governance research (one that considers the technological and environmental side).

Now, as organisations and regulators are being pushed to transform business/city models according to CE, IT professionals have to put more efforts to make this transition consistent, fast, and low cost (Nobre-gustavo *et al.*, 2019).

For example, Nobre-gustavo *et al.* (2019) investigate the big data/IoT capabilities that IT executives need to address in order to support organisations' transition to the CE, and in order to evaluate the organisation's readiness for this transition, they provide a framework to identify 39 capabilities divided into six CE principles.

Notably, their contribution is to assess the roles that modern technologies and Industry 4.0 play in the transition to CE and identify the most interesting institutions/publications worldwide (Nobre-gustavo *et al.*, 2019).

In this sense, smart contracts can build trust and support sustainable social businesses in which social and economic logics of social ventures can coexist (Devine *et al.*, 2021).

Also, Chauhan *et al.* (2022) conduct a rigorous analysis of the literature on the alignment of the CE and DTs, as DTs combined with business model innovation could enable CE.

They provide a practical systems-based framework for a digitalised CE, showing the literature linkages among the emerging research streams and providing novel insights regarding CE benefits.

Mishra and Kaushik (2021) provide an overview of blockchain and analyse the major challenges of its application in the financial sector.

This is important considering the blockchain network and technology are part of a peer-to-peer distributed system that operates in a decentralised manner, creating a secure environment that allows users to exchange transactions, contracts, and data, establishing trust among the users (Mishra and Kaushik, 2021).

In fact, blockchain provides security, performance, quality, and cost reduction in many of the banking sector's processes and services, as it is cheaper, transparent, and more effective compared to the traditional system, often seen as cumbersome, error-prone, slow, and unsafe (Mishra and Kaushik, 2021).

As blockchain is decentralised, transparent, and immutable, it can create a more customer-centric, secure, and open marketplace for stakeholders and businesses (Gleim and Stevens, 2021), and it has the potential to transform businesses.

A framework for blockchain usage in sustainable social businesses has been made possible by Soni *et al.* (2021) who examine previous papers on social businesses through an in-depth bibliometric statistical analysis of the literature on technological interventions in sustainable social business.

They focus on social innovation, DT, information systems, and decision-making for sustainability, showcasing possible future research trajectories and offering useful recommendations for future analysis in other fields.

In fact, blockchain is a technological innovation that can help social businesses towards financial and operational sustainability, as these organisations are often structurally and financially fragile, and DTs are increasingly being accepted as tools for sustainability and scalability of social businesses (Soni *et al.*, 2021).

A social business blockchain model could promote the coexistence of social and economic logics, as the implementation of this technology elicits trust relationships between stakeholders and social businesses (Devine *et al.*, 2021).

DLTs could also help solve the challenges of mandatory ESG reporting (Dario *et al.*, 2021).

In fact, even though disclosure of ESG reporting became mandatory in 2022, currently there is no standardised reporting framework to ensure the information is readable, scalable, consistent, and comparable due to the variety of ESG rating models in the market, the different interpretive approaches used by businesses, and the novelty of measures used by the authorities and supervisors on financial intermediaries.

In this context, DLTs can process and make streamlined ESG reports by creating agile, transparent, and automated data collection processes (Dario *et al.*, 2021).

4. Methodology

The present study intends to contribute to previous publications that offer insights on blockchain's impact over time through a bibliometric analysis of extant publications, to fill the void in the literature, to quantify research trends within publications, and to reveal some valuable insights to scholars and practitioners in the domain of interest.

This study can be considered a conceptual one, in which theoretical propositions derive from desk research and literature review.

As for the scientific approach, it uses a qualitative method of indirect observation, cause–effect analysis, induction, and description.

This study analyses extant research, from the oldest to the newest, to investigate how this technology informs sustainability, proposing a future agenda to foster innovation in the field.

In particular, this study is based on a literature review approach using a descriptive bibliometric method to understand the content of selected studies, while data analysis visualisation is not performed.

Regarding the theoretical lens of the research, the articles retrieved, published in the period 2020–2022, were those focusing on blockchain in business and management, along with those providing a link between sustainability, social responsibility, and CE.

The theoretical foundation is blockchain's moderating role in the transition to CE, as this phenomenon is still spreading and research has been mainly conceptual with few empirical studies.

In accordance with Böhmecke-Schwafert *et al.* (2022), this study intends to investigate the potential of this emerging technology, especially in the contexts of CE, technical challenges in its implementation, and the relationships among CE drivers and barriers.

The bibliometric method is useful for promoting the growth of specific knowledge, helping to assess the developing body of knowledge and find future research paths, considering the critical effect of research on specific areas.

Initially, for data collection, the Scopus database was utilised as the data source of this study in May 2022 because it is the largest database and includes various types of papers.

To select appropriate keywords, we reviewed previous bibliometric studies and literature reviews. We then identified and selected the papers that contributed to the development of knowledge in the specified domain and answered the research questions.

Then, we filtered the core document set considering published articles, articles in press, and book chapters to obtain an updated dataset.

Through the search query of Scopus, we selected documents (only articles in final publication status) using the primary input of "Article title, Abstract, Keywords", adopting the Boolean operator (AND-OR) in the search tool.

Therefore, we used the query with TITLE-ABS-KEY with the following research string: "Blockchain AND sustainability" OR "Blockchain AND implementation AND challenges" OR "Blockchain AND decentralisation AND governance" OR "Blockchain AND use cases AND cost AND reliability AND security".

Regarding the selection performed on Google Scholar, we included only scientific articles retrieved using the exact keyphrase, written in English, that appears in journals/books (for example, research reports and conference proceedings).

We excluded papers that were not conceptual (for example, case studies), and all the research focused on a specific geographical context and in specific industry sectors or sectors outside the business and management area.

Descriptive bibliometric indicators were defined and the main topics were investigated in the dataset to understand the extent of the literature and answer the research questions.

Therefore, the content of the papers belonging to each of the four main clusters was examined through a thematic analysis.

For each cluster, the papers containing a given keyword were grouped, and it was manually checked that each cluster contained all the papers associated with the respective keyword.

This chapter conducts a systematic mapping study on blockchain and sustainability, in line with Lund *et al.* (2019) who proposed the grouping of articles in this field based on the knowledge area, contribution type, and research type.

This study is conceptual, as a narrative and integrative literature review and a desk study are employed to develop theoretical propositions.

As for the scientific approach, this chapter uses a qualitative design of research, through indirect observations, cause–effect analysis, and predictive synthesis.

Since the subject matter is new and needs further exploration, data collection from scientific databases consisted of data source identification and data extraction.

The aim was not to look depth into use cases for blockchain technology, but to obtain a general understanding of the evolution of this concept after COVID-19.

Thus, considering that blockchain technology is still novel and rapid changes can be expected, this study only looks at papers from 2020 to 2022.

The Systematic Literature Review was conducted in June 2022: We searched for the key terms only in the title, abstract, and keywords and maintained a broad search to avoid missing any relevant papers.

For example, the search using "sustainability" returned a large number of papers (as this is also a commonly used word in other fields), showing that there is a lot of work available in the financial domain.

A crucial step in screening papers is to decide which independent and unbiased database to use: We chose the Scopus database because it is the largest abstract and citation source of peer-reviewed literature and is largely used worldwide.

We used Google Scholar to further refine the results.

The libraries were selected by looking at the most recent articles and scanning for relevant results, using the sources available to my university.

The term "sustainability" was preferable to "ESG" since it is more specific and can cover any kind of situation where blockchain technology is applied for a regenerative economy.

In fact, this study excluded the term ESG because it describes a concept that is too broad, which could limit the topics of interest, and deals with the social aspect, that in this study, would be too inaccurate.

To filter the remaining results, we used an inclusion and exclusion criteria: in particular, from the selection, we excluded the articles referring to a single geographical context (e.g., India), a single application (cryptocurrencies, smart cities, supply chain), or a single industrial sector (fashion industry, maritime transport, or education) to find generalisable solutions.

Additionally, in order to construct a high-quality study with rigorous contributions, articles not available for download were excluded, along with conference proceedings, book chapters, review articles, etc. Then, a careful abstract screening was conducted in accordance with the scope of our chapter that includes three aspects (sustainability, applications, and challenges), and only those papers providing significant results were selected, along with those published in the period 2020–2022.

In order to construct a high-quality review with rigorous contributions, by manually refining the results, we removed duplicates or articles not fully edited or those not written in the English language.

The remaining articles were mainly conceptual and primarily discussed the blockchain in terms of its current applications and benefits.

To form groups, it was necessary to read the titles, abstracts, conclusions, and keywords (if included) of the selected papers, creating a new category only if the paper did not fit an existing one.

The papers were divided into four main knowledge areas, each corresponding to a given search string, as can be seen in Table 1.

Papers that do not propose a solution in themselves (e.g., surveys) or those proposing a testbed to aid further development (since technology is only starting to develop, solutions cannot be considered definitive) were excluded.

Overall, each paper was fitted into a research type and a contribution type: To elaborate on this categorisation, the search was performed manually by accessing each paper, reading the abstract and the conclusions.

A small number of papers could potentially fit into more than one or fall slightly outside a strict categorisation, but ultimately they were systematised (see Fig. 2).

5. Findings

The academic debate triggered by the three types of studies examined (validation papers, evaluation research, and solution proposals) shows that there is a potential for utilising blockchain technology in sustainable technology. Even though not all the papers retrieved dealt directly with sustainability, in all of them distributed ledger technology played a central role and the details of implementation were discussed.

Half of the papers examined are validation papers (nine papers), while four papers have been classified as solution proposals (Table 2).

Those show the academic interest in solving the problems in applying or implementing this technology, trying to propose different ways of understanding and addressing the issues.

Furthermore, the lack of evaluation research means that researchers have not tested the proposed techniques, maybe due to the novelty of this technology, as most solution proposals have been published in the last two years.

Looking at the contribution types in Fig. 2, many represent framework proposals as well as models/methods. Thus, researchers have proposed many variations of implementations, but have few ideas on how to use them practically. As research progresses and the field matures, we will probably see more papers providing compatible solutions, tools, and testbeds that will make further developments easier.

Table 1. Key questions, explanations of the topic, and corresponding strings.

Questions of the Study	Knowledge Areas	Search Strings	Scientific Articles Retrieved
1. How is blockchain technology related to sustainability	The aim is to explore how this technology could enable sustainable investments, power the green economy and the ecological regeneration, considering that some of blockchain's use cases might have a positive effect on climate change.	Blockchain AND "sustainability"	By searching "blockchain" + "sustainability" on Scopus and limiting the selection to the Business, Management, and Accounting fields, 186 results were retrieved. Of those, 114 were articles and 103 of them (90%) published in the period 2020–2022. Refinement was conducted manually on Scopus since none of the 103 articles were published in any of the top 20 journals as per SCImago rank. After filtering the results according to the exclusion criteria, the articles considered (top three with highest citations) were Upadhyay *et al.* (2021), Khan *et al.* (2021), and Shojaei *et al.* (2021), while Parmentola *et al.* (2022) and Giesel and Nobre (2021) were also considered as they were retrieved from Google Scholar using the same keywords. A search with the same keywords was conducted on Google Scholar to find further results. By searching "blockchain" + "sustainability" on Google Scholar and filtering only scientific articles in the period 2015–2022, the search yielded 71 results, of which 60 were published in the period 2020–2022: Since 85% of the articles on this topic have been published after 2020, this could mean that in that year the subject started to gain momentum. Only scientific articles were included and the results were retrieved considering the exact keyphrase. The articles retrieved were Parmentola *et al.* (2022), Giesel and Nobre (2021), Rejeb *et al.* (2022), Jameel *et al.* (2020), Gurzhii (2022), Le and Hsu (2021), and Botene *et al.* (2021).

2. What implementation challenges in blockchain persist?	The focus will be on legislation, considering the lack of common standards, especially in the financial field.	Blockchain AND "implementation" AND "challenges"	On Scopus, filtering the results for the Business, Management, and Accounting fields, 84 articles were retrieved, but 74 were published in the period 2020–2022. Refinement was conducted manually on Scopus since none of the 74 articles were published in any of the top 20 journals as per SCImago rank. The remaining articles considered (the top three with highest citations) were Upadhyay *et al.* (2021), Rymarczyk (2020), and Jabbar and Dani (2020)
3. How can blockchain enable decentralised decisions, new governance structures and practices?		Blockchain AND "decentralisation" AND "governance"	On Scopus, filtering the results for the Business, Management, and Accounting fields, 163 articles were retrieved: 138 were published in the period 2020–2022. Considering only those published in the top 20 journals as per SCImago rank, the remaining articles were Chen *et al.* (2021), Lumineau *et al.* (2021), Chen and Bellavitis (2020), and Chawla (2020)
4. What are real-use cases that guarantee cost, reliability, and security?	For example, an interesting use of blockchain, in combination with smart contracts, is that of developing various applications on top of the protocol layer, including Initial Coin Offerings.	Blockchain AND "use cases" AND "cost" AND "reliability" AND "security"	On Scopus, filtering the results for the Business, Management, and Accounting fields, only 1 article was retrieved (Fuller and Markelevich, 2020)

Table 2. Research and contribution types.

Research Types	Contribution Types: Model: Papers Proposing New Methods to Address a Problem	Framework: Papers Introducing Frameworks for Development	Ontology: Papers Provide Guidance for Identifying and Discussing Issues
Validation research: It looks into proposing new possibilities for addressing a given problem. The papers try to prove the validity or viability of some new technique, without actually implementing it.	Jabbar and Dani (2020)	Giesel and Nobre (2021), Botene *et al.* (2021), and Chawla (2020)	Gurzhii (2022), Rymarczyk (2020), Chen and Bellavitis (2020), and Lumineau *et al.* (2021)
Evaluation research: It shows how techniques are implemented in practice (solution implementation) and evaluates benefits/drawbacks in applying the proposed solutions.	Rejeb *et al.* (2022)	Parmentola *et al.* (2022)	Upadhyay *et al.* (2021), Le and Hsu (2021), and Fuller and Markelevich (2020)
Solution proposal: It proposes a solution that can be either novel or an improvement of an existing technique. The potential benefits and the applicability of the solution are shown by an example or an argumentation.	Khan *et al.* (2021) and Jameel *et al.* (2020)	Shojaei *et al.* (2021)	Chen *et al.* (2021)

The literature surveyed included the top 20 journals with SCImago Journal Rank indicator higher than 5 in the fields of Business, Management, and Accounting, based on the 2022 Scientific Journal Rank (as of June 2022).

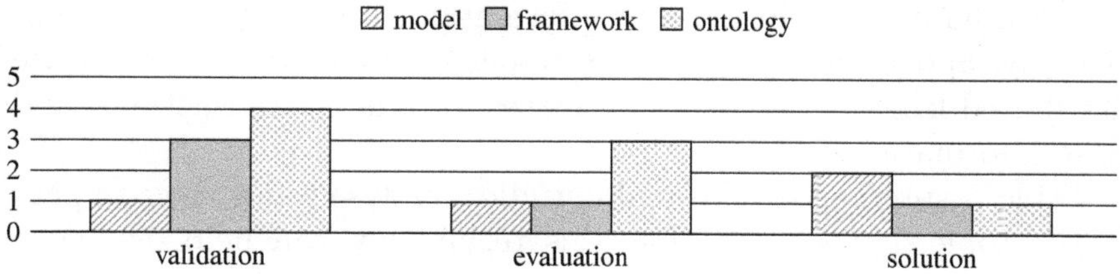

Fig. 2. Research and contribution types.

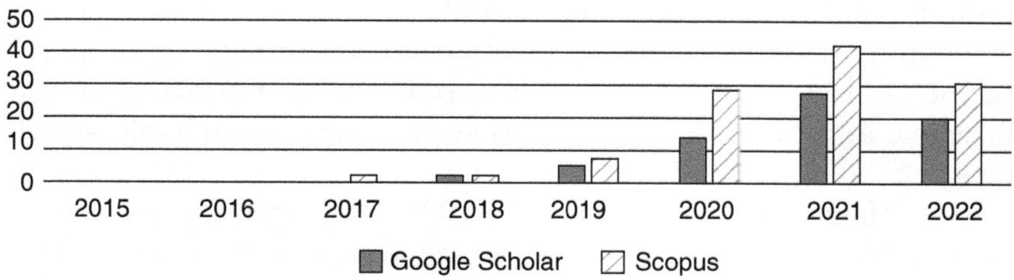

Fig. 3. Year-wise division of articles retrieved using the keyphrase "blockchain sustainability".
Note: For Scopus, we considered only results in the business, management, and accounting categories.
Source: Author's elaboration using data from Scopus and Google Scholar.

Regarding bibliographic coupling distribution among journals, considering two as the minimum number of relevant articles for a source, only the *Journal of Business Venturing Insights* was within the threshold (Chen and Bellavitis, 2020; Chawla, 2020).

Other journals (among the first 20 as per SCImago rank) that published relevant contributions in the period 2020–2022 were the *Journal of Management* (Chen *et al.*, 2021) and *Organization Science* (Lumineau *et al.*, 2021).

Over the last 2 years, it appears that there has been a significant increase in publications which look into blockchain technology applications in sustainability, compared to the scarcity of literature in this field before 2020 (Fig. 3).

The progressive academic interest emerges from the fact that articles published in 2021 were double the amount of articles published the previous year (results for 2022 are not considered since the year still hadn't ended at the time of writing this chapter), and this trend could persist in the future.

Blockchain is revolutionising information technology in a disruptive way, and organisations are striving to understand how to use distributed ledger to innovate processes, products, transactions, and share information.

Table 3 summarises the main studies analysed and their impact on the topic, considering that this technology can help overcome pressing sustainability issues.

Firstly, Parmentola *et al.* (2022) note that blockchain has no negative effects on the environment that need to be considered before adoption, and they suggest that it could instead contribute to environmentally sustainable development goals, for example, by supporting the realisation of a sustainable supply chain, improving energy efficiency, and promoting the creation of secure and reliable smart cities.

Even though Parmentola *et al.* (2022) highlight the sectors in which to focus research investments, providing a way to reward sustainable behaviour and environmental sustainability, the literature still lacks studies that explain the organisational circumstances in which blockchain can enable progress on transparency in BS, with few authors (Giesel and Nobre, 2021) advancing knowledge on the implications of the use of blockchain in transparency for business sustainability (BS).

Now, considering the increasing interest in applying blockchain to provide and improve transparency, with the latter representing a strategic asset in BS, Giesel and Nobre (2021) propose two analytical frameworks: one related to the benefits of blockchain and transparency for the economic, social, and environmental BS and the other related to the concepts of blockchain and transparency presented by the scientific literature.

Other contributions provide insights for decision-makers and managers aiming to optimise blockchain implementations in the CE, considering that this technology can help overcome pressing sustainability issues; but, to date, there have been limited studies investigating this topic (Rejeb *et al.*, 2022).

In this sense, Rejeb *et al.* (2022) provide a comprehensive review of the barriers hampering the adoption of blockchain technology in CE, a concept that comprehends various designs and choices, in addition to rewiring production, operation, and reuse cycles of useful products by implementing closed loops (Shojaei *et al.*, 2021).

Table 3. Publications reviewed and their content for each research type.

Author	Contribution to the Extant Literature	Research Type
Parmentola *et al.* (2022)	They show how blockchain technology could foster environmentally sustainable development goals.	Quantitative
Rejeb *et al.* (2022)	The authors provide a comprehensive review of the barriers hampering the adoption of blockchain technology in CE. This produces insights for decision-makers and managers aiming to optimise blockchain implementations in the CE.	Quantitative
Khan *et al.* (2021)	They examine the role of blockchain technology in transforming CE practices and business models and their impact on eco-environmental performance, which influences organisational performance.	Quantitative
Shojaei *et al.* (2021)	They provide a proof of concept regarding the feasibility of a blockchain model, tested through a synthetic case study, as an enabler of CE, as information flow through blockchain produces synergy with a smart and connected community. This is appropriate since blockchain allows a secure, fast, and accessible information network where products and materials can be traced to their sources, enabling proactive planning for reusability along with material and energy traceability.	Quantitative
Jameel *et al.* (2020)	They address some of the major issues of blockchain-enabled networks, proposing some future research avenues, along with the improvements required.	Quantitative

(*Continued*)

Table 3. (*Continued*)

Author	Contribution to the Extant Literature	Research Type
Chawla (2020)	Unlike traditional theories, blockchains highlight the technical competence and transparency dimensions of trust, and this has been compared with that in Transaction Cost Economics (TCE), Agency Theory (AT), and Resource-Based View (RBV), with the aim of offering new insights into the implications of the emergence of blockchains, which received increasing attention from entrepreneurs and researchers considering that it enabled disintermediation.	Quantitative
Giesel and Nobre (2021)	They propose two analytical frameworks related to the benefits of blockchain and transparency: one that presents the economic, social, and environmental aspects and the other as presented by scientific debate.	Qualitative–quantitative research that advances new avenues to address a given issue, trying to prove the validity or viability of some new technique, without actually implementing it.
Jabbar and Dani (2020)	Regarding conceptual research on the blockchain implementation, the authors introduce the notion of computational costs as an essential mechanism for completing operational transactions in the blockchain environment, and discuss the complexity and efficiency of smart contracts to identify potential costs.	Qualitative–quantitative research
Gurzhii (2022)	They examine the most promising areas of digitalisation, along with benefits, challenges, and barriers in blockchain adoption.	Qualitative

Chen *et al.* (2021)	The authors note that semi-decentralisation could help dominant platforms avoid trust issues regarding platform monopolies. The fact that semi-decentralisation promotes shared governance enables centralised platforms to enhance the network of the stakeholders involved, such as users and developers, increasing value in the long term.	Qualitative
Le and Hsu (2021)	The authors provide a complete literature review of blockchain, as they discuss challenges of blockchain in terms of security and performance, provide a taxonomy of blockchain-based applications, and outline some research directions. This is important since blockchain's decentralised nature can enable sustainable practices and innovative business models, providing high trust and real-time communications while reducing costs, delivery times, transaction times and fees, and waste in manufacturing and production processes.	Qualitative
Lumineau *et al.* (2021)	They outline the background and the features of blockchains, considering the social implications as well as the challenges and limitations. This helps one to understand how blockchains may change the way in which one organises collaborations or influences organisational outcomes, who is involved and affected by blockchain governance, the reasons behind its adoption, and when and where blockchains can be more (versus less) effective.	Qualitative

(*Continued*)

Table 3. (*Continued*)

Author	Contribution to the Extant Literature	Research Type
Upadhyay *et al.* (2021)	They identify and systematise the Industry 4.0 research on blockchain's impact on CE through sustainability and social responsibility, providing suggestions for future studies in this field. In particular, blockchain appears to positively contribute to the CE, for example, by helping to enhance performance and communication along the supply chain and reduce transaction and carbon footprint.	Qualitative
Fuller and Markelevich (2020)	They investigate the potential impact of blockchain on the accounting and auditing profession, with regard to data security and privacy, technology, adoption, and implementation. Thus, they suggest that blockchain usage in accounting still has to address scalability at an acceptable cost along with data security and privacy issues.	Qualitative
Rymarczyk (2020)	The author notes how blockchain will find wide applications primarily in the operations of financial market institutions, and that other industries along with non-profit institutions, governmental organisations, and local governments can take advantage of this technology as it ensures transaction security, reduces the risk of counterfeits and hacking attacks, eliminates intermediaries, and shortens implementation times.	Qualitative
Chen and Bellavitis (2020)	They evaluate potential advantages and challenges of decentralised business models (which tend to be more transparent, decentralised, innovative, and interoperable) compared to existing ones, through blockchain technology that can reduce transaction costs and distribute trust. This also broadens financial inclusion, encourages permissionless innovation and open access, and encourages innovation in finance and entrepreneurship.	Qualitative

By reviewing extant literature and using the Fuzzy Delphi method, they analyse and rank sixteen barriers to blockchain adoption in the CE and these are then validated by a panel of experts; their expert opinion survey includes mainly anonymous response, iteration and controlled feedback, and statistical group response (Rejeb *et al.*, 2022).

Then, using the best–worst method, they determine the optimal weights based on the experts' judgement on the importance of each of the ten significant barriers identified.

The findings showed that the least significant barriers were investment costs, security risks, and scalability issues, while the most significant ones were a lack of knowledge and management support, reluctance to change, and technological immaturity (Rejeb *et al.*, 2022).

Similarly, Gurzhii (2022) examines challenges and barriers from blockchain adoption, technological benefits, and the most promising areas of digitalisation, given the impact of the topic of digital transformation on the economic, social, individual, environmental, and technical aspects.

By conducting a systematic literature review of 39 empirical articles on blockchain's impact on digital transformation, this theoretical framework can be useful for academia and industries willing to expand their knowledge on the topic (Gurzhii, 2022).

In fact, the transition to new models and strategies through emerging technologies could increase business freedom, operational revenue, and affect living standards, and a real-world example can help one adopt the technology considering current limitations (Gurzhii, 2022).

Also, Jameel *et al.* (2020) address some of the major issues of blockchain-enabled IIoT networks, such as block time minimisation and transaction throughput enhancement, promoting the utility of reinforcement learning (RL) techniques and suggesting some future research directions, along with the improvements needed.

The results demonstrate that the Q-learning approach (used for minimising the occurrence of forking events by reducing the transmission delays for a miner) outperformed greedy policy, notwithstanding its complexity.

A more complete literature review of blockchain, compared with previous research, was conducted by Le and Hsu (2021), as they discussed challenges of blockchain in terms of security and performance, explained various security properties of blockchain, provided a taxonomy of blockchain-based applications, and finally outlined some research directions.

This was done considering that blockchain, due to its decentralised nature, can enable sustainable practices and innovative business models, reducing costs, transaction times, and waste in manufacturing and production processes; it also provides real-time communications, low product costs, reduced delivery times, and fast payment with reduced transaction fees (Le and Hsu, 2021).

In fact, blockchain allows one to record, in an immutable way and in a fixed period of time, various products for a specific payment: This possibility to record immutable data enables one to track the highest emitters of greenhouse gases and identify materials and products that use significant non-renewable resources (Le and Hsu, 2021).

Additionally, through blockchain's adoption, a low-trust centralised transaction ledger held by a single third party becomes a high-trust decentralised form held by various verifying nodes (Le and Hsu, 2021).

Khan *et al.* (2021) examine the role of blockchain technology in transforming CE practices and business models, and its impact on eco-environmental performance, which influences organisational performance.

Those findings lay the foundations for countries/firms that aim to achieve financial and sustainable goals by integrating this technology in CE practices (Khan *et al.*, 2021), as blockchain significantly improves CE practices (namely, circular design, circular procurement, recycling, and remanufacturing) that in turn improve firms' environmental, financial, and organisational performances (Khan *et al.*, 2021).

In this sense, Shojaei *et al.* (2021) also provide a proof of concept regarding the feasibility of the blockchain model, tested through a synthetic case study, as an enabler of a CE, as information flow through blockchain produces synergy with a smart and connected community (Shojaei *et al.*, 2021).

This is important since blockchain allows a secure, fast, and accessible information network by providing a decentralised ledger where products and materials can be traced to their sources, enabling proactive planning for reusability along with material and energy traceability, permitting the user to make predictions for the recycling and reuse of materials and goods used in the built environment (Shojaei *et al.*, 2021).

Upadhyay *et al.* (2021) identify and systematise the Industry 4.0 research on blockchain's contribution to the CE through sustainability and social responsibility, providing recommendations for future studies in this field.

In particular, blockchain appears to positively contribute to the CE, for example, by helping to enhance performance and communication along the supply chain and reduce the transaction and carbon footprints (Upadhyay *et al.*, 2021).

Blockchain also proved to be able to solve operational challenges in manufacturing and service supply chains through its platform used to execute smart contracts, a logic-based approach to trust building (Jabbar and Dani, 2020).

The remaining challenges relative to blockchain implementation for CE appear to be trust, illegal activities, and the potential for hacking, with a need to address these through suitable legislation and policy development, although the benefits are likely to exceed the challenges (Upadhyay *et al.*, 2021).

Regarding conceptual research on blockchain implementation, Jabbar and Dani (2020) introduce the notion of computational cost as an essential mechanism for completing operational transactions in the blockchain environment, and discuss the use of smart contracts and their influence on operational transactions in a supply chain from a cost perspective.

In fact, in this field, it is important to estimate the complexity and efficiency of smart contracts to identify potential costs, as the more complex the transaction, the more computational work that is required (Jabbar and Dani, 2020).

Frequency, computational costs, and intensity of transactions are measured through an experimental methodology, as they develop and implement a fully virtual public blockchain to store, validate, and maintain transactions (Jabbar and Dani, 2020).

The fact that the exponential rise of blockchain technology led to the emergence of a growing number of decentralised platforms also provided the opportunity to examine alternative governance structures (as platforms are governed through community efforts instead of their owners).

In this sense, drawing on mechanism design theory, Chen *et al.* (2021) evaluate the trade-offs between centralisation and decentralisation and provide empirical evidence from the blockchain industry on the characteristics, antecedents, and consequences of effective platform governance.

Semi-decentralisation appears to be a higher-performing governance structure, preferred by experienced leaders compared to the more decentralised digital platforms of the infrastructure layer (Chen *et al.*, 2021).

This is important considering an inverted U-shaped relationship between decentralisation and platforms' development activity, market capitalisation, and developer attention (Chen *et al.*, 2021).

Lumineau *et al.* (2021) outline the background and the features of blockchains, considering their social implications as well as their challenges and limitations.

They intend mainly to explore how blockchains may change the way to organise collaborations, including what different types of blockchains may emerge, who is involved and affected by blockchain governance, the reasons behind its adoption, when and where blockchains can be more (versus less) effective, and how blockchains influence relevant organisational outcomes (Lumineau *et al.*, 2021).

This technology enables an efficient governance mechanism, and the tacitness of the transaction is a key boundary condition as blockchain can enforce agreements and assure a new form of cooperation and coordination compared to other information technology solutions or contractual and relational governance (Lumineau *et al.*, 2021).

Chen and Bellavitis (2020) investigate the benefits of decentralised finance and evaluate promises and challenges of decentralised business models compared to existing ones.

This is imperative since blockchain technology can reduce transaction costs, distribute trust, and empower decentralised platforms, providing layers for decentralised business models, which tend to be more transparent, decentralised, innovative, and interoperable (Chen and Bellavitis, 2020).

Blockchain technology also has the potential to broaden financial inclusion, facilitate open access, encourage permissionless innovation, and create new opportunities for entrepreneurs, reshaping and innovating the structure of finance and entrepreneurship (Chen and Bellavitis, 2020).

Similarly, Rymarczyk (2020) notes how financial market institutions can take advantage of this technology that ensures transaction security, reduces the risk of counterfeits and hacking attacks, eliminates intermediaries, and shortens implementation time.

Chawla (2020) compares trust in blockchains with that in TCE, AT, and RBV, with the aim of offering new insights into the implications of the emergence of blockchains, which has changed our view of crowdfunding, platforms, organisation, and governance, enabling disintermediation that has received increasing attention from entrepreneurs and researchers.

In fact, enforcement in TCE, AT, and RBV depends on property rights, contractual obligations, and legal recourses (Chawla, 2020) while, in comparison, distributed ledgers have the following four peculiarities (Chawla, 2020):

1. Trust is based on algorithms (instead of an organisational and legal regime) and on an associated social layer that propagates and maintains the blockchain. For example, unlike TCE (that focuses on markets, hierarchies, and hybrid forms of governance), trust depends on the algorithms, their transparency, and the organisational governance of the blockchain. Moreover, if blockchains rely on a peer-to-peer network, AT relies on a principal–agent dyad.
2. Blockchain technology has different core assumptions and sources of distrust. For example, it is difficult to apply TCE to PoW blockchains, which are not economising compared to TCE that can align the transaction attributes and the governance mode. Then, compared to AT, which is based on information asymmetry, blockchain emphasises transparency for each actor who can view the transaction record, with the only problem being the ability (technical competence) of the stakeholders involved.
3. Blockchain enables stakeholders to be anonymous parties to a transaction, and this accentuates the relevance of the technical competence and transparency on which algorithmic trust relies.
4. Finally, the combination of the above factors with lack of legal recourse highlights the importance of decentralisation to blockchains. In fact, a centralised blockchain jeopardises control and the property rights of the marginal stakeholders who have no conventional legal recourse.

Distributed ledger technologies also influenced the accounting profession, promising to increase the quality of information in sustainability report and allow assurance professionals to verify more information (as stakeholders and regulators demand non-traditional metrics and sustainability reporting): This could lead to uniform standards in the evaluation of sustainability reports.

Thus, blockchain applied to the traditional reporting systems can help to overcome problems with sustainability reporting (Bakarich *et al.*, 2020).

In particular, blockchain can provide reliable tracking and custodial support (as sustainability information is often self-reported by many firms, such as greenhouse gas emissions or product origin), and enhance sustainability reporting and assurance through increased trust, transparency, and traceability (Bakarich *et al.*, 2020).

The use of DLT and AI also has the potential to lower the costs and ease the process for disclosure and benchmarking in the green bonds market, making voluntary frameworks more appealing or, when mandatory, less burdensome.

It also allows to store green energy data and to control performance after the investment; this by screening documents and making data permanent and accessible, neutralising the lack of transparency.

In this sense, examples of peer-to-peer energy trading involve "energy" tokens assigned to the producer of energy with low carbon emissions, tokens used to trade the excess of energy in peer-to-peer networks (with individuals being contemporarily producers and consumers, therefore called "prosumers") or tokens even rewarded for contributing to other green behaviours.

A publicly available blockchain enables mandatory sustainability reporting, along with helping socially responsible organisations signal their orientation towards sustainable development; however, currently only few companies adopt blockchain systems to ensure their information's reliability (Pizzi *et al.*, 2022).

In this field, Bakarich *et al.* (2020) analyse, through an exploratory content analysis, potential and current uses of blockchain technology in the US and Canada to help accountants and auditors prepare and review sustainability data.

This shows the relevance of expanding the scientific knowledge about the impacts related to the notarisation of mandatory sustainability reports, underlining the opportunity for socially responsible organisations to use notarisation, since the proliferation of mandatory non-financial reports can reduce the signalling effects of disclosing non-financial information (Pizzi *et al.*, 2022).

In fact, the notarisation of the non-financial reports through a publicly available blockchain can represent a useful tool to mitigate the asymmetric information between organisations and stakeholders, to increase their engagement (Pizzi *et al.*, 2022).

Finally, Fuller and Markelevich (2020) investigate the potential impact of blockchain on the accounting and auditing profession, with regard to data security and privacy, technology, adoption, and implementation.

They suggest that blockchain usage in accounting still requires significant investment for further development of business applications and widespread usage.

In fact, even though blockchain may be beneficial in data reliability and financial statement auditing, it raises the problems of scalability at an acceptable cost and how to adequately address risks associated with data security and privacy (Fuller and Markelevich, 2020).

Finally, Fig. 4 clearly divides the papers, as listed in Table 2, according to their divergent or convergent nature.

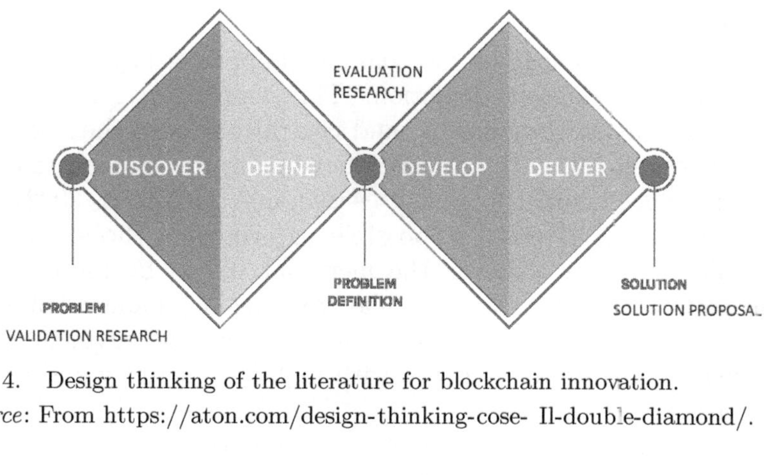

Fig. 4. Design thinking of the literature for blockchain innovation.
Source: From https://aton.com/design-thinking-cose- Il-double-diamond/.

6. Legislation in the Blockchain Environment

Currently, blockchain is still in the proof-of-concept stage; for it to reach large-scale application, four aspects appear crucial to explore, namely, technology, application, strategy, and legislation.

Regarding the last aspect, most of the regulatory challenges faced by blockchain are currently in the financial field.

In this sense, attention must be paid to digital currencies that facilitate cross-border capital flows, which may harm financial sovereignty of countries (affecting the stability of financial markets) and provide a channel for criminal activities such as money laundering and ransomware.

The issue is that regulations on blockchain supervision still do not follow uniform standards and have to be further incorporated into legal supervision and regulation to power sustainable development.

In fact, sound regulatory enforcement will reduce the risks of digital assets, encourage the participation of organisations, and increase the trust of consumers and investors.

The analysis has to expand to consider the aspect of regulatory compliance of blockchain, which requires infrastructure construction, such as Know Your Customer (KYC) or Anti Money Laundering (AML), along with on-chain and off-chain data mining, industrial audit and regulatory reporting tools, the integration of data and assets, data and credit, on-chain data and off-chain assets, and monitoring of how the transformation and circulation of data and assets will become increasingly secure.

Blockchain technology innovations should prevent payment fraud, bank runs, and deposit depletion: This emphasises the role of financial institutions, regulators, and central banks in the diffusion of digital currencies, with the aim of reducing tax evasion, money laundering, and terrorist financing (Aysan and Al-Ansari, 2022).

Digital currencies make it possible to overcome the shortcomings of fiat currency, such as the fact that it can be more easily employed for illicit transactions like tax evasion, money laundering, and terrorist financing, representing a form of payment that is cheaper to operate in countries with high fiat currency and check use (Soderberg *et al.*, 2022).

Now, even though digital currencies are considered by many economists as the future of money, their usage will increase the complexity for local banks, and the banking sector will have to change its organisation to remain able to provide competitive products (Deloitte, 2021).

Additionally, in order to reduce their risks, some authors suggest restricting digital currencies balances or taxing the use/balances after a certain limit (Soderberg *et al.*, 2022).

This is done by establishing restrictions on the remuneration of digital currencies and quantitative restrictions on their holdings and transactions (Soderberg *et al.*, 2022).

In this context, the role of the central bank is to issue electronic coins or accounts that are backed by the government's credit. Central banks started to explore digital currencies mainly for the following reasons (Deloitte, 2021):

a. Digital currencies could streamline central banks' function of providing legal tender and support digitisation of economies, offering access to digital payments at lower cost.
b. These could improve the efficiency of payment systems, even in peer-to-peer transactions, by speeding payment contestability, reducing operational costs and risks associated with managing traditional currency, and ensuring faster settlements and extended settlement hours.
c. These could improve monetary and fiscal policy, simplifying the distribution of government benefits and improving transaction control. Additionally, these could enhance financial stability by managing liquidity changes and offering public alternatives to private digital currencies.
d. Improving financial inclusion: Digital currencies could improve the competitiveness of local currency in regions that are trying to be less dependent on the US dollar.

7. Limitations of the Study and Concluding Remarks

The last decade witnessed a significant increase in academic publications on CE and digitalisation, with many studies focusing on barriers to digitalisation-led CE transition (such as policy-related concerns and information vulnerability), as CE could leverage emerging DTs, in particular blockchain, IoT, and AI (Chauhan *et al.*, 2022). As this technology is evolving, new features and capabilities are being developed and its usage has increased enormously over the last decade, expanding to other fields (such as audit) that can equally benefit from a shared, secure ledger (Fuller and Markelevich, 2020).

According to the literature examined, it seems possible to address sustainability issues using blockchain, as this technology ensures the data are stored and updated in a secure, tamper-proof, and irreversible way, where ledgers or databases are connected in a peer-to-peer, decentralised, open-access network.

In fact, blockchain is a decentralised, secure, and auditable solution for exchanging and authenticating information via transactions, without the need for a trusted third party.

Therefore, blockchain-enabled IoT networks may support next-generation networks and Industry 4.0, for the uberisation of Internet services (Jameel *et al.*, 2020); the effects of these current breakthrough inventions and technological phenomena of the fourth industrial revolution (IoT, advanced robots, cloud computing, big data, augmented/simulated reality, AI, blockchain) will emerge worldwide as soon as they are implemented by economies.

In any case, unlike traditional theories, blockchains highlight the ability (technical competence) and transparency or dimensions of trust, but unfortunately the trust shifts to the algorithmic layer much more than the conventional organisational or social layers (Chawla, 2020).

From a methodological standpoint, it has to be considered that, in this study, articles have been retrieved only through Scopus and Google Scholar, so this probably does not cover all the literature on cybersecurity in management accounting, auditing, and governance.

Additionally, this study is limited to the business, management, and accounting fields, so it would be useful to develop case studies about the application in other related fields or business networks to foster the adoption and establishment of best practices.

The first unfolding step of the present study denotes that blockchain, in combination with smart contracts and large databases, presents great potential in many sectors, including sustainable finance, and certifies the supply chain of enterprises and certain "green aspects", and the insights provided could pave the way for rapid adoption of blockchain technology and further development of blockchain-enabled IIoT networks (Jameel *et al.*, 2020).

Additionally, the diversified demand regarding the integration of blockchain with other cutting-edge information technologies (such as AI, big data, cloud computing, and IoT) appears to be a field of investigation that promotes integrated innovation.

Furthermore, a distributed network of global infrastructure supports more democratic forms of governance, and this technology enables individuals to transact energy among them without the need for central oversight from profit-seeking intermediaries (Gardner, 2019).

Moreover, implementation challenges persist: for example, DLT and big data have to face extremely high level of energy consumption to support sustainable finance.

To overcome this obstacle and support the deployment of blockchain in the green investment sector, it could be relevant to discuss other less energy-consuming forms of consensus methods or structures which should also reduce the time lapse between transaction validations and reduce operational risk.

Additionally, the problems of wrongful assessments (because of possible data inaccuracy or errors in the algorithm design or impossibility to cover all customers' characteristics), opacity (lack of transparency about the evaluation process), and financial exclusion (the elderly might face obstacles in accessing the services) must be confronted in depth.

In fact, the use of algorithms, AI, and big data in credit scoring, insurance underwriting, or robo-advice presents risks relating to data protection, accessibility, and reliability of data, portability, and interoperability: To solve interoperability problems, the focus should be on how to create trustless bridges and cross-chain applications that guarantee cost, reliability, or security.

Other issues to explore remain lower comparability (caused by the extreme personalisation of the evaluation), granular segmentation, possible unclear attribution of responsibilities, and lack of understanding by the customer about the importance of the information provided.

Finally, blockchain's advantages and disadvantages have not been sufficiently studied, despite dynamic development in all areas (Gurzhii, 2022; Rejeb *et al.*, 2022).

In this sense, further research could expand the number of successful use cases (that still appear to be limited) and handle open issues, such as monitoring the application of blockchain beyond the financial field and the digital currencies of central banks of countries, which will play a pivotal role in the global monetary system in the coming years.

Thus, the propositions open future directions of investigation to studies that aim to test them, qualitatively or quantitatively.

References

Aysan A. F. and Al-ansari K. A. (2022). Central bank digital currencies. Internet of things, and islamic finance: Blockchain prospects and challenges. *Internet of Things, and Islamic Finance: Blockchain Prospects and Challenges*. Available at: http://dx.doi.org/10.2139/ssrn.4128096.

Bakarich, K. M., Castonguay, J. J., and O'brien Pe (2020). The use of blockchains to enhance sustainability reporting and assurance accounting perspectives, 19(4), pp. 389–412. doi:10.1111/1911-3838.12241.

Balaguer Rasillo, X. (2020). Alternative economies, digital innovation and commoning in grassroots organisations: Analysing degrowth currencies in the Spanish region of Catalonia, *Environmental Policy* Gov. Available at: https://onlinelibrary.wiley.com/doi/abs/10.1002/eet.1910 e1910.

Benkler, Y. (2006). *The Wealth of Networks: How Social Production Transforms Markets and Freed*om (New Haven, CT: Yale University Press).

Benkler, Y. (2017). Peer production, the commons, and the future of the firm, *Strategic Organization*, 15(2), pp. 264–274. doi:10.1177/1476127016652606.

Böhmecke-Schwafert, M., Wehinger, M., and Teigland, R. (2022). Blockchain for the circular economy: Theorising blockchain's role in the transition to a circular economy through an empirical investigation, *Business Strategy and the Environment*. doi:10.1002/bse.3032.

Botene, P. H. R., De Azevedo, A. T., De Arruda, and Ignácio, P. S. (2021). Blockchain as an enabling technology in the COVID-19 pandemic: A systematic review, *Health and Technology*, 11(6), pp. 1369–1382.

Chauhan, C., Parida, V., and Dhir, A. (2022). Linking circular economy and digitalisation technologies: A systematic literature review of past achievements and future promises, *Technological Forecasting and Social Change*, 177, art. No. 121508. doi:10.1016/j.techfore.2022.121508.

Chawla, C. (2020). Trust in blockchains: Algorithmic and organizational. *Journal of Business Venturing Insights*, 14, pp. 2, 13–14.

Chen, Y., and Bellavitis, C. (2020). Blockchain disruption and decentralized finance: The rise of decentralized business models. *Journal of Business Venturing Insights*, 13, p. 1.

Chen, Y., Pereira, I., and Patel, P. C. (2021). Decentralised governance of digital platforms, *Journal of Management*, 47(5), pp. 1305–1337.

Dario, C., Sabrina, L., Landriault, E., and De Vega, P. (2021). DLT to boost efficiency for financial intermediaries. An application in ESG reporting activities, *Technology Analysis and Strategic Management*. doi:10.1080/09537325.2021.1999921.

Deloitte, (2021). CBDC: The next disruptor. Available at: https://www2.deloitte.com/us/en/pages/financial-services/articles/cbdc-central-bankdigital-currency.html.

Devine, A., Jabbar, A., Kimmitt, J., and Apostolidis, C. (2021). Conceptualising a social business blockchain: The coexistence of social and economic logics, *Technological Forecasting and Social Change*, 172, art. no. 120997. doi:10.1016/j.techfore.2021.120997.

Ezekiel, A., and Ismaila M. M. (2022). Introducing decentralised decision to our institutional platforms: Algorand and choice coin, doi:10.21203/rs.3.rs-1265770/v1.

Fuller, S. H., and Markelevich, A. (2020). Should accountants care about blockchain? *Journal of Corporate Accounting and Finance*, 31(2), pp. 34–46.

Gardner, J. (2019). Peer-to-peer energy trading and blockchain: The future of distributed energy resources, *Natural Resources of Environment*, 33 (4), 8–11.

Giesel, H. D., and Nobre, F. S. M. (2021) Implications of blockchain and transparency for business sustainability: An integrative review, *Revista de Administracao Mackenzie*, 22(6), art. no. eRAMD210033. doi:10.1590/1678-6971/ERAMD210033.

Gleim, M. R., and Stevens, J. L. (2021). Blockchain: A game changer for marketers? *Marketing Letters*, 32(1), pp. 123–128. doi:10.1007/s11002-021-09557-9.

Gunderson, R., Stuart, D., Petersen, B., and Yun, S. (2018). Social conditions to better realise the environmental gains of alternative energy: Degrowth and collective ownership, *Futures*, 99, pp. 36–44.

Gurzhii, A. (2022). Blockchain for digital transformation: A systematic literature review. Lappeenranta-Lahti University of Technology LUT, LUT School of Engineering Science, Master's thesis.

Howson, P. (2019). Tackling climate change with blockchain, *Nature Climate Change*, 9(9), pp. 644–645.

Howson, P. (2021). Distributed degrowth technology: Challenges for blockchain beyond the green economy, *Ecological Economics*, 184,

107020, ISSN 0921-8009, Available at: https://doi.org/10.1016/j.ecolecon.2021.107020.

Howson, P., Oakes, S., Baynham-Herd, Z., and Swords, J. (2019). Cryptocarbon: The promises and pitfalls of forest protection on a blockchain, *Geoforum*, 100, pp. 1–9.

Introna, L. D. (2016). Algorithms, governance, and governmentality on governing academic writing, *Science, Technology & Human Values*, 41(1), pp. 17–49. doi:10.1177/0162243915587360.

Jabbar, A., and Dani, S. (2020). Investigating the link between transaction and computational costs in a blockchain environment, *International Journal of Production Research*, 58(11), pp. 3423–3436.

Jameel, F., Javaid, U., Khan, W. U., Aman, M. N., Pervaiz, H., and Jäntti, R. (2020). Reinforcement learning in blockchain-enabled IIoT networks: A survey of recent advances and open challenges, *Sustainability*, 12(12), p. 5161.

Kavanagh, D. and Ennis, P. (2020). Cryptocurrencies and the emergence of blockocracy, *Information Society*, 36(5), pp. 290–300.

Khan, S. A. R., Razzaq, A., Yu, Z., and Miller, S. (2021). Industry 4.0 and circular economy practices: A new era business strategies for environmental sustainability, *Business Strategy and the Environment*, 30(8), pp. 4001–4014. doi:10.1002/bse.2853.

Le, T. V. and Hsu, C. L. (2021). A systematic literature review of blockchain technology: Security properties, applications and challenges, *Journal of Internet Technology*, 22(4), pp. 789–802.

Li, Z., Zhong, R. Y., Tian, Z. G., Dai, H. N., Barenji, A. V., and Huang, G. Q. (2021). Industrial blockchain: A state-of-the-art survey, *Robotics and Computer–Integrated Manufacturing*, 70, art. No. 102124.

Lumineau, F., Wang, W., and Schilke, O. (2021). Blockchain governance — A new way of organising collaborations? *Organization Science*, 32(2), pp. 500–521.

Lund, E. H., Jaccheri, L., Li, J., Cico, O., and Bai, X. (2019). Blockchain and sustainability: A systematic mapping study, in *IEEE/ACM 2nd International Workshop on Emerging Trends in Software Engineering for Blockchain* (WETSEB), pp. 16–23.

Macchiavello, E., and Siri, M. (2020). Sustainable finance and fintech: Can technology contribute to achieving environmental goals? A preliminary assessment of 'Green FinTech', EBI Working Paper Series No. 71.

Massaro, M., Dal Mas, F., Chiappetta Jabbour, C. J., and Bagnoli, C. (2020). Crypto-economy and new sustainable business models: Reflections and projections using a case study analysis, *Corporate Social Responsibility and Environmental Management*, 27(5), pp. 2150–2160. doi:10.1002/csr.1954.

Mishra, L. and Kaushik, V. (2021). Application of blockchain in dealing with sustainability issues and challenges of financial sector, *Journal of Sustainable Finance and Investment*. doi:10.1080/20430795.2021.1940805.

Nandi, S., Hervani, A. A., Helms, M. M., and Sarkis, J. (2021). Conceptualising circular economy performance with non-traditional valuation methods: Lessons for a post-pandemic recovery, *International Journal of Logistics Research and Applications*. doi:10.1080/13675567.2021.1974365.

Nobre-Gustavo G. C., Rodrigues-Elaine E. M. T., and De Lima-Miriane M. S. P. (2019). Assessing the role of Big Data and the Internet of Things on the transition to Circular Economy: a conceptual framework proposal through a literature review. *Journal Encontro da ANPAD*, Issue XLIII, Publisher: ANPAD.

Parmentola, A., Petrillo, A., Tutore, I., and De Felice, F. (2022). Is blockchain able to enhance environmental sustainability? A systematic review and research agenda from the perspective of sustainable development goals (SDGs), *Business Strategy and the Environment*, 31(1), pp. 194–217. doi:10.1002/bse.2882.

Pizzi, S., Caputo, A., Venturelli, A., and Caputo, F. (2022). Embedding and managing blockchain in sustainability reporting: A practical framework, *Sustainability Accounting, Management and Policy Journal*, 13(3), pp. 545–567. doi:10.1108/SAMPJ-07-2021-0288.

Rejeb, A., Rejeb, K., Keogh, J. G., and Zailani, S. (2022). Barriers to blockchain adoption in the circular economy: A fuzzy Delphi and best-worst approach, *Sustainability*, 14(6), p. 3611.

Rusch, M., Schöggl, J.-P., and Baumgartner, R. J. (2022). Application of digital technologies for sustainable product management in a circular economy: A review, *Business Strategy and the Environment*. doi:10.1002/bse.3099.

Rymarczyk, J. (2020). Technologies, opportunities and challenges of the industrial revolution 4.0: Theoretical considerations, *Entrepreneurial Business and Economics Review*, 8(1), pp. 185–198.

Schulz, K., Gstrein, O. J., and Zwitter, A. J. (2020). Exploring the governance and implementation of sustainable development initiatives through blockchain technology, *Futures*, 122, art. no. 102611. doi:10.1016/j.futures.2020.102611.

Shojaei, A., Ketabi, R., Razkenari, M., Hakim, H., and Wang, J. (2021). Enabling a circular economy in the built environment sector through blockchain technology, *Journal of Cleaner Production*, 294, art. no. 126352. doi:10.1016/j.jclepro.2021.126352.

Soderberg, G., Bechara, M., Bossu, W., Che, N., and Yoshinaga, A. (2022). Behind the scenes of central bank digital currency, IMF, February

2022. Available at: https://www.imf.org/en/Publications/fintech-notes/Issues/2022/02/07/Behind-the-Scenes-of-Central-Bank-Digital-Currency-512174.

Soni, G., Mangla, S. K., Singh, P., Dey, B. L., and Dora, M. (2021). Technological interventions in social business: Mapping current research and establishing future research agenda, *Technological Forecasting and Social Change*, 169, art. no. 120818. doi:10.1016/j.techfore.2021.120818.

Talafidaryani, M., Jalali, S. M. J., and Moro, S. (2021). Digital transformation: Toward new research themes and collaborations yet to be explored, *Business Information Review*, 38(2), pp. 79–88. doi:10.1177/0266382120986035.

Tawiah, V., Zakari, A., Li, G., and Kyiu, A. (2022). Blockchain technology and environmental efficiency: Evidence from US-listed firms, *Business Strategy and the Environment*. doi:10.1002/bse.3030.

Upadhyay, A., Mukhuty, S., Kumar, V., and Kazancoglu, Y. (2021). Blockchain technology and the circular economy: Implications for sustainability and social responsibility, *Journal of Cleaner Production*, 293, art. no. 126130. doi:10.1016/j.jclepro.2021.126130.

https://doi.org/10.1142/9781800614604_0003

Chapter 3

Blockchain Technology and Material Flow Analysis to Track Food Waste and Enhance Food Security and Sustainability

Christian Bux* and Vera Amicarelli†

Department of Economics, Management and Business Law, University of Bari Aldo Moro, Bari, Italy

*christian.bux@uniba.it

†vera.amicarelli@uniba.it

One of the main challenges with food waste minimisation relates to measurement and traceability across the food system. Complete, comprehensive, and transparent data are required to track progress on reduction targets, explore environmental impacts, and suggest mitigation strategies. The present chapter focuses on the use of material flow analysis and its utility in end-to-end traceability powered by blockchain technology, which stores digitised records in a decentralised and immutable manner and promotes trust and transparency across the entire food chain. The authors develop a food loss and waste measurement framework based on a mixed approach. On the one hand, material flow analysis emerges as an essential tool to quantify and qualify food loss and waste streams in the food system; on the other side, blockchain technology enables the optimisation of partnership networks and implementation of circular economy paradigms, thereby reducing food loss and waste.

Keywords: Food waste; food security; sustainability; material flow analysis; blockchain technology; circular economy; environmental accountancy; food loss; industrial symbiosis; sustainability; waste management

1. Introduction

Food security, which is when "when all people, at all times, have physical and economic access to sufficient safe and nutritious food to meet their dietary needs and food preferences for a healthy and active life" (United Nations, 1975; Pinstrup-Andersen, 2009), represents one of the main pillars of the Sustainable Development Goals (SDGs) of the UN, as highlighted by Goal 2 ("End hunger, achieve food security and improve nutrition and promote sustainable agriculture") and Goal 12 ("Ensure sustainable production and consumption patterns") (United Nations, 2022a). Among others, the SDGs call for the following: (a) 100% access to adequate food all year round; (b) all food systems to be sustainable; and (c) zero loss or waste of food (United Nations, 2022b). Overall, it is estimated that more than 1.3 billion tons of food is lost or wasted in the food system (FAO *et al.*, 2019), approximately 48% during upstream stages (i.e., agricultural production, postharvest, transportation, industrial processing, and retail) and more than 52% during downstream stages (i.e., household consumption and food services) (Xue *et al.*, 2017). To enhance food security, the SDGs aim to halve per capita global food waste (assessed as a range from 95 to 115 kg per person in Europe and North America, and from 6 to 11 kg per person per year in sub-Saharan Africa, and South and Southeast Asia) at retail and consumer levels and reduce food losses during upstream stages by 2030 (United Nations Environment Programme, 2021).

One of the main challenges of food waste minimisation relates to food waste measurement and traceability across the food system, as highlighted by the European Union Commission Delegated Decision (EU) 2019/1597 in "common methodologies and minimum quality requirements for the homogeneous assessment of food waste quantities and composition" (OJEU, 2019). Complete, comprehensive, and transparent data are a prerequisite for tracking progress on reduction targets, exploring environmental impacts, and suggesting mitigation strategies towards food security (Xue *et al.*, 2017). However, data inconsistencies and deficiencies in measurement programming still emerge as relevant issues. Different measurement methodologies, such as food diaries, surveys, direct measurement, mass balance approach, or waste composition analysis, and different functional units or system boundaries can lead to high uncertainties in results.

Although food waste has raised several concerns in the scientific literature, few articles have measured and tracked food waste along the entire food supply chain, providing updated and reliable data as required by the Commission Delegated Decision 2019/1597 (Amicarelli and Bux, 2020). A vast majority of authors have investigated households and hospitality sectors (Sehnem *et al.*, 2022), whereas the agricultural stage (Zavyalova *et al.*, 2022), as well as industrial processing and the retail sector (Eičaitė *et al.*, 2022) are still under-researched. Moreover, a majority of authors apply self-reporting analyses, such as questionnaires and in-depth interviews, whereas more consistent analyses, such as those relying on the mass balance approach and material flow analysis (Bux and Amicarelli, 2022), have been rarely used in academic research. However, such approaches could enhance food security by delivering both quantitative and qualitative information to companies and consumers (Damiani *et al.*, 2021).

This chapter highlights the need to develop comparable and replicable tools to measure food loss and food waste under a quantitative or qualitative perspective. Starting with a theoretical introduction related to the main concepts such as food security, food waste, and environmental sustainability (Section 2), this chapter focuses on the use of material flow analysis (Section 3.1), defined as a "systematic assessment of the state and change of materials flow and stock in space and time" (Brunner and Rechberger, 2017), and its utility in end-to-end traceability powered by blockchain technology (Section 3.2), which stores digitised records in a decentralised and immutable manner, and promotes trust and transparency across the entire food chain. The authors develop a food loss and waste measurement framework based on a mixed approach (Section 4): on the one hand, using material flow analysis; on the other hand, using blockchain technology.

The final aim of this chapter is to provide a theoretical framework to companies and consumers by implementing material flow analysis and blockchain technology as fundamental tools to boost food security, as well as drivers to enhance environmental sustainability and environmental entrepreneurship. This analysis adds an extra step in environmental research, since to the best of the authors' knowledge there is no research, which develops a mixed approach based on material flow analysis and blockchain technology. Moreover, the theoretical framework presented in this chapter could inform consumers on sustainable accountancy tools and help food companies achieve more sustainable performances and acquire market competitiveness.

2. Theoretical Background

2.1. *Food security*

In light of the global dimension of agricultural production and the elated economic, social, and health conditions imposed by the market, food security depends on food production and consumption patterns. In Europe, Regulation (EC) No. 178/2002 of the European Parliament and the Council lays down the general principles and requirements of food law, as well as general procedures in matters of food safety, aiming to guarantee at the same time human health, consumer interests, and market stability with a view towards sustainability along the entire agri-food chain (OJEU, 2002).

As regards its definition, food security has a dual nature: On the one hand, "food security" concerns socioeconomic factors in terms of food resource availability; on the other hand, "food safety" concerns the hygiene and health conditions of food production and consumption. Considering the socioeconomic aspects, food security means "a situation in which the entire population, at all times, has physical, social and economic access to food resources that are sufficient from a hygienic and nutritional point of view, and which meet the needs of supply nutritional and the daily preferences of consumers" (FAO *et al.*, 2019). Based on this definition, two levels of food insecurity could be identified: "moderate" and "severe". Moderate food insecurity concerns circumstances in which the population is unable to obtain food in sufficient quantity or quality to meet its energy needs and essentially depends on individual food budgets or other resources. Severe food insecurity corresponds to the complete absence of food for one or more consecutive days, and places the health of human beings at high risk.

Food insecurity must be considered a multilevel issue, with three fundamental and equally important pillars that can be distinguished (FAO, 2018):

- *Food availability*: The availability of food resources is a necessary but not sufficient factor to ensure global food security. Food availability is intended as the amount of food present in a given geographical area in terms of national production, import–export, and stocks present, representing the more strictly "commercial" aspect of food safety.
- *Food access*: Access to food mainly concerns the physical, economic, financial, and social dimensions of the acquisition of food resources. In physical terms, access to food concerns the presence/absence of transport infrastructure between the country of production and the country of purchase. In economic/financial terms, it essentially depends on the monetary value (e.g., income level, food price) that consumers assign to the purchase of sufficient food. In sociocultural terms, access to food concerns the specific characteristics of each country, within which it is possible that some ethnic minorities (or gender groups) cannot freely access food resources. Lastly, access to food takes into account the legislative profile of each country (e.g., presence/absence of social subsidies).
- *Food utilisation*: Although available and accessible, a further characteristic of food resources concerns the quality/quantity in terms of hygiene, health, and nutrition in order to meet the energy needs of every human being. Food utilisation is configured as a dimension strictly connected to the habits, needs, and methods of consumption of every human being, and can change very quickly over time and space.

The contextual presence of food availability, access, and utilisation guarantees the existence of "food stability".

Among the SDGs, food security plays a prominent role. In particular, the second goal (*Goal 2, Zero Hunger*) is dedicated to the reduction of hunger in the world, whereas the twelfth goal (*Goal 12, Sustainable production and consumption*) aims to reduce food loss and waste by halving per capita global food waste at the retail and consumer levels and reduce food losses along production and supply chains by 2030 (United Nations, 2022a, 2022b).

2.2. *Food loss and waste*

Among the main economic, environmental, and social challenges that the agri-food industry must address, food waste deserves special attention. If "food" means any substance which, however processed, semi-processed, or raw, is intended for human consumption (including beverages or other substances used for the production, preparation, and storage of food), (Nebbia, 1995), then "food loss" and "food waste" could also be defined as a decrease in the quantity or quality of food intended for human consumption (Pinstrup-Andersen, 2009; Food Loss and Waste Protocol, 2016a, 2016b). However, there is no single definition of "food waste".

The first categorisation concerns the distinction between food loss and food waste. Food loss could be explained as a decrease in the quantity and quality of food for human consumption which occurs essentially in the phases of agricultural production, processing, and distribution, excluding the stages of final consumption. Food losses are due to problems encountered during the collection, storage, processing, packaging, transport, and distribution activities, as well as due to technical malfunctions of the production system (Lipińska *et al.*, 2019; Nicastro and Carillo, 2021). Further, food waste could be defined as a decrease in the quantity and quality that occurs mainly in the distribution and final consumption phases for various reasons (e.g., due to excessive purchase of food followed by the impossibility of consumption before the expiration date).

An additional distinction takes into consideration the difference between "avoidable", "possibly avoidable", and "inevitable waste". Avoidable waste means "any food or drink thrown away, at any stage prior to disposal, in most cases still edible", while possibly avoidable waste refers to food and drinks that some people consume and others do not consume for reasons of taste (e.g., crusty bread), or which can become edible only if cooked in a certain way (e.g., potato skin). Unavoidable waste is generated during food preparation and cannot be destined for human consumption (e.g., bones).

Lastly, one more definition concerns the distinction between "absolute waste" and "relative waste". Relative waste indicates each food, which can find a commercial (and market) setting under other forms (e.g., animal feed, compost, and source of biogas), while absolute waste means what is intended solely and exclusively for disposal.

To conclude, food waste takes place along the entire production chain, from the agricultural to the final consumption stage, and each phase differs from the others in terms of causes and waste typologies. On average, although food waste measurement essentially depends on the definition and the analysis breakdown adopted, it is estimated that about 11–23% of food waste occurs along the agricultural production phase, 17–19% during the industrial transformation phase, 8–17% during the distribution phase, and more than 50% during the final consumption phase.

2.3. *Food loss and waste measurement*

Food loss and waste represent a health, social, economic, and environmental challenge. The issue, already included in the 2030 Agenda for Sustainable Development and in the European plan entitled "Closing the Loop — An EU Action Plan for the Circular Economy", has recently been included as a useful variable for the purpose of the "monitoring framework for the circular economy". Food loss and waste, explicitly mentioned in the context of European sustainability strategies, have been further analysed through the implementation of a specific indicator, called the "food waste index", and included among the 10 indicators of the circular economy (Moraga *et al.*, 2019; Eurostat, 2020).

One of the main problems related to food waste is the absence of a homogeneous definition, the lack of data availability (both quantitative and qualitative), and the absence of a standardised methodology for its measurement. Five measurement methods have been suggested in the context of the Delegated Decision (EU) 2019/1597 of the Commission of May 3, 2019: (i) food diaries; (ii) direct measurement; (iii) mass balance approach; (iv) food questionnaires; and (v) waste analysis composition. The measurement methods integrate the previous Directive 2008/98/EC and recommend a common methodology and minimum quality requirements for the uniform measurement of food waste levels.

The Delegated Decision (EU) 2019/1597 establishes that the quantities of food loss and waste must be measured separately for each phase of the agri-food chain, in the context of primary production, processing, and manufacturing; retail or other forms of food distribution; restaurants and catering services; and households. Technically, the standard establishes that member states must measure the quantity of food waste for a given stage of the food chain at least once every four years, and the quantities of waste must be expressed in metric tons of fresh mass. The measurements, carried out in accordance with the proposed methodologies, must be based on a representative sample of the population and must adequately reflect the changes in the data related to the quantities of food waste to be measured. In addition, the measurements must be based on the best information available in a given geographic area.

As regards food loss and waste typologies, Table 1 shows their classification based on Delegated Decision (EU) 2019/1597, distinguishing them according to their stage of generation.

2.4. *Environmental sustainability*

Overall, food waste has significant environmental impacts, especially with regard to climate change, water consumption, soil erosion, and the loss of biodiversity. Considering the footprint indicators of food waste, such as the carbon and water footprints (i.e., production of climate-altering gases by product, service, organisation, event, or individual), the first has accounted for over 3.3 billion tons of CO_2 equivalent, while the second (i.e., consumption of surface and ground water resources) exceeds the value of 250 km^3, approximately equivalent to the water transported annually by the Volga River. With regard to land consumption (i.e., quantity of land occupied for the production of food produced but not consumed), it is estimated that every year more than 1.4 billion hectares (approximately 30% of the total area agriculture) is dedicated to the production of wasted food (FAO, 2013).

Considering that the above-mentioned food waste carbon footprint is equal to 3.3 billion tons of CO_2 equivalent, it is possible to estimate that about 35% of the emissions are derived from the waste of cereals (1.15 billion tons), followed by meat and vegetables, which produce about 20% of the emissions (0.65 billion tons). From a geographical point of view, industrialised Asia represents the area with the greatest impact, contributing to about 35% of CO_2-equivalent

Table 1. Food loss and waste typologies and generation stage based on Delegated Decision (EU) 2019/1597.

Generation Stage	**Food Loss and Waste Typologies**
Waste from primary production	Primary production waste includes food losses from agriculture, forestry, and fishing, and also includes animal tissue waste and plant tissue waste.
Processing and manufacturing waste	Waste from processing and manufacturing includes waste derived from manufacturing activities, whether from the food or beverage industries. In addition, the following wastes are considered: • preparation and processing of meat, fish, and other foods of animal origin; • preparation and processing of fruit, vegetables, cereals, edible oils, cocoa, coffee, tea, and tobacco, as well as wastes from the production of canned food, production of yeast, yeast extract, preparation and fermentation of molasses; • sugar refining; • dairy industry; • confectionery and bakery industry; • production of alcoholic and non-alcoholic beverages (except coffee, tea, and cocoa).
Waste from retail sale or other forms of food distribution	Sales waste includes that derived from wholesale and retail trade, as well as biodegradable waste from kitchens and canteens, edible oils and fats, unsorted municipal waste, market waste, and organic waste other than the previous ones.
Waste from restaurants and catering services	Waste from restaurants and catering services (so-called hospitality) includes that derived from accommodation and catering services, as well as biodegradable waste from kitchens and canteens, edible oils and fats, and unsorted municipal waste. Hospitality services include canteens, hospitals and nursing homes for the elderly, hotels, schools, restaurants, and universities.
Household waste	Household waste includes biodegradable kitchen and canteen waste, edible oils and fats, and unsorted municipal waste.

emissions. On average, a ton of wasted food produces about 4.2 tons of CO_2 equivalent; thus, is it possible to estimate that Italy produces greenhouse gas quantities of over 8 million tons (Gaiani, 2013). As regards the water footprint, over 50% of the food waste-related water footprint comes from grain waste, followed by fruit waste. The geographical area causing the most impact is Southeast Asia. The Italian food waste-related water footprint is estimated at approximately 5.3 km^3 per year (Segré and Falasconi, 2011). Lastly, in the case of land consumption (agricultural and pastureland) associated with food waste, it refers to the portion of land destined for the production of uneaten food. Meat and milk together contribute to about 80% of global land use associated with food waste (1.12 billion hectares).

Sustainability associated with food waste can be considered under the environmental, the economic and the social perspective. Sustainable management of resources, generally understood as "a management that allows the present generation to meet their own needs without compromising the ability of future generations to satisfy their own" (United Nations, 2022), must be based on the following essential pillars:

- End hunger (and all forms of malnutrition) and ensure that all people have secure access to nutritious and sufficient food throughout the year.
- Double the agricultural productivity and income of small and medium-sized agricultural producers through safe and equitable access to land, resource and production inputs, know-how, financial services, and market opportunities.
- Ensure sustainable food production systems and implement resilient agricultural practices that increase productivity and land production, while protecting ecosystems and strengthening adaptive capacities to climate change, extreme weather conditions, drought, floods, and natural disasters.
- Preserve the genetic diversity of seeds, cultivated plants, farm and domestic animals, and related wild species.
- Increase investment, through the improvement of international cooperation, in rural infrastructure, agricultural research and training, and technological development, in order to improve agricultural production capacities in developing countries.

- Correct and prevent trade restrictions and distortions in world agricultural markets.
- Adopt measures to ensure the proper functioning of the markets for food raw materials and their derivatives, and facilitate rapid access to market information, including that relating to food reserves.

3. Measurement Methodologies

3.1. *Material flow analysis*

Material flow analysis is a "systematic assessment of the state and change of flows and stocks of materials within a system defined in space and time" (Brunner and Rechberger, 2017). It allows connection between resources, flows, and paths of disposal of materials, and is mainly based on the law of conservation of matter (principle of conservation of mass), which states that matter cannot be created or destroyed in an isolated system (Sterner *et al.*, 2011). Thus, since during any physical or chemical change the total mass of finished products (output) remains equal to the total mass of resources (inputs) (Ball *et al.*, 2011), the results of material flow analysis can be checked by comparing the inputs, stocks, and outputs of a defined process. Simplified mass balance represents a useful and intuitive support methodology for decisions regarding the environmental management of natural resources and waste. Material flow analysis deals with a coherent set of information on flows and stocks in a defined time and space, managing energy, natural resources, emissions, and socioeconomic issues. More generally, it connects the anthroposphere (guided by man) with the environment (governed by nature).

Within the objectives of material flow analysis, it is possible to distinguish the following:

- Investigation (and understanding) of the qualitative characteristics of a metabolic system well defined in space and time through the selection of the most relevant processes, the main material flows, and the most representative stock levels. In this context, material flow analysis offers the opportunity to choose different boundaries and connect (discretionally) processes and flows.
- Investigation (and understanding) of the quantitative characteristics of flows, processes, and stocks within a system, allowing

researchers to track inputs, outputs, waste, and emissions from the beginning to the end of the process.

- Observation of a metabolic system over time, with the ability to focus attention on past trends or evaluate future opportunities. Furthermore, material flow analysis allows one to simulate the functioning of a certain metabolic system by modifying drivers (e.g., consumption behaviours) or by introducing new technologies within the process.
- Reduction of a complex process to a simplified flowchart, while ensuring a meaningful and robust basis for public and private decision-makers.
- Application of the mass balance principle to control and verify the efficiency of the process, as well as identify deficiencies in the methodology or data. The use of the law of conservation of mass, unlike data of an economic nature, makes it possible to apply a scientific method of great precision.
- Presentation of easy and ready-to-use results, facilitating transparency, universal understanding, and communication to a wider audience of interested parties.
- Creation of an adequate basis for the implementation of other methodologies and indicators such as life cycle assessment, input–output analysis, or water or carbon footprints.

In any case, material flow analysis does not focus on the identification and assessment of environmental impacts, but on the creation of a material inventory (in terms of resources and waste) that is useful for subsequent environmental impact evaluations.

One of the main steps in conducting a material flow analysis is identifying a mass balance of goods, since it represents the basis for determining the balance of substances. The identification of a goods–substances binomial is crucial, since substance balances without asset balances cannot provide complete information for researchers, industrial plants, and public and private decision-makers. First, it is essential to identify good flows on which the system is based. Subsequently, the research must focus on the concentration of substances in the given good. Finally, it will be possible to identify any errors that cannot otherwise be found for single goods or for single substances.

A further step in conducting a material flow analysis is material accounting, often called "materials bookkeeping", indicating a systematic and comprehensive routine for updating the results by key flow and key stock measurements. This accounting also provides time series and allows the identification of trends at multiple levels, from micro to macro (Brigenzu *et al.*, 1997).

From a procedural point of view, material flow analysis consists of several phases. Mainly, it begins with the definition of problems, as well as with the identification of objectives and purposes. Subsequently, the assets, the substances, and the key processes will be selected, as well as the suitable system boundaries, thus enabling completing the so-called "qualitative model" (Brunner and Rechberger, 2017). Furthermore, all goods and substances will have to be identified on the basis of the mass balance principle, and any uncertainties will have to be considered.

One of the main steps in conducting a material flow analysis is defining the spatial system boundaries, in line with the objectives and purposes of the analysis. The boundaries often coincide with regions or companies, or other larger or smaller geographic areas (e.g., states, cities). Often, political and/or administrative boundaries are adopted as they appear more adequate and coherent with the objectives and purposes of the analysis (Brunner and Rechberger, 2017).

Subsequently, in order to conduct the first mass balance within the system, data are acquired from the literature, official reports (i.e., secondary data), or from company sources (i.e., primary data). Usually, non-influent material flows, representing less than 1% of the whole system, are ignored. At this stage, it is necessary to define all the processes included in the system, the number of which depends on the objectives of the analysis. In case the system is extremely complex, the processes can be divided into sub-processes. On the contrary, if you want to increase the simplification of the system, you can opt for the unification of the sub-processes in a single macro process. The reference literature considers systems with more than 15 processes to be extremely clumsy and complex.

Finally, a crucial point concerns the collection of data which are usually acquired from databases or measured directly or indirectly. However, most of the data come from regional, national, or international statistics, as well as from industry reports (e.g., private or public associations) or consumer organisations (Kelly and Matos, 2014). Further inventories could be found in scientific articles, deeds, and manuals, requiring more or less wide levels of approximation or estimation.

3.2. *Blockchain technology*

The agri-food chain industry is responsible for economic, environmental, and social challenges, and the increased demand for safe, high-quality food with less environmental impacts has made the availability of information along the entire agri-food chain necessary, so as to boost consumers' reliance and reduce information asymmetry (Galati *et al.*, 2019). As a consequence, innovative technologies have been introduced, aimed at ensuring an effective traceability system in the agri-food chain and guaranteeing food safety and security as well as consumer acceptance, maximising companies' economic benefits (Li *et al.*, 2017). Blockchain has been introduced to enhance food traceability, among other reasons. Blockchain can be considered as shared and immutable ledger that facilitates the process of recording transactions and the traceability of assets in a commercial network. An asset can be tangible (e.g., food or food waste) or intangible. Virtually anything of value can be tracked and traded on a blockchain network, reducing risks and costs for all concerned (IBM, 2022). Its utility can be identified not only under the environmental perspective (i.e., reduced food waste, reduce environmental impacts) but also under the economic one (i.e., sold food waste, increased profits for companies). It is clear that each business is based on information, and the faster and more accurate the information, the better. In the light of these circumstances, blockchain allows the transmission of immediate, shared, and completely transparent data in an immutable ledger that only authorised network members can access. Further, considering the ancillary opportunities of blockchain, it is possible track orders, payments, accounts, production, and other features, enhancing (also) trade of by-products, co-products, and food waste better intended as secondary raw materials. Blockchain technology collects all the details of an end-to-end transaction, thus generating greater trust, as well as new opportunities in terms of efficiency, profitability, and environmental sustainability (IBM, 2022).

Overall, blockchain technology can facilitate food waste tracking along the food supply chain due to its scrupulous structure, which consists of (i) *blocks*, (ii) *chains*, and (iii) *transactions* (European Environmental Agency, 2021). Blockchain, defined as "a public ledger consisting of all transactions taking place across a peer-to-peer network" (Adamashvili *et al.*, 2018) and described as a decentralised and transparent peer-to-peer distributed database secured by cryptography, where transactions are registered in a constantly growing list of records which are immutable and append-only, relies on the following three items (IBM, 2022):

(1) *Blocks of data.* Each time a transaction occurs, it is recorded as a "block" of data. Such transactions represent the movement of an asset which can be tangible (e.g., food or food waste) or intangible. Each block provides transparent and comprehensive information, such as "who", "what", "when", "where", and "how much", and other types of information, such as the temperature of a food shipment, the organoleptic quality of the by-products, as well as the possible applications in other sectors according to the principles of circular economy and the industrial ecology.
(2) *Chains of data.* Each block is linked to those that precede it and follow it. Such blocks form a chain of data as an asset moves from place to place or changes ownership. The blocks attest to the exact time and sequence of transactions, and the blocks connect securely to each other to prevent one of them from being tampered with or sandwiched between two existing blocks.
(3) *Irreversible transactions.* Each additional block strengthens the verification of the previous block and therefore of the entire blockchain. This makes blockchain tamper-proof, offering the key element of immutability. This eliminates the possibility of malicious tampering and creates a transaction log that network members can trust.

Records can be updated through specific agreements among peers, and untrusted transactions are not agreed upon and not included in the chain (Chandra *et al.*, 2019; Casino *et al.*, 2019). The first attempts to use blockchain technology were to support cryptocurrency trade, but later such technology was introduced to store all information related to several commodities and service sectors, such as automotive, banking and finance, healthcare, life sciences, manufacturing, and agribusiness (Antonucci *et al.*, 2019). Blockchain has been applied with success, even in education, privacy, and security, as well as in governance (e.g., notary, law). Among its goals are increasing transparency and visibility for all stakeholders from agricultural production to distribution and the final consumption stage. Through its application, all raw materials suppliers, manufacturers, distributors, wholesalers, retailers, and final consumers increase their chance to store all transactions and obtain a (quite) complete guarantee on the trustworthiness of products and contacts. Blockchain records procedures and makes documents unalterable, providing certification cost savings from 70% to 90% (Tan *et al.*, 2020), but some effort from local governments, industrial associations, and dominant customers is needed. Blockchain technology can be accessed by any of the supply chain actors, but none of them can modify the succession of information shared among all nodes in the system. It means that the history of the network is immutable (European Environmental Agency, 2021).

Among its benefits, blockchain increases the following: (i) trust among members, since members receive accurate and timely data, and the confidential blockchain records will only be shared with granted members of the network; (ii) security, since data accuracy consent is required for all network members, all validated transactions are immutable, and not even a system administrator can delete them; and (iii) efficiency, since the availability of a distributed and shared ledger among members can avoid useless reconciliations. Further, to speed up transactions, a set of rules, the so-called smart contract, can be stored on blockchain and executed automatically, improving the exchange (sale–purchase) of secondary raw materials and food loss and waste.

4. Material Flow Analysis and Blockchain Technology to Track Food Waste

4.1. *Theoretical framework*

Material flow analysis and blockchain technology could be integrated within a measurement framework which could help track food waste with high levels of detail and enhance food security and sustainability at companies' level (e.g., at single industrial plants). On the one hand, material flow analysis appears to be an essential tool to quantify and qualify food loss and waste streams in the food system, from agricultural production to distribution, retail, and final consumption. On the other hand, blockchain technology enables the optimisation of partnership networks, enhancing secure transactions and efficacy through, for instance, smart contracts among companies.

Material flow analysis allows one to quantify the amount of food waste in the context of single agri-food companies that are part of a network, while blockchain allows one to structure, in a reliable, safe and constant way, transactions of purchase–sale of the aforementioned food waste. If the material flow analysis approach is applied within a single company, it will not be necessary to resort to uncertainties or estimates, since the individual company can calculate the mass balance internally. Furthermore, considering that food waste is constantly monitored through the blockchain system, this can facilitate the identification of standardised and consistent measurement methodologies at an international level, allowing each member state to know "in detail" the amount of waste generated. Finally, considering the use of smart contracts, it is possible to facilitate the purchase and sale of food waste (which will become secondary raw material for another industry), improving environmental performance and therefore the sustainability of the entire agri-food chain. Overall, it is more likely to increase circular economy paradigms and reduce food loss and waste.

However, it seems essential to understand the main definitions and times which must be accounted in the measurement process (Table 2).

Figure 1 illustrates a simplified material flow analysis diagram, highlighting either positive outputs (i.e., livestock, carcasses, and final products) or negative outputs (i.e., food losses and food wastes) from farm to retail, the food industry, and food service. The simplified diagram illustrates the meat chain system, as developed by Bux and Amicarelli (2022). Each supply chain stage is identified with a single company, as to develop the idea that each company must conduct a material flow analysis at the single industrial plant level and provide quantitative and qualitative data to the network. Although the entire meat chain system is encompassed within the entire agri-food system, which accounts for feed production companies as well as other companies involved, for instance, livestock transportation or final product transportation, the simplified flow diagram focuses solely on the meat chain. Material flow analysis, intended as an environmental accounting method which identifies in a transparent and clear manner either quantitative or qualitative

Table 2. Definitions and items included in the research framework.

Item	Definition
Substances	A substance is any chemical element or substance made up of uniform units. All substances are characterised by a single and identical constitution and are therefore homogeneous.
Goods	Goods are defined as economic entities of matter with a positive or negative economic value. The assets consist of one or more substances.
Materials	Material is used as a generic term for both substances and goods.
Process	Process means the transformation, transport, or storage of materials. The term "process" implies that something has changed in its quality, while the term "stock" is primarily concerned with changes in quantity.
Flow	Flow is defined as a mass flow rate. Flux represents the ratio of mass to time flowing through a conductor. The flow unit can be expressed in units of kg/s or t/year.
Flux	Flux is defined as one flow per cross section.
System	The system is the real object of the investigation. It is defined by a group of elements, by the interaction between them, and within the boundaries between them, as well as in terms of space and time. It is a group of physical components connected or correlated in such a way as to form and/or act as an entire unit.
Activity	An activity is defined as the set of several processes, flows, stocks of goods, and substances that are relevant and necessary to satisfy a specific human need.
Anthroposphere	"The sphere of human life — a complex system of flows of energy, material, and information in space — is called the anthroposphere." It can be divided into four compartments: (a) agriculture; (b) industry, commerce, and exchange; (c) domestic consumption; and (d) waste management.
Metabolism	The metabolism of a system consists in the transfer, storage, and transformation of materials within the system, as well as in the exchange of materials with its environment.

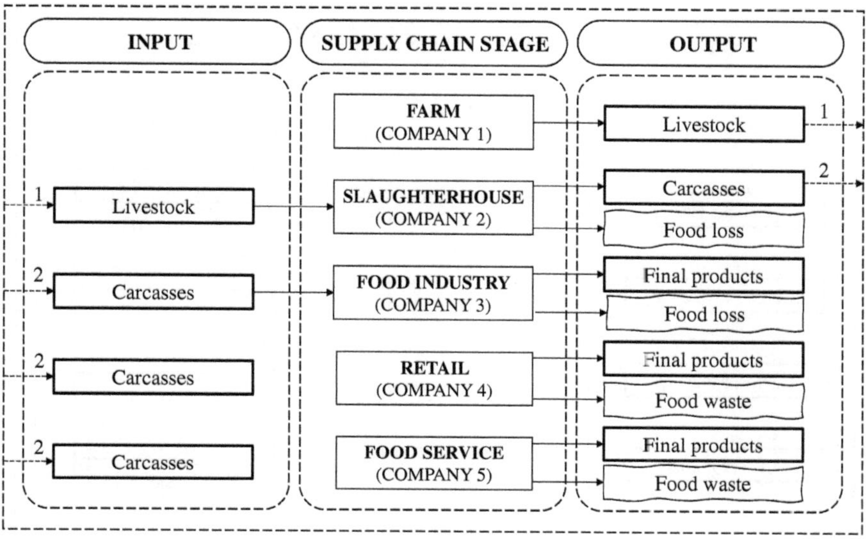

Fig. 1. Simplified diagram of material flow analysis of the meat chain system.

Notes: Boxes in bold indicate flows of positive inputs and/or edible food. Curved boxes indicate flows of food losses and food waste. Dashed lines indicate system boundaries.

flows across the system, should be conducted by each company involved in the meat supply chain. It means that each company keeps an account of all material flows in a detailed and precise manner, from raw material procurement to transformation in both positive and negative outputs. For instance, each company could adopt proper input–output tables (Marco *et al.*, 2009).

Figure 2 provides an example of material flow analysis in the meat sector from farm to retail, without considering final consumption. The proposed process starts with 100 kg in terms of livestock passing from farm (Company 1) to the slaughterhouse plant (Company 2), where the first generation of positive and negative outputs takes place, approx. 60 kg of useful carcasses to be sent to other companies in the supply chain and approx. 40 kg of food losses (e.g., by-products, co-products), respectively. For the latter, it is necessary to know in detail the quantity, quality, and product characteristics to make possible their use as secondary raw materials in other companies often producing high added-value products, instead of being considered useless waste. Subsequently, the 60 kg of carcasses are

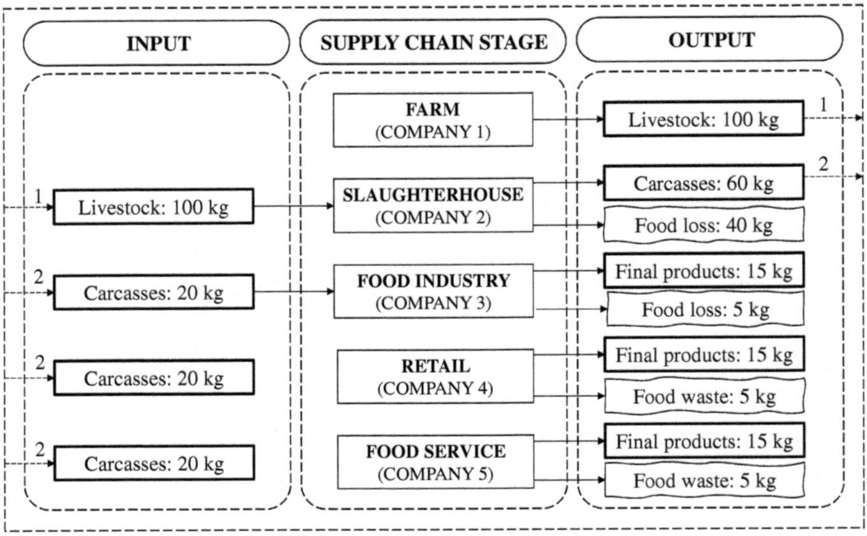

Fig. 2. Simplified diagram of material flow analysis of the meat chain system in numbers (kg).

Notes: Boxes in bold indicate flows of positive inputs and/or edible food. Curved boxes indicate flows of food losses and food waste. Dashed lines indicate system boundaries.

sent to the food industry (Company 3), to retail (Company 4), and to food services (Company 5). At the end of the supply chain, therefore, 45 kg of finished products useful for human nutrition will be generated, 45 kg of food loss, and 10 kg of food waste. As in the case of food loss (45 kg), in the case of food waste (10 kg), it is necessary to ensure that such waste is sent to companies that produce high added-value products, so that the material is not considered simple and useless waste.

Once quantitative (i.e., amount of food loss and waste in weight) and qualitative (e.g., organoleptic characteristics, food healthiness, origin) data have been collected at a single industrial plant, companies (from 1 to 5) must record data in the blockchain system as to guarantee trust and provide transparent and comprehensive information, such as "who", "what", "when", "where", "how much", and others (e.g., possible applications in other sectors according to the principles of circular economy and industrial ecology). Such data are immutable and cannot be modified by any user.

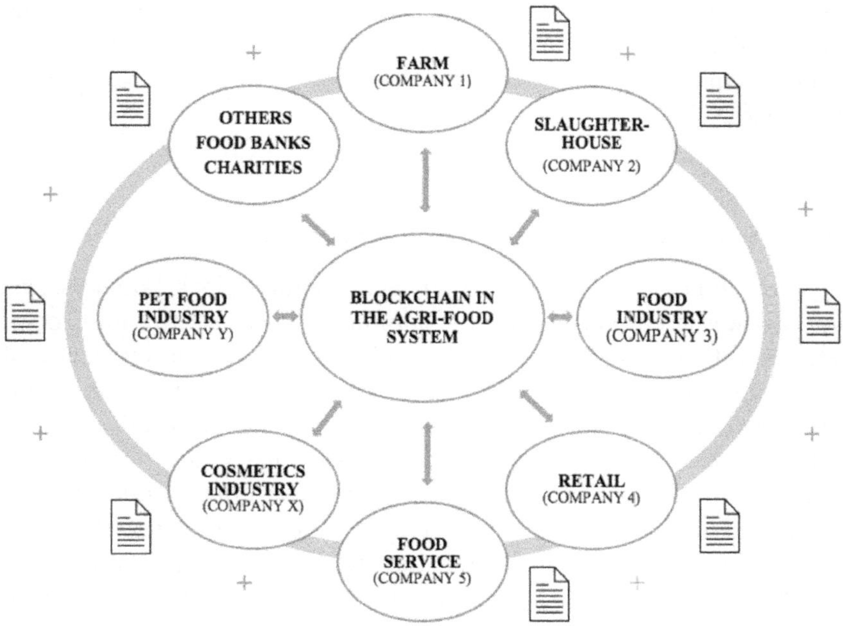

Fig. 3. Hypothetical blockchain technology in the agri-food system.

Figure 3 illustrates the input–output flow of information along the meat supply chain (from Company 1 to Company 5) in particular and along the agri-food and non-food system (e.g., Company X, Y, Z) in general in the hypothetical blockchain system.

Figure 3 highlights the input–output flows, which have been tracked according to material flow analysis and whose data are included in the blockchain system. Once data have been recorded in-depth, companies or other members of the network can speed up transactions through, for instance, smart contracts and start trading food loss and waste according to their characteristics, their needs, and their geographical allocations. It means that food losses from slaughterhouse (Company 2), for instance, could be purchased by other companies included in the network, such as cosmetics companies (Company X) or pet food production companies (Company Y) (Amicarelli *et al.*, 2021a).

The same applies for food waste produced in retail (Company 4) or food services (Company 5), which could be purchased as secondary raw materials and transformed in high added-value products in other companies towards the enhancement of environmental entrepreneurship. Finally, food services (Company 5) could share data with food banks or charities, enhancing food security and tackling still edible food waste.

4.2. *Practical and managerial implications*

The adoption of secure, transparent, and certified blockchain systems could allow the enhancement of economic, environmental, and social sustainability by improving the incoming and outgoing efficiency of each single company belonging to the network. The first step concerns the quantification and qualification of the material outputs, so that they can stop being considered worthless waste but re-enter the production chain, through principles of circular economy, and be economically exploited by other companies. The use of food loss and waste as secondary raw materials, undoubtedly, generates positive advantages both for the companies that sell, which do not have to incur disposal costs and can at the same time improve profits, and for the companies that buy, which can obtain discounts and more competitive prices on the market. Furthermore, the reuse of waste as secondary raw materials also improves environmental performances: The reference literature has underlined how food waste impacts twice, that is, when it is produced and when it is disposed (Amicarelli *et al.*, 2021b). Improving the transactions of food waste among companies, therefore, prevents industrial systems from disposing of waste with evident environmental consequences (e.g., CO_2 emissions) and, at the same time, prevents raw materials from being taken out of the biosphere (Rana *et al.*, 2021).

In the field of food security, if in the agricultural and industrial processing stages material flow analysis and blockchain technology allow the enhancement of waste and by-products towards environmental sustainability/entrepreneurship, in the field of the hospitality (e.g., collective catering, restaurants, school canteens) and the retail, such tools allow the identification of food products that are close to expiry, for example, and therefore still edible and addressable to human consumption. The chance of tracking these foods and sharing their quanti-qualitative information through stakeholders, which can either be private or public companies (e.g., charities), could undoubtedly increase food security and allow the distribution of packaged and still edible foods that would otherwise end up in the garbage (Santeramo, 2021).

Companies applying material flow analysis and participating in blockchain technology can be the following: (a) agri-food companies interested in by-product valorisation, which can reduce the environmental load associated with raw material withdrawals and waste disposal, and can therefore enhance environmental sustainability; and (b) food banks and charities, which can collect still edible food from retail, restaurants, canteens, etc. (Damiani *et al.*, 2021). Therefore, the key to reduce the environmental impacts and enhance food security lies in the availability of information and in its dissemination "in real time", so that interested stakeholders can exchange food waste (or still edible food) in very short times and 0 km.

A final, essential remark concerns the planning of material flow analysis in each single company that takes part in the blockchain network. Companies must be aware that data are crucial for achieving sustainable development goals and must be considered an essential prerequisite for assessing the environmental, social, and economic effectiveness of their productions. Therefore, companies taking part in the blockchain network must establish a commonly accepted definition of food loss and waste and then programme a common way of conducting material flow analysis.

5. Conclusions

The present research develops a food loss and waste measurement framework mixing two approaches: material flow analysis and blockchain technology. The first appears to be an essential tool to quantify and quality food loss and waste streams in the food system, while the second enables the optimisation of partnership networks and increases circular economy paradigms. The proposed framework could be considered a useful tool to reduce food loss and waste and enhance environmental, economic, and social sustainability. It emerges that blockchain technology could make agri-food supply chains more transparent, avoiding both social and environmental impacts. Further, blockchain technology could create more awareness in users participating in the network, thereby enabling better decisions related to food and non-food productions. This research highlights the need to develop integrated platforms which encompass new technologies and environmental accounting methods, promoting a circular economy approach by preventing food disposal and increasing food waste valorisation and reuse using material flow analysis and blockchain technology. The spread of blockchain technology at single industrial plant levels can lead to the increase in industrial symbiosis networks.

To boost food security and ensure, at the same time, health and reduced hunger, undernourishment, and overweight, companies must perform reliable, secure, and transparent analyses, implementing sustainable production models, rebalancing the current inadequate food system, and pursuing environmentally friendly practices. In light of this, the participation in blockchain networks could help in speeding up these improvement processes and moving from a (still) linear economy to a circular economy.

References

Adamashvili, N., Gallo, C., Rana, R. L., and Faccilongo, N. (2018). Blockchain technology–The tool for revolutionise the agri-food supply Chain, in *Proceedings of the Dynamics and Recent Trends of Vary Industries in Eu and Georgia: Icts Adoption in Supply Chain Management*, Tiblisi, Georgia, 17–19 October 2018.

Amicarelli, V. and Bux, C. (2020). Food waste measurement toward a fair, healthy and environmental-friendly food system: A critical review, *British Food Journal*, 123(8), pp. 2907–2935. doi:10.1108/BFJ-07-2020-0658.

Amicarelli, V., Lagioia, G., and Bux, C. (2021a). Global warming potential of food waste through the life cycle assessment: An analytical review, *Environmental Impact Assessment Review*, 91, art. no. 106677.

Amicarelli, V., Rana, L. R., Lombardi, M., and Bux, C. (2021b). Material flow analysis and sustainability of the Italian meat industry, *Journal of Cleaner Production*, 299.

Antonucci, F., Figorilli, S., Costa, C., Pallottino, F., Raso, L., and Menesatti, P. (2019). A review on blockchain applications in the agri-food sector, *Journal of Science and Food Agriculture*, 99, pp. 6129–6138.

Ball, D. W., Hill, J. W., and Scott, R. J. (2011). *The Basics of General, Organic, and Biological Chemistry* (Boston, United States: Flatworld).

Brigenzu, S. (1997). Material flow analyses for sustainable development of regions, in *Proceedings of the ConAccount Conference*, 11–12 September 1997, Wuppertal Special, 6, pp. 57–66.

Brunner, P. H. and Rechberger, H. (2017). *Handbook of Material Flow Analysis. For Environmental, Resource and Waste Engineers*, 2nd edition (Boca Raton, London, New York, NY: CRC Press, Taylor & Francis Group, LLC).

Bux, C. and Amicarelli, V. (2022). Material flow cost accounting (MFCA) to enhance environmental entrepreneurship in the meat sector: Challenges and opportunities, *Journal of Environmental Management*, 313, art. no. 115001.

Casino, F., Dasaklis, T. K., and Constantinos, P. (2019). A systematic literature review of blockchain-based applications: Current status, classification and open issues, *Telematics Information*, 36, pp. 55–81.

Chandra, G., Liaget, I. M., and Sharma, B. (2019). Blockchain redefining: The halal food sector, in *Proceedings of the 2019 Amity International Conference on Artificial Intelligence (AICAI)*, Dubai, United Arab Emirate, 4–6 February 2019.

Damiani, M., Pastorello, T., Carlesso, A., Tesser, S., and Semenzin, E. (2021). Quantifying environmental implications of surplus food redistribution to reduce food waste, *Journal of Cleaner Production*, 289, art. no. 125813. doi.org/10.1016/j.jclepro.2021.125813.

Eičaitė, O., Baležentis, T., Ribašauskienė, E., Morkūnas, M., Melnikienė, R., and Štreimikienė, D. (2022). Food waste in the retail sector: A survey-based evidence from Central and Eastern Europe, *Journal of Retailing and Consumer Services*, 69, art. no. 103116. doi.org/10.1016/j.jretconser.2022.103116.

European Environmental Agency (2021). Blockchain and the environment. Available at: https://www.eea.europa.eu/publications/blockchain-and-the-environment, accessed 20/05/22.

Eurostat (2020). Monitoring framework — Circular economy. Available at: https://ec.europa.eu/eurostat/web/circular-economy/monitoring-framework, accessed 13/11/2023.

FAO (2013). *Food Wastage Footprint. Impacts on Natural Resources* (Rome: Food and Agriculture Organization of the United Nations).

FAO (2018). *World Food and Agriculture — Statistical Pocketbook 2018* (Rome, Italy: Food and Agriculture Organization of the United States).

FAO, IFAD, UNICEF, WFP, and WHO (2019). *The State of Food Security and Nutrition in the World 2019.* Safeguarding against economic slowdowns and downturns. (Rome: FAO).

Food Loss and Waste Protocol (2016a). *Food Loss and Waste Accounting and Reporting Standard.* Available at: https://flwprotocol.org/, accessed 20/05/22.

Food Loss and Waste Protocol (2016b). *Guidance on FLW Quantification Methods.* Available at: https://flwprotocol.org/, accessed 20/05/22.

Gaiani, S. (2013). Household food waste in Italy: Estimations, drivers and impacts. Doctoral Research Thesis in Economics and Environmental and Agricultural Policy, University of Bologna.

Galati, A., Tulone, A., Moavero, P., and Crescimanno, M. (2019). Consumer interest in information regarding novel food technologies in Italy: The case of irradiated foods, *Food Research International*, 119, pp. 291–296.

IBM (2022). Cos'è la tecnologia blockchain? Available at: https://www.ibm.com/it-it/topics/what-is-blockchain, accessed 20/05/22.

Kelly, T. D., and Matos, G. R. (2014). Historical statistics for mineral and material commodities in the United States (2016 version). U.S. Geological Survey Data Series, 140.

Li, Z., Liu, G., Liu, L., Lai, X., and Xu, G. (2017). IoT-based tracking and tracing platform for prepackaged food supply chain, *Industrial Management and Data Systems*, 117(9), pp. 1906–1916.

Lipińska, M., Tomaszewska, M., and Kołożyn-Krajewska, D. (2019). Identifying factors associated with food losses during transportation: Potentials for social purposes, *Sustainability*, 11(7), 2046. doi.org/10.3390/su11072046.

Marco, O. D., Lagioia, G., Amicarelli, V., and Sgaramella, A. (2009). Constructing physical input-output tables with material flow analysis (MFA) data: Bottom-up case studies, in Suh, S. (eds.), *Handbook of Input–Output Economics in Industrial Ecology* (Springer, Dordrecht: Eco-Efficiency in Industry and Science), p. 23.

Moraga, G., Huysveld, S., Mathieux, F., Blengini, G. A., Alaerts, L., Van Acker, K., de Meester, S., and Dewulf, J. (2019), Circular economy indicators: What do they measure? *Resources, Conservation and Recycling*, 146, pp. 452–461.

Nebbia, G. (1995). *Lezioni di Merceologia* (Rome: Laterza & Figli Spa).

Nicastro R. and Carillo P. (2021). Food loss and waste prevention strategies from farm to fork, *Sustainability*, 13(10), 5443. doi.org/10.3390/su13105443.

OJEU (Official Journal of the European Commission) (2002). Regolamento (CE) N. 178/2002 del Parlamento Europeo e del Consiglio del 28 gennaio 2002.

OJEU (Official Journal of the European Union) (2019). Commission Delegated Decision (EU) 2019/1597 of 3 May 2019 supplementing Directive 2008/98/EC of the European Parliament and of the Council as regards a common methodology and minimum quality requirements for the uniform measurement of levels of food waste.

Pinstrup-Andersen, P. (2009). Food security: Definition and measurement, *Food Security*, 1(1), pp. 5–7.

Rana, R. L., Tricase, C., and De Cesare, L. (2021). Blockchain technology for a sustainable agri-food supply chain, *British Food Journal*, 123(11), pp. 3471–3485.

Santeramo, F. G. (2021). Exploring the link among food loss, waste and food security: what the research should focus on? *Agriculture & Food Security*, 10, 26. doi.org/10.1186/s40066-021-00302-z.

Segré, A. and Falasconi, L., (2011), Il libro nero dello spreco: il cibo. Edizioni Ambiente.

Sehnem, S., Pereira, L. H., Junior, S. S., Bernardy, R. J., and Lara, A. C. (2022). Management of food waste in restaurants by way of circular practices, *Journal of Material Cycles and Waste Management*, 24, pp. 1020–1036. doi.org/10.1007/s10163-022-01377-x.

Sterner, R. W., Small, G. E., and Hood, J. M. (2011). The conservation of mass, *Nature Education Knowledge*, 3(10), pp. 1–20.

Tan, A., Gligor, D., and Ngah, A. (2020). Applying blockchain for halal food traceability, *International Journal of Logistics Research Applications* doi:10.1080/13675567.2020.1825653.

United Nations (1975). *Report of the World Food Conference.* Rome (5–16 November 1974, New York).

United Nations (2022a). *The 17 Goals.* Available at: https://sdgs.un.org/goals, accessed 20/05/22.

United Nations (2022b). *Transforming Our World: The 2030 Agenda for Sustainable Development.* Available at: https://sdgs.un.org/2030agenda, accessed 20/05/22.

United Nations Environment Programme (2021). *Food Waste Index Report 2021* (Nairobi, Kenya, United Nations Environment Programme Publications).

Xue, L., Liu, G., Parfitt, J., Liu, X., Van Herpen, E., Stenmarck, Å., O'Connor, C., Ostergren, K., and Cheng, S. (2017). Missing food, missing data? A critical review of global food losses and food waste data, *Environmental Science Technology*, 51(12), pp. 6618–6633.

Zavyalova, E. B., Krykanov, D. D., and Patrunina, K. A. (2022). Gaps and constraints in the agricultural production and supply chains as a source of food waste and loss, in Popkova, E. G., and Sergi, B. S. (eds.), *Sustainable Agriculture. Environmental Footprints and Eco-design of Products and Processes* (Singapore: Springer). Available at: https://doi.org/10.1007/978-981-19-1125-5_10.

https://doi.org/10.1142/9781800614604_0004

Chapter 4

China's Green Revolution — Can Fintech & Green Digital Finance Empower Sustainable Development in a Coal-Reliant Economy?

Lucía Morales*,‡ and Bernadette Andreosso-O'Callaghan†,§

School of Accounting, Economics and Finance, Faculty of Business, Technological University Dublin, Republic of Ireland

†*Department of Economics, Kemmy Business School, University of Limerick, Republic of Ireland*

‡*lucia.morales@tudublin.ie*

§*bernadette.andreosso@ul.ie*

Financial technologies and digital finance emerge as new elements to support countries in their quest for green transformation and sustainable economic models. The green revolution is a complex process supported by policies and reforms that achieve a well-grounded institutional, financial, and economic framework. This chapter focuses on analysing China's green revolution and the importance of prioritising technologies within the financial ecosystem to achieve energy and environmental sustainability. In particular, the country's financial system, the innovations associated with the fintech sector, green digital finance, and particularly Beijing's financial incentives through its state-dominated banking sector are critical to driving China's green revolution. However, the scale of the required operations, infrastructure, and innovations is enormous, and financial support to empower the green economy will be crucial. China's five largest state-owned commercial banks are poised to take a decisive role in realising the country's ambitious plan of becoming a more environmentally friendly economy. It is expected that green finance should promote high-quality economic development through its positive impact on the ecology, generating economic efficiencies and achieving solid economic structures. Nevertheless, Chinese authorities face a daunting task in moving away from a heavily coal-dependent energy model that has become a predicament as political leaders are confronted with the reality of managing the ongoing energy crisis. Policy-makers must balance the new economic realities and their existing energy and economic models to ensure an appropriate balance between sustainability and political and economic interests. In order to progress towards China's 2060 "carbon-neutral" agenda and to shift towards a *high-quality growth* vision, the Chinese authorities must engage in a cautious and slow approach to change and transform so as to avoid destabilising the country's economy.

Keywords: China; green growth; fintech; digital finance; big five; coal; sustainable development

1. Introduction

Understanding the concept of sustainable growth is essential to framing the role played by the financial sector, particularly by the fintech industry and green digital finance. Green growth means fostering economic growth and development while ensuring that natural assets continue to provide the resources and environmental services on which our well-being relies. Sustainability is another aspect that needs to be considered in the context of economic growth. The United Nations General Assembly (1987, p. 43) defines sustainable development as *development that meets the needs of the present without compromising the ability of future generations to meet their own needs.* This definition is only a starting point in the discussion on sustainable development. Over a short period, the Chinese authorities have achieved remarkable progress in building a green financial system that has become one of the world's dominant systems (Meng *et al.*, 2021). The country's fintech market is developing rapidly, with a defined agenda focused on promoting and managing green finance initiatives (Wernberg-Tougaard, 2020). The Communist Party of China's Central Committee embraced the green revolution with the State Council's issuance of the Integrated Reform Plan for Promoting Ecological Progress in September 2015 (Choi and Heller, 2021, p. 1). Further progress was made with the introduction of the Guidelines for Establishing a Green Financial System jointly issued by the People's Bank of China and six ministries and commissions in August 2016 (Choi *et al.*, 2021; Choi *et al.*, 2020). As a result of the introduced initiatives, China's green credit and green bond market have become the largest across the globe (Meng *et al.*, 2021). Furthermore, in collaboration with the UN Environment Programme (UNEP), the Ant Group, formally known as Ant Financial Services — an affiliate company of the Chinese Alibaba Group — launched the Green Digital Finance Alliance. The alliance's objective is to empower business innovations to foster the transition towards a new economic model based on *high-quality growth*. In order to progress with the current green agenda, digital finance offers significant potential to help reshape the financial system and contribute to its better alignment with the needs and demands of sustainable development (Green Digital Finance Alliance, 2022).

Central to the green transformation and reform process, we identify the role of the country's financial system, particularly the state-dominated banking sector. The scale of the required operations and innovations is enormous, and financial support to empower the green economy will be critical. China's five largest state-owned commercial banks are poised to take a crucial role in realising the country's ambitious plan of becoming a more environmentally friendly economy. Certainly, the goal is very ambitious, and significant challenges surround its implementation. The country's ability to curtail its greenhouse emissions is vital to the success of its economic transition. China needs to reduce its carbon emissions rapidly to align with President Xi Jinping's pledge to achieve *carbon neutrality* by 2060.[a] In comparative terms, China's greenhouse gas emissions account for 27% of global emissions, while the US emits 14%, and the EU-27 and India's emissions represent 7% each (Borrell, 2020). Therefore, China's pledge to transition towards a green economic model is critical if the international community wishes to accomplish global *net-zero* commitments. As such, comprehensive policies and guidelines to enable coordination combined with economic and political stability would be fundamental to avoid destabilising the world's

[a]It is important to bear in mind the fact that carbon dioxide (CO_2) is essential to the process of photosynthesis, without which there is no life at all on earth; scientifically, a zero-CO_2 economy is a fallacy. In this article, we nevertheless use the expressions "carbon neutrality" and "zero-carbon economy" to imply the reduction in polluting emissions from all economic activities (or the minimisation of negative externalities).

second-largest economy and ensure steady and adequate progression. However, the Chinese authorities face a daunting task as transitioning from a heavily coal-dependent energy model has become a dilemma. The country faces significant pressures due to the international community's demands and increasing levels of uncertainty derived from a heavily volatile and fossil-fuel-dependent energy market (Madi *et al.*, 2022; Chen and Chen, 2021). Within the outlined framework, this research chapter proposes a comprehensive analysis of China's green practices framed within the country's economic and financial ecosystem. This chapter offers insights into the *big five* to help us unveil the country's reality in meeting decarbonisation targets while being cognisant of challenges associated with its ambitious plan to transition from a planned to a market economy (Choi *et al.*, 2020).

To accomplish this goal, the chapter is structured into six main sections as follows: Section 2 discusses China's economic transition from a planned to a market economy model. Section 3 analyses how the fintech sector and green digital finance can drive growth. Section 4 identifies and analyses the state-led solid initiatives and innovative solutions guided by the country's largest banks — *the big five*. Section 5 critically assesses China's fossil fuel dependency and its implications on Sustainable Economic Development. Section 6 appraises the fintech sector regulatory vacuum and the connected risk implications. Section 7 goes into green economic policy and its implications for *high-quality growth*, and some concluding remarks are suggested in the last section.

2. China's Economic Transition from a Planned to a Market Economy Model

China's economic departure from a full-fledged economic planning model started 40 years ago, as the country began its economic reforms aiming to open to the global economy. At the time, China exhibited very high poverty levels, with a meagre 2% contribution to the global share of GDP in terms of purchasing power parity. Nowadays, the country's position has shifted to a representation of more than 18%, showing the magnitude of changes and the significant contribution to the global economy. The debate surrounding the reasons for the country's economic success has been focused on three main areas: (i) the role played by the market as emphasised in many studies, (ii) the critical element represented by significant state intervention according to other authors, and (iii) the claim by another group of authors that the success is due to the country's ability to implement a hybrid model that combines both elements, and as such that credit should be subject to government policies and market forces alike.

The transformation started with the first decade of the *reform and opening-up* (1978–1988). The policies implemented contributed to differentiating China's new economic model that, early in the 1980s, was defined by a GDP per capita ratio in alignment with the world's poorest economies until it became the proverbial *workshop of the world* (Weber, 2022). The country initiated a process of rapid economic expansion followed by high growth rates that led to three decades of economic success. But the economic miracle was compounded by several drawbacks: cheap labour created collateral damage by rapidly raising the levels of inequality; unprecedented challenges were faced by the depletion of natural resources combined with continuous deterioration of the environment; and a demographic policy that prolonged sub-replacement fertility rates led to China facing significant demographic challenges (Fadanelli, 2022; IIDS, 2015, p. 7; Davis, 2014).

The reforms were followed by adjustments that resulted from the dual division between the agricultural and industrial sectors that arose as an essential characteristic of the planned economy. The idiosyncrasies associated with the post-1978 Chinese economic model that aided the country in becoming a global powerhouse have significant implications on the economic model that characterises Western economies, but with essential distinctions leading academics to refer to it as, for example, *Capitalism with Chinese Characteristics* (Bello, 2019; Huang, 2008). To understand China's economic miracle, one must look back at how the country started its economic revolution and the significant achievements that took place over a brief period. Labour productivity was a defining factor, as the urban sector experienced impressive allocation efficiency gains across the state-owned and private sectors. The redefinition of the labour market in the 1980s was combined with its downsizing in the state-owned sector, favouring the private sector; this is considered as being a decisive element in enabling labour productivity levels to grow at significant rates parallel to a high level of return of capital. According to Yuan *et al.* (2022), China's economic miracle can be explained by the significant improvements experienced by the labour market at the early stages of the economic transition that started in 1978. The labour market achieved a more efficient allocation of human capital across different sectors. The country benefited from vast amounts of cheap labour, which was the defining feature of the market for decades (Beamish, 2006). Quite remarkably, despite increasing levels of capital input, high return of capital was maintained, leading to a significant misalignment with the principles associated with traditional neoclassical economic models that started to emerge as a defining feature of the Chinese economic scenery (Yuan *et al.*, 2022). The Chinese industrialisation process enabled an efficient reallocation of "surplus labour" in both the manufacturing sector and services.

A rapid urbanisation process followed in the 1990s, which also helped to explain the Chinese economic miracle. Since then, the country has been able to enjoy three consecutive decades of stellar economic growth, defined by an annual average growth rate of up to 10% that was interrupted by the 2008 Global Economic and Financial Crisis (The World Bank, 2022). According to Weber (2022), significant distinctions should be considered when differentiating China's economic development and its connotations from the capitalist models. The first point of interest is how the country seems to have escaped from the *Washington Consensus* doctrine and challenged it by defining its own rules on what became to be known as the *Beijing Consensus*. The Washington Consensus was designed as a comprehensive package of policies that should be implemented in order to liberalise as many markets as possible; in the case of planned economies, this package resonates with the principles of economic shock therapy. It can be noted that *the Washington Consensus describes an extreme and dogmatic commitment to the belief that markets can solve all problems, and this axiomatic conviction is valid for all places and at all times, leading to the idea that "one-size-fits-all"*. The precepts of shock therapy meant that planned economies should undergo a major shock at once to enable their economic transition towards the market economy. But, in reality, such an approach can lead to a doctrine of economic destruction. The transition towards a market economy requires significant time, given the need for institutional privatisation and trade liberalisation, requiring very complex and lengthy processes and profound policy adjustments. In this regard, China's restructuring process was based on a gradual approach towards policy reforms that proved to be quite successful in terms of economic performance without accounting for costly externalities. However, what became known as the "Beijing Consensus" might be understood as a way of implementing the "Washington Consensus" with gradual changes mindful of the Chinese context and the reality of a transition economy.

Consequently, the Beijing Consensus is based on a pragmatic mix of state direction and intervention and market incentives that support economic development in line with China's aspiration to be seen as a market economy. To meet the challenge, the Chinese government sought to use a practical combination of market incentives and state direction that, to some extent, turned the Chinese economy into a vibrant capitalist economy, defined by a mixed market- and state-driven development model (Weber, 2022; Turner, 2017). Some of the core defining characteristics of the Chinese economic model and its connection to the state can be summarised as follows:

(a) The state's role is entrenched as part of its economic development machinery, where the state uses the market as a tool to achieve developmental goals.
(b) The state preserves a significant degree of control that translates into solid levels of economic sovereignty that cushion its economy against the dynamics of the global markets. As notable examples, it is possible to identify how China navigated the effects of the 1997/1998 Asian Financial Crisis and the 2008 Global Economic and Financial Crisis, where rapid government intervention led to significant economic resilience.
(c) China managed to escape the shock therapy experiment, which meant that the state maintained the capacity to insulate its economy and provided the required levels of economic stability and growth for quite some time as it progressed with its integration into global capitalism.

The country's ability to avoid the destructive elements associated with shock therapy and the inadequate guidelines offered by the strict *Washington Consensus* doctrine to transition economies led the country to emerge as a global economic powerhouse. The government focused its economic expansion on the international markets, fuelled by its competitive advantage of unlimited supply of low-cost labour and coal as the dominant energy resource. According to Rodrik (2020) and *The Economist* (2018), everyone now recognises that China's manufacturing prowess is not the result of unfettered market forces. Its successful state-driven economic model defines the country's economic premises. In parallel, significant levels of experimentation enabled the identification of policies that worked well and could be replicated from policies that did not provide the desired outcomes and needed to be discarded. In this regard, researchers acknowledge that the Chinese authorities engaged in what could be understood as a living lab of economic practice, offering quite an interesting combination of elements that turn out to be critical factors when explaining the nature of the Chinese success. Therefore, understanding the country's economic history is critical to understanding its current reality and to reconsidering how the current green revolution might be enacted.

Once more, the Chinese government is facing a significant challenge as it tries to navigate a needed economic transition towards its new vision for *high-quality* economic growth embedded in the sustainability dogma. Therefore, the following section discusses the role of innovation, particularly the importance of the fintech sector and green digital finance as potential enablers of a new phase of sustainable economic growth.

3. Fintech and Green Digital Finance to Drive Sustainable Growth

Research studies examining the connection between mainstream finance, financial innovation and technologies (fintech), and sustainable finance goals that lead to their application to digital finance innovations are quite limited (UN Environment Inquiry, 2018).

Fintech can be understood as a broader extension of the financial ecosystem as it integrates innovations in payment systems, blockchain-assisted technology, cryptocurrencies, credit markets, and insurance markets that play a significant role in the development of smart contracts (Thakor, 2020; Anagnostopoulos, 2018;

Gomber *et al.*, 2017). Green digital finance is geared to finance initiatives with a sustainable development goal, aiming to speed up the allocation of capital towards carbon-neutral assets (BBVA, 2022). As a result, the fintech sector can foster and nurture significant changes in the financing conditions of a country in order to drive sustainability and the transition to greener economic and financial models. An aspect to be considered relates to how financial services are structured; this represents a substantial point of interest when considering China's need to introduce adequate policies that help address economic and financial distortions between the private and the public sectors. Additionally, innovation is of paramount importance when trying to achieve competitive advantages. It has also been suggested that the country faces significant innovation challenges due to the state's heavy intervention level, which is mainly focused on stimulating innovation from the top and with limited scope for encouraging innovation from the bottom. Furthermore, the political context poses severe concerns due to the importance, broad reach, and dominance of the country's schools, universities, and business operations, which are very much circumscribed and can threaten creativity and innovative practices.

On the other hand, China's technological innovation levels are constantly improving and evolving; these are driven by the needs of its population and by the evolving nature of consumer behaviour and emergent patterns. The country's new demographic reality requires a shift in the labour market as its pool of young workers is decreasing amidst a growing ageing population. Quite remarkably, China's innovation ecosystem is characterised by a population that exhibits significant levels of hyper-adoptive and hyper-adaptive consumers willing to use new technologies. On that front, China does not seem to have many competitors (Dychtwald, 2021). Consequently, a critical factor that can contribute to using fintech and digital finance to drive sustainable growth relates to the transformational dimension that can be achieved if rapid adoption is experienced, as it will enable the introduction of changes on a large scale. However, some remaining worrying aspects relate to the reality of the current innovation landscape in the country that is revealing a significant spatial differentiation between the eastern region, which is experiencing high levels of growth, and the central and western regions, which are lagging behind. Current dynamics are also combined with growing levels of state control and monitoring from Beijing.

In parallel, there are critical economic and policy imbalances, suggesting heterogeneous impact in terms of implementing strict carbon policies that will result in substantial hardship for regions that are heavily reliant on exploiting fossil fuels. In particular, the country's coal reliance could undermine the objectives settled in the 2060 "carbon-neutral" agenda. On this front, technological innovation can affect the production and operation of enterprises by changing their financing conditions through, for example, the provision of financial services that create a positive synergy between the desired green growth and the association with relevant stakeholders. Consequently, technology and innovation can be used to accelerate the transition towards more conscious business activities. Another element relates to consumption patterns; by targeting innovation and investment that encourage environmentally based consumption, the country could take the lead towards the transformation of the economy into a "greener" model. The integration of financial technology and digital finance practices is opening a broad range of innovative lines of credit that can favour and nurture the development of the green economy. As such, China's ability to embrace faster and broader levels of adoption will be critical. Relevant aspects to be considered relate to the role to be played by financial technologies and the extent to which they can impact consumer behaviour by supporting business activities. Policy efforts need to explore the mechanism contributing to rearranging their traditional business models based on polluting activities and the intensification of greenhouse emissions. China's heavy reliance on the consumption of natural resources is driven by traditional state-owned enterprises (SOEs) that are characterised by low levels of technological innovation; this highlights the need to bring alternative financial options focused on preserving the environment. Undeniably, the task is quite daunting, as green growth factors are multifaceted and subject to significant change like technological innovation, financial aspects, enterprises' features, the political and social system, dominant economic models, and power balance dynamics at the global level.

Moreover, there is currently a significant lack of research studies examining the impact that fintech and digital finance can have on the development of green economic growth, particularly in terms of financial synergies and efficiencies. While there is little written on the impact of fintech innovation on green growth, some emerging research suggests a positive association between fintech, digital finance, and green growth. For instance, Yang *et al.* (2021a, 2021b) offer insights suggesting that green finance comprehensively promotes high-quality economic development through its positive impact on the ecological environment, economic efficiency, and economic structure. By introducing and enhancing green lines of credit capacity, focusing on growing green investment volumes and structures, and accelerating industrial optimisation, it would be possible to offer solid support to the transition from fossil-fuel-reliant energy models to renewable energies.

The environmental perspective and its integration into policy-making are relevant to the current debates seeking to bring changes to promote green growth. At the centre of the debate, we identify the importance of the financial system and its contribution. For example, by enabling green credit policies, it might be possible to improve the financial performance and competitiveness of the global business network. As such, encouraging commercial and investment banks to turn into green types of investment is critical, but financial changes on their own are insufficient. Moreover, there is a need to provide additional support to the business network to help devise the required mechanisms that enable green transition. The government can promote green growth through green credit policies by improving banks' financial performance and core competitiveness and encouraging commercial banks to lend to green enterprises. Still, the policy dimension needs to articulate the necessary conditions conducive to synergies between the financial system, the business sector, and consumers (Zhang *et al.*, 2021a, 2021b). From the perspective of environmental constraints, green credit, credit scale, environmental regulation, technological progress, and industrial structure all play an essential role in promoting energy-efficient utilisation. Therefore, while green credit can positively impact the efficient utilisation of energy, they require appropriate conditions to articulate sustainable structural changes.

In short, some recent research suggests that green finance, which comprehensively promotes high-quality economic development, has a positive impact on the ecology (Yang *et al.*, 2021a, 2021b). This emerging research suggests that fintech and digital finance might provide the required conditions for the optimal allocation of credit resources and for the improvement of financial efficiency, which as a result, should promote green growth.

4. China's State-Led Initiatives and Innovative Solutions Guided by the "Big Five"

China has entered a new developmental phase that requires coordination to support its green transformation as it tries to shift towards new high-quality growth with certain environmental characteristics. The development of green finance in the country aligns with the state intervention approach that ensured its rapid development. Beijing followed a leading top-down approach with high-level directives that guided the process and enabled a fast market response (Choi *et al.*, 2020). The guidelines for establishing the green financial system were launched in 2016. Since then, the growth of green credit policies has been remarkable, leading to a direct impact on the state-owned banks that experienced a significant expansion of their green credit portfolios (The People's Bank of China, 2016). The country's green investment has undergone a process guided by four core factors — (i) the national economic growth effect (NEG); (ii) national green investment structure effects (NIS); (iii) homothetic regional green investment competition effects (HRIC), and (iv) regional green investment allocation effects (RIA) — that have increased green investment between 2002 and 2017. Over the years, state-led initiatives and innovative solutions have been characterised by growth patterns with declining trends, highlighting the need for coordinated efforts in green investment across the country's regions (Eyraud *et al.*, 2013). China's financial sector is dominated by a few commercial banks and by significant levels of control exerted by the government, which indirectly leads to the promotion of political competition among local governments, which might end up being counterproductive. Moreover, state-owned financial institutions and banks provide soft lines of credit to SOEs and to real estate enterprises; this helps to create an imbalanced system of financial distribution that favours the public sector.

It has been argued that the main purpose of the "big four" banks is to support the development of Chinese corporations so that they can maintain competitive levels that consolidate their position in the global financial market guided by the directives of the state. In 2021, the "big four" maintained their leading positions, consolidating themselves as the world's most prominent financial institutions, as illustrated in Table 1. China's major banks have managed to widen their leadership position with expanded balance sheets when compared to the world's most important banks (S&P Global Market Intelligence, 2021). More specifically, the "big four" experienced a significant expansion as their aggregate assets grew approximately 10.2% in 2021, expanding from US$17.321 trillion registered in 2020 to a position of US$19.081 trillion in 2021. Significant levels of growth are justified by Beijing's pressures seeking to inject liquidity into lending so as to incentivise economic dynamics to speed up economic recovery; the country indeed experienced a significant slowdown in the second half of 2021 as it faced a significant wave of bond defaults by property developers and the lagging effects from the ongoing global health crisis (China Monetary Policy Report, 2021).

The following are the specific elements that the banks have considered:

(a) The People's Bank of China (PBoC) articulated its green programme by creating green incentives supported by relending policies. This means that green loans are now part of the standing lending facility (SLF) and that green bonds (AA rating) are admitted as collateral in its medium-term lending facility (MLF). In addition, banks' green performance is integrated as part of the bank macroprudential framework (MPA) that gives banks further incentives to grow and develop their green portfolios.

(b) The Industrial and Commercial Bank of China (ICBC) was the first bank to establish its Green Loan Framework, and the Agricultural Bank of China (ABC) secured the first-ever GLPs compliance loan, securing US$200 million from a syndicate of five banks.

(c) ICBC is a major player with a significant green portfolio associated with the Belt and Road Initiative Projects with a substantial level of attraction to green investment at the international level. However, the level of operations is considered quite limited when taking into account the bank's size.

(d) Chinese banks have expanded their green instruments to provide diversified and specialised tools and instruments across different sectors, particularly enabling mechanisms that facilitate international green finance cooperation.

(e) The vast majority of green finance has been focused on supporting the development of clean transport and clean energy, accounting for almost 70% of green finance in 2019.

(f) Green loans are associated with better performance metrics than traditional loans, suggesting that green loans are less risky than other types of lending. However, a point to consider is that green loans are significantly linked to infrastructural projects.

(g) Two banks (Industrial Bank and Shanghai Pudong Development Bank) have achieved specialisation in green finance.

The People's Bank of China supports green initiatives, which provide guidelines to ensure that China's banking sector is increasing and expanding its green efforts due to the significant implications for sustainable growth in the region (BNP Paribas, 2019). Furthermore, the financial system provides favourable capitalisation conditions and interest rate benefits that add additional incentives to the development of the green investment. The sector continues to grow under challenging economic circumstances derived from low growth rates, trade frictions with the US, pressures to deleverage, growing concerns about the energy markets, and the lasting challenges of the global health crisis. From a monetary policy perspective, it is important to consider that the approach for 2021 was focused on enabling liquidity to ensure adequate support to the financial system. Liquidity was kept adequate at a reasonable level. Using a mix of monetary policy instruments for liquidity injections, the PBC cut the required reserve ratio (RRR) for financial institutions by 0.5 percentage points in July and in December, respectively, which released RMB2.2 trillion of long-term funds. Financial institutions were guided to make proper credit arrangements for the turn of the year so that the stability of aggregate credit growth was improved. Financial institutions were guided to make proper credit arrangements to improve the stability of aggregate credit growth (China Monetary Policy Report, 2021, p. 1). The introduced measures aimed to stabilise the overall financing costs and were associated with

Table 1. The world's 10 largest banks.

Ranking of the World's 10 Largest Banks						
Current Rank	**Previous Rank**	**Current vs. Previous**	**Bank Name**	**Head-quarters**	**Accounting Principle**	**Total Assets (US$B)**
1	1	NC	Industrial & Commercial Bank of China Limited	China	IFRS	5,536.53
2	2	NC	China Construction Bank Corporation	China	IFRS	4,762.46
3	3	NC	Agricultural Bank of China Limited	China	IFRS	4,575.95
4	4	NC	Bank of China Limited	China	IFRS	4,206.53
5	6	▲	JPMorgan Chase & Company	US	US GAAP	3,743.57
6	5	▼	Mitsubishi UFJ Financial Group Incorporated	Japan	Japanese GAAP	3,176.84
7	9	▲	Bank of America Corporation	US	US GAAP	3,169.50
8	8	NC	HSBC Holding Public Limited Company	UK	IFRS	2,953.64
9	7	▼	BNP Paribas Société Anonyme	France	IFRS	2,905.83
10	10	NC	Crédit Agricole Group	France	IFRS	2,674.35

Note: Abbreviations: NC: No change; IFRS: International Financial Reporting Standards; GAAP: Generally Accepted Financial Practices

Source: S&P Global Market Intelligence (2021).

a slight decline in innovations seeking to promote a sustainable economy.

Policy reforms and green financial reforms are of significant importance in China due to the scale of its state-owned banks, which are the largest banks in the world with combined assets of over US$14.8 trillion (Choi *et al.* 2020). The Bank of China, the Industrial and Commercial Bank of China (the largest lender), China Construction Bank, Agricultural Bank of China, and China Development Bank are also known as the *big five*, with four of them being the largest banks in the world; these banks will be critical to the success of the Chinese green revolution (S&P Global Market Intelligence, 2021). However, the "big four" are also the major contributors to the country's coal mining activities, which might appear as being an apparent contradiction of the country's ambition to meet decarbonising targets.

5. China's Fossil Fuel Dependency and Implications on Sustainable Economic Development

China has enjoyed significant growth and development at the cost of environmental degradation derived from significant pollution levels. At the centre of the country's dilemma, we identify its economic model that for years has been focused on achieving economic goals that have led to a trade-off between economic gains and sustainability and negative impact on the environment. The country's overreliance on fossil fuels and its dependency on coal amidst an ongoing global energy crisis raise significant doubts and concerns regarding the Chinese authorities' ability to reach its carbon neutrality goals by 2060. Undoubtedly, environmental goals need to be revisited to understand the extent to which they are realistic not only in the context of transition economies but also for developed economies when compared to the macroeconomics dynamics of the most advanced countries due to the ongoing conflict between Russia and Ukraine. The energy crisis has proven to be quite challenging and has provided a reality check to world economies and their fossil fuel dependency. There is a critical need to reconsider how countries invest in developing alternative energy sources for their needs and reassess economic models that pursue high levels of "better" growth. It is naïve to

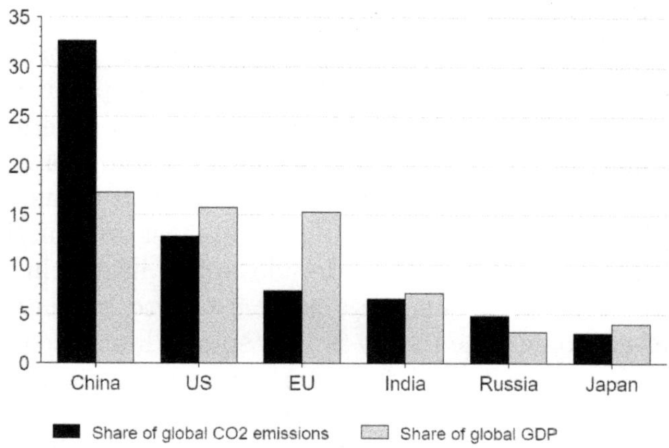

Fig. 1. Global CO_2 emissions and GDP.

expect that emerging and less developed economies would be willing to compromise their growth rates for the sake of environmental gains when economic and political agendas are taking the lead. A starting point in terms of economic realities can be found in issues that relate to economic and political instability, sectoral instability, and the need for structural transformation that account for economic efficiencies. In the context of productivity measures, factor allocation and quality growth strategies that foster economic growth aligned with sustainability goals while being cognisant of the crucial differences between the world's most developed and less developed economies can be an excellent way to start.

China is considered as being the world's largest polluter, accounting for nearly one-third of global CO_2 emissions and with an 18.8% representation of the share of global GDP (see Fig. 1). The impact of China's banking system goes beyond borders. Together, China's leading banks *the big four* have contributed to the fossil fuel industry with investments of over US$240 billion, with approximately 44% of the contribution going towards coal mining and coal power activities. As a result, *the big four* are considered the most prominent financiers of coal at the global level. An evident controversy emerges; on the one hand, China is making significant progress in its green transition by, for example, subsidising solar panels and wind turbines, which has resulted in a considerable decline in the cost of renewable energies (IEA, 2022a); on the other hand, the Chinese authorities are consolidating their investment in the fossil fuel market. In particular, securing a supply of coal emerges as a critical priority for the country's energy needs, but coal is the world's most polluting energy resource, representing over one-third of global energy generation and, as such, is not a problem confined to the Chinese energy context (IEA, 2022b). Then, is it realistic to expect a swift transition from coal towards renewable energies? The gradualist reform that took place in China over the past four decades offers interesting insights regarding the country's potential approach toward its energy sector and greener economy. The reality is that since China's economy has slowed down and since its coal dependency is very strong, the Chinese authorities are reassessing the country's energy transition model. The Chinese authorities are on the path to catch up, to reindustrialise, and to reintegrate into global capitalism in alignment with international pressures on fostering green economies. A point of reflection relates to core lessons for the government as the country transitioned from being one of the world's poorest economies to becoming an economic miracle without precedent. China escaped from a harsh shock therapy model with negative implications on economic development. As such, it is expected that the lessons learned through that transition process will play a significant role in designing and implementing the country's vision for future economic, financial, and energy transformation. Undoubtedly, China's experience positions the country in an advantageous place in finding its way around the required reforms but without the need to cut the umbilical cord to its existing economic model in a drastic manner that could compromise its economic stability.

Therefore, by gradually moving away from coal as the dominant energy resource, the country will be able to ensure that the required transformation does not destabilise its economic system.

6. Fintech Sector Regulatory Vacuum and Risk Implications

Barefoot (2020) argues that innovation offers enormous potential to drive changes in the financial system so as to enable a more competitive sector. But, on the other hand, technological advances within the financial system are associated with benefits and dangers that are often interwoven and create significant challenges for policy-makers as the latter seek to promote quality activities and control the downside risks. To monitor and prevent the emergence of risks, it is vital to consider the role of regulating the technological sector and to define the extent to which regulations can play a dual role, either by improving the functioning of the sector or by contributing to worsening it and compromising its stability. Therefore, countries need to consider the importance of enabling the development of effective and efficient financial regulation to prevent or minimise risks that can undermine the sector's development, threaten the financial system's stability, and have dangerous ramifications for the macroeconomy. Failing to address the issue of a sound regulatory framework can materialise in adverse spillover effects on the economic system and lead to a dual shock. But, at the centre of the worries are the regulators who struggle to keep pace with the content and scope of technologies. There is no doubt that traditional regulation is not able to manage the challenges associated with the fintech sector and the development of digital technology.

The levels of growth experienced by the fintech sector since the 2008 GEFC have been quite remarkable, resulting in a significant regulatory vacuum as financial regulators have not been able to progress at the same pace, posing significant risks to the financial system (Morales *et al.*, 2022). The risks associated with fintech are unknown, and the scale of the potential reach is a significant source of concern as there is a prevalent assumption that systemic risk is associated with the domination of large, systematically important financial institutions. In the Chinese context, the dominance of the "big four" throughout the banking sector requires careful attention due to their powerful position at the national and international levels.

The following are a few significant risks associated with fintech:

(a) Consumers are significantly exposed as their privacy is affected due to the compromised use of their data, manipulation of consumer behaviour, cybersecurity threats, and growing levels of fraud, to name but a few.
(b) Erosion of financial literacy due to a lack of understanding of financial contracts, transactions, and services will translate into vulnerability towards technology and will leave consumers exposed to technology failure and to predatory practices.

(c) There is a proliferation of small-scale providers that are difficult to control and regulate. While small start-ups might bring significant improvements and additions through their new ideas, they can be associated with unregulated operations, fraud, and significant rates of failure that can leave customers stranded.
(d) Interlinkages between the small fintech sector and the traditional financial system are another source of concern due to the potential of hidden systemic risk.
(e) Lack of to be removed, the point would be: International financial regulation and enforcement procedures prevent growing levels of illicit activities and their impact on capital flows.
(f) There is a disconnect between financial regulators and the fast pace of development of the fintech sector and digital technologies.

According to Zhou *et al.* (2022), there is a significant lack of research examining the impact of fintech and green finance on green growth and the mechanisms that enable materialising potential positive synergies between financial resources and the development of the green economy. In addition, there is a lack of understanding of the potential risks associated with a fast-emerging sector and the threats that it poses to the stability of the economic and financial system. The fintech sector and digital finance are developing too fast, challenging both policy-makers and regulators. While research studies reveal a positive association between fintech innovation and its role in promoting green economic growth, the risk dimension is not fully and adequately understood. In particular, the role of green credit and investment activities is critical in the transition towards a greener economic model, but articulating adequate mechanisms that enable the transition remains a blur. An aspect that requires further insights relates to potential downside risks that might emerge within the fintech sector and green digital finance and to which extent they could destabilise national, regional, and global economic systems.

7. Green Economic Policy and Implications for "High-Quality Growth"

The world economy has entered a phase that requires the re-evaluation and assessment of existing economic models and the importance of offering alternatives that drive sustainable growth. In this regard, enabling sustainable growth is closely tied to the critical need for investment in the development of human capital and talent due to its critical role in identifying, designing, and implementing the required changes and adopting reforms. The reform process has an overarching dimension as a profound transformation process requiring adjustments across institutions, sectors, and business activities globally, where the financial system has an important role to play. However, as pointed out by Yuan *et al.* (2022), today's Chinese industry and labour markets exhibit significant differences from the industry and labour market dynamics that characterised the reforms during the early stages of its economic transition, leading to the achievement of important efficiency gains. In particular, the financial system is affected by massive distortions due to the *political pecking order of financing* that creates significant divisions across different sectors. The country's state-owned sector receives substantial support, while private firms are pointedly discriminated against and face significant constraints when trying to access credit on the market. In this regard, there is an urgent need to reform the financial sector so that market-oriented policies are introduced to facilitate the efficient allocation of financial resources, which should lead to the creation of dynamic efficiencies. However, implementing market reforms is inherently associated with a trade-off process between state control and fuelling marketisation. Our recent history has provided us with painful evidence of how unregulated processes are conducive to high levels of uncertainty that can bring the global economy to its knees. We just need to look back at the events that unfolded during the 2008 GEFC. The GEFC can be considered a significant example of how the US financial system, which is regarded as one of the world's most sophisticated and developed systems, failed to regulate and monitor its operations. The banking sector was significantly challenged by speculative investment and arbitrage activities, cemented by regulatory failure, which led to a global financial debacle with serious and painful ramifications for the global economy. Lax regulation led to significant economic and financial mayhem. As such, in the context of China's financial reforms, regulation is needed to promote appropriate balance and the development of a healthy relationship between the market and the government that helps to correct the misallocation of financial resources and the pervasive effect on the private sector while favouring and cushioning the financial needs of the local governments and the SOEs. Therefore, the lack of guidelines and best practice type of approaches with regard to what constitutes the best mix of regulatory interventions is an important hindrance as countries seek to navigate the complexities of financial innovation and its role in driving green and sustainable growth. Moreover, another significant challenge that needs to be confronted is how China is experiencing significant problems when trying to balance socioeconomic and environmental dynamics. A rapidly ageing population, a deteriorating environment, and rising hostilities from the world's developed economies that perceive China's economic progress as a major threat are fuelling national and international frictions that can destabilise its economic and political system (Andreosso-O'Callaghan and Morales, 2022).

Researchers have identified key macroeconomic drivers that can boost economic growth. The financial system has been highlighted as a critical player, as sound financial dynamics can provide the required conditions for quality green growth (Yao and Yang, 2022). By offering low-interest rates, exercising pressure on the use of fuels, and introducing policy interventions that target prices combined with schemes supported by *feed-in-tariffs*, appropriate conditions could be created to make green investment attractive. From a microeconomic perspective, Murovec *et al.* (2021) suggest that policy measures need to be strongly supported by a solid track record of environmental investment that consolidates the use of environmental technologies. Policies could focus on firms and consumer performance that incentivise positive synergies towards green investment.

The government faces significant challenges as it needs to address problems associated with a distorted structure that is affecting its economy and that the structural reforms initiated in 1998 are not able to address. As China continues to deepen its engagement with the global economy, appropriate and updated policies that enable economic stability and risk controls are needed. According to the latest report from Deloitte (2022), the banking sector's prospects include technological advances coupled with growing external shocks and environmental pressures that can lead to *triple pressure* from demand contraction, supply shocks, and weakening expectations. Core challenges for the fintech industry are emerging in the context of regulatory policy changes and in the disconnection between the sector and the regulatory authorities as the financial system reshapes and market competition increases. In addition, bank runs and additional signs of distress at the level of small lenders are on the rise, with significant concern affecting the top of the banking sector in terms of the growing levels of corruption and disruption that are also involving regulators (*The Economist*, 2022). China's financial system is considered to be notoriously opaque. As such, the financial sector requires more clarity regarding a regulatory framework that enables more robust control of financial risks. Moreover, there is a need for further effort that supports the required deep financial reform so that the digital transformation process aligns with required corporate social responsibilities, transparency, accountability, and compliance, with an environmental and social governance agenda (ESG). There is no doubt that the existing tools are insufficient to manage the needs of the economic and financial system and the country's new ambition to achieve *high-quality* growth.

As additional examples of critical problems that need to be addressed, we find state-owned monopolies in upstream industries, the new real estate bubble, the government monopoly of land supply, and local government debt problems. The reality is that a new round of structural reforms is needed, grounded in careful consideration of how to enable and facilitate the development of the fintech sector and green digital finance to ensure that they can help drive sustainable and *high-quality* growth. The Chinese authorities are facing a dilemma in terms of the trade-off between growth stabilisation, growth sustainability, and risk prevention. An inadequate policy response would trigger further economic and financial distortions that could weaken the economy and be conducive to potential systemic risk. However, the need to take the path to green growth is not confined to China and it requires the world's unanimous commitment, which in the current context, is only a fallacy (Zhou *et al.*, 2022; Sun *et al.*, 2020; Vargas-Hernandez, 2020; Liu *et al.*, 2019 and Capasso *et al.*, 2019).

8. Conclusions

The Chinese economy has undergone a significant reform process, and it has now embarked on a decisive stage to try and balance its transition towards a greener economic model. A critical learning from the shock therapy model is that the shift towards a green sustainable economic model implies that China will need to find its own way around the required reforms. Countries economic system cannot be subject to shock therapy types of changes as dramatic changes or the destruction of existing models will lead to the collapse of the whole system. As such, a gradual approach to reform and change is needed so that the appropriate balance between the old economic structures and the new ones can be found. Policy-makers need to find a proper balance of integration and coexistence with new economic realities that should take place slowly and smoothly to avoid endangering the existing systems and structures. A critical learning outcome from the conducted research is that a country could not just *jump to the market economy* (Weber, 2022), and that there is a need to differentiate between economic developmental needs associated with countries and their different phases of economic progress. The same applies to the required transition towards a greener economy, and we cannot expect that China will *just jump into it.* In this regard, the fintech sector and digital green finance might offer significant opportunities to help countries change their economic models and to lead a transition towards a new economic and financial model that is sustainable economically, financially, environmentally, and sociopolitically, thus reshuffling large parts of the vision enshrined in the United Nations 2030 Agenda for Sustainable Development (UN, 2015). At the same time, we need to be mindful of the risks and regulatory vacuums surrounding the fintech sector and the integration of technological advancements to enable capital flows as we immerse ourselves in the digital transformation process. There is a clear need to improve efficiency and transparency that contribute to the development of green policies guiding business social responsibility, and the financial system has a significant role to play therein. A critical challenge faced by the Chinese authorities relates to the imperative need to reconcile development and economic growth with environmental sustainability goals due to China's current energy model that is heavily reliant on fossil fuels. Therefore, the Chinese banks will be essential in the country's quest for sustainability (Choi *et al.*, 2020). The *big five* will be critical in offering specialised tools and instruments that promote sustainable development as they execute the mandate of the government. Consequently, the financial system and banking activities seeking to open and consolidate national and international green credit lines, foster green capital flows, and encourage international green finance cooperation would be at the centre of the new green revolution.

To conclude, the Chinese energy model has become the country's sword of Damocles as it has driven its economic development at the cost of its environment. The country is facing additional challenges due to the lack of an appropriate framework that integrates fintech, innovation, and green growth, which helps design and implement adequate policies and regulations to guide the transition towards sustainable economic development. Bearing in mind that green growth has become an important development goal for all countries around the world and that the rapid integration of finance and technology poses a significant regulatory vacuum, it is necessary for future research to focus on studying the mechanisms that connect fintech innovation, digital finance, green growth, and growth. Countries are in much need of high-quality research studies that provide some enlightenment on the green economic transformation while ensuring economic, financial, and sociopolitical stability.

References

Anagnostopoulos, I. (2018). Fintech and regtech: Impact on regulators and banks, *Journal of Economics Business,* 100, pp. 7–25.

Andreosso-O'Callaghan, B. and Morales, L. (2022). China's economic connectivity to the world economy. F1000Research, 11, p. 317.

Barefoot, J. A. (2020). Digital Technology Risks for Finance: Dangers Embedded in Fintech and Regtech. Harvard Kennedy School. Mossavar-Rahmani Center for Business Government. M-RCBG Associate Working Paper Series, No. 151.

BBVA (2022). Green digital finance: What it is and what it involves. Available at: https://www.bbva.com/en/sustainability/green-digital-finance-what-it-is-and-what-it-involves/.

Beamish, P. W. (2006). The high cost of cheap chinese labour. *Harvard Business Review. Finance and Investing.* Available at: https://hbr.org/2006/06/the-high-cost-of-cheap-chinese-labor.

Bello (2019). Capitalism with Chinese characteristics. Available at: https://fpif.org/capitalism-with-chinese-characteristics/.

BNP Paribas (2019). Seeding China's banks with sustainable lending. Available at: https://cib.bnpparibas/seeding-china-s-banks-with-sustainable-lending/.

Borrell, J. (2020). Available at: https://www.eeas.europa.eu/eeas/china-carbon-neutrality-2060-possible-game-changer-climate_en.

Capasso, M., Hansen, T., Heiberg, J., Klitkou, A., and Steen, M. (2019). Green growth–a synthesis of scientific findings, *Technological Forecasting and Social Change*, 146, pp. 390–402.

Chen, X. and Chen, Z. (2021). Can green finance development reduce carbon emissions? Empirical evidence from 30 Chinese Provinces. Sustainability, 13(21). doi.org/10.3390/su132112137.

China Monetary Policy Report, Q4 (2021). Monetary Policy Analysis Group of the People's Bank of China. Available at: http://www.pbc.gov.cn/en/3688229/3688353/3688356/4271098/4515014/2022032411414559365.pdf.

Choi, J. and Heller, T. C. (2021). The potential for scaling climate finance in China. *Climate Policy Initiative.* Available at: https://www.climatepolicyinitiative.org/publication/the-potential-for-scaling-climate-finance-in-china/.

Choi, J., Escalante, D., and Larsen, M. L. (2020). Green banking in China — Emerging trends. With a spotlight on the Industrial and Commercial Bank of China (ICBC). CPI Discussion Brief, August 2020. Available at: https://www.climatepolicyinitiative.org/publication/green-banking-in-china-emerging-trends/.

Davis, D. S. (2014). Demographic challenges for a raising China. Daedalus. Available at: https://www.amacad.org/publication/demographic-challenges-rising-china.

Deloitte (2022). Forging ahead together for a better future. Chinese Banking sector 2021. Review and 2022 Outlook. Published 27 April 2022. Available at: https://www2.deloitte.com/cn/en/pages/financial-services/articles/chinese-banking-sector-2021-review-and-2022-outlook.html.

Dychtwald, Z. (2021). China's new innovation advantage. *Harvard Business Review.* Available at: https://hbr.org/2021/05/chinas-new-innovation-advantage.

Eyraud, L., Clements, B., and Wane, A. (2013). Green investment: Trends and determinants, *Energy Policy*, 60, pp. 852–865.

Fadanelli, J. (2022). China's demographic trends in the context of economic competition. Center for Strategic and International Studies. Available at: https://www.csis.org/blogs/new-perspectives-asia/chinas-demographic-trends-context-economic-competition#:~:text=Just%20before%20it%20reaches%20high,prospects%20will%20be%20negatively%20impacted.

Gomber, P., Koch, J. A., and Siering, M. (2017). Digital finance and FinTech: Current research and future research directions, *Journal of Business Economics*, 87, pp. 537–580.

Green Digital Finance Alliance (2022). Green growth knowledge partnership. Available at: https://www.greenfinanceplatform.org/about-us.

Huang, Y. (2008) *Capitalism with Chinese Characteristics: Entrepreneurship and the State* (Cambridge: Cambridge University Press). doi:10.1017/CBO9780511754210.

IEA (2022a). Renewable energy market update. Available at: https://www.iea.org/reports/renewable-energy-market-update-may-2022/renewable-electricity.

IEA (2022b). Coal. Available at: https://www.iea.org/fuels-and-technologies/coal.

IISD (2015). Greening China's financial system. International Institute for Sustainable Development. Available at: https://www.iisd.org/system/files/publications/greening-chinas-financial-system.pdf.

Liu, R., Wang, D., Zhang, L., and Zhang, L. (2019). Can green financial development promote regional ecological efficiency? A case study of China, *Nature Hazards*, 95, pp. 325–341.

Madi, I., Morales, L., and Andreosso-O'Callaghan, B. (2022). China's rise in the Middle East: Fuelling a tired dragon? in Andreosso-O'Callaghan, B., Rey, S., and Taylor, R. (eds.), *Sustainable Development in Asia.* Contributions to Economics (Springer, Cham.). doi.org/10.1007/978-3-030-94679-1_5.

Meng, A. X., Xie, W., Shao, H., Shang, J., and Qiqige, Z., (2021). China green bond market report. Climate Bonds Initiative and China Central Depository and Clearing Research Centre. Available at: https://www.climatebonds.net/files/reports/cbi_china_sotm_2021_0.pdf.

Morales, L., Gray, G., and Rajmil, D. (2022). Emerging risks in the fintech industry — Insights from data science and financial econometrics analysis, *Economics, Management & Financial Markets*, 17(2), pp. 9–36. doi:10.22381/emfm17220221.

Murovec, N., Erker, R. S., and Prodan, I. (2021). Determinants of environmental investments: Testing the structural model, *Journal of Cleaner Production*, 37, pp. 265–277.

Rodrik, D. (2020). China as economic Bogeyman. Project Syndicate. Available at: https://www.project-syndicate.org/commentary/west-should-stop-criticizing-china-industrial-policy-by-dani-rodrik-2020-07.

S&P Global Market Intelligence (2021). The world's 100 largest banks, 2021. Available at: https://www.spglobal.com/marketintelligence/en/news-insights/research/the-worlds-100-largest-banks-2021.

Sun, Y., Ding, W., Yang, Z., Yang, G., and Du, J. (2020). Measuring China's regional inclusive green growth, *Science of Total Environment*, 713, art. no. 136367.

Thakor, A. V. (2020). Fintech and banking: What do we know? *Journal of Finance Intermediation*, 41, art. no. 100833.

The Economist (2018). Seeking lessons from China's long economic boom. Available at: https://www.economist.com/finance-and-economics/2018/12/14/seeking-lessons-from-chinas-long-economic-boom.

The Economist (2022). Trouble at the top and bottom of China's financial sector. Available at: https://www.economist.com/china/2022/05/26/trouble-at-the-top-and-bottom-of-chinas-financial-sector.

The People's Bank of China (2016). The People's Bank of China and six other agencies jointly issue guidelines for establishing the green financial system. Available at: http://www.pbc.gov.cn/english/130721/3131759/index.html.

The World Bank (2022). The World Bank in China. Country overview. Available at: https://www.worldbank.org/en/country/china/overview.

Turner, A. (2017). China vs. the Washington consensus. Available at: https://www.project-syndicate.org/commentary/china-versus-washington-consensus-by-adair-turner-2017-10.

UN (2015). Transforming our world: The 2030 agenda for sustainable development. Available at: https://sdgs.un.org/2030agenda.

UN Environment (2018). Green digital finance. Mapping current practice and potential in Switzerland and beyond, UN Environment Inquiry Discussion Paper. Available at: https://wedocs.unep.org/bitstream/handle/20.500.11822/34499/GDF.pdf?sequence=1&isAllowed=y.

United Nations General Assembly (1987). Report of the world commission on environment and development: Our common future. Oslo, Norway: United Nations General Assembly, Development and International Co-operation: Environment. Vargas-Hernandez, J. G. (2020). Strategic transformational transition of green economy, green growth, and sustainable development: An institutional approach, *International Journal of Green Computation*, 11, pp. 34–56.

Weber, I. (2022). How China became a global economic powerhouse through an idiosyncratic approach to market capitalism, Promarket. Stigler Center for the Study of the Economy and the State. Chicago Booth. Available at: https://www.promarket.org/2022/02/27/how-china-became-a-global-economic-powerhouse-through-an-idiosyncratic-app roach-to-market-capitalism/.

Wernberg-Tougaard, E. (2020). Greening China — How fintech drives Green Finance in China. China Experience. Insights for Future Business. Available at: https://www.china-experience.com/china-experience-insights/how-fintech-accelerates-chinas-sustainable-finance-ambitions.

Yang, X., Zhang, J. Ren, S., and Ran, Q. (2021a). Can the new energy demonstration cicty policy reduce environmental pollution? Evidence from quasi-natural experiment in China. *Journal of Cleaner Production*, Vol. 287. Available at: https://doi.org/10.1016/j.jclepro.2020.125015.

Yang, X., Wu, H., Ren, S., Ran, Q., and Zhang, J. (2021b). Does the development of the internet contribute to air pollution control in China? Mechanism discussion and empirical test. *Structural Change and Economic Dynamics*, Vol. 56, pp. 207–224. Available at: https://doi.org/10.1016/j.strueco.2020.12.001.

Yao, L. and Yang, X. (2022). Can digital finance boost SME innovation by easing financing constraints? Evidence from Chinese GEM-listed companies, *PLOS ONE*, 17(3), e0264647. Available at: https://doi.org/10.1371/journal.pone.0264647.

Yuan, Z., Vercueil, J., and Boyer, R. (2022). A Growth Model with Chinese Characteristics, *Revue de la régulation* [En ligne], 21 | 1er semestre/Spring 2017, mis en ligne le 20 juin 2017, consulté le 23 juillet 2022.

Zhang, D., Mohsin, M., Rasheed, A. K., Chang, Y., and Taghizadeh-Hesary, F. (2021a). Public spending and green economic growth in BRI region: Mediating role of green finance. *Energy Policy*, Vol. 153. Available at: https://doi.org/10.1016/j.enpol.2021.112256.

Zhang, S., Wu, Z., Wang, Y., and Hao, Y. (2021b). Fostering green development with green finance: An empirical study on the environmental effect of green credit policy in China. *Journal of Environmental Management*, Vol. 296. Available at: https://doi.org/10.1016/j.jenvman.2021.113159.

Zhou, G., Zhu, J., and Luo, S. (2022). The impact of fintech innovation on green growth in China: Mediating effect of green finance. *Ecological Economics*, Vol. 193. https://doi.org/10.1016/j.ecolecon.2021.107308.

Part II

Digital Currency, Banking, and Society

https://doi.org/10.1142/9781800614604_0005

Chapter 5

Carbon Footprint and Market Value of Cryptocurrencies and the Real Economy

Gang Nathan Dong

Department of Finance, Boston College, Chestnut Hill, MA, USA
nathan.dong@bc.edu

The competitive process of creating blocks in blockchains — the technological backbone of cryptocurrencies — is computation intensive and consumes a large amount of energy. However, its environmental impact may not be significant, or at least not significant enough to undermine the application of digital currency as both a medium of exchange and a store of value. This chapter uses a unique dataset from the United States Environmental Protection Agency (EPA) to compare the carbon footprints of various industry sectors in the US with that of Bitcoin. Overall, the equivalent amount of greenhouse gas emissions from the Bitcoin network in 2020 is about one-third of the amount emitted by the entire mining sector in the US. In cross-sectional analysis, Bitcoin has a significantly larger carbon footprint than many companies and even industries after controlling for the economic value created. What is alarming is the rate of increase in Bitcoin's energy consumption since 2017 and the possibility that its carbon footprint may eventually surpass all industries in the near future.

Keywords: Blockchain; cryptocurrency; Bitcoin mining; PoW; energy consumption; carbon; footprint; fintech; market value; CBECI

1. Introduction

The growing popularity of cryptocurrencies is due, in part, to the fact that they are digital money with low transaction costs and minimum regulatory restrictions (Enoksen *et al.*, 2000). Cryptocurrency ownership and use among Americans has increased dramatically from 1% of US consumers owning Bitcoin in 2015 (Pew Survey, 2021) to about 12% owning various types of digital currencies in 2021 (Federal Reserve, 2022). While the blockchain technology underpinning cryptocurrencies is revolutionary in the digital economy, significantly changing methods of payment and ways of life, its consensus mechanism of Proof of Work (PoW) is clearly out of touch with modern economic realities, raising concerns about the potentially high environmental costs of blockchain mining (Cho, 2021; John *et al.*, 2022).

Many of the harshest critics of cryptocurrencies have been environmentalists (*Guardian*, 2021; *New York Times*, 2022). As miners compete fiercely to post new transactions on the Bitcoin blockchain, its energy consumption and associated carbon emissions rise to levels that are not likely sustainable, highlighting an important environmental issue confronting blockchain (Corbet *et al.*, 2021; Jiang *et al.*, 2021). It is suggested that if Bitcoin follows the same rate of adoption of other technologies, such as automobiles, televisions, computers, smartphones, and social media, it could produce enough greenhouse gas emissions to cause an increase of two degrees Celsius in global temperature (Mora *et al.*, 2018).

Of course, the counterargument of cryptocurrency enthusiasts is not without validity. Blockchain technology actually contributes to sustainability by eliminating paper-based money and improving business process efficiency (Rieger *et al.*, 2022), and many companies and industries in the real economy consume more electricity that is produced from fossil fuel sources than the use of cryptocurrencies. For example, the use of other high-tech services such as watching YouTube's online streaming is responsible for 300 megatons of CO_2 emissions in a year. For comparison, Bitcoin mining alone is only responsible for about 30–40 megatons of greenhouse gas emissions. It seems that the climate impacts of cryptocurrency mining remain relatively modest (Kamiya, 2020).

Some critics from both business and academia even claim that there is no justification for the relatively high energy consumption as cryptocurrencies have no financial value. The reason why they do not carry or create value is that cryptocurrencies do not generate income and utility or have a relationship with economic fundamentals; therefore, they cannot store value or be considered as an investable asset (Goldman Sachs, 2021). However, the design feature of artificial scarcity or limited supply embedded in many cryptocurrencies such as Bitcoin and Ethereum allows them to serve as a store of value. Inflation with fiat currencies backed by governments can occur when more paper currencies are created to dilute the money supply, causing fiat currencies to lose value. This is not the case for Bitcoin and Ethereum because both blockchains are programmed to be scarce, making the currencies deflationary and resistant to inflation. This is the main source of their economic value (Kelleher, 2022; Chiu and Koeppl, 2021).

The critical issue in the debate over the increasing carbon footprint in blockchain-related activities is whether they are economically justifiable. On the one hand, value is created not only by the cryptocurrencies themselves but also by the fintech applications of blockchain technology, such as initial coin offerings (ICOs) for easily raising capital from investors without the services of an underwriter. On the other hand, all activities around blockchains, including communication between computer servers and storing ledgers in data centres, require enormous amounts of energy to operate. Therefore, it boils down to the simple question of whether the economic value they create does or does not exceed the environmental costs.

Nonetheless, regulatory attention has been drawn to the importance of creating rules to slow down the rapid growth of the cryptocurrency industry. Senator Elizabeth Warren called for a crackdown on Bitcoin mining in a Senate Banking Subcommittee hearing (Daniel, 2021): *Bitcoin requires so much computing activity that it eats up more energy than entire countries. One of the easiest and least disruptive things we can do to fight the climate crisis is to crack down on environmentally wasteful cryptocurrencies.* The question of how to regulate the industry with a priority on environmental impacts remains unanswered by the government and the claim of "environmental wasteful cryptocurrencies" has been unsubstantiated by rigorous analysis to date.

The purpose of this article is to determine empirically whether cryptocurrencies are environmentally wasteful by comparing the carbon footprint and the market value of publicly traded companies with those of Bitcoin. In other words, do Bitcoin mining activities emit more greenhouse gases than a company with a comparable market capitalisation? The answer to this question would have profound implications for investment decisions in cryptocurrencies, particularly the inclusion of cryptocurrencies in ESG portfolios. The present article will first describe the data used in the analysis and then will estimate the total amount of greenhouse gases emitted by each industry sector and Bitcoin. The subsequent sections will attempt to analyse the relationship between emission amount and market value at the firm level, to determine whether Bitcoin has a market value at a reasonable environmental cost.

2. Data Sources

This research constructs two samples using historical data from four main sources: firm-level greenhouse gas emissions, financial characteristics of publicly traded companies, Bitcoin's electricity usage, and Bitcoin's historical market value. The first sample is a panel dataset consisting of firm-level greenhouse gas emissions in each calendar year. The amount of emissions of a company is based on the Greenhouse Gas Reporting Program (GHGRP) regulated by the United States Environmental Protection Agency (EPA). The program collected facility-level greenhouse gas emission data from 2011 to 2020 from large manufacturers, suppliers of fossil fuels and industrial gases that result in greenhouse gas emissions when used, and businesses that inject carbon dioxide underground. The amount of facility-level emissions is aggregated at the holding company level to describe the carbon footprint of individual companies rather than individual facilities.

The second panel dataset is a Compustat-matched sample created by matching the company names in the EPA GHGRP database to the publicly traded companies in the Compustat database. The market value of each company is calculated using the number of shares outstanding and the year-end stock price reported in the Compustat. It is noted that more than a half of the samples in the EPA GHGRP database do not have a match in Compustat, suggesting that many private companies have voluntarily reported their greenhouse gas emissions to the EPA.

The annual energy demand of the Bitcoin network is obtained from the Cambridge Bitcoin Electricity Consumption Index (CBECI). The index is produced by the Cambridge Centre for Alternative Finance (CCAF), an academic research centre at the University of Cambridge. The CBECI was designed to report the environmental footprint of the cryptocurrency mining industry from 2011 to 2022. This index uses eight different economic and technological factors to estimate the Bitcoin network's daily electricity load including hash rate, new coin issuance, miner fees, mining difficulty, equipment efficiency, electricity cost, power usage effectiveness, and daily market price of Bitcoin (CBECI, 2022). The techno-economic model underlying the index to approximate Bitcoin's electricity consumption uses a bottom-up approach based on the work of Bevand (2017a, 2017b) and Krause and Tolaymat (2018). The amount of electricity consumption each year is then converted to Bitcoin's equivalent greenhouse gas emission using a method to be described in the next section.

The historical data of Bitcoin price and the total number of Bitcoins outstanding are collected from the Coinbase website. Because the market value of Bitcoin has increased (and fluctuated) dramatically since 2017 (Kufeoglu and Ozkuran, 2019) and the greenhouse gas emission data from the EPA is available till 2020, the final sample period is narrowed to 2017–2020. There are 10,673 firm-year observations with company-level greenhouse emission data in the EPA sample over the period of 2017–2020. The sample size is reduced to 1,238 firm-year observations when the companies in the EPA sample are matched to the financial statement and stock price data in the Compustat database. Four observations of Bitcoin's equivalent greenhouse gas emissions and market value, one for each year, are added to both the EPA sample and the Compustat-matched sample, increasing the sample sizes to 10,677 and 1,242, respectively.

3. Empirical Analysis

3.1. *Carbon footprint*

The first analysis presents a univariate comparison of the carbon footprint of the real economy and that of the Bitcoin network. Companies in the real economy are categorised into 12 industry sectors based on their 2-digit NAICS code reported in the EPA GHGRP database. The total amount of carbon dioxide emitted directly into the atmosphere by an industry sector in a given year is measured in megaton (1,000,000 metric tons) of carbon dioxide equivalent (Table 1). Among the 12 industries, the largest carbon-emitting sector is electric utilities, followed by the manufacturing sector. The three smallest emitters are agriculture, hospitality, and finance. The carbon footprint of Bitcoin, or its equivalent greenhouse gas emission, is estimated by converting the network's electricity consumption in kilowatt-hour (kWh) to CO_2 emission in metric ton. The total US electricity generation by the electric power industry in 2020 is 4.01 trillion kWh from all energy sources. This resulted in the emission of 1.55 billion metric tons of carbon dioxide (EIA, 2020).

Table 1. Total carbon dioxide emissions in megaton (1,000,000 metric tons).

Sector	**2017**	**2018**	**2019**	**2020**
Agriculture, forestry, fishing, and hunting	0.197	0.188	0.132	0.129
Construction	2.586	2.667	2.554	2.435
Education and health services	9.618	10.132	10.506	9.875
Financial activities	0.331	0.465	0.419	0.585
Leisure and hospitality	0.439	0.451	0.469	0.318
Manufacturing	788.234	758.374	687.084	606.434
Mining, quarrying, and oil and gas extraction	114.872	114.229	107.608	92.657
Professional and business services	218.056	215.712	210.929	190.257
Public administration	71.367	67.379	60.126	40.094
Transportation and warehousing	292.276	292.810	584.781	535.865
Utilities	2,584.534	2,624.011	2,075.424	1,748.65
Wholesale trade	39.536	55.542	41.354	34.114
Bitcoin	5.307	16.001	20.492	26.373
Sample size	2,711	2,795	2,598	2,573

Therefore, the conversion ratio from electricity consumption to CO_2 emission is 0.000378 metric ton per kWh (1,550,000,000 metric tons/4,100,000,000,000 kWhs).

Bitcoin's equivalent greenhouse gas emission of 5.3 megatons in 2017 is less than one-twentieth of the mining and energy sector's carbon footprint (114 megatons). Over the following next three years, it has increased substantially to 26 megatons in 2020, which is almost one-third of the mining and energy sector's greenhouse gas emissions (92 megatons). This implies an annualised growth rate of 71% from 2017 to 2020, and none of the sectors in the real economy has a carbon footprint that has increased at a rate faster than the Bitcoin network over the same period. For comparison, the fastest growing sector in terms of carbon footprint is transportation and warehousing with an annualised growth rate of 22%.

The second analysis uses the Compustat-matched sample including only the publicly traded companies that have reported annual greenhouse gas emissions to the EPA's Greenhouse Gas Reporting Program. Given the higher degree of scrutiny publicly traded companies have received, they are more likely to report accurate information to regulators than their private counterparts. This is particularly true in the case of financial statement reporting, since external audits are required for publicly listed firms but are voluntary for private ones (Lennox and Pittman, 2011). Companies in this smaller sample are also divided into 12 industry sectors based on the 2-digit NAICS code reported in the Compustat database. Table 2 shows the total emissions of carbon dioxide equivalent (in megatons) in each industry sector and the equivalent greenhouse gas emission by the Bitcoin network.

Bitcoin's equivalent greenhouse gas emission of 5.3 megatons in 2017 is about one-12th of the mining and energy sector's carbon footprint (63 megatons). This ratio is smaller than the ratio of one-twentieth found in the first sample that includes both public and private firms. The reduced magnitude of Bitcoin's carbon footprint is due to the fact that the number of publicly traded companies in the Compustat-matched sample (304 firms in 2020) is much smaller than the number of all companies in the entire sample (2,573 firms in 2020). This ratio decreases to one-quarter of the mining and energy sector's greenhouse gas emissions in 2020, which is similar to the ratio of one-third found in the first sample.

Table 2. Total carbon dioxide emissions of publicly traded companies in megaton (1,000,000 metric tons).

Sector	2017	2018	2019	2020
Agriculture, forestry, fishing, and hunting	0.875	—	0.117	0.097
Education and health services			0.070	0.073
Financial activities	3.159	5.234	6.363	6.029
Information and technology	0.001	0.066	0.071	0.318
Leisure and hospitality	0.244	0.243	0.250	0.142
Manufacturing	402.468	401.195	387.065	367.693
Mining, quarrying, and oil and gas extraction	63.232	58.104	60.890	59.337
Professional and business services	39.483	37.685	38.045	36.894
Retail trade	0.051	0.053	0.509	0.410
Transportation and warehousing	34.267	31.162	146.378	119.859
Utilities	975.934	818.413	803.234	760.258
Wholesale trade	2.417	2.804	2.614	1.955
Bitcoin	5.307	16.001	20.492	26.373
Sample size	313	307	318	304

3.2. *Market value*

It is important to emphasise that the summary statistics presented in the previous section obscure the connection between a company's carbon footprint and its business size and growth opportunities. The size of a company can be measured by the total assets reported in its financial statement, whereas the growth opportunities can be measured by the market value of its equity or the market capitalisation. In fact, market capitalisation reflects both the current value creation (the size effect) and the expectations regarding the company's ability to grow and create value in the future (the growth effect). The higher the market capitalisation of a company, the larger its scale of operations, and the more growth opportunities it would have. Therefore, the hypothesis can be that publicly traded companies with the objective of market value maximisation need to increase capital investment and ramp up production, consequently driving up energy consumption.

Table 3 reports the market capitalisation (in billion dollars) for each of the 12 industry sectors and Bitcoin. The market value of all outstanding Bitcoins was US$233 billion in 2017, which is about half

Table 3. Total market capitalisation (US$ billion) of publicly traded companies.

Sector	2017	2018	2019	2020
Agriculture, forestry, fishing, and hunting	51.334	—	22.128	28.787
Education and health services			21.975	24.344
Financial activities	119.116	132.710	21.460	20.612
Information and technology	7.652	6.972	927.639	1,184.580
Leisure and hospitality	30.107	19.830	29.988	31.028
Manufacturing	5,141.729	4,582.565	4,913.968	5,861.651
Mining, quarrying, and oil and gas extraction	503.912	376.141	414.454	341.454
Professional and business services	362.839	166.856	227.110	241.077
Retail trade	8.350	10.922	22.286	18.767
Transportation and warehousing	243.109	261.561	977.386	823.505
Utilities	789.148	704.547	910.662	846.770
Wholesale trade	4.817	30.369	385.44	4.719
Bitcoin	233.526	64.363	129.971	539.443
Sample size	313	307	318	304

of the mining and energy sector's market cap (US$503 billion). Over the next three years, Bitcoin's market value increased to US$539 billion, surpassing the size of the mining and energy sector in 2020.

3.3. *Relationship between carbon footprint and market value*

To quantify the relationship between carbon footprint and market value, the 12 industry sectors of all publicly traded companies and Bitcoin in the Compustat-matched sample are plotted in Fig. 1 with market capitalisation on the x-axis and the amount of greenhouse gas emissions on the y-axis. The values on both axes are linearised using the natural logarithm function. Clearly, there is a positive relationship between market capitalisation and carbon footprint. Larger industry sectors like manufacturing, transportation, and utilities consume more energy and have a much bigger carbon footprint, whereas smaller sectors like agriculture, education, and hospitality emit much less. This is consistent with the hypothesis that companies with higher market value run larger operations, have more growth opportunities, and hence emit more greenhouse gases.

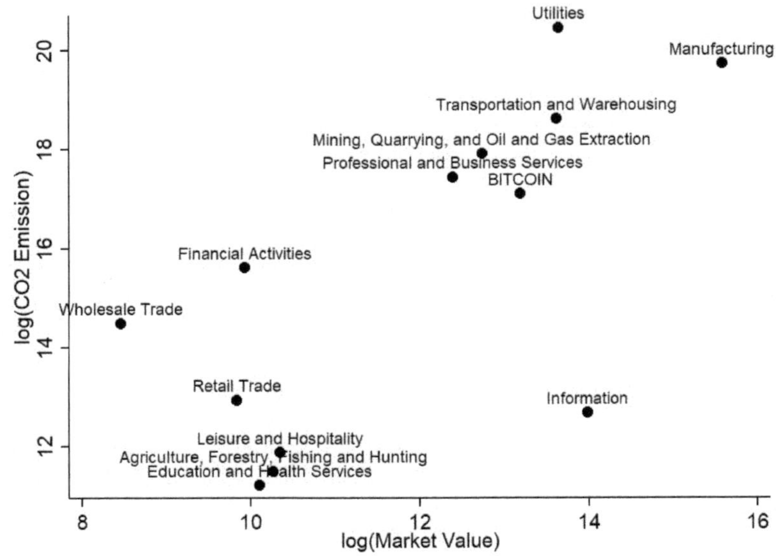

Fig. 1. Industry sector-level relationship between market capitalisation and carbon footprint.

In the scatter plot of Fig. 1, Bitcoin does not appear to be an outlier in the relationship between carbon footprint and market capitalisation. In fact, it is in the middle of both distributions. In order to answer the question of whether the Bitcoin network consumes more energy than its industrial counterparts in the real economy, it is necessary to use multivariate regression analysis to control for market capitalisation. The hypothesis of the test is that the mining activities of Bitcoin do not emit more greenhouse gases than other industries after controlling for size and growth opportunities. The baseline model is as follows:

$$\text{CarbonEmission}_{i,t} = \alpha + \beta\text{MarketValue}_{i,t} + \gamma\text{Bitcoin}_t + \text{FixedEffect}_{i,t} + \varepsilon_{i,t}$$

This regression fits a line to the points in the scatter plot as shown in Fig. 1. The variable "MarketValue" in the equation is the total market capitalisation of an industry or Bitcoin. Its coefficient (β) reflects the statistical relationship between an industry's carbon footprint and its ability to create economic value. The coefficient estimate of β can be used to predict the average value of carbon emissions for a specific industry given its market value. This feature of "regressing towards the mean" does not imply that an individual industry's actual emission amount must lie on the line. In fact, a particular industry or Bitcoin can be systematically far from the line, meaning emitting far more or less greenhouse gases given its value creation. To specifically capture this "outlier", a dummy variable "Bitcoin" is included in the equation. It has a value of one if observation i in the panel dataset is Bitcoin in year t, and zero otherwise. There are three possible interpretations for the coefficient of the dummy variable Bitcoin (γ). If the value of γ is statistically insignificant, Bitcoin mining is just like an average industry in terms of the relationship between its market value and carbon emissions. If the value of γ is positive and statistically significant, Bitcoin-related activities can be a serious environmental concern because they emit more greenhouse gases than the comparable industries. Finally, if the value of γ is negative and statistically significant, Bitcoin actually has a smaller carbon footprint than the average industry. This outcome would suggest that investing in Bitcoin can be considered like investing in any other ESG stock for socially responsible investment portfolios.

The regression specification in column (1) of Table 4 uses all industry-year observations, adjusts standard errors by clustering at the industry level, and includes both year fixed effects. The positive and statistically significant coefficient of the market capitalisation variable confirms the positive relation between carbon footprint and market value. In column (2), eleven dummy variables indicating industry sectors (excluding the sector of agriculture, forestry, fishing, and hunting) and Bitcoin are added to the specification. While the coefficient of market capitalisation remains significant, the positive coefficient of the dummy variable "Bitcoin" indicates that the Bitcoin network does consume more energy than the average industry. Columns (3) and (4) repeat the same specifications of columns (1) and (2) but exclude the two largest sectors in terms of direct CO_2 emissions (manufacturing and utilities), and columns (5) and (6) also exclude the sector of mining and energy. Across these specifications, Bitcoin is shown to have a larger carbon footprint after controlling for market value. Among the 12 industry sectors in the real economy, seven of them emit significantly fewer greenhouse gases than Bitcoin: agriculture (omitted variable to avoid perfect collinearity), education and healthcare, finance, information technology, leisure,

Table 4. Industry-level relationship between carbon emission and market capitalisation.

Dependent Variables: log(emission)	**(1)**	**(2)**	**(3)**	**(4)**	**(5)**	**(6)**
log(market capitalisation)	1.330***	0.494***	1.199***	0.484**	1.094**	0.476**
	(5.82)	(3.18)	(3.59)	(3.10)	(2.86)	(2.93)
Bitcoin		3.331***		3.347***		3.358***
		(9.77)		(9.32)		(8.74)
Education and health services		−1.098***		−1.147***		−1.170***
		(−6.63)		(−5.81)		(−5.22)
Financial activities		2.880***		2.883***		2.884***
		(18.19)		(16.07)		(14.56)
Information and technology		−2.442***		−2.433***		−2.428***
		(−10.47)		(−9.63)		(−8.87)
Leisure and hospitality		0.0413		0.0386		0.0342
		(0.47)		(0.35)		(0.27)
Manufacturing		4.961***				
		(5.81)				
Mining, quarrying, and oil and gas extraction		4.348***		4.373***		
		(9.37)		(9.08)		
Professional and business services		4.144***		4.163***		4.176***
		(10.79)		(10.35)		(9.74)
Retail trade		0.0439		0.0346		0.0249
		(0.42)		(0.31)		(0.21)
Transportation and warehousing		4.355***		4.381***		4.399***
		(8.91)		(8.65)		(8.19)

Utilities		6.634***				
		(11.63)				
Wholesale trade		2.841***		2.830***		2.820***
		(25.17)		(23.56)		(22.03)
Intercept	−0.251	6.845***	0.948	6.858***	1.946	6.898***
	(−0.09)	(4.30)	(0.26)	(4.32)	(0.49)	(4.22)
All industries	Yes	Yes				
Excluding manufacturing industry			Yes	Yes	Yes	Yes
Excluding utilities industry			Yes	Yes	Yes	Yes
Excluding mining industry					Yes	Yes
Year fixed effects	Yes	Yes	Yes	Yes	Yes	Yes
SE clustered at industry level	Yes	Yes	Yes	Yes	Yes	Yes
Sample size	49	49	41	41	37	37
Adjusted R-squared	0.569	0.942	0.390	0.907	0.308	0.890

Note: The t-statistics of coefficient estimates are shown in parentheses below the coefficient. ***, ** and * indicate significance at the 1%, 5% and 10% levels.

retail, and wholesale. The other five industries, on the other hand, emit more than Bitcoin: manufacturing, mining and energy, business services, transportation and warehousing, and utilities. This finding is consistent with the summary statistics reported in Tables 1 and 2.

3.4. *Firm-level evidence*

It is likely that the results from the industry sector-level analysis in the previous section may not be able to account for the full complexity of carbon footprint patterns by overlooking the possibility that a small group of super-large companies in a sector can emit the majority of greenhouse gases of this sector. To capture this aspect of data granularity, it is necessary to conduct a firm-level analysis and identify the link between market capitalisation and carbon footprint on a more granular level. In Fig. 2, all publicly traded companies and Bitcoin in the Compustat-matched sample are plotted with market capitalisation on the x-axis and carbon footprint on the y-axis. The values on both axes are linearised using the natural logarithm function. While it is impossible to label the industry of each company

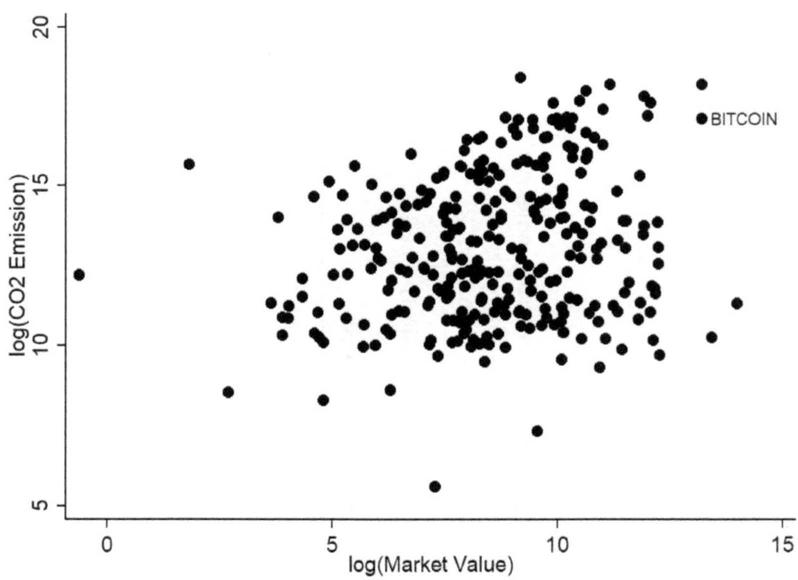

Fig. 2. Firm-level relationship between market value and carbon footprint.

(dot) in the scatter plot, the positive relationship between market capitalisation and carbon footprint is similar to the one evidenced in the industry sector-level analysis. The difference is that companies with a large market capitalisation, regardless of their industries, are the ones with a larger carbon footprint. In other words, companies with higher market value run larger operations, have more growth opportunities, and hence emit more greenhouse gases. Similar to the scatter plot using the industry-level data, Bitcoin does not appear to be an outlier in this relationship using the firm-level data.

To answer the question of whether the Bitcoin network consumes more energy than its individual company counterparts, it is critical to control for company-level market capitalisation in the multivariate regression analysis. The regression specification in column (1) of Table 5 uses all firm-year observations, adjusts standard errors by clustering at the firm level, and includes both year and industry fixed effects. The industry fixed effect is based on the 2-digit NAICS code reported in the Compustat database. While the positive and statistically significant coefficient of the market capitalisation variable confirms the positive relation between carbon footprint and market value, the positive coefficient of the dummy variable "Bitcoin" indicates that the Bitcoin network does consume more energy than the average firm in the real economy. The second specification uses firm fixed effects that can help capture unobserved time-invariant characteristics of individual companies. The result in column (2) also shows the significantly larger carbon footprint of Bitcoin, whereas the market capitalisation effect becomes insignificant. Bitcoin's carbon footprint remains significant in the next four specifications where the samples are limited to various combinations of information technology, finance, and service industries in columns (3)–(6).

3.5. *Separating the size and growth effects*

While the results in the previous sections are consistent with the idea that a company or an industry's greenhouse gas emission is positively related to its market capitalisation, and even after taking this relationship into consideration, the Bitcoin network still has a larger carbon footprint, they should be interpreted with caution. Market capitalisation reflects both the current value creation (i.e., the size

Table 5. Controlling for the relationship between emissions and market capitalisation at the firm level.

Dependent Variables: log(emission)	**(1)**	**(2)**	**(3)**	**(4)**	**(5)**	**(6)**
Log(market capitalisation)	0.315***	0.0533	0.206	0.120	−0.265	0.199
	(5.19)	(0.73)	(0.87)	(0.61)	(−0.64)	(0.64)
Bitcoin	4.385***	2.072***	5.475***	5.434***	8.497**	5.383**
	(18.07)	(2.91)	(3.33)	(18.26)	(2.86)	(2.42)
Intercept	8.191***	13.73***	8.287***	9.497***	10.50***	8.328***
	(16.26)	(71.65)	(6.96)	(3.45)	(4.74)	(5.60)
All firms	Yes	Yes				
Information technology firms			Yes	Yes		
Financial service firms			Yes	Yes	Yes	Yes
Business professional service firms			Yes	Yes	Yes	Yes
Year fixed effects	Yes	Yes	Yes	Yes	Yes	Yes
Industry fixed effects	Yes		Yes		Yes	
Firm fixed effects		Yes		Yes		Yes
SE clustered at firm level	Yes	Yes	Yes	Yes	Yes	Yes
Sample size	1,231	1,231	96	96	31	31
Adjusted R-squared	0.428	0.957	0.524	0.885	0.751	0.937

Note: The t-statistics of coefficient estimates are shown in parentheses below the coefficient. ***, ** and * indicate significance at the 1%, 5% and 10% levels.

effect) and the expectations regarding the company's ability to grow and create value in the future (i.e., the growth effect). It is empirically important to distinguish between the size effect, which simply means that a large scale of operations consumes more energy, and the growth effect, which might suggest an underestimation of the carbon footprint. To illustrate, take the example of the positive coefficient of the market capitalisation variable in the firm-level analysis with firm fixed effects in column (2) of Table 5. If the existence of more growth opportunities in a company (growth effect), rather than its large operations (size effect), leads to a higher market capitalisation, the predicted (or fitted) greenhouse gas emission of this company from the regression model would be much higher than the average of all firms. Therefore, the fixed effect of this firm in the regression model must be negative in order to bring the predicted emission value close to the observed (or actual) value. While the coefficient estimates of all firms' fixed effects are omitted from the table for brevity, the dummy variable "Bitcoin" is essentially the fixed effect of the Bitcoin network.

To control for the size effect and growth effect separately, the natural logarithm of a company's total assets (book value in each fiscal year) is added to the regression specifications. Unfortunately, there is no total asset value for Bitcoin as it is a network of computer nodes; therefore, it is necessary to use a proxy variable to measure Bitcoin's book value. For simplicity, the book value of Bitcoin's total assets in each year is the average daily price of Bitcoin traded on the open market over the previous year. For example, the book value in 2020 was the average daily price in 2019. In contrast, the market capitalisation value is the daily price on the last day of 2020 multiplied by the number of Bitcoins outstanding on that day. The regression results are reported in Table 6. The positive coefficient of total assets in column (1) of Table 6 does suggest the pure size effect in the cross-sectional specification with both year and industry fixed effects, and Bitcoin is still shown to have larger greenhouse gas emissions after controlling for size effect. However, the statistical significance of the Bitcoin variable vanishes in the regression with firm fixed effects (column 2). When both total assets and market capitalisation are included in the same specification (column 3), only the coefficient of total assets (not the market capitalisation) has a

Table 6. Relationship between carbon emission and market capitalisation after controlling for size.

Dependent Variables: log(emission)	**(1)**	**(2)**	**(3)**	**(4)**	**(5)**	**(6)**
log(total assets)	0.366***	0.339**	0.262**	0.355**	0.618	0.407**
	(4.81)	(2.06)	(1.98)	(2.10)	(1.48)	(2.38)
log(market capitalisation)			0.103	−0.0154	−0.313	0.0653
			(1.01)	(−0.21)	(−0.66)	(0.29)
Bitcoin	4.486***	−0.559	4.403***	−0.597	5.838***	6.000***
	(18.73)	(−0.25)	(18.14)	(−0.27)	(16.42)	(14.70)
Intercept	7.978***	13.31***	7.927***	13.38***	7.557**	5.187
	(13.52)	(28.47)	(13.73)	(26.16)	(2.52)	(1.44)
All firms	Yes	Yes	Yes	Yes		
Information technology firms					Yes	Yes
Financial service firms					Yes	Yes
Business professional service firms					Yes	Yes
Year fixed effects	Yes	Yes	Yes	Yes	Yes	Yes
Industry fixed effects	Yes		Yes		Yes	
Firm fixed effects		Yes		Yes		Yes
Sample size	1,231	1,231	1,231	1,231	96	96
Adjusted R-squared	0.457	0.971	0.434	0.958	0.562	0.888

Note: The t-statistics of coefficient estimates are shown in parentheses below the coefficient. ***, ** and * indicate significance at the 1%, 5% and 10% levels.

significant coefficient, suggesting that it is the size effect that drives the previous results.

Again, after replacing the year and industry fixed effects by the firm fixed effects in column (4), Bitcoin is no longer shown to have a larger carbon footprint than publicly traded companies after controlling for both size and growth effects. The statistically insignificance of Bitcoin in the specifications with firm fixed effects in column (2) and column (4) deserves some attention. The use of fixed effects at the firm level essentially de-means each the amount of emissions by the average amount in the same company (or Bitcoin as it is considered as a firm in the panel dataset). This allows the regression to show the year-to-year changes in carbon footprint, also known as the "within estimation". One possible explanation for the insignificant Bitcoin effect is that the variation in size captures the variations in changes of greenhouse gas emissions in both publicly traded companies and the Bitcoin network. As a result, Bitcoin's de-meaned emission does not show a large deviation from the regression line based on the estimation of the entire sample. This is certainly not the case in a smaller sample that includes only information technology, finance, and service companies. The coefficient estimate of Bitcoin remains statistically significant regardless of the use of fixed effects in columns (5) and (6).

4. Discussion and Implications

With two exceptions, all specifications in the regression analysis (Tables 4–6) yield significant positive Bitcoin coefficients, suggesting that the amount of greenhouse gases emitted by the Bitcoin network has exceeded that of an average company (and even an industry) in the real economy with a similar market value of Bitcoin. The empirical work has been guided by the assumption that an average-sized company should have an average-sized carbon footprint. While Bitcoin is still within a reasonable range given that many US publicly traded companies of similar size also emit much more CO_2 than the average, the rapid pace of growth in Bitcoin's carbon footprint is more concerning. In other words, the economic value Bitcoin and other cryptocurrencies created would become unjustifiable in the near future.

As with any study, the empirical results have several limitations. First, Bitcoin's equivalent greenhouse gas emission is estimated using the annual energy demand from the Cambridge Bitcoin Electricity Consumption Index (CBECI) and the market price of Bitcoin is one of the eight factors in CBECI's techno-economic model underlying the index. The dependence of Bitcoin network's electricity load on Bitcoin's market price makes the positive coefficient of market capitalisation in regression results less surprising. Furthermore, the EPA's Greenhouse Gas Reporting Program does not collect data of indirect emissions of CO_2 associated with the use of computer equipment. For example, Google, a subsidiary of Alphabet Inc., used 15.5 terawatt hours of electricity in 2020, and the majority of that goes to its data centres (*CNBC*, 2021). This translates to 5.9 megatons of indirect CO_2 emissions in that year. However, the entire information and technology industry of publicly traded companies in Table 2 reports only 0.3 megatons of direct emissions in 2020. In fact, this amount of indirect emissions is reported as direct emissions by the utility companies that supply electricity to Google's data centres. This explains why the utility industry has the highest direct emissions in the same year (760 megatons). Such distortion does not appear to affect the results from the sub-sample without utility companies. Finally, the finding of a larger carbon footprint of Bitcoin than that of companies in the real economy from the cross-sectional regression analysis relies on the market value of equity shares traded in the US. Any attempt to extrapolate to private companies (i.e., not publicly traded) in the US or companies outside the US is necessarily speculative.

Despite these limitations, we provide novel evidence of the existence of Bitcoin's excessive environmental wastefulness, as claimed by Senator Elizabeth Warren. While such a substantial size of carbon footprint can be attributed to Bitcoin's exceptional creativity or unusual technical risks in its development, a simple comparison with the world's most innovative and risk-taking company (according to FastCompany 2019 and Forbes 2019) may make it appear less justifiable. Google, a company of US$900 billion market capitalisation in 2020, has 5.9 megatons of indirect greenhouse gas emissions, whereas Bitcoin, an Internet-based network of US$539 billion market capitalisation, has 26 megatons in the same year. Bitcoin's carbon footprint is more than three times larger than that of Google, but its market value is only half that of Google. Indeed, it is time to replace the PoW consensus in Bitcoin's blockchain with a less energy-intensive mechanism. Nonetheless, concerns about the carbon footprint of cryptocurrencies should not hold back the application of blockchain technology in the real economy, from replacing fiat money in banking and finance to enabling businesses to manage carbon emissions. In the end, there is always a balance between the social and environmental costs and the benefits of using them in creative and efficient ways (Howson, 2019).

References

Bevand, M. (2017a). Electricity consumption of Bitcoin: a market-based and technical analysis. March 10, 2017. Available at: http://blog.zorinaq.com/bitcoin-electricity-consumption/.

Bevand, M. (2017b). Op Ed: Bitcoin miners consume a reasonable amount of energy — And it's all worth it. *Bitcoin Magazine*. April 7, 2017. Available at: http://bitcoinmagazine.com/business/op-ed-bitcoin-miners-consume-reasonable-amount-energy-and-its-all-worth-it/.

CBECI (2022). Methodology of Cambridge Bitcoin electricity consumption index, Judge Business School, University of Cambridge. Available at: http://ccaf.io/cbeci/index/methodology.

Chiu, J. and Koeppl, T. V. (2021). The economics of cryptocurrencies — Bitcoin and beyond, Bank of Canada Working Paper.

Cho, R. (2021). Bitcoin's impacts on climate and the environment, state of the planet, Columbia University's Climate School, 20 September.

CNBC (2022). How Google plans to use 100% carbon-free energy in its data centers by 2030, Catherine Clifford, *Consumer News and Business Channel (CNBC)*, 13 April. Available at: http://www.cnbc.com/2022/04/13/google-data-center-goal-100percent-green-energy-by-2030.html.

Corbet, S., Lucey, B., and Yarovaya, L. (2021). Bitcoin-energy markets interrelationships — New evidence, *Resource Policy*, 70, art. no. 101916.

Daniel, W. (2021). Elizabeth Warren calls for a crackdown on 'environmentally wasteful cryptocurrencies' to fight the climate crisis. Jun 10, 2021, 2:04 PM. Business Insider.

EIA (2020). How much carbon dioxide is produced per kilowatthour of US electricity generation? US Energy Information Administration.

Enoksen, F. A., Landsenes, C. J., Lucivjanska, K., and Molnar, P. (2000). Understanding risk of bubbles in cryptocurrencies, *Journal of Economic Behavior & Organization*, 176, pp. 129–144.

FastCompany (2019). Most innovative companies: Google, *FastCompany Magazine*. Available at: http://www.fastcompany.com/company/google/.

Federal Reserve (2022). Economic well-being of US households in 2021, Board of Governors of The Federal Reserve System, May 2022.

Forbes (2019). The most innovative companies of 2019 according to BCG, Louis Columbus, 24 March, *Forbes Magazine*. Available at: http://www.forbes.com/sites/louiscolumbus/2019/03/24/the-most-innovative-companies-of-2019-according-to-bcg/.

Goldman Sachs (2021). Crypto: A new asset class?, Top of mind, *Goldman Sachs Global Macro Research*, 98, p. 3.

Guardian (2021). Environmentalists sound alarm at US politicians' embrace of cryptocurrency, K. Gammon, 18 November, *The Guardian*. Available at: http://www.theguardian.com/technology/2021/nov/18/cryptocurrency-bitcoin-environmentalist-alarm-us-politicians/.

Howson, P. (2019). Tackling climate change with blockchain, *Nature Climate Change*, 9, pp. 644–645.

Jiang, S., Li, Y., Lu, Q., Hong, Y., Guan, D., Xiong, Y., and Wang, S. (2021). Policy assessments for the carbon emission flows and sustainability of Bitcoin blockchain operation in China, *Nature Communications*, 12, p. 1938.

John, K., O'Hara, M., and Saleh, F. (2022). Bitcoin and beyond, *Annual Review of Financial Economics*, 14, pp. 2.1–2.21.

Kamiya, G. (2020). Factcheck: What is the carbon footprint of streaming video on Netflix? *Carbon Brief*, 13(8).

Kelleher, J. P. (2022). Why do Bitcoins have value? reviewed by J. R. Brown and fact-checked by P. Rathburn, *Investopedia*.

Krause, M. J. and Tolaymat, T. (2018). Quantification of energy and carbon costs for mining cryptocurrencies, *Nature Sustainability*, 1, pp. 711–718.

Kufeoglu, S. and Ozkuran, M. (2019). Bitcoin mining: A global review of energy and power demand, *Energy Research & Social Science*, 58, art. no. 101273.

Lennox, C. S. and Pittman, J. A. (2011). Voluntary audits versus mandatory audits, *The Accounting Review*, 86(5), pp. 1655–1678.

Mora, C., Rollins, R. L., Taladay, K., Kantar, M. B., Chock, M. K., Shimada, M., and Franklin, E. C. (2018). Bitcoin emissions alone could push global warming above 2C, *Nature Climate Change*, 8(11), pp. 931–933.

New York Times (2022). Bitcoin miners want to recast themselves as eco-friendly, D. Yaffe-Bellany, March 22, 2022, *The New York Times.* Available at: http://www.nytimes.com/2022/03/22/technology/bitcoin-miners-environment-crypto.html.

Pew Survey (2021). 16% of Americans say they have ever invested in, traded or used cryptocurrency, Pew Research Center, 11 November.

Rieger, A., Roth, T., Sedlmeir, J., and Fridgen, G. (2022). We need a broader debate on the sustainability of blockchain, *Commentary, Joule*, 6(6), pp. 1137–1141.

https://doi.org/10.1142/9781800614604_0006

Chapter 6

Green Cryptocurrencies and Investor Attention: The Case of Cardano Coin

Zeliha Can Ergün
Faculty of Business, Aydın Adnan Menderes University, Aydın, Turkey
zeliha.can@adu.edu.tr

This research aims to examine the relationship between Cardano (ADA) return, which is used as a proxy for green cryptocurrency, and Google search volume (GSV), which is used as a proxy for investor attention. The weekly data cover the period from January 2018 to June 2022. To analyse the causal relationship between investor attention and Cardano returns, the VAR model and Granger causality tests are implemented. As a result, it is found that there is a bidirectional relationship between Cardano returns and investor attention. However, while changes in investor attention have little impact on the Cardano returns, changes in Cardano returns have a substantial impact on investors' search intensity. Finally, it is concluded from the VAR results that both variables positively affect each other.

Keywords: Cryptocurrency market; investor attention; Google search volume; causality; Cardano coin; behavioural finance; green cryptocurrencies; proof of stake (PoS); energy efficiency; green finance

1. Introduction

Rapid and trustworthy financial transaction systems are in high demand as a result of technological advancements. In this regard, cryptocurrencies have recently gained popularity, and their projected market capitalisation has already surpassed the hundreds of billions of dollars level. The most significant distinction between cryptocurrencies and fiat currencies is that cryptocurrencies are not established by governments and do not adhere to the rules of any country. Cryptocurrencies have gained media and investment attention due to their low transaction fees, peer-to-peer network, and lack of central authority (Shen *et al.*, 2019). With a market capitalisation of US$795 billion, Bitcoin is the most popular cryptocurrency today. However, besides its popularity, it is also the most harmful cryptocurrency to the environment. Recent concerns related to climate change have increased the importance of sustainability and a greener global economy.

Due to the market's increasing need for greener cryptocurrencies and the current trend towards greener businesses, an increasing number of environmentally friendly cryptocurrencies have been developed (Ren and Lucey, 2022). As stated by Ul Haq *et al.* (2022), since Elon Musk (CEO of Tesla) announced that Tesla will no longer accept Bitcoin as payment for electric vehicles, green cryptocurrencies have attracted a lot of attention. The mining of green cryptocurrencies uses less non-renewable resources (i.e., coal and fossil fuels) and requires lower-powered computers and electricity than mining conventional cryptocurrencies (Ul Haq *et al.*, 2022). The most well-known green cryptocurrency, Cardano (ADA), has the biggest market capitalisation among them, and overall, it is also the eighth-largest cryptocurrency (as of June 2022). Cardano was created by the co-founder of Ethereum.

On the other hand, in psychology, attention is regarded as a limited resource because people can pay attention to only one or two things at the same time. The concept of investor attention was discussed for the first time by Merton (1987) who argued that investor attention influences stock prices and their liquidity. Odean (1999) explained the effect of attention as follows: Since investors have limited capability of evaluating each security in the market, they tend to prefer securities that draw their attention. Empirical evidence suggests that investor attention has an influence on the financial markets, and researchers used various indirect proxies to measure the attention in a variety of financial markets (i.e., abnormal trading volume, analysts' coverage, and media coverage). Besides these indirect proxies, Google search volume (GSV) is mostly used as a direct proxy for investor attention.

When the previous studies about investor attention and the cryptocurrency market are evaluated, it is observed that the authors mostly focused on the impact of investor attention on Bitcoin price dynamics (i.e., Jafarinejad and Sakaki, 2018; Philippas *et al.*, 2019; Neto, 2021). Furthermore, a few studies have examined the relationship between investor attention and the major cryptocurrencies (i.e., Piccoli and Chaudhury, 2019; Guindy, 2021; Lin, 2021). Different from the previous research, this study focuses on the probable relationship between investor attention and green cryptocurrencies. Currently, more investors are requesting environmentally friendly investments due to concerns about climate change. Therefore, regulators might promote green financing by better understanding the connection between investor attention and the market performance of green cryptocurrencies.

In light of the above explanations, the purpose of this study is to examine the relationship between Cardano (ADA) returns, which serve as a proxy for green cryptocurrency, and GSV, which serves as a proxy for investor attention. The weekly data cover the period from January 2018 to June 2022. To investigate the causal relationship between investor attention and Cardano returns, the VAR model and Granger causality tests are implemented.

In this chapter, first, the green cryptocurrencies, their importance, and information about green cryptocurrencies with the highest market capitalisation will be explained. Second, investor attention and the related literature will be summarised. Third, data and the methodology will be explained with the results. Finally, the chapter will be concluded with the interpretation of the results, policy implications, and suggestions for future studies.

2. Green Cryptocurrencies

Bitcoin is currently the most popular cryptocurrency, but it is also the most environmentally destructive one. According to the Bitcoin Energy Consumption Index, while the estimated annual energy usage of Bitcoin mining was 9.59 TWh (Terawatt hours) in February 2017, it increased rapidly to 129.63 TWh in June 2022, which is comparable to the power consumption of Norway. Moreover, a single transaction of Bitcoin is projected to consume around 1450.16 kWh electricity, which is equivalent to the amount of power consumed by a US household for more than 49.71 days.[a]

Bitcoin's high energy usage is due to its inefficient mining technique, known as proof of work (PoW), which necessitates the use of extremely powerful and energy-intensive systems. Therefore, recently, cryptocurrencies that use non-PoW mechanisms have become popular. Green cryptocurrencies such as Cardano (ADA), Stellar (XLM), and Cosmos (ATOM) are based on the energy-efficient mechanism called proof-of-stake (PoS) algorithm. As indicated by Košťál *et al.* (2018) with PoS, on the blockchain network, there are no mining computers; only validating machines are in use, so the network is protected without consuming a lot of power.

The top seven green cryptocurrencies as measured by market capitalisation as of 30 June 2022 are shown in Table 1. The most well-known green cryptocurrency, Cardano (ADA), has the biggest market capitalisation among them, and overall, it is also the eighth-largest cryptocurrency. Cardano is the PoS blockchain platform that has been built on peer-reviewed research and developed using evidence-based techniques.[b] The second green cryptocurrency, Tron (TRX), is the thirteenth-largest cryptocurrency overall, which is

Table 1. Top seven green cryptocurrencies.

Cryptocurrency	**Market Capitalisation ($)**	**Overall Rank**
Cardano (ADA)	14,862,514,434	8
Tron (TRX)	5,821,244,044	13
Avalanche (AVAX)	4,545,062,212	17
Stellar (XLM)	2,675,481,356	24
NearProtocol (NEAR)	2,332,006,369	25
Algorand (ALGO)	2,053,514,113	26
Cosmos (ATOM)	2,041,905,274	27

Note: This table shows the top seven green cryptocurrencies based on their market capitalisation as of 30 June 2022.

[a]Retrieved from https://digiconomist.net/bitcoin-energy-consumption.
[b]Retrieved from https://cardano.org/.

defined as the world's fastest-growing public chain.[c] The third green cryptocurrency, Avalanche (AVAX), is the 17th-largest cryptocurrency overall. It is the blockchain industry's fastest platform for smart contracts according to time to finality.[d]

On the other hand, the remaining green cryptocurrencies' market capitalisations are very close to each other. Stellar (XLM), the 24th-largest cryptocurrency overall, is a decentralised platform for trading various types of currencies (including Dollars, Pesos, and Bitcoin), and it describes itself as being quicker, less expensive, and more energy efficient than traditional blockchain systems (i.e., Bitcoin and Ethereum).[e] Near Protocol (NEAR) is the 25th-largest cryptocurrency overall, and it is defined as a developer-friendly, PoS, and public blockchain.[f] Algorand (ALGO) is the 26th-largest cryptocurrency overall, which is also a sustainable blockchain and defines itself as the most energy-efficient blockchain.[g] Lastly, Cosmos (ATOM) is the 27th-largest cryptocurrency overall, and is a fast-growing network of autonomous, interconnected blockchains that were created with the aid of developer-friendly application components, linked together using the revolutionary inter-blockchain communication (IBC) protocol.[h]

3. Literature Review

While most studies on investor attention have focused on its connection to the stock markets (i.e., Da *et al.*, 2011; Aouadi *et al.*, 2013; Wang *et al.*, 2021), more studies have recently examined its relationship with the cryptocurrency market. The studies primarily used direct proxies (i.e., GSV, number of tweets, and Wikipedia) for investor attention to investigate its relationship with the market dynamics of the cryptocurrencies (i.e., prices, returns, volatilities, and trading volume). Additionally, several recent studies have

[c]Retrieved from https://tron.network/index?lng=en.
[d]Retrieved from https://www.avalabs.org/.
[e]Retrieved from https://www.stellar.org/learn/intro-to-stellar.
[f]Retrieved from https://coinmarketcap.com/currencies/near-protocol/#About.
[g]Retrieved from https://www.algorand.com/.
[h]Retrieved from https://cosmos.network/intro.

examined some of the other top cryptocurrencies, even though most studies have used Bitcoin as a benchmark for the cryptocurrency market.

One group of studies investigated the relationship between investor attention and Bitcoin prices, as summarised in Table 2. Kristoufek (2013) used Google Trends and Wikipedia search terms as a proxy for investor attention, and as a result of the vector error correction model (VECM), a positive and bidirectional relationship was found between the variables. The other research that focused on the effect of investor attention on the price of Bitcoin was conducted by Skaug and Bratlie (2019). Different from previous studies, they constructed an attention index by using principal component analysis, which is composed of the search queries on Google Trends, Wikipedia, and Bitcointalk. Similar to Kristoufek (2013), they found a positive relationship and also concluded that

Table 2. Studies about investor attention and the prices of cryptocurrencies.

Author(s)	**Investor Attention Proxy**	**Cryptocurrencies**	**Effect**
Kristoufek (2013)	Google Trends & Wikipedia	Bitcoin	Positive, bidirectional
Skaug and Bratlie (2019)	Constructed index	Bitcoin	Positive
Philippas *et al.* (2019)	Google Trends & Twitter	Bitcoin	Yes
Ibikunle *et al.* (2020)	Google Trends	Bitcoin	Yes
Piccoli and Chaudhury (2019)	Google Trends	Bitcoin, Ethereum, Ripple	Bidirectional
Piccoli and Chaudhury (2019)	Google Trends	Bitcoin, Ethereum, Ripple	Yes, but weaker for Ripple
Raza *et al.* (2022)	Google Trends	Bitcoin, New Economy Movement (NEM), Dash, Ethereum, Ripple, Litecoin	Yes, for all, except Dash

investor attention could predict the future Bitcoin price changes with a 51.42% accuracy. Moreover, Philippas *et al.* (2019) used Google Trends and Twitter to represent investor attention and suggested that there is a partial effect of attention on Bitcoin prices, and this effect increases in the periods with more uncertainty. On the other hand, Ibikunle *et al.* (2020) decomposed Bitcoin prices into efficient and noise components and revealed that the efficient side is driven by arbitrage, while the noise side is driven by high levels of attention as determined by Google Trends.

Besides Bitcoin, a few studies analysed the effect of investor attention, proxied by Google Trends, on other top cryptocurrencies' prices. Investor attention was found to have a weak relationship with the prices of Ethereum and Ripple by Piccoli and Chaudhury (2019), but a strong bidirectional relationship with the price of Bitcoin. Additionally, Subramaniam and Chakraborty (2020) discovered that investors primarily pay attention to ranked cryptocurrencies (Bitcoin and Ethereum), whereas they only pay attention to younger cryptocurrencies such as Ripple when they perform better. Lastly, Raza *et al.* (2022) examined the effect of Google Trends on the prices of Bitcoin, New Economy Movement (NEM), Dash, Ethereum, Ripple, and Litecoin. It is found that investor attention is a good predictor of all the analysed cryptocurrencies' prices, except Dash.

The second group of studies investigated the relationship between investor attention and the cryptocurrencies' returns as shown in Table 3. It is observed that these studies generally used Google Trends as a proxy for investor attention. Similar to previous groups of studies, a majority of analyses are implemented for the Bitcoin returns. Investor attention and Bitcoin returns are causally related in both directions, according to Dastgir *et al.* (2019). Moreover, although Neto (2021) observed unidirectional causality at first, it was found that it becomes bidirectional when the time delay increases. On the other hand, quantile and time-varying causality was reported by Hang and Zhang (2021) when they investigated the time-varying quantile causality between variables. Together with Bitcoin, the other studies examined the top five (i.e., Ethereum, Litecoin, Ripple, Bitcoin Cash, and Tether) cryptocurrencies in the market. Lin (2021) concluded that the attention of investors increases with the higher past performance of cryptocurrencies. Moreover, as found by Su *et al.* (2021), large positive gains are realised when investors pay

Table 3. Studies about investor attention and returns of cryptocurrencies.

Author(s)	Investor Attention Proxy	Cryptocurrencies	Effect
Dastgir *et al.* (2019)	Google Trends	Bitcoin	Bidirectional
Neto (2021)	Google Trends	Bitcoin	Unidirectional, becomes bidirectional with the time delay
Hang and Zhang (2021)	Google Trends	Bitcoin	Quantile and time-varying causality
Lin (2021)	Google Trends	Top five cryptocurrencies	Positive
Su *et al.* (2021)	Google Trends	Top five cryptocurrencies	Positive
Neto (2022)	Google Trends	Top five cryptocurrencies	Nonlinear

more attention to cryptocurrencies. Neto (2022) also found a nonlinear relationship between investor attention and cryptocurrencies' returns.

The last group of studies focused on the impact of investor attention on other market dynamics of cryptocurrencies (i.e., volatility, trading volume, and liquidity) as listed in Table 4. The connection between investor attention and Bitcoin returns, trading volume, and volatility was studied by Urquhart (2018) and Shen *et al.* (2019). Urquhart (2018) demonstrated unidirectional causality from volatility and trading volume to the next day's investor attention using Google trends as a proxy for investor attention. On the other hand, Shen *et al.* (2019) observed that investor attention strongly influences next-day trading volume and volatility of Bitcoin using Twitter as a proxy for investor attention. Furthermore, Zhang and Wang (2020), Zhu *et al.* (2021), and Aslanidis *et al.* (2022) investigated investor attention and the cryptocurrencies' return and volatility relationship in their studies. By using Google Trends as a proxy for investor attention, Zhang and Wang (2020) found both linear and nonlinear bidirectional relationships between variables for the 20 largest

Table 4. Studies about investor attention and other market dynamics.

Author(s)	Investor Attention Proxy	Cryptocurrencies	Market Dynamic	Effect
Urquhart (2018)	Google Trends	Bitcoin	Returns, trading volume, volatility	Unidirectional for volatility and trading volume
Shen *et al.* (2019)	Twitter	Bitcoin	Returns, trading volume, volatility	Positive for trading volume and volatility
Zhang and Wang (2020)	Google Trends	20 largest cryptocurrencies	Return, volatility	Bidirectional (linear and nonlinear)
Zhu *et al.* (2021)	Google Trends	Bitcoin	Return, volatility	Linear and nonlinear
Aslanidis *et al.* (2022)	Google Trends index	Top five cryptocurrencies	Return, volatility	Bidirectional
Smales (2022)	Google Trends	20 largest cryptocurrencies	Return, volatility, liquidity	Positive
Choi (2021)	Twitter	Bitcoin	Liquidity	Positive
Yao *et al.* (2021)	Google Trends	452 cryptocurrencies	Idiosyncratic risk	Positive
Smales (2021)	Google Trends	20 largest cryptocurrencies	Crash risk	Positive
Bashir *et al.* (2021)	Google Trends	Top five cryptocurrencies	Herding	Negative
Tang and Liu (2022)	Google Trends	Bitcoin	Speculation	Positive

cryptocurrencies. Similarly, Zhu *et al.* (2021) concluded that investor attention causes changes in Bitcoin return and volatility linearly and nonlinearly. Different from previous studies, Aslanidis *et al.* (2022) constructed the Google Trends index and examined its relationship with the returns and volatilities of five major cryptocurrencies. They detected a bidirectional causal relationship between attention and returns, but it was found that the causal relationship from Bitcoin volatility to attention was stronger than the one in the opposite direction. Together with the return and volatility, Smales (2022) also investigated the investor attention effect on the cryptocurrencies' liquidity and found a positive relationship between the variables. Likewise, Choi (2021) also found a positive impact of investor attention on Bitcoin liquidity by measuring it with the number of tweets. In addition, because investor attention increases liquidity, Yao *et al.* (2021) suggested that it reduces the idiosyncratic risks of cryptocurrencies.

On the other hand, several studies examined the interaction between the remaining aspects of the cryptocurrencies (crash risk, herding, and speculation) and investor attention. Smales (2021) investigated the crash risk of the 20 largest cryptocurrencies and found a positive relationship. Bashir *et al.* (2021) examined the interaction of investor attention and herding in the cryptocurrency market and found a negative relationship. Lastly, Tang and Liu (2022) analysed the effect of investor attention on Bitcoin speculation and found a positive effect.

In sum, when the previous literature is evaluated, it is observed that investor attention is a significant predictor in the cryptocurrency market. Concordantly, this study aims to examine the relationship between Cardano (ADA) returns, which serve as a proxy for green cryptocurrency, and GSV, which serves as a proxy for investor attention. In the following part, the data, methodology, and results will be evaluated.

4. Data and Methodology

Among the green cryptocurrencies (i.e., Cardano, Avalanche, Near, and Cosmos), the one with the largest market capitalisation is the Cardano (ADA) coin. That is why, as a representative of green cryptocurrencies, US dollar closing prices of Cardano coin are taken into consideration, which can be obtained from www.investing.com. On the other hand, as a proxy for investor attention, GSV is used, which is derived from the "Google Trends" website (www.google.com/trends) by using the keyword "Cardano".

GSV is a scaled indicator of the frequency of searches with the total number of searches across all potential queries, which is scaled from 0 to 100. A score of 100 indicates that the given search keyword is very popular during the chosen period and in the chosen area. In this study, the global search volume is considered since

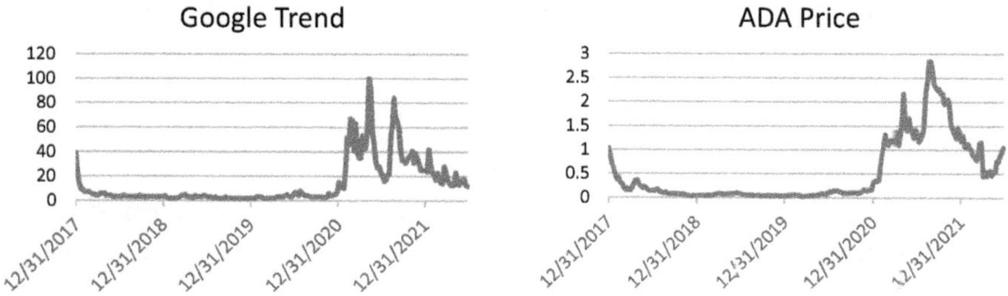

Fig. 1. Google searches for Cardano (index from 0 to 100) and Cardano price (USD).

cryptocurrencies are traded internationally. Google Trends provides weekly data; hence in this chapter, the weekly data are used, which cover the period from January 2018 (the Cardano price is available as of 31 December 2017) to June 2022.

Figure 1 illustrates the GSV of Cardano coin and its price between January 2018 and June 2022. The price of Cardano (ADA) ranges between 0.026 and 2.847 (USD). On the other hand, investor attention proxied by Google Trends ranges between 2 and 100. While the investor attention was 19 at the beginning of the period, it decreased rapidly in the following times. Investor interest was roughly in line until December 2020. After January 2021, it had increased rapidly, which may be due to the effect of the COVID-19 outbreak. Investors started searching for a safer investment as a result of the COVID-19 outbreak, which elevated their level of worry about the financial markets. Investors used cryptocurrencies as a hedging tool at the beginning of the outbreak, which substantially increased interest in the market (Bashir *et al.*, 2021). The attention reached its peak point on 9 May 2021 with the top point of 100. After the end of August 2021, it again started to fall. Cardano's price, on the other hand, was 1.036 (USD) at the beginning of the period. Like Google Trends, it started to decline and stayed at a similar amount until December 2020. After January 2021, it again started to increase and reached its peak point on the 22 August 2021 at 2.846 (USD) prices. In sum, it is noticeable from both graphs that the changes in the GSV and Cardano prices may be interrelated.

For the empirical analysis, the natural logarithmic returns of Cardano prices and the logarithmic change in the Google Trends search queries are calculated in line with several studies (i.e., Dastgir *et al.*, 2018; Piccoli and Chaudhury, 2019; Zhang and Wang, 2020). The related equations are as follows, respectively:

$$r_{i,t} = \ln\left(\frac{p_{i,t}}{p_{i,t-1}}\right) \tag{1}$$

where $r_{i,t}$ indicates the logarithmic return of Cardano on day t, $p_{i,t}$ shows the closing price of Cardano on trading day t, and $p_{i,t-1}$ denotes the closing price of Cardano on trading day $t-1$.

$$\text{GSV}_{i,t} = \ln\left(\frac{\text{Trends}_{i,t}}{\text{Trends}_{i,t-1}}\right) \tag{2}$$

where $\text{GSV}_{i,t}$ indicates the logarithmic change in the GSV on day t, $\text{Trends}_{i,t}$ shows the GSV of Cardano on trading day t, and $\text{Trends}_{i,t-1}$ denotes the GSV of Cardano on trading day $t-1$.

The linear Granger causality test following the unrestricted VAR(k) model is used to examine the Granger causality (Granger, 1969) between Cardano returns ($r_{i,t}$) and investor attention ($\text{GSV}_{i,t}$) in the following manner:

$$\begin{aligned} r_{i,t} &= \alpha_0 + \alpha_1 r_{t-1} + \cdots + \alpha_k r_{t-k} + \omega_1 \text{GSV}_{t-1} \\ &\quad + \cdots + \omega_k \text{GSV}_{t-k} + \varepsilon_t \end{aligned} \tag{3}$$

$$\begin{aligned} \text{GSV}_{i,t} &= \alpha_0 + \alpha_1 \text{GSV}_{t-1} + \cdots + \alpha_k \text{GSV}_{t-k} + \omega_1 r_{t-1} \\ &\quad + \cdots + \omega_k r_{t-k} + \varepsilon_t \end{aligned} \tag{4}$$

where k is the optimal lag length obtained from Schwartz Information Criterion. The null hypothesis of Granger non-causality is tested that if ω parameters are zero, GSV does not cause r in Eq. (3), and r does not cause GSV in Eq. (4).

5. Empirical Results

Before applying the Granger causality test, the Augmented Dickey–Fuller (ADF) and Philips–Perron (PP) unit root tests, as indicated in Table 5, were used to check the series' stationary property. Since the results are statistically significant, the null hypotheses are rejected, which means all of the series are stationary.

After confirming that Cardano returns and GSV are stationary, vector autoregression (VAR) equation is estimated to examine

Table 5. Unit root test statistics.

Tests	ADA_Return	GSV
Augmented Dickey–Fuller	−13.48111***	−16.02962***
Philips–Perron	−13.50473***	−16.11114***

Note: The null hypothesis in these tests is that the series contains a unit root. *** denotes statistical significance at the 1%, 5%, and 10% levels, respectively.

Table 6. Granger causality test results.

Null Hypothesis	Chi-sq	Prob.
GSV does not Granger-cause ADA return	2.791506	0.0948*
ADA_Return does not Granger-cause GSV	18.65068	0.0000***

Note: ***, * denote statistical significance at the 1%, 5%, and 10% levels, respectively.

the Granger causality between the series. One lag is considered for the Granger causality based on the Schwarz Information Criteria. The Granger causality results are indicated in Table 6. The first row shows that the GSV does not Granger-cause Cardano returns. The second row demonstrates that Cardano returns do not Granger-cause GSV. According to the Granger causality test results, both null hypotheses are rejected. This result suggests that GSV Granger-causes Cardano returns, and vice versa. Cardano returns and GSV are shown to be bidirectionally causally related; however, the statistical significance that Cardano returns Granger-cause GSV is stronger. In other words, while changes in GSV have a little impact on the Cardano returns, changes in Cardano returns have a substantial impact on investors' search intensity.

For the second step, the VAR model of Cardano returns and GSV is evaluated, which is reported in Table 7. The Cardano returns and GSV are shown as dependent variables in the first and second columns, respectively. It is found that historical Cardano returns have a remarkable positive effect on future investor attention in the suggested model with one lag. On the other hand, the historical GSV has a smaller positive effect on the future Cardano returns.

Table 7. VAR (1) estimation results.

	Dependent Variables	
	ADA_Return_t	**GSV_t**
Intercept	0.001158	−0.003286
	(0.103778)	(−0.207928)
ADA_Return_{t-1}	0.065378	0.445924
	(0.896631)	(4.318643)***
GSV_{t-1}	0.0829983	−0.180174
	(1.670780)*	(−2.561702)***

Notes: Cardano returns and GSV are shown as the dependent variables in the first and second columns, respectively. Each VAR model has one lag, and the number in parentheses represents the *t*-statistics for that model. The VAR (1) system satisfies the stability criteria since no roots exist beyond the unit circle. ***, * denote statistical significance at the 1%, 5%, and 10% levels, respectively.

6. Conclusion

The demand for the cryptocurrency market has substantially increased during the last few years. Due to this expansion, the market experienced tremendous market capitalisation. The most widely used cryptocurrency, Bitcoin, is also the most damaging to the environment. For that reason, recently, environmentally friendly cryptocurrencies have begun to receive greater investor attention. The primary distinction between green cryptocurrencies and conventional ones is that they favour the energy-efficient oS algorithm over the more powerful and energy-intensive PoW systems.

Psychologists believe that attention is a limited resource, and evidence suggests that investor attention has a significant impact on the financial markets. Although several researchers have examined how investor attention affects the cryptocurrency market, this study aims to demonstrate how investor attention and green cryptocurrencies are related. Accordingly, Cardano (ADA) coin was selected as a representative of green cryptocurrencies due to its higher market capitalisation among others. GSV, on the other hand, was used as a proxy for investor attention. The weekly data spans from January 2018 to

June 2022, and the VAR model and Granger causality tests are used to investigate the causal linkages between investor attention and Cardano returns.

The Granger causality test results indicate a bidirectional relationship between investor attention and Cardano returns. However, the statistical significance of the "Cardano returns Granger-cause investor attention" is stronger than the other way around. This means that while changes in investor attention have little impact on the Cardano returns, changes in Cardano returns have a substantial impact on investors' search intensity. Moreover, the VAR results suggest that past Cardano returns have a remarkable positive effect on future investor attention, and past GSV has a little positive impact on future Cardano returns.

Overall, the findings imply that investor attention is significantly influenced by historical Cardano returns, particularly greater prior returns increasing investor attention, and vice versa. These findings offer useful information for green cryptocurrency investors who can make money by investing in green cryptocurrencies on the days after there has been greater investor attention. Additionally, as there is a strong correlation between investor attention and the performance of the green cryptocurrency market, policymakers might support more environmentally friendly financing.

Future research may study the association between investor attention and green cryptocurrencies using nonlinear models. The analyses might also include other green cryptocurrencies besides Cardano, and in addition to returns, their volatility, trading volumes, and liquidities could be considered to highlight their relationship with the investor attention.

References

Al Guindy, M. (2021). Cryptocurrency price volatility and investor attention, *International Review of Economics & Finance*, 76, pp. 556–570.

Aouadi, A., Arouri, M., and Teulon, F. (2013). Investor attention and stock market activity: Evidence from France, *Economic Modelling*, 35, pp. 674–681.

Aslanidis, N., Bariviera, A. F., and López, Ó. G. (2022). The link between cryptocurrencies and Google Trends attention, *Finance Research Letters*, 47, pp. 1–8.

Bashir, H. A., Kumar, D., and Shiljas, K. (2021). Investor attention and herding in the cryptocurrency market during the COVID-19 pandemic, *Applied Finance Letters*, 10, pp. 67–77.

Choi, H. (2021). Investor attention and bitcoin liquidity: Evidence from bitcoin tweets, *Finance Research Letters*, 39, pp. 1–9.

Da, Z., Engelberg, J., and Gao, P. (2011). In search of attention, *The Journal of Finance*, 66(5), pp. 1461–1499.

Dastgir, S., Demir, E., Downing, G., Gozgor, G., and Lau, C. K. M. (2019). The causal relationship between bitcoin attention and bitcoin returns: Evidence from the copula-based Granger causality test, *Finance Research Letters*, 28, pp. 160–164.

Granger, C. W. (1969). Investigating causal relations by econometric models and cross-spectral methods, *Econometrica: Journal of the Econometric Society*, 37(3), pp. 424–438.

Hang, J. and Zhang, X. (2021). Time-and quantile-varying causality between investor attention and bitcoin returns: A rolling-window causality-in-quantiles approach, *Complexity*, 2021, pp. 1–12.

Ibikunle, G., McGroarty, F., and Rzayev, K. (2020). More heat than light: Investor attention and bitcoin price discovery, *International Review of Financial Analysis*, 69, pp. 1–5.

Jafarinejad, M. and Sakaki, H. (2018). The role of investor attention in bitcoin mania. Available at SSRN: https://ssrn.com/abstract=3137284.

Košt'ál, K., Krupa, T., Gembec, M., Vereš, I., Ries, M., and Kotuliak, I. (2018). On transition between PoW and PoS, in *2018 International Symposium ELMAR*, pp. 207–210.

Kristoufek, L. (2013). BitCoin meets Google Trends and Wikipedia: Quantifying the relationship between phenomena of the Internet era, *Scientific Reports*, 3(1), pp. 1–7.

Lin, Z. Y. (2021). Investor attention and cryptocurrency performance, *Finance Research Letters*, 40, pp. 1–7.

Merton, R. (1987). A simple model of capital market equilibrium with incomplete information, *Journal of Finance*, 42, pp. 483–510.

Neto, D. (2021). Are Google searches making the bitcoin market run amok? A tail event analysis, *The North American Journal of Economics and Finance,* 57, pp 1–6.

Neto, D. (2022). Examining interconnectedness between media attention and cryptocurrency markets: A transfer entropy story, *Economics Letters*, 214, pp. 1–6.

Odean, T. (1999). Do investors trade too much? *American Economic Review*, 89 (5), pp. 1279–1298.

Philippas, D., Rjiba, H., Guesmi, K., and Goutte, S. (2019). Media attention and bitcoin prices, *Finance Research Letters*, 30, pp. 37–43

Piccoli, P. and Chaudhury, M. (2019). Dynamic relationship of cryptocurrency prices and investor attention. Available at SSRN: https://ssrn.com/abstract=3327232.

Raza, S. A., Yarovaya, L., Guesmi, K., and Shah, N. (2022) Google Trends and cryptocurrencies: A nonparametric causality-in-quantiles analysis, *International Journal of Emerging Markets*. Available at https://doi.org/ 10.1108/IJOEM-10-2021-1522.

Ren, B. and Lucey, B. (2022). A clean, green haven? — Examining the relationship between clean energy, clean and dirty cryptocurrencies, *Energy Economics,* 109, pp. 1–29.

Shen, D., Urquhart, A., and Wang, P. (2019). Does twitter predict bitcoin?, *Economics Letters,* 174, pp. 118–122.

Skaug, N. and Bratlie, M. M. (2019). How does investor attention impact the price of bitcoin? (Master's thesis, Handelshøyskolen BI).

Smales, L. A. (2021). Investor attention and cryptocurrency price crash risk: A quantile regression approach, *Studies in Economics and Finance*, 39(3), pp. 490–505.

Smales, L. A. (2022). Investor attention in cryptocurrency markets, *International Review of Financial Analysis*, 79, pp. 1–17.

Su, X., Zhan, W., and Li, Y. (2021). Quantile dependence between investor attention and cryptocurrency returns: Evidence from time and frequency domain analyses, *Applied Economics*, 53(55), pp. 6439–6471.

Subramaniam, S. and Chakraborty, M. (2020). Investor attention and cryptocurrency returns: Evidence from quantile causality approach, *Journal of Behavioral Finance*, 21(1), pp. 103–115.

Tang, C. and Liu, X. (2022). Bitcoin speculation, investor attention and major events. Are they connected?, *Applied Economics Letters*, 30(8), pp. 1–9.

Ul Haq, I., Maneengam, A., Chupradit, S., and Huo, C. (2022). Are green bonds and sustainable cryptocurrencies truly sustainable? Evidence from a wavelet coherence analysis, *Economic Research-Ekonomska Istraživanja*, 36(1), pp. 1–20.

Urquhart, A. (2018). What causes the attention of bitcoin?, *Economics Letters*, 166, pp. 40–44.

Wang, H., Xu, L., and Sharma, S. S. (2021). Does investor attention increase stock market volatility during the COVID-19 pandemic?, *Pacific-Basin Finance Journal*, 69, pp. 1–11.

Yao, S., Kong, X., Sensoy, A., Akyildirim, E., and Cheng, F. (2021). Investor attention and idiosyncratic risk in cryptocurrency markets, *The European Journal of Finance*, 27, pp. 1–19.

Zhang, W. and Wang, P. (2020). Investor attention and the pricing of cryptocurrency market, *Evolutionary and Institutional Economics Review*, 17(2), pp. 445–468.

Zhu, P., Zhang, X., Wu, Y., Zheng, H., and Zhang, Y. (2021). Investor attention and cryptocurrency: Evidence from the bitcoin market, *PLoS One*, 16(2), pp. 1–28.

https://doi.org/10.1142/9781800614604_0007

Chapter 7

Needs and Perspectives on Emerging Banking Trends in the Age of Fintech

Adalberto Rangone*,‡ and Sarmad Ali†,§

Department of Law, University of Perugia, Via Alessandro Pascoli, Perugia, Italy

†*Department of Management and Business Administration, Gabriele d'Annunzio University of Chieti and Pescara, Viale Pindaro, Pescara, Italy*

‡*adalberto.rangone@unipg.it*

§*sarmad.ali@unich.it*

This work aims to understand current trends in the financial sector. Many trends are the technological solutions provided by new players operating in the financial sector (fintech), leading to different perspectives for the future awaiting private citizens and companies. This work presupposes the need to understand how the traditional financial system is able to keep up with the continuous and changing demands of a society that is evolving towards 4.0 and is increasingly aiming to meet environmental, social, and governance sustainability criteria. Above all, this chapter requires an understanding of the real reasons why systems such as decentralised finance are taking over despite the presence of well-established players. In this work, the authors aim to investigate the players, the battleground of a clash between tradition and innovation in the financial field, and whether the measures adopted by the banking system to adapt to the trends of technological innovation are sufficient to stand up to a real model of innovative development which sees a closer relationship between stakeholders and companies and which is far from the traditional banking–company system.

Keywords: Fintech; DeFi; CeFi; banking system; financial system; blockchain; bank-based systems; market-based systems; SMEs; corporate ownership

1. Introduction

In the context of the relationship between bank and firm, technological innovation is now leading to extremely important and ever-changing phenomena. In recent years, three specific phenomena have characterised the evolution of the financial environment: the introduction of new formidable technologies, the development of "fintech", and the increase in the number of 4.0 companies. Taken together, these phenomena have led to a new development model, requiring the formulation of financial products to support entrepreneurial initiatives.

To keep up with the times, the traditional banking system had to start offering new services to its customers, not only towards the more sophisticated and complex corporate sector but also towards the retail sector.

According to the Observatory Fintech & Insurtech (Politecnico di Milano, 2021), the most widespread fintech services are utilised in the following:

- mobile payment;
- P2P payment;
- family budget services;
- chatbot;
- cardless withdrawal;
- data transfer from the banking account.

In line with this perspective, efforts have been focused on services provided via API, and aimed at making it easier to use on-demand activities. In addition, the use of big data and advanced analytics allows one to maximise the information baggage of company data, giving the banking system the opportunity to more efficiently outline the profile of its customers and offer tailored services (Caccavale and Righi, 2018). Today, the objective of the traditional banking system is clearly aimed at redefining the criteria of supply chain finance, enhancing the digitisation of the sales force, achieving an upgrade of back-end infrastructures, and above all creating a solid platform of global transaction banking.

These prospects have certainly redefined the way banking is done, but above all they have pushed the credit system towards new paradigms of competitiveness, a competitiveness that is expressed in a constantly changing context and is dictated by the most innovative fintech offerings.

At the international level, clear examples of this approach can now be found in the following partnerships:

- HSBC and Tradeshift;
- Deutsche Bank and Traxpay;
- Banking Circle and SIA;
- N26 and TransferWise;
- ABN AMRO and Subaio.

However, this approach requires at least two factors:

- The creation of funds to support specific investments in the fintech sector.
- The ability to best meet the user experience.

Alternatively, the traditional banking system is destined to be hit hard. The risks include, firstly, a loss of the number of customers eager to receive innovative and high-performance services and, secondly, a strategic targeting of third parties in the payment world to optimise costs. Therefore, the perspective that emerges does not consider simple remote banking, but rather digital consulting services on potential forms of funding, new forms of collaboration in outsourcing with new fintech companies to meet specific customer needs, and having a strategic impact on customers when managing suppliers and cash flow (Caccavale and Righi, 2018). However, in order to understand the new level at which traditional and new players in international finance are confronted, it is appropriate to outline the reasons that have led to the spread of fintech initiatives. Generally, there is a tendency to mention important aspects which — especially thanks to blockchain — express (Kamat and Seo, 2019; Durnev *et al.*, 2018; Gervais *et al.*, 2016) the following:

- programmable capacity;
- simplification of processes;
- transparency.

The *programmable capacity* is due to the coding of the entire business logic. This includes data privacy, compliance, and identity aspects. The *simplification of processes* is due to improved operational efficiency, including real-time regulation of transactions, reporting, and auditing.

Transparency, on the other hand, ensures that the data processed are intact and are authentically transcribed into the systems. They are complemented by the potential economic benefits defined by improved operating costs, lower infrastructure costs, and lower transaction costs.

Although these aspects require continuous and additional work so that they can be properly disseminated at a global level in every financial area, they are already present on the market. These aspects are part of a technology which has now been developed and which does not seem to determine the ultimate objective of the current evolutionary process.

Is it possible, therefore, that these are only lean and digital operations?

While outlining perspectives to anticipate trends means looking at and understanding the evolving context, it is considered essential in this work to analyse and understand (as far as possible because of the constraints imposed) the motivations and context in which the main players are involved. The analysis of decentralised finance — opposed to centralised financial system promoted by traditional banking players — in our view provides essential information to understand the current trend and its ratio. This last area, which for simplicity can be understood as an extremisation of high-tech financial aspects, is in fact intended to exclude any form of intermediation that traditional credit institutions may represent. Decentralised finance platforms are in fact able to distribute profits while leaving users and the community to "control" and govern them.

This is because decentralised networks generate "consensus" (Xiong *et al.*, 2022), i.e., no entity has the power to alter or censor the data circulating on them. The community involved would therefore be the master of the processes and would feed itself from many points of view, primarily financial and legal. This statement thus leads us to the logic of this work linked to two fundamental questions: why and how. The starting point is certainly inherent in the reasons why the adoption of technological innovations is leading to an extreme financial evolution dictated by the marginal role of credit institutions. This first analytical context allows us to define some key themes:

- evolution of the financing needs of SMEs;
- evolution of key players in the fintech and decentralised finance world;
- the new role of stakeholders in investment projects (i.e., green ones).

And again, how can the traditional and innovative coexist in light of current trends and emerging prospects. Thus, the key perspectives of this context are as follows:

- the role of international regulation and the influence on first movers in DeFi;
- the conversion scenarios of the players involved.

2. Understanding Current Firms' Needs

2.1. *Old customers with new needs*

In the European Union, small and medium-sized enterprises account for almost all enterprises and about 65% of global turnover.

Despite this undeniably important fact, small and medium-sized enterprises are the main victims of an overly complex legal, fiscal, and administrative environment which still entails exorbitant costs. These factors ultimately discourage new initiatives, investment in innovation in existing companies, and recruitment of new employees. Stimulating the creation of new small and medium-sized enterprises, based on new technologies — through better access to finance, the marketing of research products, the provision of instruments to facilitate research and innovation, and the promotion of the use of new information technologies — is therefore a significant need in the post-globalisation era (Mastroiacovo, 2019) and in the society of the European Union (Paccagnella, 2020). As already evidenced in numerous studies (Rangone, 2013a, 2013b, 2018, 2020), banks and other financial institutions have continued to move away from the events of the real economy to focus on financial intermediation based on securities markets. This trend has allowed relationships between providers of capital and users to become increasingly "anonymous" and mistrustful. Small businesses are the ones who suffer most from this depersonalisation of the economy and finance. This is due to the fact that the bank has always been the "successful stakeholder", which does not forget the relationship with the client and maintains a long-term relationship of trust. It has always been one of the essential features of Europe's financial market culture and should therefore not give way to any other temptation or fad that characterises the new globalisation of the economy. The main task of the European banking and financial system is to promote the creation and consolidation of an autonomous middle class in the countries of Central and Eastern Europe which are currently undergoing change.

In fact, as we have already pointed out, these same institutions are able to promote the local savings market. In other words, the relationship between small and medium-sized enterprises and the financial and banking sector must be closely linked. The creation of small businesses and their development in terms of efficiency and productivity in the context of continuous and constant competitive conditions imposed by globalisation cannot be separated from a vision of financial management.

In addition to an appropriate cost control policy, credit information system, and inventory control, as well as product organisation and sponsorship techniques, small and medium-sized enterprises often lack appropriate technical knowledge on the sources of development finance and working capital. It is therefore necessary to give some thought to this matter.

2.2. *Firms' needs and investment logic*

The creation or restructuring of a company is certainly a complex process and, in order to obtain benefits, it requires a careful and thoughtful search for the various possibilities to be pursued.

The choice of the most appropriate form of investment is important for the success of the investment.

The health of a firm thus remains closely linked to its ability to receive financing from credit institutions or to be able to allocate new shares on the market. The interaction between business and credit institutions has a long tradition and in Europe it has certainly acquired a preponderance over the search for capital on the financial market (Tarantola, 2007). Until the creation of DeFi, the banking system was perhaps the only point of contact for small and medium-sized enterprises with the financial world.

However, the international economic crisis has made this relationship fragile and more difficult, dictated by a substantial decrease in the supply of credit (Wehinger, 2014). In such a context, it is interesting to highlight how the business logic (Rangone, 2018) is progressively related to the evolution of the system of indebtedness that is useful to carry out actions of corporate restructuring (for companies already started) but also to provide capital for new initiatives

In order to develop this analysis, it is necessary first to identify the main criteria influencing the choice of financing from a business point of view:

- The cost of the loan (expressed in particular in the cost of capital which varies according to the products obtained and in the related administrative costs).
- The terms of the financing (may be short-term or medium-term if the project is highly remunerated or long-term if the project is less profitable but involves more expensive operations).
- The effects of taxation, allowing tax deductions to be made on part of the interest accrued on loans.
- The value of the company's assets collateralised for the financing.
- The special conditions imposed by the lenders.
- The ability of the firm to have sufficient liquidity to repay the financing.

However, the relationship between the business world and the financial capital to develop their projects is not unambiguous, so it cannot be seen only in light of the business perspective. It is therefore important to understand whether, and to what extent, the degree of access to credit is constrained by the performance of companies or, in the current context, financial trends in credit offered by the system have become a dominant variable.

The credit offer is linked to a number of factors which — without any claim to be exhaustive — can be summarised here.

Essentially, the solutions are based on the degree of risk involved in the business initiative (Ruozi, 2016) and the company's presence on the stock market. The latter condition has a significant impact on the granting of financing, as it is more likely to attract back-up facilities, merchant banking operations, or simply the attention of international investors. However, a more complete analysis cannot disregard macroeconomic variables, which are here understood as determinants and which in some contexts may themselves be conditioned (for example, inflation may vary according to access to credit, tax policies, and the consumer price index).

In recent years, due to the economic and financial crisis, some authors have shown that the credit offer has suffered an enormous contraction in Italy, highlighting the impact (Fig. 1) of some specific factors (Morettini, 2013).

However, in this context, it has been possible to find that, at least in Italy, there are categories of companies for which access to credit is more available and others for which it is more difficult (Rangone, 2018).

Looking at the data (Table 1) provided by the Bank of Italy, the answer seems obvious.

As early as 2016, the survey clearly shows how unfavourable access to credit is for the category of medium-sized companies which, in the case of the takeover under consideration, includes partnerships and sole proprietorships, which already have difficulty competing with medium and large sized companies in global market conditions.

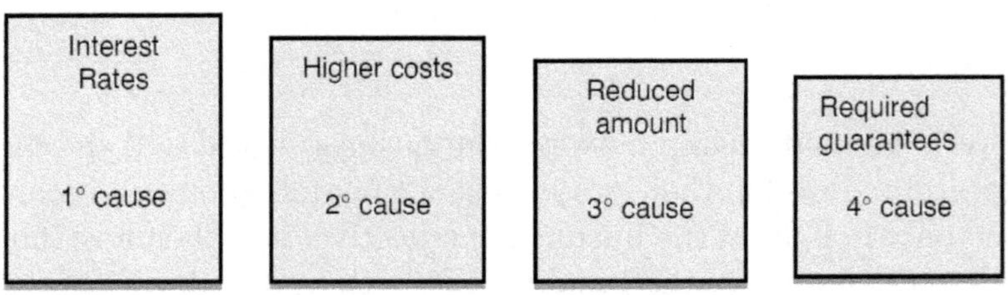

Fig. 1. Factors of the credit crunch in Italy.

Table 1. Bank interest rates on short-term loans in 2016 in Region of Italy.

Regions	Small Companies (%)	Medium–Large Cc. (%)
Northwest	7.33	3.92
Northeast	6.39	3.95
Centre	7.57	4.58
South and Isles	8.65	5.73

Source: Bank of Italy (2017).

This brief review of business needs in light of the financial possibilities on the market thus allows us to outline some key aspects in understanding the reasons why (as we shall see in more detail below) the volume of decentralised finance has increased exponentially and the traditional banking system has found itself in a situation of forced adaptation to the new market conditions.

The difficult supply of credit by the traditional banking system is increasingly having the effect of a vortex in which the less flexible or less enterprising companies fall, but so do those companies which are anchored in the territory of reference by type of product or service offered.

Just think of a small company operating in highly traditional sectors, which hardly resorts to the transfer of its registered office, the opening of foreign branches, or the creation of production units abroad. If it invests, it will have to limit itself to the financial offerings provided by the system in which it operates and, as is often the case, it may not be able to access them due to the inability to bear the high rates, the operating costs, or the refusal of the banking system, which does not consider it sufficiently performing.

These data and projections are further supported by recent findings of the Fintech & Insurtech Observatory, and demonstrate not only the degree of diffusion of fintech among Italian companies but also the sector in which the traditional banking and insurance system are committing enormous resources. The Politecnico di Milano (2021) argues the following:

The SME sector is also dealing with this Italian digital revolution in finance and insurance, while maintaining a more traditional demand. A significant proportion of SMEs reported using financial products and services aimed at businesses such as Invoice Trading, Medium-Long-Term Loans, Investments, Factoring, Letter of Credit, Cash Flow Forecasting Tools. However, when it comes to accessing these services, there is a balance between physical channels (branch or consultant) and digital channels (Internet Banking from PCs). Only for payment services (such as wire transfers, F24, RI.BA, etc.) the digital channel clearly prevails. Italian micro-enterprises (with fewer than 10 employees) still tend to prefer banks and insurance companies for the demand for financial and insurance services. In general, no non-traditional player in the financial sector (i.e., start-ups, gas/electricity suppliers, insurance companies, supermarkets, telephone operators) is currently trusted by more than 7% of micro-enterprises for financial services and 12% for insurance services (authors' translation).

On the basis of the considerations and the data presented, the question arises as to whether it is right for the traditional banking system to continue in this race towards digitisation or whether it is right for it to return to its more traditional role of assisting business development.

And again, the question arises as to whether small and medium-sized enterprises will necessarily have to look for the many financial products in the decentralised finance market — a system which, as we shall see later on, due to its intrinsic characteristics, aims to provide the necessary tools to enterprises (even those not performing) without particular limitations.

3. Decentralised Finance: Status Quaestionis and Spheres of Influence

3.1. *Definition and role*

According to the most authoritative and widely used definitions, the term Decentralised Finance (also DeFi) refers to a financial system that provides ervices based on infrastructures without any hierarchy (Qin *et al.*, 2021; Schär, 2020). By means of these systems, which allow financial transactions to be carried out using

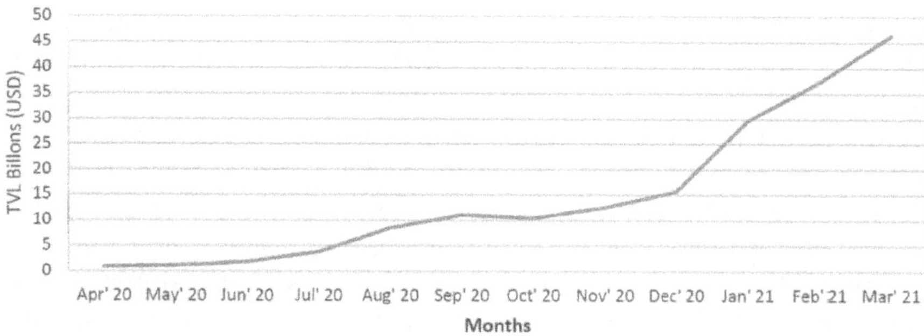

Fig. 2. The current state of TVL in decentralised finance.
Source: From DeFi Pulse (2021).

cryptocurrencies (Zhou and Shen, 2022), users of all kinds are thus able to access any banking service without resorting to a traditional intermediary.

Through decentralised finance, it is possible to exchange digitalised assets, engage in monetary speculation, and even get fast loans. With this in mind, payments and transactions are accessible to all, which inevitably leads to a rapid increase in the rate of use of the system in both the private and public sectors. Unlike traditional finance, decentralised finance has broadened financial inclusion while playing a pivotal role in encouraging permissionless innovation and facilitating open access to financial networks.

Digital technology as an essential component of decentralised finance reduces transaction costs, supports peer-to-peer transactions, enlarges transaction scope, and stimulates the process of innovation (Chen *et al.*, 2019). The current state of decentralised finance is still at the initial stage of its evolution. According to DeFi Pulse (2021), however, the total value of tokens circulated in DeFi exceeds US$45 billion as of March 30, 2021, as shown in Fig. 2.

The total figure may sound substantial because most tokens lack sufficient liquidity to trade in crypto markets (Sharma, 2021). The technological innovation in decentralised finance has become the need of the hour and increased our dependence to handle the complex large volumes of digitalised data on more open, shared networks and multi-platforms (Termeer, 2009). Before the emergence of decentralised finance, financial institutions acted as intermediaries to execute economic transactions. To facilitate the process of transactions, intermediaries established trust among parties to perform transactions (Roth, 2015). However, some concerns over the monopolistic approach of intermediaries raised, as they often take control over shaping economic transactions as well as exercise their substantial power to maintain self-interests (Srnicek, 2017; Cohen, 2019). Blockchain technology as an important tool of decentralised finance may prove to be the next step in the progression of disintermediation to carry out financial transactions through distributed trust and decentralised networks. Hence, the impact of this disruptive technology on governance mechanisms, such as financial reporting, internal and external auditing, shareholders, the board of directors, and regulations, calls for studies (Brennan *et al.*, 2019).

This new paradigm is based on distributed trust as opposed to traditional finance that focuses on opportunism because the transactions on a blockchain network are verified through shared consensus and protected by cryptography. Blockchain-based products such as cryptocurrencies compete with traditional financial institutions by proposing an alternative form of corporate governance (Narayanan *et al.*, 2016; Seidel, 2018). According to the Financial Stability Board (2019), DeFi backed up by blockchain technology not only reduces the role of financial intermediaries but also builds an open financial infrastructure to create new business opportunities through broad financial inclusion and permissionless innovation (Fig. 3).

However, a system of governance is still needed to govern the design and operations of blockchain within organisational constellations.

3.2. *A new perspective for firms' access to financial capital*

Decentralised finance reshapes the dynamics of the current era of finance by providing a new landscape to establish new platforms for innovators and entrepreneurs to get easy access to financial capital, showcasing the benefits and shortcomings of decentralised business models. Using blockchain technology, the new financial system involves a decentralised form of currencies, payments, financing, and

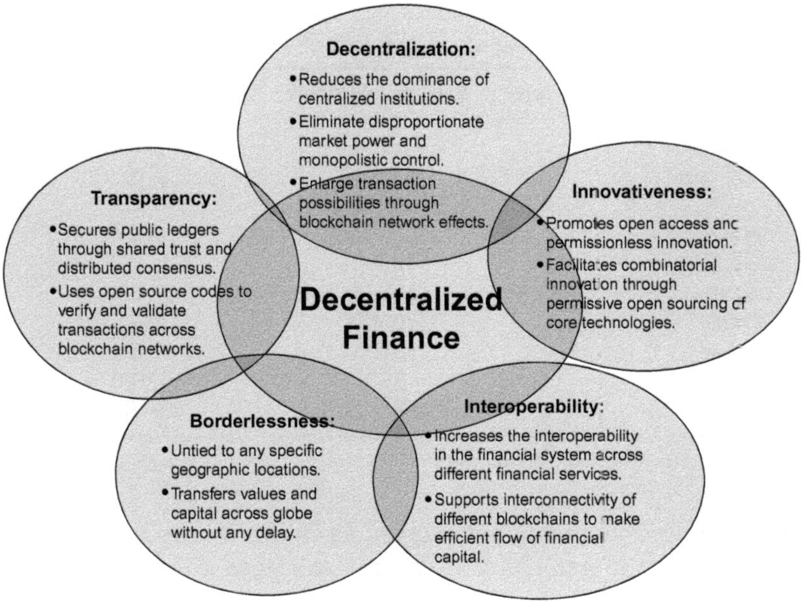

Fig. 3. Features of decentralised finance.
Source: Inspired by Chen and Bellavitis (2020).

contracting as an integral part of modern business models. Bitcoin is the most common type of decentralised cryptocurrency and can be issued without any intermediaries. Unlike fiat currency, bitcoins are anti-inflationary due to their fixed supply schedule and are not tied to a specific country's government and central bank economic policies (Chen and Bellavitis, 2020). Decentralised payments, such as payment networks of Libra and Ripple, have unleashed a new way of making cross-border and inexpensive payments by relying on blockchain technology.

As opposed to centralised finance, decentralised payments are less costly, more secure, and faster. The rise of decentralised global cryptocurrencies over the last year reached US$1.83 trillion from just US$179 million in March of the previous year. It is in contrast to traditional fundraising, where potential investors have to build strong network ties to win trust, and often involves several constraints in the financing process.

Table 2. List of small privately held technological companies in decentralised finance — values in US dollar.

Name of the Company	Capital Raised	No. of Employees
Uniswep	11 M	5 or less
Compound	33.2 M	5–10
Eco	35 M	10–25
Metaco	17 M	10–25
Monolith	16.7 M	10–25
Argent	16 M	10–25
MODE	10.4 M	10–25
Finality	63.2 M	25–50
Celo	65 M	50–100
Bitcoin Suisse	48.9 M	50–100

Source: Adapted from Topionetworks (2021).

Decentralised financing has evolved as an innovative financing tool that has given opportunities to various start-ups to raise capital by attracting global investors. At present, 65 start-ups are operating in 18 related markets that have raised US$390 million in total funding (Ellicott, 2021). The list of small private technology companies that are more inclined towards the decentralised finance ecosystem is shown in Table 2.

Blockchain technology is an integrated network that changes the landscape of decentralised financing (Chen, 2018). The most prominent forms of decentralised financing are initial coin offerings (ICO) and initial exchange offerings (IEO). The ICO uses public blockchain to sell the project-specific token to investors to raise capital. On the other hand, the IEO relies on cryptocurrency exchanges to create a connection between high-quality projects and potential investors (Martino *et al.*, 2019; Chen and Bellavitis, 2020).

For centuries, the parties involved in transactions relied on financial institutions for financial contracting at low transaction cost by establishing trust (Murray *et al.*, 2019). Over the last few years, blockchain has substituted the role of centralised institutions with smart contracts, which leads to a new paradigm of peer-to-peer financial contracting. Smart contracts not only solve the issues of adverse selections and contingencies associated with contracting but also reduce transaction costs, delays, and frictions in their programming process due to their automaticity and transparency (Cong and He, 2019).

3.3. *Changing approaches in the landscape of corporate governance*

Blockchain technology emerges as one of the most prominent and core technologies in the industrial revolution 4.0 (Kim *et al.*, 2020). It has the potential to completely transform the way the financial system works: It eliminates traditional processes and offers opportunities for existing business units to flourish and new ones to expand (Morkunas *et al.*, 2019). While there is a reduction in cost and improvement in the overall efficiency of decentralised financial systems, practitioners observe that blockchain will create new forms of "economic organisation and governance" (Davidson *et al.*, 2016a, 2016b). On the other hand, corporate governance includes a set of monitoring principles aiming to ensure accountability and transparency (Gillan, 2016). The decentralised form of blockchain tied to greater speed and transparency has an impact on those contributing to corporate governance scenarios. The unpredictable and rapidly evolving nature of technological changes is more likely to collide with traditional approaches to governance which are hierarchical and less self-regulated (Gans, 2016). The implications of blockchain are then an essential component of decentralised finance for corporate governance, mainly focusing on financial reporting transparency, corporate ownership, shareholders' voting, and stock trading transparency, as well as regulatory mechanisms as emerges from the recent literature (Yermack, 2017; Kimani *et al.*, 2020).

Major stock exchanges across the world are now looking for the possibility of using blockchain technology to keep a record of stocks issued by companies and to monitor subsequent trading activities related to such stocks (Yarmack, 2017). The unparalleled transparency feature of blockchain technology could help investors to ascertain the real-time ownership status of the debt and equity investors and combat ill practices on the part of exchanges, registered companies, and regulators (Singh *et al.*, 2019). This has not only replaced the traditional corporate practices but also provides a great degree of transparency, accuracy, and efficacy in stock ownership and corporate voting as well as reducing corporate misbehaviour and wrongdoings noticeably (Nasdaq, 2017).

The codes in their respective digital wallets within the permissioned blockchain technology such as distributed ledger technology (DLT) could help trace the shareholder's identity. The technology also benefits investors in trading of shares as the blockchain minimises the processing time of share-based transactions due to its lower reliance on clearinghouses as opposed to the traditional financial system; consequently, it reduces the settlement time for the delivery of the shares and eliminates paper shares to a greater extent. While conceptualising the wider implications of blockchain technology for different types of assets, Yermack (2017) argued that "innovators continuously now considering the suitability of blockchain for recording the ownership of various types of assets from stocks and bonds to automobile titles, real state and works of art". A decentralised financial system could solve the issue of lack of shareholder engagement that has been highlighted in the corporate governance codes; the shareholder engagement system could be improved through blockchain technology as it affects the dynamics of power among managers, the board of directors, and shareholders, therefore minimising the agency problems. The decentralised blockchain organisations interrupt traditional principle and agent relationships through blockchain technology at the core of corporate governance. The developers write the rules, such as software codes, in a decentralised way instead of board members, CEOs, or senior managers. The stakeholders exercise power and govern the blockchain technology at a varying level in different arrangements (Narayanan *et al.*, 2016).

Moreover, the chances of conducting insider trading and stock backdating are nearly impossible as the users in some types of permissioned or permissionless blockchain technologies will not be allowed to hide or change the original entries of the stock, so decentralised finance has also provided a solution to the issues relating to stock ownership of employees. The data integrity, speed, and cost of financial innovations certainly improve "timely record-keeping" of stocks in real time. Every participant in the shared or distributed network can invigilate the trading patterns of all major stakeholders. Blockchain technology impacts managerial stock options, for instance, reducing their ability to gain personal profit by using internal information. Thus, people cannot enjoy hefty incentives through stock-based compensation due to the greater vigilance of their transactions over blockchain (Yarmack, 2017).

Another feature of the distributed nature of the decentralised finance ecosystem is the digital vote or e-vote system that makes the manipulation of shareholder voting difficult in the annual general meeting while appointing board members, something that was easily done in the past under the traditional finance system. Now, it will be much easier for shareholders to cast votes on a blockchain network. This leads to the reduction of election and voting cost and in turn achieves better voting turnout with less possibility of rigging (Lafarre and Van der Elst, 2018). The strategies used in corporate voting, such as "No Vote", that were intended to misuse voting rights are now not easy to execute furtively in a decentralised finance ecosystem (Yermack, 2016; Sisli-Ciamarra, 2012). Furthermore, the shareholders are motivated to participate actively in corporate governance and demand votes on highly sensitive issues with a greater degree of enhanced transparency due to the blockchain nature of decentralised finance (Haque, 2018).

3.4. *The implications for accounting systems*

Previously, it has been mentioned that decentralised finance has been able to change the corporate reporting and disclosure landscape since the inception of blockchain technology. There are several implications of blockchain technology for accounting systems. Piazza (2017) and Yarmack (2017) predict its unprecedented role in keeping records of financial data, especially on permissionless public blockchains. The stakeholders requiring financial information do not necessarily have to rely on the verification of the auditors. Instead, they could make an accounting judgement, for instance, on non-cash adjustments such as inventory revaluation and deprecation, with their trust in the available financial data on corporate blockchains (Deloitte, 2016). It improves the trustworthiness of financial reports as it enables real-time accounting due to the daily updating of accounting entries and fewer chances of alteration in the blockchain ledger (Byström, 2019). The books of accounts and all kinds of financial information are now easily accessible; the companies could submit financial reports and returns to various regulatory bodies and institutions to fulfil the formalities in real time. Corporate information (key performance indicators, financial reports, and strategic management reports) can be disclosed flexibly and these disclosure blocks are generated on a platform for the auditor's verification and countersign to file them in the national storage system (NSM).

The disclosure of financial information in a decentralised blockchain system will be more likely easy, compatible, timely, and cost effective from the preparer's perspective. Similarly, it will be more engaging, useable, credible, and contextual from the user's point of view (Financial Reporting Council, 2018). Nevertheless, there are some limitations to the use of blockchain-based decentralised finance. Commentators questioned the immutability of blockchain and its technological relevance. Davidson *et al.* (2016a, 2016b) and Rückeshäuser (2017) argued that blockchain may not prevent fraud and the senior manager will still be able to commit fraud. Hence, the integrity of data using blockchain could be challenged. For efficient blockchain performance, its size should be large to speed up the transaction process which would ultimately lead to higher transaction costs.

Decentralised finance will also transform the accounting profession because of blockchain technology. Lazanis (2015) argued that the role of auditors will be greatly condensed or even eliminated. Since the financial records on blockchain could not be manipulated or tampered, and if corporates maintain all their record on a shared network, there will be no need for an external auditor's judgements or opinions on the financial statement (Byström, 2019). On the other hand, the blockchain transforms internal audits into a continuous process because internal auditors could continuously perform internal audits with account analysis and audit trails using blockchain at the push of a button (Vasarhelyi *et al.*, 2015). However, the blockchain-based internal audit brings some challenges since internal auditors need to have access to information in new formats to maximise the real-time value of continuous information (Rooney *et al.*, 2017).

4. Scenarios and Perspectives

4.1. *Relations with stakeholders in the context of corporate sustainability*

The evolution of new paradigms aimed at meeting the financial and business needs of enterprises 4.0 requires analyses also inherent to the new figures of stakeholders.

If, for example, one considers the green environment, now more than ever the focus of international attention (Rangone and

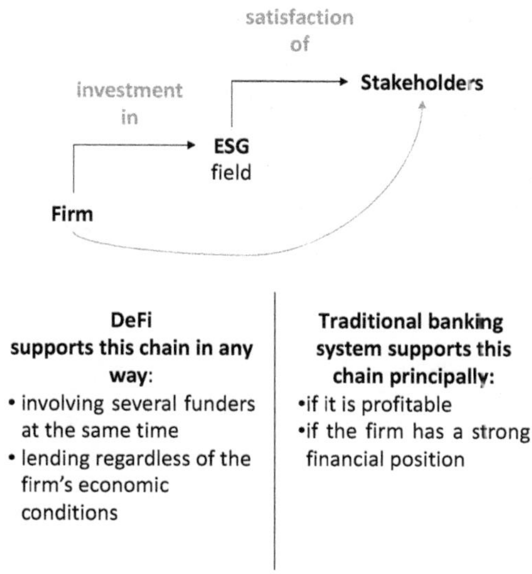

Fig. 4. Different perspectives of financial support in the firm–stakeholder relation.

Ali, 2021), a business development plan may require particular investments and resources that a micro-small company can hardly achieve (at least in the short term).

As we have explained in the course of this work, certain fintech technologies (the ones that define decentralised scenarios) are able to support initiatives that protect stakeholders, unlike traditional financial players that mainly support initiatives with high economic returns (Fig. 4).

In this regard, interaction with the public world is an equally important aspect which cannot be overlooked. There are still few initiatives that involve public players and the fintech world in a sustainable way.

An outstanding example of this is the fintech initiative launched by the Monetary Authority of Singapore, which began in 2015 and which has made Singapore one of the world's leading fintech hubs.

Project "Greenprint", in fact, manages to combine the power of finance with the opportunities and prospects provided by technology.

The Monetary Authority of Singapore will collaborate and act as coordinator to develop digital utilities to facilitate the efficient flow of reliable ESG data. Above all, the project (Fig. 5) aims to support financial institutions and businesses in mobilising capital

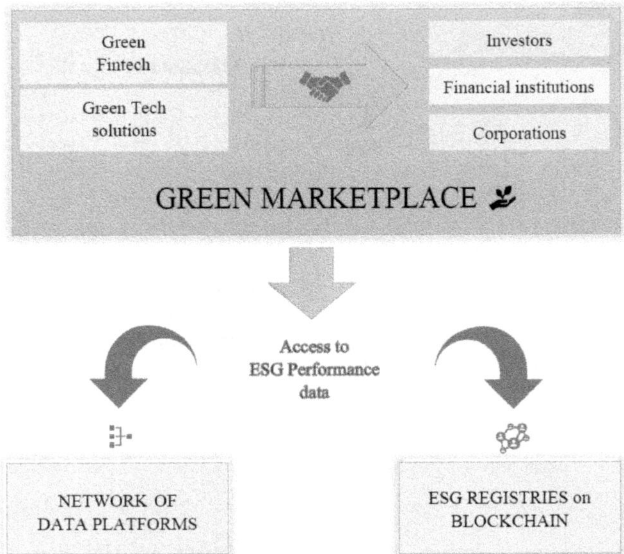

Fig. 5. Project greenprint platforms.
Source: Adapted from Monetary Authority of Singapore (2022).

for sustainable projects, monitoring commitments, and measuring impact.

The Greenprint marketplace will facilitate the growth of a vibrant green fintech ecosystem by connecting fintech and green tech suppliers to investors, financial institutions, and companies.

The digital platform will provide accurate lists of solution providers, solution seekers, and investors to facilitate discovery, acceleration of partnerships, and channelling investments towards green and sustainable solutions and initiatives. The launch is planned for 2023 (Monetary Authority of Singapore, 2022).

Examples of such public–private interaction are, however, very limited in the world, and there is a risk in involving large corporate players rather than small and medium-sized enterprises.

This last protocol is no longer acceptable. Small and medium-sized enterprises are also called upon to make their contribution in a sustainable manner (OECD, 2017). This contribution, however, is not always very profitable and would therefore not be possible at a time when traditional credit providers do not support the "risky" initiatives of SMEs.

Hence, the need to raise funds directly on the market and join forces with multiple partners and financiers to collaborate on projects that are not exclusively dependent on economic and financial factors but can fulfil the highest-sounding task of corporate sustainability.

In the decentralised market, stakeholders can become an active part of initiatives contributing to the successful implementation of projects.

In the environmental field, faced with this emerging reality, in 2020, several scholars proposed blockchain-enabled green bond issuance architecture. Malamas *et al.* (2020) have proposed a system which also acts as a transparent but fully controllable decentralised authority where funds for environmentally friendly projects can be traced. This is because in a "traditional" context, for example, bond issuance is a highly technical and complicated process. It sometimes involves stakeholders who do not trust each other and sometimes have conflicting objectives. Therefore, (Malamas *et al.*, 2020) have worked to propose an adaptable and efficient system that reduces brokerage costs and provides compliance, scalability, confidentiality, and security.

This is not the only study on green bonds. Schletz *et al.* (2020), for example, have applied an inductive approach based on the qualitative evidence of expert feedback to assess the potential of blockchain-based security tokens in the face of multiple market failures that have constrained green investment vehicles.

Evidence shows how tokenised securities, although evolving, can contribute to a genuine democratisation of green finance.

There are, however, sources that provided considerations about constraints and risks as well.

Among these, Schletz *et al.* (2020) highlight software risk, regulatory uncertainty, and investment infrastructures that are still immature at present.

While infrastructure development and software risk depend on strictly focused efforts in the technology field, the regulatory aspect may initially require the development of pilot use cases and the creation of regulatory sandboxes (Bank of Italy, 2022); however, these should not be considered sufficient as the regulatory environment affects many aspects (as described in the following).

4.2. *The evolution of financial systems*

In light of what has been analysed from many points of view, the outlook now seems clear. The traditional banking system will no longer be limited to managing innovative processes to deliver technologically advanced products. Business needs are becoming more complex every day, especially for small businesses. This is the reason why so many fintech companies have sprung up and, above all, the system of decentralised finance has spread.

Traditional banks invest heavily in new technologies and powerful security systems that can guarantee stability, transparency, and fairness (Caccavale and Righi, 2018). However, we must not forget that the most important need of companies is credit. This is the premise of the bank–business relationship, and in recent years, due to the imposition of risk conditions and the economic and financial crisis, SMEs have been increasingly neglected by the banking system. This has certainly fostered the conditions for a transition from traditional to innovative financing. Some authors (Qin *et al.*, 2021) expect CeFi and DeFi to coexist, to complement, to strengthen, and to learn from each other's experiences, mistakes, and innovations. This prospect could also be realised but, in our view, not without a radical change in the order now taking place.

Until the birth of decentralised finance, there was talk of bank-based and market-based systems (Boadi *et al.*, 2019; Rangone, 2017).

Today, the scenario is undergoing profound change, or rather the order of these two financial systems is evolving (Table 3).

If, according to the literature, market-based systems have mainly characterised "Anglophone" countries, we propose the hypothesis that with the advent of decentralised finance this system may change in relation to the size and new needs of companies.

The fintech financial market will be better able to meet the needs of small and medium-sized enterprises in terms of technological innovation, credit, and new partners as they are leaner because they are less constrained by economic, legal, and institutional constraints.

On the contrary, the provision of advice linked to strategic business development plans will increasingly become the prerogative of

Table 3. Perspective in the evolution of financial systems.

<table>
<tr><th>Subject</th><th>Objectives</th><th>Needs</th><th>System</th><th>Solutions</th></tr>
<tr><td rowspan="2">SME</td><td>New business models</td><td>Smart tech</td><td rowspan="2">Market-based</td><td>Fintech</td></tr>
<tr><td rowspan="2">Investments</td><td rowspan="2">Credit</td><td>DeFi</td></tr>
<tr><td rowspan="2">Large Co.</td><td rowspan="2">Bank-based</td><td rowspan="2">Traditional banks/ Institutional investors</td></tr>
<tr><td>Strategic planning</td><td>Consulting</td></tr>
</table>

large traditional banking players and institutional investors, who will see medium-to-large companies as their main clients.

This work, therefore, presents a new geographical scenario in which market-based and bank-based systems are more diluted within their territorial boundaries but better differentiated according to the perspective of the services offered.

4.3. *The need for complete mechanisms of regulation*

In this context, it is not possible to think that the evolutionary process will take place without potential problems. Some thought must therefore be given to the way in which the decentralised system will develop.

The massive development seen in recent years has been mainly driven by technological solutions on the market today, by the pressing needs of micro and small or medium-sized enterprises, but also by a lack of regulation.

However, a lack of regulation is unacceptable and will require action to ensure an appropriate balance. Unlike traditional banks bound by risk standards and regulatory thresholds, most of the players in DeFi and some fintechs can now operate almost completely independently by meeting market demands, particularly those of start-ups, micro-enterprises, and SMEs.

According to KPMG (2019) studies, the absence of precise regulation defines the emergence of the following potential new risks:

- Risks to consumers and investors: mis-selling of products and services, privacy, data protection, and information security.
- Risks to financial intermediaries: sustainability of the business model, governance, technological risk, operational resilience, data management, use of artificial intelligence, and anti-money laundering issues.
- Risks to financial stability: risk of concentration, uncontrolled spread of alternative financial intermediation channels, use of crypto assets, and vulnerability.

With the emergence and spread of an increasingly decentralised financial system, a level playing field will be required to achieve equal regulatory treatment.

To this end, the European Fintech Action Plan (European Commission, 2018) in this case aims to do the following:

- reduce the risks of recycling;
- reduce the number of infringements;
- create greater transparency towards customers and users.

Without precise development models and a clear regulatory framework, fintech companies may find themselves unable to cope with the exponential growth in funding requests. However, this is only one of many contexts which should be regulated. The key challenge is not just in the adoption of blockchain technology but in the way it is going to be regulated since the technology serves different purposes in tandem with several regulatory constraints. For instance, each cryptocurrency has its own set of self-regulation. The recent literature argued that blockchain technology is likely to facilitate and disrupt the traditional corporate governance mechanisms. Governments and firms around the world require a regulatory framework before the adaption of blockchain technologies since the unregulated technological innovations might pose hazards in the business operations (Leong *et al.*, 2017). In some countries, the political and regulatory situations are conducive, such as the UK, Australia, Sweden, and especially Singapore that is leading in developing a user-friendly regulatory framework to facilitate the implementation of digital decentralised technologies (Lee and Shin, 2018). Setting a regulatory agenda promotes the proliferation of blockchain to settle payment proceeds and to raise capital without the presence of traditional financial systems (Zhu and Zhou, 2016). Blockchain technologies in decentralised finance are expected to revolutionise the financial industry to deter money laundering or fraudulent financial reporting tactics which have remained a part of a debate in the literature on blockchain adoption (Kimani *et al.*, 2020).

The regulators play a decisive role in setting standards and the agenda of governance. The disruptive innovations of blockchain will need to expand into more agile and real-time policy-making. In setting boundaries of governance, regulators could have access to blockchain to review real-time transactions. A smooth transition towards disruptive innovations requires best practices, skills, and new rules of law (Chartered Professional Accountants Canada, 2016). Tormen (2019) emphasised the importance of blockchain to ensure that strong governance is in place to define the roles and responsibilities of every participant in the network to design blockchain infrastructure in a decentralised ecosystem. Yarmack (2017) also suggests the establishment of new governance models to govern blockchain, a process in which participants agree to protocols for the underlying software encryptions to be changed. A governance model should address six regulatory issues as presented by Cermeño (2016) before the adoption of blockchain technology: *These are legal nature of blockchain and distributed ledger, recognition of immutability, source of tamper-proof truth, the rights to be forgotten, the legal validity of the documents that are stored in the blockchain and validity of financial instruments using smart contracts.* Trust could be built through collaborative governance to make sure that all stakeholders act according to agreed rules. Regulations concern laws to control behaviours, while governance engages collaboration, stewardship, and incentives to act on mutual interests. Governments need to regulate blockchain technologies as a collaborative peer with other societal constituents instead of relying only on law (Tapscott and Tapscott, 2016). The lack of collaborative governance is one of the main impediments to realising the real-time societal benefits of blockchain technology. However, it can be achieved with the formulation of policies, mechanisms, procedures, and enforcement (Janssen *et al.*, 2020).

5. Conclusions

At the end of this work, which was conceived of as a proposal for the understanding of the perspectives and needs of the players operating in the new international financial scenario dictated by DeFi, we can summarise some aspects more than others.

Born during the Renaissance period, banks have been the engine of transnational capitalist development, financing productive enterprises and governments, fostering socioeconomic change from a typically feudal society to an eminently mercantile one and, in the following centuries, to an industrial one.

However, the long process of financialisation of the economy has led the traditional banking system to take on a new face, no longer as a successful stakeholder of local businesses, but as an important player in global development.

While in some ways this trend has enabled banks to meet internal performance and external regulatory compliance criteria, on the other hand it has pushed them towards a real speculative entrepreneurial structure aimed at allocating liquidity to the financial markets, favouring profitable investments mainly in the short term.

This competitiveness policy, however, has caused the traditional banking system to neglect the economic and social development of the local territory, while at the same time contributing to global bubbles, which have already been observed over time and more recently felt with the 2007 crisis.

It is believed that this change of strategic action by the banking system has had an enormous impact on the economic and social crisis, with repercussions of a political and institutional nature, which we are still experiencing dramatically today.

These are the roots which, in our view, have been a major influence on the development and application of new technological solutions for the financial world. The services offered by DeFi relate to all the areas needed to support the initiatives or activities already undertaken by companies.

In fact, we can find debt capital, equity, insurance, currency exchange, trading, assets, and even business partners; in short, DeFi offers the entire financial world at a "click" and without the need for an intermediary to arrange transactions or impose heavy constraints.

At a time when companies languish because of credit barriers, international economic instability, and difficult regulatory compliance, the wide "availability of heterogeneous solutions" offered by decentralised finance is an interesting alternative.

However, this is not the only aspect to consider. Even more important are the prospects that this trend presents, as better analysed in this work.

We have looked at the effort that the traditional banking system is concentrating on technological reconfiguration projects.

While such initiatives may lead to more up-to-date services, it is felt that they will not help to meet the millennium challenge.

The battles will see an exchange of witnesses, but the victory in the war between DeFi and CeFi systems will be owned only by those who are able to best serve the customer.

In our view, given the current conditions, the solutions offered by fintech initiatives can simplify the operations of companies and private citizens for limited operations and thereby arouse the admiration of the more mature generations. However, the generations that were born shortly before the spread of blockchain — and even more so those born after — are by nature predisposed to searching the online market for the solution to their private and professional problems.

This will define for these generations a limited relationship with fintech solutions, thus an increasingly *marginal relationship* with the traditional banking system, while establishing a deep *core relationship* with DeFi.

The only way to limit this process is in two actions: firstly, a return to the original role of the banking system alongside the local business. Here, we refer to the long-standing role of successful stakeholders able to support, advice, and facilitate SMEs even in critical development situations.

A second targeted action is the deep and careful regulation of the financial market dictated by DeFi. Only compliance constraints can limit the operation of a system designed to be autonomous and independent. But this will not be easy, given the interests at stake.

References

Bank of Italy (2017). Banks and Money: National Data — 2017. Available at: https://www.bancaditalia.it/pubblicazioni/moneta-banche/2017-moneta/index.html?com.dotmarketing.htmlpage.language=1.

Bank of Italy (2022). Regulatory Sandbox. Available at: https://www.bancaditalia.it/focus/sandbox/index.html?com.dotmarketing.htmlpage.language=1.

Boadi, I., Osarfo, D., and Boadi, P. (2019). Bank-based and market-based development and economic growth: An international investigation, *Studies in Economics and Finance*, 36(3) pp. 365–394.

Brennan, N. M., Subramaniam, N., and van Staden, C. J. (2019). Corporate governance implications of disruptive technology: An overview, *British Accounting Review*, 51(6). Available at: https://www.sciencedirect.com/science/article/pii/S089083891930085X?via%3Dihub.

Byström, H. (2019). Blockchains, real-time accounting, and the future of credit risk modeling, *Ledger*, 4, pp. 40–47.

Caccavale, A. and Righi, S. (2018). *Tech Bank. The Technological Revolution of Credit Analysed by the Heads of the Banking System* (Milan, Italy: goWare & Edizioni Guerini e Associati). (Translated from Italian: *Banca tech. La rivoluzione tecnologica nel credito vista dai vertici del sistema bancario, goWare & Edizioni Guerini e Associati, Milano*).

Cermeño, J. S. (2016). Blockchain in financial services: Regulatory landscape and future challenges for its commercial application, BBVA Research Paper, 16, p. 20.

Chartered Professional Accountants Canada (2016). *Technological Disruption of Capital Markets Reporting? Introduction to Blockchain* (Toronto: CPA Canada).

Chen, M. A., Wu, Q., and Yang, B. (2019). How valuable is FinTech innovation? *The Review of Financial Studies*, 32(5), pp. 2062–2106.

Chen, Y. (2018). Blockchain tokens and the potential democratisation of entrepreneurship and innovation, *Business Horizons*, 61(4), 567–575.

Chen, Y. and Bellavitis, C. (2020). Blockchain disruption and decentralised finance: The rise of decentralised business models, *Journal of Business Venturing Insights*, 13, e00151.

Cohen, J. E. (2019). *Between Truth and Power: The Legal Constructions of Informational Capitalism* (Oxford: Oxford University Press).

Coinmarketcap (2021). *Global Cryptocurrency Charts, Total Market Capitalization.* Available at: https://coinmarketcap.com/charts/.

Cong, L. W. and He, Z. (2019). Blockchain disruption and smart contracts, *The Review of Financial Studies*, 32(5), pp. 1754–1797.

Davidson, S., De Filippi, P., and Potts, J. (2016a). Disrupting governance: The new institutional economics of distributed ledger technology, Available at: SSRN 2811995.

Davidson, S., De Filippi, P., and Potts, J. (2016b). Economics of block chain. Available at: SSRN 2744751.

DeFi Pulse. (2021). Total value locked (USD) in DeFi. Available at: https://defipulse.com/.

Deloitte (2016). *Blockchain Technology a Game-Changer in Accounting?* Available at: https://www2.deloitte.com/content/dam/Deloitte/de/Documents/Innovation/Blockchain_A%20game-changer%20in%20accounting.pdf.

Durnev, V. G., Murin, D. M., Sokolov, V. A., and Chalyy, D. J. (2018). On some approaches to the solution of the "useful proof-of-work for Blockchains" task, *Automatic Control and Computer Sciences*, 52, pp. 880–884.

Ellicott, K. (2021). Decentralised finance (DeFi) (Blockchain). Available at: https://www.topionetworks.com/markets/decentralized-finance-defi-blockchain-5d8dda6d9490493107b30e93.

European Commission (2018). Communication from the commission. FinTech action plan: For a more competitive and innovative European financial sector. Available at: https://eur-lex.europa.eu/legal-content/EN/TXT/?uri=CELEX:52018DC0109.

Financial Reporting Council (2018). Blockchain and the future of corporate reporting. Available at: https://www.frc.org.uk/getattachment/58866565-ab3b-44d3-93e1-1ef7158968d5/Blockchain-and-the-future-of-corporate-reporting-how-does-itmeasure-up-(June-2018).pdf.

Financial Stability Board (2019). Decentralised financial technologies: Report on financial stability, regulatory and governance implications. Available at: https://www.fsb.org/2019/06/decentralised-financial-technologies-report-on-financial-stability-regulatory-and-governance-implications/.

Gans, J. (2016). *The Disruption Dilemma* (Cambridge: MIT Press).

Gervais, A., Karame, G. O., Wüst, K., Glykantzis, V., Ritzdor, H., and Capkun, S. (2016). On the security and performance of proof of work blockchains, in *Proceedings of the 2016 ACM SIGSAC Conference on Computer and Communications Security*, pp. 3–16.

Gillan, S. L. (2006). Recent developments in corporate governance: An overview. *Journal of Corporate Finance*, 12(6). Available at: https://deliverypdf.ssrn.com/delivery.php?ID=036104118122116086064065021119066091118034032080036086072003117090126070118100028095039031120001116015022099022070104127006114001062026011107098006103064126099055077078096025114116090098003008125117003069006125109003117118100116066109101092013000&EXT=pdf&INDEX=TRUE.

Haque, F. (2019). Ownership, regulation and bank risk-taking: Evidence from the Middle East and North Africa (MENA) region, *Corporate Governance: The International Journal of Business in Society*, 19, pp. 23–43.

Janssen, M., Weerakkody, V., Ismagilova, E., Sivarajah, U., and Irani, Z. (2020). A framework for analysing blockchain technology adoption: Integrating institutional, market and technical factors, *International Journal of Information Management*, 50, pp. 302–309.

Kamat, J. and Seo, K. (2019). Blockchain-based mobile fingerprint verification and automatic log-in platform for future computing, *The Journal of Supercomputing*, 75, pp. 3123–3139.

Kim, S., Park, H., and Lee, J. (2020). Word2vec-based latent semantic analysis (W2V-LSA) for topic modeling: A study on blockchain technology trend analysis, *Expert Systems with Applications*, 152, art. no. 113401.

Kimani, D., Adams, K., Attah-Boakye, R., Ullah, S., Frecknall-Hughes, J., and Kim, J. (2020). Blockchain, business and the fourth industrial revolution: Whence, whither, wherefore and how? *Technological Forecasting and Social Change*, 161, art. no. 120254.

KPMG (2019). Regolamentazione e vigilanza nel settore fintech. Available at: https://home.kpmg/it/it/home/insights/2019/04/regolamentazione-e-vigilanza-nel-fintech.html.

Lafarre, A., and Van der Elst, C. (2018). Blockchain technology for corporate governance and shareholder activism, European Corporate Governance Institute (ECGI)-Law Working Paper No. 390.

Lazanis, R. (2015). How technology behind Bitcoin could transform accounting as we know it. TechVibes. Available at: https://techvibes.com/2015/01/22/howtechnology-behind-bitcoin-could-transform-accounting-as-we-know-it-2015-01-22.

Lee, I. and Shin, Y. J. (2018). Fintech: Ecosystem, business models, investment decisions, and challenges, *Business Horizons*, 61(1), pp. 35–46.

Leong, C., Tan, B., Xiao, X., Tan, F. T. C., and Sun, Y. (2017). Nurturing a FinTech ecosystem: The case of a youth microloan startup in China, *International Journal of Information Management*, 37(2), pp. 92–97.

Malamas, V., Dasaklis, T., Arakelian, V., and Chondrokoukis, G. (2020). A block-chain framework for increased trust in green bonds issuance, 16 September. Available at: https://ssrn.com/abstract=3693638.

Martino, P., Bellavitis, C., and DaSilva, C. M. (2019). Blockchain and initial coin offerings (ICOs): A new way of crowdfunding. Available at: SSRN 3414238.

Mastroiacovo, V. (2019). Le sovranità nell'era della post globalizzazione (Pacini, Pisa).

Monetary Authority of Singapore (2022). Green FinTech. Available at: https://www.mas.gov.sg/development/fintech/Green-FinTech.

Morettini, L. (2013). Analisi dell'evoluzione del sistema finanziario e della struttura bancaria, *Istituto di Studi Regionali Federali e sulle Autonomie*. Available at: http://issirfa-spoglio.cnr.it/regioni_sistemacreditizio/studi-interventi/papers/178-l-morettini-analisi-dell-evoluzione-del-sistema-finanziario-e-della-struttura-bancaria.

Morkunas, V. J., Paschen, J., and Boon, E. (2019). How blockchain technologies impact your business model, *Business Horizons*, 62(3), pp. 295–306.

Murray, A., Kuban, S., Josefy, M., and Anderson, J. (2019). Contracting in the smart era: The implications of blockchain and decentralised autonomous organisations for contracting and corporate governance, *Academy of Management Perspectives*. Available at: https://journals.aom.org/doi/full/10.5465/amp.2018.0066.

Narayanan, A., Bonneau, J., Felten, E., Miller, A., and Goldfeder, S. (2016). *Bitcoin and Cryptocurrency Technologies: A Comprehensive Introduction* (Princeton: Princeton University Press).

Nasdaq (2017). *Blockchain* comes to corporate governance with AST proxy voting. Available at: https://www.nasdaq.com/articles/blockchain-comes-corporate-governance-ast-proxy-voting-2017-05-18.

OECD (2017). Enhancing the contributions of SMEs in a global and digitalised economy. *Meeting of the OECD Council at Ministerial Level*, Paris, 7–8 June. Available at: https://www.oecd.org/mcm/documents/C-MIN-2017-8-EN.pdf.

Ølnes, S., Ubacht, J., and Janssen, M. (2017). Blockchain in government: Benefits and implications of distributed ledger technology for information sharing, *Government Information Quarterly*, 34(3), pp. 355–364.

Paccagnella, L. (2020). *Open Access. Conoscenza aperta e società dell'informazione* (Milano: Il Mulino).

Piazza, F. S. (2017). Bitcoin and the blockchain as possible corporate governance tools: Strengths and weaknesses, *Bocconi Legal Papers*, 9, p. 125.

Politecnico di Milano (2021). *Cresce il Fintech in Italia: quali sono le startup e i numeri e della rivoluzione*. L'Osservatorio Fintech & Insurtech. Available at: https://blog.osservatori.net/it_it/fintech-in-italia?hsLang=it-it#servizi.

Politecnico di Milano (2022). Fintech. Definizioni, servizi e protagonisti della Tecnofinanza. L'Osservatorio Fintech & Insurtech. Available at: https://blog.osservatori.net/it_it/fintech-significato.

Qin, K., Zhou, L., Afonin, Y., Lazzaretti, L., and Gervais, A. (2021). CeFi vs. DeFi — comparing centralised to decentralised finance. *Crypto Valley Conference on Blockchain Technology*. Available at: https://arxiv.org/pdf/2106.08157v2.pdf.

Rangone, A. (2013a). Analysis on the ongoing crisis. Historical economic, financial and corporate governance motivations (II), *Romanian Journal of Economics*, 37, 2(46), pp. 53–66.

Rangone, A. (2013b). Analysis on the ongoing crisis. Historical economic, financial and corporate governance motivations (I), *Romanian Journal of Economics*, 36, 1 (45), pp. 71–84.

Rangone, A. (2017). *International Perspectives on Corporate Governance: Empirical Evidence Concerning the Foundations of Banking Origin.* (Roma: Rirea Aziende).

Rangone, A. (2018). *La Logica di Impresa. Fenomeni e Relazioni di Influenza nell'Attuale Contesto Economico* (Roma: Aracne).

Rangone, A. (2020). *Managing Corporate Innovation. Determinants, Critical Issues and Success Factors* (Cham: Springer).

Rangone, A. and Ali, S. (2021). European green deal and sustainable development: The green bonds as an integrated intervention tool to support agribusiness in italy. *Economia Aziendale Online*, 12(3), pp. 313–328.

Rooney, H., Aiken, B., and Rooney, M. (2017). Q&A. Is internal audit ready for blockchain? *Technology Innovation Management Review*, 7(10), pp. 41–44.

Roth, A. E. (2015). *Who Gets What — And Why: The New Economics of Matchmaking and Market Design* (Houghton Mifflin Harcourt).

Rückeshäuser, N. (2017). Do we really want blockchain-based accounting? Decentralised consensus as enabler of management override of internal controls. Institute of Computer Science and Social Studies, Department of Telematics, Freiburg, Germany. Available at: https://wi2017.ch/images/wi2017-0112.pdf.

Ruozi, R. (ed.) (2016). *Economia della Banca* (Milano: Egea).

Sandner, P. (2021). Decentralised finance will change your understanding of financial systems. Available at: https://www.forbes.com/sites/philippsandner/2021/02/22/decentralized-finance-will-change-your-understanding-of-financial-systems/?sh=522255f55b52.

Schär, F. (2020). Decentralised finance: On blockchain-and smart contract-based financial markets. Available at: SSRN 3571335.

Seidel, M. D. L. (2018). Questioning centralised organisations in a time of distributed trust, *Journal of Management Inquiry*, 27(1), pp. 40–44.

Sharma, R. (2021). Decentralised finance (DeFi) *Definition.* Available at: https://www.investopedia.com/decentralized-finance-defi-5113835 #citation-1.

Singh, H., Jain, G., Munjal, A., and Rakesh, S. (2019). Blockchain technology in corporate governance: Disrupting chain reaction or not? *Corporate Governance: The International Journal of Business in Society*, 20, pp. 67–86.

Sisli-Ciamarra, E. (2012). Monitoring by affiliated bankers on board of directors: Evidence from corporate financing outcomes, *Financial Management*, 41(3), pp. 665–702.

Srnicek, N. (2017). *Platform Capitalism* (Cambridge: Polity Press).

Tapscott, D. and Tapscott, A. (2016). *Blockchain Revolution: How the Technology Behind Bitcoin is Changing Money, Business, and the World* (London: Penguin).

Tarantola, A. M. (2007). Banca e Impresa. Nuovi scenari, nuove prospettive, in seminario *Banche e imprese: opportunità e sfide alla luce di Basilea II.*

Termeer, C. J. (2009). Barriers to new modes of horizontal governance: A sense-making perspective, *Public Management Review*, 11(3), pp. 299–316.

Topionetworks (2021). Companies of decentralised finance (DeFi) (block chain). Available at: https://www.topionetworks.com/markets/decentralized-finance-defi-blockchain-5d8dda6d9490493107b30e93/companies?item_layout=list.

Tormen, R. (2019). *Blockchain for Decision Makers: A Systematic Guide to Using Blockchain for Improving Your Business* (Birmingham: Packt Publishing Ltd.).

Vasarhelyi, M. A., Kogan, A., and Tuttle, B. M. (2015). Big data in accounting: An overview, *Accounting Horizons*, 29(2), pp. 381–396.

Wehinger, G. (2014). SMEs and the credit crunch: Current financing difficulties, policy measures and a review of literature, *OECD Journal: Financial Market Trends*, 2013(2), pp. 1–34. doi.org/10.1787/fmt-2013-5jz734p6b8jg.

Xiong, H, Chen, M, Wu, C, Zhao, Y., and Yi, W. (2022). Research on progress of blockchain consensus algorithm: A review on recent progress of blockchain consensus algorithms. *Future Internet*, 14(2), p. 47. doi.org/10.3390/fi14020047.

Yermack, D. (2016). Corporate governance and blockchains, *Review of Finance.* Available at: https://papers.ssrn.com/sol3/papers.cfm?abstract_id=2700475.

Yermack, D. (2017). Corporate governance and blockchains, *Review of Finance*, 21(1), pp. 7–31.

Zhou, Z. and Shen, B. (2022). Toward understanding the use of centralised exchanges for decentralised cryptocurrency. ArXiv, abs/2204.08664.

Zhu, H. and Zhou, Z. Z. (2016). Analysis and outlook of applications of blockchain technology to equity crowdfunding in China. *Financial Innovation*, 2(1), p. 29.

https://doi.org/10.1142/9781800614604_0008

Chapter 8

Green Banking Regulation and Cross-Border Lending

Le Thanh Ha[*,‡] and Doan Ngoc Thang[†,§]

*Faculty of Economics,
National Economics University, Hanoi, Vietnam

†Faculty of International Business,
Vietnam Banking Academy, Hanoi, Vietnam

‡halethanh.kt@gmail.com

§ngocthangdoan@hvnh.edu.vn

This chapter uncovers the effects of green banking regulation (GBR) on cross-border lending using panel data of 2,814 country pairs from 1995 to 2019. We label banking regulations as *de jure* and *de facto* ones. The former captures whether a central bank has explicit sustainability objectives or supports the government's policies to pursue sustainability goals. The latter reflects whether a central bank takes on green activities or not. We use panel data of 2,814 country pairs from 1995 to 2019. The empirical results show that while *de jure* regulation acts as a brake, *de facto* regulation fosters cross-border banking flows (CBFs). When both genres of regulation are matched, the joint effects are positive. GBR mitigates the detrimental effects of environmental risks. These results are robust for alternative measures of green finance regulation and when we take the endogeneity into account. Our findings suggest important policy implications that central banks should engage in green banking activities to spur CBFs.

Keywords: Cross-border banking flows; *de jure* and *de facto* regulations; green banking; environmental risks; green finance regulation; endogeneity; IV checks; green finance policies; sustainable development

1. Introduction

In recent times, the public has been affirming that environmental protection and active environmental consequence mitigating policies should have gained special attention from economists, policy-makers, and authorities in designing and implementing policies, both domestically and internationally, and in all aspects and sectors of the economy. In this current trend, the important role of central banks in resolving risks pertaining to environmental degradation and in promoting green finance has been mainly mentioned by scholars such as Batten *et al.* (2016), Campiglio *et al.* (2018), Dikau and Volz, (2019), and Volz *et al.* (2015). The term "green finance" is also mentioned numerous times in the 2030 United Nations Sustainable Development Goals (SDGs) and the Paris Climate Accord. It can be seen that green finance has become an inevitable trend in the contemporary era.

The literature has used various terms, such as "sustainable finance", "environmental finance", or "green investment" to refer to green finance (Akomea-Frimpong *et al.*, 2021). Since scholars are concerned about different aspects of green finance, there are diverse definitions of green finance, leading to diversity in understanding green finance. While green finance can be defined as the confines of investment products preserving the environment (IFC, 2017), it is also associated with policies designed and implemented by financial institutions to meet sustainability standards. Weber and ElAlfy (2019) indicate that the term "finance" refers to the use of financial systems for capital allocation and investment. In addition to ensuring the conventional goal of economic development, banks should also allocate financial resources towards environmental protection, green and clean energy, and the resolution of climate change in all sectors of the economy (Urban and Wójcik, 2019; Yuan and Gallagher, 2018).

In the current transformation trend towards a low-carbon and resilient climate economy, central banks (and other relevant financial regulatory agencies) play a critical role in addressing environmental risks and promoting sustainable finance by integrating environmental considerations into their operation and reviewing the public financial governance policies (Dikau and Volz, 2021). Therefore, it is vital to orient the financial system with sustainable development so that the decisions on investments and lending are based on environmental risk assessment to comply with sustainability standards (Akomea-Frimpong *et al.*, 2021; Dikau and Volz, 2021). However, green finance has not been implemented in many regions in the world at the current stage (Akomea-Frimpong *et al.*, 2021; Dikau and Volz, 2021). In order to scale up green finance, a central bank should provide detailed and appropriate guidance to help commercial banks integrate environmental issues into their business models.

Fostering green finance could help target countries benefit from different aspects. Green finance may lead to diversity in investment opportunities and sources by mobilising both private and institutional capital. Furthermore, the flow of resources may be redirected from environmentally damaging activities to environmentally friendly ones, thus expanding sustainable and green businesses. Besides, green finance can reduce credit default risks of borrowers of banks that mitigate commercial banks' overall risks. Consequently, green finance can help countries address environmental problems while promoting and facilitating long-term production transformation in many developing countries.

The literature has indicated a rise in interest of scholars in research pertaining to green finance topics. For example, the limited dimensions of the internal practices of green banking are investigated by Sarma and Roy (2021), while green finance in a general context, but not in the specific banking sector, is examined by Zhang *et al.* (2019). Most recently, Dikau and Volz (2021) investigated how resolving climate-related risks and promoting mitigation and adaptation policies fit into the mandates of 135 central banks across the world. However, the scanty literature still constitutes unexploited niches on topics such as banks' actions, green finance products, and drivers of green finance in banks. Furthermore, there is no study exploring the effect of green bank regulation on the different aspects of the economy such as the international bank flows.

There has been a striking rise in international bank flows over the last two decades. The development of global banking operations via the expanding links between physical branches and subsidiaries in foreign markets is considered a key determinant of this rise. As argued by Bremus and Fratzscher (2015), the targeting countries may face a double-edged sword created by international capital flows. On the one hand, a boost in economic growth and inducing welfare gains may stem from a rise in international capital flows that provide opportunities for productive investments. On the other hand, inflationary pressures and deficits in capital accounts may arise due to surges in international capital flows. These make the country more susceptible to external shocks. Additionally, the performance of the economy can get worse if capital retrenchment occurs. Among various genres of capital flows, scholars have paid a lot of attention to credit flows via global banks, as global banks have shifted their transactions towards foreign markets since the 2000s. Furthermore, Dell'Ariccia *et al.* (2008) contend that the instability of cross-border banking flows (CBFs) raises the likelihood of banking crises that mitigate the potential for economic growth of the economy where banks play a critical role via lending and investment channels.

In order to fill these gaps in the literature, this chapter examines how green banking regulation (GBR) gaps across countries shape the structure of CBFs. Green bank regulation has been illustrated to have a striking effect on banks' risk and lending activities. There are at least two plausible reasons to explain our belief. First, banks are more likely to lend their money to riskier domestic borrowers under a lax regulation regime Khwaja and Mian, 2008; Thakor, 1996; Gao and Jang, 2021). Participating in the global capital market can be considered as a way to alleviate regulatory pressure (Gao and Jang, 2021). Second, the stringent green bank regulation, defined as those that consider environmental risk, markedly affects the short-term and long-term stability and development of both the macroeconomy and financial market as well as market failure with regard to missing or incomplete financial market (Dikau and Volz, 2021). These may either discourage or encourage investors to lend their capital outside the border.

To investigate the GBL–CBF nexus, we use a structural gravity model combining panel data of 2,814 country pairs from 1995 to 2019. While the data on bilateral cross-border banks claims are sourced locational banking statistics (LBS) as global banking flows (GBFs) from the Bank for International Settlements (BIS), we take data on GBR comes from the IMF's Central Bank Legislation Database as in Dikau and Volz (2021). We also classify green central banking regulation into two criteria: *de jure* and *de facto*. *De jure* regulation represents whether the central bank has explicit sustainability objectives or supports the government's policies that consist of sustainability goals. *De facto* regulation captures whether or not a central bank takes on green activities. By controlling for gravity factors, country, year, and pair fixed effects, we find that while *de jure* regulation acts as a brake, *de facto* regulation fosters CBFs. When both types of regulation are matched, the joint effects are positive. Furthermore, the GBR mitigates the detrimental effects of environmental risks on the cross-border flow of banking investment activities. We also conduct robustness checks by using alternative measures of GBR and the Instrumental Variables (IVs) approach to deal with the potential issue of endogeneity arising from the reverse causality between GBR and global bank claims and unobserved variables. The checks confirm that our findings are robust and reliable.

This chapter makes at least three contributions to the literature. First, to the best of our knowledge, this chapter is the first to investigate the nexus between GBR and the formation of a global banking network. Second, our study is also the first to distinguish between the heterogeneous effects of *de jure* and *de facto* GBR. Third, based on our argument, this chapter is also the first to provide empirical evidence to prove that environmental risks can be an effective channel through which the GBR transfers its effects on global bank lending activities.

The rest of this chapter is organised into five sections. The following section discusses the theoretical background, establishing the link between GBR and CBFs. In Section 3, this chapter describes the variables and the methodological approach. The results from the empirical analysis are presented in Section 4. In Section 5, we conclude the chapter by discussing future research and the policy implications of our findings.

2. Theoretical Background and Hypothesis Development

2.1. *Green bank regulation and cross-border bank flows*

This study attempts to investigate how GBR gaps across countries shape the structure of cross-border bank flows. The following are some reasons that support our belief: First, the literature has indicated that bank regulation has an effect on cross-border bank flows. As revealed by Khwaja and Mian (2008), Thakor (1996), and Gao and Jang (2021), under lax regulation regimes, banks are more likely to lend their money to riskier domestic borrowers. Barth *et al.* (2004) also argue that the stringent bank regulation in the home country leads to fewer non-performing loans. Moreover, restrictive regulation causes banks to have an incentive to approach risky but profitable loans overseas (Gao and Jang, 2021). Under strict regulation, banks participate in the global capital market as a way to reduce regulatory pressure. Frame *et al.* (2020), Houston *et al.* (2012a, 2012b), and Karolyi and Taboada (2015) have provided evidence that banks pursue risky loans outside the border to circumvent tight regulations in the home country. More stringent regulations in the home country also lead to a decrease in lending standards of banks overseas (Ongena *et al.*, 2013). It can be seen that stringent bank regulation leads to a rise in cross-border lending.

Second, tighter green bank regulation, our biggest concern in this chapter, has been demonstrated to impact banks' risk appetite and cross-border lending activities profoundly. The reasons are as follows. Green central banking, defined as banking that considers environmental risk, significantly influences both the macroeconomy and financial market's short-term and long-term stability and development (Dikau and Volz, 2021). The process of addressing environmental risks and promoting sustainability-pertaining issues is taken into consideration by green central banking when designing and implementing monetary policy and financial regulations in the pursuit of its traditional core goals of safeguarding macroeconomic and financial stability. As contended by Dikau and Volz (2021), this description is for passive green central banks since they need to incorporate environmental factors into the existing conventional system instead of solely pursuing sustainability-related goals. However, Dafe and Volz (2015) argue that active central banks can be mandated to employ tools to discourage brown investment, encourage green investment, and obtain developmental goals. In this chapter, we provide a strong discussion that the pursuit of sustainability goals by green central banks can guarantee the safeguarding of macroeconomic and financial stability, but can either positively or negatively affect lending outside the border. On the one hand, macroeconomic stability, like control for price variability, becomes difficult to achieve under the rise in frequency and severity of extreme climate change and other weather events. For example, droughts and floods may adversely impact agricultural productivity and create supply shocks, which lead to a sustained rise in food prices and cost-push inflation. The consequences become extremely severe for agriculture-oriented economies since they have a more substantial influence on income and employment in these countries. On the other hand, as contended by Volz (2017), there are potential impacts of policies mitigating climate change on energy production and prices. Furthermore, the monetary policy regimes may change due to the climate policy regime, like carbon policies (McKibbin *et al.*, 2017). In particular, the introduction of a carbon tax leads to a reduction in output and a spike in inflation. Some inflation-targeting countries may respond to this spike of inflation by increasing the interest rate, which slows the economy and causes exchange rate appreciation. Both lead to a more substantial decline in aggregate output. McKibbin *et al.* (2017) recommend that the central bank pay attention to environmental effects on food, energy, and other prices and policies dealing with environmental issues since they have potentially critical impacts on inflation. We argue that either more stability or fluctuations in the macroeconomy may happen due to the policies towards mitigating the environmental issues, which, respectively, discourage and encourage investors to lend their capital outside the border.

Regarding the effects on the financial sector, there is an emerging consensus that environmental problems and policies related to resolving these problems will generate considerable impacts on the functioning of financial systems (Bank of England, 2015; Carney, 2015). On the one hand, the natural hazard risks or the physical risks, as defined by Carney (2015), produce direct and indirect damages through the disruption and changes in global supply to an economy and thus financial stability (Bank of England, 2015). Considering physical risks when designing the policies can play an essential role in avoiding these adverse repercussions on the economy, especially the valuation of long-term investments. A more stable financial sector can discourage cross-border banking investments. On the other hand, Carney (2015) also emphasises that there exists uncertainty pertaining to changes in policy, price, and valuation as central banks introduce policies to mitigate or limit consequences of climate changes and reduce carbon emissions. Powerful policies like extensive environmental regulations and an introduction of carbon taxes are required to pursue international environmental goals. These policies adversely influence the valuation of carbon-intensive businesses and make coal, gas, and oil companies' assets less valuable (Dikau and

Volz, 2018, 2021). At the same time, the new technologies intended for mitigating environmental issues may make existing technology redundant. These things lead to more volatility in the financial sectors (Volz, 2017).

Another issue raised by Dikau and Volz (2018, 2021) is that the GBR plays an essential role in mitigating market failure regarding missing or incomplete financial markets. By contrast, green bank regulation can be considered a type of stringent capital regulation (Dikau and Volz, 2021) that leads to reluctance to undertake lending in the home country while promoting lending overseas to circumvent tight regulations regarding mitigating environmental consequences.

Based on our discussion, we hypothesise the following:

H1a: Green bank regulation discourages motivation to undertake to lend overseas.

H1b: Green bank regulation encourages motivation to undertake to lend overseas.

2.2. *De jure and de facto green bank regulation and cross-border bank flows*

2.2.1. *De jure and de facto regulation*

Scholars have emphasised distinctions between *de jure* and *de facto* regulations concerning central bank independence or the independence of regulatory agencies (Hanretty and Koop, 2013; Melton and Ginsburg, 2014; Voigt *et al.*, 2015). According to Lewkowicz and Metelska-Szaniawska (2020), *de jure* refers to a state of affairs that is restrictive within the framework of the law. This type of regulation is defined as "rule laid down for the guidance of an intelligent being by an intelligent being having power over him" (Austin, 1885, p. 86) or a "rule of conduct, prescribed by the supreme power in a state, commanding what is right and prohibiting what is wrong" (Blackstone, 1979, p. 44). On the other hand, the *de facto* concept is more sophisticated. *De facto* is defined as a state of affairs that is true in fact. While *de jure* reflects the understanding of authority in formal ways, the sociological understanding of authority represents manifestation of authority in a behavioural way, which is grasped by *de facto*. (Busch *et al.*, 2020). Green (2014) and Busch *et al.* (2020) use the terms *de jure* and *de facto* to grasp two basic understandings of how authority is manifested. Concentrating on distinguishing between the *de jure* and *de facto* institutions, Lewkowicz and Metelska-Szaniawska (2020) show that *de facto* is actual human interaction and may vary in nature but still fulfils the condition of being actually operative.

Emerging discussions reveal that *de jure* and *de facto* do not always conform. Indeed, it is not possible to grasp the functioning of law while not referring to social norms (Posner, 1997). There is a case where social actors comply with *de jure* regulation when it is imposed and implemented in society. As *de facto* regulation differs from *de jure* regulation in a given sphere of human interaction, *de jure* and *de facto* regulations may converge, then cause a change in social behaviour (Lewkowicz and Metelska-Szaniawska, 2020). The *de jure* regulation becomes a *de facto* one if the *de jure* regulation is perfectly enforced. In this case, *de jure* and *de facto* overlap, and they can boost each other. It can be seen that *de jure* and *de facto* regulations are mutual in nature. However, Fehr and Gaechter (2011) and Frey and Oberholzer-Gee (1997) indicate that *de jure* rule and regulation can be substituted for social norms, and there is a possibility that societies can function based on *de facto* or informal rules without the need for costly *de jure* rules. By contrast, Cassotta and Mazza (2014) argue that there is a distinction between *de jure* and *de facto* laws and regulations when they study the effects of climate change and explain the problem of exploration and exploitation of oil and gas, and then environmental protection.

Scholars have contended that there is a time lag between the formal introduction of law and the development of *de facto* regulation (Mechkova *et al.*, 2019). There are two reasons for this time lag. First, there is a need for a certain level of capacity and development of society for the implementation of *de facto* rules and regulations (Fukuyama, 2011). Second, the stickiness and historically developed processes and patterns require more time for profound institutional change (Katznelson and Weingast, 2005).

2.2.2. *Effects of de jure and de facto bank regulation*

In this section, we argue that *de jure* and *de facto* rules and regulations may have an effect on the economy, which in turn can cause changes in cross-border lending behaviour. First, an introduction of *de jure* and *de facto* rules and regulations in all sectors, including banking, creates transaction costs of legislation, such as costs of announcing new laws, costs of adjustments incurred, costs of regulatory instability, or costs of law enforcement (Lewkowicz and Metelska-Szaniawska, 2020). A rise in these transaction costs of legislation then makes the institutions and the overall economy less effective (Rothstein and Teorell, 2008). In the case where *de facto* regulation inhibits *de jure* regulation, these costs increase more. By contrast, these costs decrease if the *de jure* and *de facto* boost each other. Hence, a decrease or increase in transaction costs of legislation and final effects on the economy is inevitably conditional upon the beneficial and detrimental nature of *de jure* regulation and its relationship with *de facto* regulation. Regarding green bank regulation, introducing rules and regulations for protecting the environment or mitigating consequences of environmental issues and incorporating them into central bank policies in designing and implementing policies also include the transaction costs of legislation. As argued, these costs depend on the nature of *de jure* regulation and its association with *de facto* regulation. The dynamics and opacity of the home economy may disincentive the motivations of investors in the domestic market and then redirect their investments to foreign markets to avoid these risks.

Second, the primary objective of green central banks may be affected when imposing the new regulation regarding controls for environmental issues. The interaction between *de jure* and *de facto* regulation then impacts the real outcome of legislation. It could be the fact that the rise in the gap between *de jure* and *de facto* implies limited credibility of government promises, which influences the efficiency in providing a predictable framework for functioning economic agents or boosting investment activities (Henisz, 2000).

In this chapter, we contend that the *de jure* bank regulation may not be effective. In addition to an emphasis on the distinction between *de jure* and *de facto* laws and regulations, the study by Cassotta and Mazza (2014) has provided empirical evidence on the ineffectiveness of environmental regulations and policies. While the United Nations Environmental Programme is a good example that issues a number of practices integrating environmental issues into developing plans and policies, including trade and investments, the Arctic environmental law applied to the oil and gas industry is considered ineffective in obtaining environmental protection goals.

This ineffectiveness is attributed to many omissions and delays in implementing international agreements. They also indicate that there is a vicious circle stemming from a contrast between *de jure* and *de facto* regulations in the case of Greenland. The contrast between *de jure* and *de facto* environmental regulations is reflected by the business exploitation of natural resources and environmental protection. This contrast creates difficulties in finding a balance between constructing new environmental rules and integrating environmental aspects into investment laws (Cassotta and Mazza, 2014). In this example, *de facto* implies concrete environmental protection measures are not taken, thus influencing the possibility of having effective remedies to treat environmental damage, especially in the case where *de jure* rules cannot be enforced. Regarding international Arctic law, there is a need to find equilibrium between *de jure* and *de facto* laws.

We also contend that, for simplicity, *de jure* or *de facto* may be just a matter of measure for green bank regulation. In the study about financial openness, Kose *et al.* (2011) indicate that both *de jure* and *de facto* measures contain essential information, but they recommend using *de facto* measures. Busch *et al.* (2020) contended that positive authority gaps feature the limitations of authority's management form the international public administration, and the *de facto* authority is more likely to be preferred to the *de jure* authority. In this spirit, the *de facto* authority can be a good measure in investigating the effects of policy variables on the economy.

Based on our discussion, we hypothesise the following:

H2a: *De jure* green bank regulation discourages motivation to undertake to lend overseas.
H2b: *De jure* green bank regulation encourages motivation to undertake to lend overseas.
H2c: *De facto* green bank regulation discourages motivation to undertake to lend overseas.
H2d: *De facto* green bank regulation encourages motivation to undertake to lend overseas.

2.3. *Environmental risks channel*

Environmental degradation may have the following three risks on financial activities: transitional risk, physical risk, and liability risk

(Carney, 2015). Transitional risk refers to the uncertainty related to policy, price, and value changes that tend to happen in alleviating climate change and cutting carbon emissions. The movement towards a low-carbon economy will cause a paradigm shift in the economic structure (Semieniuk *et al.*, 2021). International objectives, including restraining global warming to two degrees, will call for demanding policy initiatives like the application of carbon taxes or widespread environmental regulation, which will influence the worth of carbon-intensive firms and might reduce the asset value of fossil fuel firms if the policy changes have not been priced in. Volz (2017) contended that the improvement of new technologies during the course of climate change moderation might lead to redundant technologies and the related reassessment of assets which could possibly cause financial instability that may have systemic consequences.

Physical risk reflects the risk of natural hazards, consisting of floods and earthquakes, which may directly destroy an economy and indirectly disrupt global production chains. Climate-associated harms and risks may induce disruptions for single firms or industries and generate systemic consequences for the whole economy and financial stability. A rise in the levels of physical risk is likely to have severe repercussions for the insurance industry. As revealed by the Bank of England (2015), climate and other environmental changes have important implications for central banks as they may trigger instability of financial systems. Climate vulnerability may influence fiscal position and debt sustainability (Kling *et al.*, 2018; Volz *et al.*, 2020). Pricing in physical risks is a usual measure of escaping these detrimental problems and plays a vital role in the assessment of long-term investments. Lastly, liability risk captures climate or environmental risks that happen due to uncertainty arising from potential financial losses and compensation claims induced by climate change-related natural disasters (Bank of England, 2015; Carney, 2015). For example, agents may claim compensation for financial losses from carbon emitters and environmental polluters, generating consequences for the insurance industry that offers third-party liability insurance, which then has inferences for financial regulators like central banks (Bank of England, 2015).

Regarding the relationship between bank regulation and the risk-taking of banks, Gonzalez (2005) contended that regulatory restrictions raise banks' risk-taking incentives by reducing their charter value. Banks located in nations with lower regulatory constraints have greater charter values that incentivise them to obey conservative policies. By contrast, banks in nations with stricter regulation possess smaller bank charter values and, thus, higher risk-taking incentives. Meanwhile, gaps in banking regulation may be vital push-or-pull determinants for global banking lending (Bremus and Fratzscher, 2015; Houston *et al.*, 2012b), and, therefore, for credit home bias. If regulatory environments are different across countries, banks may find regions applying a less stringent regulation appealing. A determinant that could lessen cross-border claims is more constrained regulations that make international lending more costly.

Based on these arguments, we hypothesise the following:

H3: The effects of GBR on CBFs are transferred through the environmental risk channel.

3. Empirical Methodology

3.1. *Data and summary statistics*

3.1.1. *Measuring cross-border bank lending*

We collected the total cross-border bank claims from the BIS Consolidated Banking Statistics database that is available on a quarterly basis. Our regression sample includes 25 reporting source countries and 186 recipient countries. A list of countries can be found in Table A.2 of Appendix. The data capture outstanding claims of internationally active banks located in source countries against their cross-country counterparties. Inter-office positions are dropped, so claims within a multinational banking institution are excluded. As most of our explanatory variables are available at a yearly frequency only, we take yearly averages of the quarterly stocks of cross-border claims. In order to escape from outliers influencing the results, we exclude (the few) negative values of cross-border claims from our sample.

3.1.2. *Measuring green banking regulation*

Data on GBR come from Dikau and Volz (2021). The authors use information from the IMF's Central Bank Legislation Database and access central banks' websites to obtain sustainability-related policies that the respective central banks have implemented in practice. Based on their analysis, we classify green central banking regulation into two criteria: *de jure* and *de facto*. *De jure* regulation represents whether a central bank has explicit sustainability objectives or supports the government's policies that consist of sustainability goals. *De facto* regulation captures whether or not a central bank takes on green activities.

Concerning *de jure* regulation, we construct a variable (*Dejure*) that takes a value of 1 if a country has explicit or implicit sustainability objectives and 0 otherwise. Further, to distinguish between sustainability and other objectives, the variable (*DirectDejure*) takes a value of 1 if a country has explicit sustainability goals and 0 if that country has implicit sustainability ones. Indeed, 75% of source countries ($Dejure_i$) have mandates that promote sustained growth or development, while the percentage of target countries is 44%. However, only 3% of *de jure* source countries have explicit environmental goals, whereas 21% of target countries have them.

The *de facto* regulation reflects the fact that central banks take actual green activities to solve climate risks and sustainability problems. The purposes of these activities are to integrate climate change-related risks into the financial system and more general ESG risks into the activities of financial institutes by offering them instruments, know-how, and comprehensive green instructions. We construct a variable GCBA_{it} that takes a value of 1 if country i's central bank takes green activity in year t and 0 otherwise. As these activities have long-lasting effects, such as becoming a member of SBN and NGFS, we construct a variable TotalGCBA_{it} to capture the accumulated effects. In particular, TotalGCBA_{it} is the sum of GCBA_{it} up to a year t.

Figure 1 plots the evolution of cross-border banking claims (CC) and GCBA over time. As shown in this figure, bank claims portray a slight increase in the period 1995–2011 before falling considerably. By contrast, the GCBA series were stable before 2012 but increased dramatically after 2012. Moreover, there are opposite trends between the CC and GBR series before and after 2012. In particular, the historical data show that there are procyclical associations between the dynamics of the bilateral cross-border banking lending and GCBA in the pre-2012 period, while the enlargement of GCBA

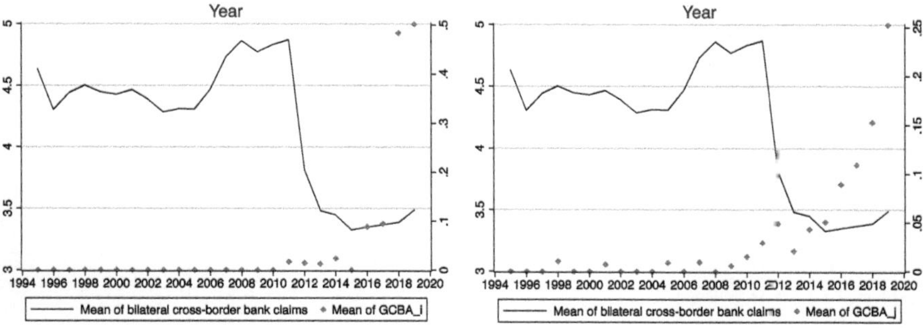

Fig. 1. Distribution of average CC and GBR over year.
Note: The mean value of bank claims is on the left-hand scale, and the mean value of GCBA is on the right-hand scale.

seemingly causes a substantial reduction in CC in the post-2012 period.

We also plot the average value of CC and GCBA series for the source and target countries in Fig. 2. We exploit the nexus between the two series by sorting countries based on the decreasing trend in CC. GCBA and bilateral GBF are shown in 2,814 pairs of 186 developing and developed countries.[a] Figure 2 reveals that the countries that most often apply more GCBA also have the greatest volume of bank claims. Figure 2 presents the positive correlation between the distribution of average banking flows and GCBA for source countries. Figure 3 displays the distribution of the average value of TotalGCBA over time. Two points are worth mentioning. First, the average value of TotalGCBA in the target countries is more likely to be higher than that in the source country. Second, the difference between the source and target countries became clearer after 2010.

3.1.3. *Control variables*

Besides our main variables of interest, we follow Choi and Furceri (2019), and Doan *et al.* (2021) to include a set of additional variables in the following regressions in order to take macroeconomic conditions and economic structure in the source and target countries into account. *CONTROL* consists of a set of control variables,

[a]For detailed information on these countries, please see Table A.1 in the Appendix.

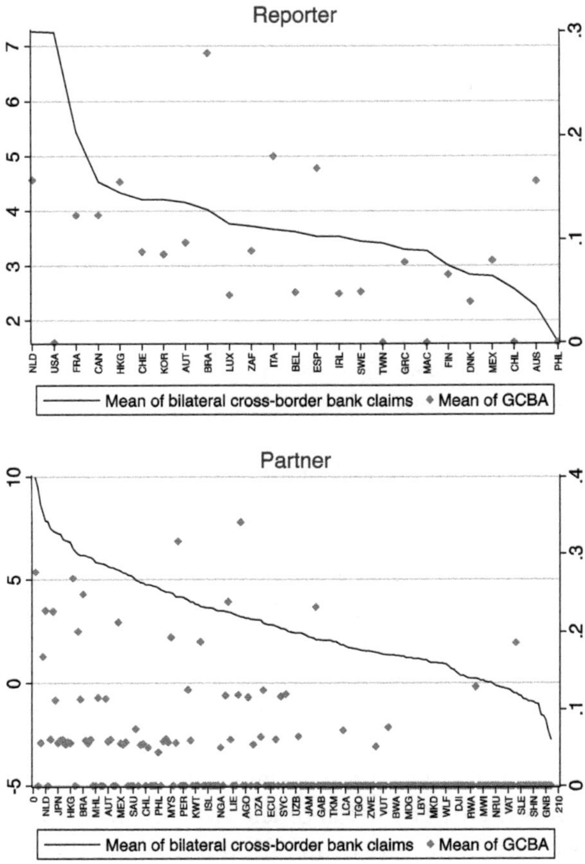

Fig. 2. Distribution of average CC and GCBA over target and source countries. *Note*: The mean value of bank claims is on the left-hand scale, and the mean value of GCBA is on the right-hand scale.

including GDP per capita and other common gravity variables that capture weighted distance (D), common religion (*comrelig*), common coloniser post 1945 (*comcol*), common official language (*comlang_off*), and same regional trade agreements (*rta*). While GDP is taken from The World Bank database, the gravity variables are obtained from the Centre dd'EtudesProspectives et dd'InformationsInternationales (CEPII). Table A.3 in the Appendix provides a detailed description of all the variables. Table 1 reports the statistical summary of variables.

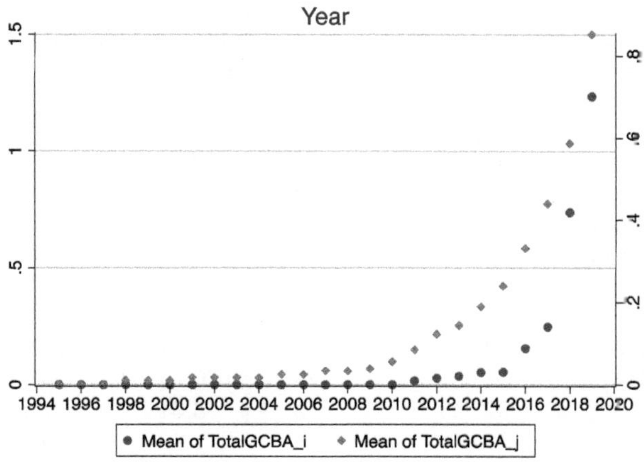

Fig. 3. Distribution of average of *TotalGCBA* over year.
Note: The mean value of GCBAi is on the left-hand scale, and the mean value of GCBAj is on the right-hand scale.

3.2. *Model specification*

We specify the following model to examine the effect of GBR on cross-border lending:

$$\begin{aligned}\mathrm{CC}_{ijt} &= \beta_0 + \beta_1 \mathrm{GBR}_{i,t-1} + \beta_2 \mathrm{GBR}_{j,t-1} \\ &\quad + \beta_3 \mathrm{CONTROL}_{ij,t} + v_t + \lambda_i + \gamma_j + \alpha_{ij} + \varepsilon_{ijt} \qquad (1)\end{aligned}$$

in which subscripts i, j, and t denote country i, country j, and year t, respectively. v_t, λ_i, γ_j, and α_{ij} denote year, source-country fixed, host-country fixed, and pair fixed effects, respectively. CC_{ijt} are bilateral cross-border banking claims in country i and j in year t that are obtained from LBS. $\mathrm{GBR}_{it} = \{\mathrm{Dejure}_{it}, \mathrm{DirectDejure}_{it}, \mathrm{GCBA}_{it}, \mathrm{TotalGCBA}_{it}\}$ and $\mathrm{GBR}_{jt} = \{\mathrm{Dejure}_{jt}, \mathrm{DirectDejure}_{jt}, \mathrm{GCBA}_{jt}, \mathrm{TotalGCBA}_{jt}\}$ are, respectively, sets of green banking regulations applied in country i and j in year t. The other control variables are included and represented by *CONTROL.*

This chapter first regresses GBFs in year t, GBF_{ijt}, on global banking regulation in year $t-1, \mathrm{GBR}_{i,t-1}$, with a set of other control variables and full of fixed effects. The empirical findings are expected to provide insights into the impacts of GBR international banking networks. For further analysis, we examine moderating effects of environmental risk by adding the interaction between GBR variables and

Table 1. Statistical summary.

Variables	Observation	Mean	Std. Dev.	Min	Max
LnC	32,643	4.45	3.28	−6.91	13.95
Dejure_i	32,643	0.75	0.43	0.00	1.00
Dejure_j	32,643	0.44	0.50	0.00	1.00
DirectDejure_i	24,594	0.03	0.16	0.00	1.00
DirectDejure_j	14,488	0.21	0.41	0.00	1.00
GCBA_i	32,643	0.09	0.28	0.00	1.00
GCBA_j	32,643	0.06	0.24	0.00	1.00
TotalGCBA_i	32,643	0.18	0.54	0.00	5.00
TotalGCBA_j	32,643	0.23	0.75	0.00	6.00
GF_i	32,643	1.73	3.04	0.00	18.00
GF_j	32,643	0.65	1.87	0.00	18.00
EPS_i	16,994	2.34	0.91	0.38	4.13
EPS_j	7,126	2.00	1.00	0.38	4.13
EPI_i	32,643	71.45	9.38	35.25	82.86
EPI_j	32,643	50.26	16.96	2.57	82.86
LnGDP_j	32,449	2.02	1.53	−2.27	4.78
LnGDP_i	32,643	3.70	0.58	1.18	4.78
D	32,643	8.46	0.94	4.95	9.89
comlang_off	32,643	0.17	0.37	0.00	1.00
comcol	32,643	0.01	0.07	0.00	1.00
comrelig	32,643	0.21	0.27	0.00	0.96
rta	32,643	0.38	0.49	0.00	1.00

variables reflecting the natural disasters and level of uncertainty. For a robustness check, we use alternative measures of GBR, and since there potentially exists an endogeneity issue arising from simultaneity between GBR variables and global bank lending, we apply the IVs method to resolve this issue.

4. Empirical Results

4.1. *Baseline results*

The main purpose of this article is to investigate the nexus between GBR and cross-border bank flows. By employing the bank-pair-year panel data, we report the estimation results of this analysis in Table 2, which outline the effects of *de jure* GBR (*Dejure)* in Column (1), *de facto* GBR (*GCBA*) in Columns (2)–(5), and both

Table 2. *De jure* estimation results.

	(1)	(2)	(3)	(4)	(5)	(6)	(7)
	De jure			*De factor*		Both	
Variables	**LnC**	**LnC**	**LnC**	**LnC**	**LnC**	**LnC**	**LnC**
Dejure_i	–2.63***						
	(0.362)						
Dejure_j	0.07						
	(0.525)						
GCBA_i		0.16***	0.17***				
		(0.041)	(0.041)				
GCBA_j		0.22***	0.21***				
		(0.036)	(0.036)				
TotalGCBA_i				0.16***	0.16***		
				(0.041)	(0.042)		
TotalGCBA_j				0.13***	0.13***		
				(0.028)	(0.028)		
DejureGCBA_i						0.08*	
						(0.044)	
DejureGCBA_j						0.17***	
						(0.041)	
DejureTotalGCBA_i							0.11***
							(0.041)
DejureTotalGCBA_j							0.06*
							(0.032)
LnGDP_i	0.72***	0.72***	0.72***	0.69***	0.70***	0.73***	0.73***
	(0.076)	(0.075)	(0.076)	(0.076)	(0.076)	(0.076)	(0.076)
LnGDP_j	0.40***	0.42***	0.43***	0.41***	0.42***	0.41***	0.41***
	(0.132)	(0.132)	(0.133)	(0.133)	(0.133)	(0.132)	(0.133)
D	–1.47***	–1.47***		–1.46***		–1.47***	–1.47***
	(0.056)	(0.056)		(0.056)		(0.056)	(0.056)
comlang_off	0.61***	0.61***		0.62***		0.61***	0.61***
	(0.113)	(0.113)		(0.113)		(0.113)	(0.113)
comcol	0.47	0.47		0.47		0.47	0.48
	(0.313)	(0.314)		(0.314)		(0.313)	(0.314)
comrelig	0.80***	0.80***		0.80***		0.80***	0.80***
	(0.223)	(0.223)		(0.223)		(0.223)	(0.223)
rta	–0.02	–0.01	–0.01	–0.00	–0.00	–0.02	–0.01
	(0.073)	(0.072)	(0.076)	(0.072)	(0.076)	(0.073)	(0.072)
Observations	32,643	32,643	32,643	32,643	32,643	32,643	32,643
Number of pair	2,814	2,814	2,814	2,814	2,814	2,814	2,814
Pair FE	No	No	Yes	No	Yes	No	No
Country FE	Yes	Yes	Yes	Yes	Yes	Yes	Yes
Year FE	Yes	Yes	Yes	Yes	Yes	Yes	Yes
R-squared	0.728	0.728	0.095	0.728	0.097	0.728	0.728

Note: *, **, and *** represent a 90%, 95% and 99% significance level, respectively.

de jure and *de facto* GBR in Columns (6) and (7). For each model, we consider the existence of GBR in both the home and host country. Concerning the *de jure* GBR, Column (1) reveals that *de jure* GBR has a negative sign, as proposed in hypothesis H2a. The results suggest that there is an adverse influence of *de jure* GBR on cross-border banking investment flows. However, our results show that only *de jure* GBR in the home country reduces the likelihood of making foreign banking investments.

Concerning the *de facto* GBR, Columns (2) and (3) of Table 2 reveal that the more stringent *de facto* GBR in both home and host countries leads to a rise in cross-border banking investment activities. The findings imply that the incorporation of sustainability standards into policies designed and implemented by financial institutions in both the home and host countries can promote a bilateral collaboration of banks from these two countries. However, our results suggest that the GBR in the host country may play a more critical role in attracting the flows of banking investment. In particular, the stringent *de facto* GBR in a home country increases the global bank claims by about 16%, and there is a rise in bank lending due to the existence of *de facto* GBR in a host country. It is worth noting that the value of R-squared decreases significantly when controlling bank-pair fixed effects in Column (3). We report the within-value R-squared in this table when we use the fixed-effect model. This R-squared represents how much variation in the dependent variable within the bank-pair units is captured by our model (or how well our model accounts for changes in the dependent variable within each of the bank pairs over time). The within R-squared is obtained assuming that groups (bank pairs, in our case) are fixed quantities, so their effects are removed from the model. Consequently, R-squared decreased significantly. By using the variable capturing the number of green activities integrated into climate change-related risk sustainability problems in the financial systems (*TotalGCBA*), our estimates also indicate the importance of GBR in promoting bilateral banking investment activities. Our empirical findings support hypothesis H2d. In our sample, there are mismatches between the effect of *de jure* and *de facto* GBR on cross-border bank lending. Chappell *et al.* (2020) also indicated a similar finding when they studied the distinction in the way that the government manages fresh water by law and in practice.

The flows of banking investment are more likely to be directly to environmentally friendly destinations. The expansion of sustainable and green banking investments can be explained by the diversity in investment opportunities and sources and the reduction in credit default risks of banks' borrowers. Our findings of this analysis are in line with those of Gao and Jang (2021), who studied impacts of stringent conventional bank regulation on the likelihood of forming a global banking network. To provide more insights on the heterogeneous impacts of *de jure* and *de facto*, we concentrate on the home and host countries having explicit or implicit sustainability objectives and simultaneously taking on green activities to address climate risks and sustainability problems (*DejureGCBA*). We also add interactions between *de jure* and the number of green activities (*DejureTotalGCBA*) and report the results in Column (7). The statistically positive signs of these variables confirm the importance of GBR in promoting cross-border banking investments.

Subsequently, we turn to analyse the effects of other control variables on cross-border bank lending. In general, our findings are consistent with those of other studies, such as Doan *et al.* (2021), Ha *et al.* (2021), and Petersen and Rajan (2002). In particular, there is a statistically positive and significant impact of GDP_i and GDP_j as well as a common language (*comlang_off*) and common religion (*comrelig*), while the geographical distance between home and host country is negatively associated with cross-border bank claims. The remaining variables, including *comcol* and *rta*, do not affect the likelihood of global banking investments.

4.2. *The role of green bank regulation in controlling environmental risks*

In the following analysis, we examine the roles of green bank regulation in controlling the adverse effects of environmental risks on the formation of a global banking network. To capture the environmental risks, we follow Baker and Bloom (2013) and use diverse information about natural disasters, including the number of events that hit the home (*Totaldisaster*) and host countries and their consequences, including the number of deaths (unit: thousand victims)

(*Totaldeaths*) and total damages (*Totaldamages*) caused by natural disasters (unit: billion dollars). The data are sourced from CRED.[b] The *Totaldeaths* and *Totaldamages* are rescaled[c] and then taken to the natural logarithm. To investigate the moderating roles of GBR in controlling detrimental effects of environmental risk, we add variables reflecting information about natural disasters and their interactions with GBR variables into Eq. (1). The results are then reported in Table 3, in which (*a*) reports the estimation results when we incorporate the interaction between environmental risk and *de facto* GBR, while those in (*a*) and (*c*) are the cases when the country has sustainability objectives and simultaneously takes green activities to resolve climate risks and sustainability problems. We use the dummy capturing *de facto* GBR in (*b*) and the number of green activities in (*c*). The statistically positive coefficients of interactions between variables reflecting environmental risks and GBR variables in the home country suggest that the GBR can alleviate the adverse impacts of environmental risks on cross-border banking investment activities. In other words, our empirical results advocate the hypothesis H3 that the effects of GBR on CBFs are transferred through the environmental risk channel. Our estimates imply that the GBR is only effective in dealing with environmental risks arising in the home country, while similar evidence cannot be found if there are environmental risks in the host country.

To further check on our argument that environmental risk can be considered an effective channel to transfer the impacts of GBR on the flows of global banking investments, we raise a similar discussion for other types of uncertainty. In this analysis, we use the World Uncertainty Index, which employs the frequency of appearance of the word "uncertainty" (*Uncertainty_Word*) or the number of pages having the word "uncertainty" (*Uncertainty_Page*). The uncertainty data are taken from the Economist Intelligence Unit (EIU). We consider uncertainty arising in the home and host country. We outline the results in Table 4. Our results show that the consequences of

[b]To download the data, we access www.emdat.be.

[c]We rescale *Totaldeaths* and *Totaldamages* by dividing by 10^3 and 10^6, respectively.

Table 3. Natural disasters.

	(1)	(2)	(3)	(4)	(5)	(6)
	Total Disaster		**Total Deaths**		**Total Damages**	
Variables	**LnC**	**LnC**	**LnC**	**LnC**	**LnC**	**LnC**
(a)						
$GCBA_i$	–0.06*	0.10***	0.19***	0.09***	0.16***	0.09***
	(0.031)	(0.029)	(0.041)	(0.036)	(0.046)	(0.036)
$GCBA_j$	0.18***	0.15***	0.13***	0.19***	0.13***	0.15***
	(0.030)	(0.037)	(0.033)	(0.036)	(0.033)	(0.040)
$LnGDP_i$	0.73***	0.73***	0.71***	0.85***	0.72***	0.85***
	(0.076)	(0.076)	(0.085)	(0.080)	(0.085)	(0.080)
$LnGDP_j$	0.47***	0.41***	0.58***	0.41***	0.57***	0.41***
	(0.132)	(0.132)	(0.143)	(0.148)	(0.143)	(0.148)
rta	–0.02	–0.02	0.08	–0.03	0.08	–0.03
	(0.076)	(0.076)	(0.074)	(0.077)	(0.074)	(0.077)
$Disaster_i$	–0.01		–0.01*		0.02*	
	(0.004)		(0.004)		(0.014)	
$DisasterGCBA_i$	0.07***		0.14**		0.13*	
	(0.010)		(0.056)		(0.077)	
$Disaster_j$		0.00		0.00		0.01
		(0.004)		(0.001)		(0.014)
$DisasterGCBA_j$		0.01		–0.03		0.05
		(0.005)		(0.023)		(0.036)
Constant	0.90*	1.13**	0.78	1.18**	0.81	1.20**
	(0.543)	(0.542)	(0.573)	(0.599)	(0.572)	(0.597)
Observations	32,643	32,643	22,277	21,771	22,277	21,771
R-squared	0.097	0.095	0.114	0.099	0.114	0.099
Number of pair	2,814	2,814	2,697	2,502	2,697	2,502
Pair FE	Yes	Yes	Yes	Yes	Yes	Yes
Country FE	Yes	Yes	Yes	Yes	Yes	Yes
Year FE	Yes	Yes	Yes	Yes	Yes	Yes
(b)						
$DejureGCBA_i$	–0.15***	0.02	0.10**	–0.00	0.10**	–0.00
	(0.035)	(0.032)	(0.045)	(0.039)	(0.048)	(0.039)
$DejureGCBA_j$	0.14***	0.15***	0.08*	0.13***	0.08*	0.15***
	(0.036)	(0.044)	(0.040)	(0.042)	(0.040)	(0.046)

(Continued)

Table 3. (*Continued*)

	(1)	(2)	(3)	(4)	(5)	(6)
	Total Disaster		**Total Deaths**		**Total Damages**	
Variables	**LnC**	**LnC**	**LnC**	**LnC**	**LnC**	**LnC**
(b)						
LnGDP_i	0.73***	0.74***	0.72***	0.86***	0.72***	0.86***
	(0.076)	(0.077)	(0.085)	(0.081)	(0.085)	(0.081)
LnGDP_j	0.47***	0.41***	0.56***	0.41***	0.56***	0.41***
	(0.133)	(0.133)	(0.144)	(0.148)	(0.144)	(0.148)
rta	–0.02	–0.02	0.08	–0.03	0.08	–0.03
	(0.076)	(0.076)	(0.075)	(0.077)	(0.075)	(0.077)
Disaster_i	–0.01		–0.01**		0.03**	
	(0.004)		(0.004)		(0.014)	
Disaster*Dejure GCBA_i	0.07***		0.18***		0.20	
	(0.011)		(0.055)		(0.152)	
Disaster_j		0.00		–0.00		0.02
		(0.004)		(0.001)		(0.015)
Disaster*Dejure GCBA_j		–0.00		–0.03		–0.11
		(0.007)		(0.022)		(0.066)
Constant	0.96*	1.20**	0.93	1.28**	0.93	1.27**
	(0.544)	(0.544)	(0.573)	(0.600)	(0.574)	(0.600)
Observations	32,643	32,643	22,277	21,771	22,277	21,771
R-squared	0.096	0.094	0.112	0.097	0.112	0.097
Number of pair	2,814	2,814	2,697	2,502	2,697	2,502
Pair FE	Yes	Yes	Yes	Yes	Yes	Yes
Country FE	Yes	Yes	Yes	Yes	Yes	Yes
Year Fe	Yes	Yes	Yes	Yes	Yes	Yes
(c)						
DejureTotal GCBA_i	–0.02	0.08**	0.02	0.08*	0.03	0.08*
	(0.040)	(0.033)	(0.041)	(0.039)	(0.038)	(0.039)
DejureTotal GCBA_j	0.07**	0.09***	0.04	0.05*	0.04	0.05*
	(0.027)	(0.032)	(0.029)	(0.030)	(0.029)	(0.030)

Table 3. (*Continued*)

	(1)	(2)	(3)	(4)	(5)	(6)
	Total Disaster		**Total Deaths**		**Total Damages**	
Variables	**LnC**	**LnC**	**LnC**	**LnC**	**LnC**	**LnC**
(c)						
LnGDP_i	0.73***	0.74***	0.72***	0.86***	0.72***	0.86***
	(0.076)	(0.076)	(0.085)	(0.081)	(0.085)	(0.080)
LnGDP_j	0.45***	0.42***	0.53***	0.42***	0.52***	0.42***
	(0.133)	(0.134)	(0.144)	(0.150)	(0.145)	(0.150)
rta	−0.02	−0.02	0.09	−0.02	0.09	−0.02
	(0.076)	(0.076)	(0.075)	(0.077)	(0.075)	(0.077)
Disaster_i	−0.01		−0.01**		0.02	
	(0.004)		(0.004)		(0.015)	
Disaster*Dejure TotalGCBA_i	0.02***		0.21***		0.07*	
	(0.005)		(0.073)		(0.039)	
Disaster_j		0.00		0.00		0.02
						(0.015)
Disaster*Dejure TotalGCBA_j		−0.01		−0.01		−0.01
		(0.005)		(0.021)		(0.024)
Constant	1.00*	1.05*	1.02*	1.11*	1.07*	1.11*
	(0.553)	(0.554)	(0.581)	(0.616)	(0.586)	(0.616)
Observations	32,643	32,643	22,277	21,771	22,277	21,771
R-squared	0.096	0.095	0.112	0.098	0.112	0.098
Number of pair	2,814	2,814	2,697	2,502	2,697	2,502
Pair FE	Yes	Yes	Yes	Yes	Yes	Yes
Country FE	Yes	Yes	Yes	Yes	Yes	Yes
Year FE	Yes	Yes	Yes	Yes	Yes	Yes

Note: Robust standard errors in parentheses. $^{***}p < 0.01$, $^{**}p < 0.05$, $^{*}p < 0.1$.

uncertainty on global bank claims become less severe if the home and host countries have the GBR.

4.3. *Robustness checks*

4.3.1. *Alternative measures*

For a robustness check, we employ an alternative measure of GBR. First, we collect data from the Green Finance Measures Database,

Table 4. Uncertainty.

	(1)	(2)	(3)	(4)
	Uncertainty_Word		**Uncertainty_Page**	
	Home	**Host**	**Home**	**Host**
Variables	**LnC**	**LnC**	**LnC**	**LnC**
$GCBA_i$	–0.22	0.09***	–0.38*	0.09***
	(0.150)	(0.030)	(0.202)	(0.030)
$GCBA_j$	0.13***	–0.05	0.13***	–0.15
	(0.030)	(0.125)	(0.030)	(0.162)
Uncertainty	0.26**	–0.32**	0.18	–0.42***
	(0.124)	(0.123)	(0.154)	(0.152)
Uncertainty*GCBA	0.37**	0.27*	0.59**	0.40*
	(0.188)	(0.159)	(0.260)	(0.211)
$LnGDP_i$	0.77***	0.79***	0.77***	0.78***
	(0.079)	(0.079)	(0.079)	(0.079)
$LnGDP_j$	0.69***	0.44***	0.68***	0.44***
	(0.131)	(0.140)	(0.130)	(0.140)
rta	0.03	–0.06	0.03	–0.06
	(0.076)	(0.081)	(0.076)	(0.081)
Constant	–0.13	1.41**	–0.04	1.51**
	(0.541)	(0.586)	(0.545)	(0.591)
Observations	29,709	28,014	29,709	28,014
R-squared	0.116	0.104	0.116	0.104
Number of pair	2,642	2,328	2,642	2,328
Pair FE	Yes	Yes	Yes	Yes
Country FE	Yes	Yes	Yes	Yes
Year FE	Yes	Yes	Yes	Yes

Note: Robust standard errors in parentheses. $^{***}p < 0.01$, $^{**}p < 0.05$, $^{*}p < 0.1$.

which consists of policy and regulatory measures promulgated by public authorities such as governments, central banks, financial regulators, and public financial institutions. We construct a variable GF_i, the total measures of environmental policy or regulation in the banking asset class issued by country i in year t. By nature, GF is broader than *TotalGCBA*. The average values of GF are, respectively, 1.73 and 0.65 in the home and host countries. Meanwhile, those of *TotalGCBA* are 0.18 and 0.23, respectively. Figure 4 displays a distribution of GF over year.

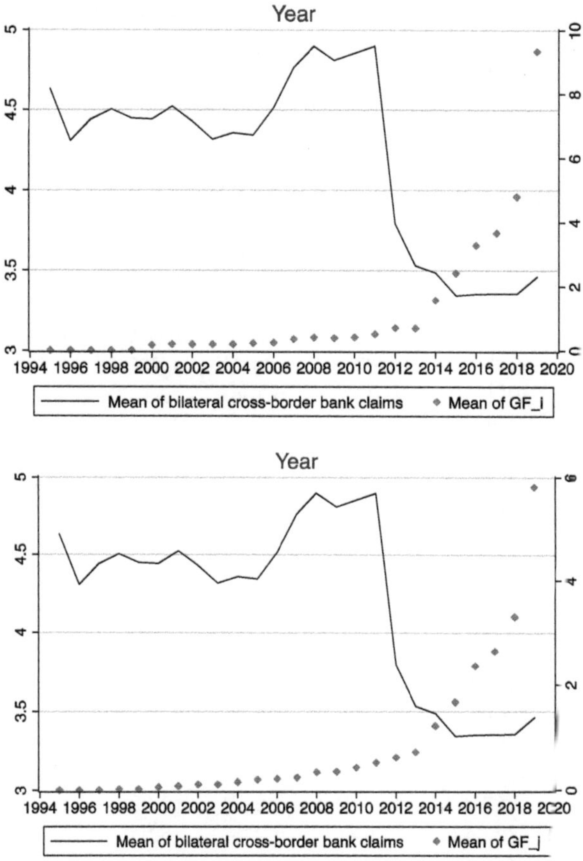

Fig. 4. Distribution of average CC and GF over year.
Note: The mean value of bank claims is on the left-hand scale, and the mean value of GF is on the right-hand scale.

Second, we utilise the OECD Environmental Policy Stringency Index (EPS), a country-specific and internationally comparable measure of the stringency of environmental policy. OECD defines stringency as the degree to which environmental policies impose an explicit or implicit premium on environmentally detrimental activity. Third, we use the Environmental Performance Index (EPI), which is a method of calculating and numerically scoring the environmental performance of a country's policies.

We re-regress the model (1) and report the estimation results in Table 5. Our estimates reveal that the baseline results are robust for alternative measures of GBR.

Table 5. Alternative measures of GBR.

	(1)	(2)	(3)	(4)	(5)	(6)
	GF		EPS		EPI	
Variables	**LnC**	**LnC**	**LnC**	**LnC**	**LnC**	**LnC**
$Alter_i$	0.04***	0.04***	0.11**	0.11**	0.01***	0.01***
	(0.013)	(0.013)	(0.054)	(0.053)	(0.004)	(0.004)
$Alter_j$	0.06***	0.06***	0.15***	0.15***	–0.01	–0.01
	(0.013)	(0.013)	(0.053)	(0.054)	(0.005)	(0.005)
$LnGDP_i$	0.76***	0.76***	1.25***	1.25***	0.72***	0.72***
	(0.076)	(0.077)	(0.136)	(0.137)	(0.075)	(0.076)
$LnGDP_j$	0.46***	0.47***	1.17***	1.21***	0.46***	0.47***
	(0.134)	(0.135)	(0.229)	(0.229)	(0.132)	(0.132)
D	–1.47***		–1.15***		–1.47***	
	(0.056)		(0.101)		(0.056)	
comlang_off	0.61***		0.21		0.61***	
	(0.112)		(0.189)		(0.113)	
comcol	0.51				0.47	
	(0.314)				(0.313)	
comrelig	0.79***		1.67***		0.80***	
	(0.223)		(0.319)		(0.223)	
rta	–0.00	–0.00	–0.09	–0.11	–0.02	–0.02
	(0.072)	(0.076)	(0.110)	(0.118)	(0.073)	(0.076)
Constant	12.16***	0.69	9.25***	–1.79*	12.16***	0.51
	(0.706)	(0.570)	(1.230)	(0.993)	(0.757)	(0.709)
Observations	32,643	32,643	5,943	5,943	32,643	32,643
R-squared	0.729	0.096	0.789	0.351	0.728	0.095
Number of pair	2,814	2,814	465	465	2,814	2,814
Pair FE	No	Yes	No	Yes	No	Yes
Country FE	Yes	Yes	Yes	Yes	Yes	Yes
Year FE	Yes	Yes	Yes	Yes	Yes	Yes

Note: Robust standard errors in parentheses. $^{***}p < 0.01$, $^{**}p < 0.05$, $^{*}p < 0.1$.

4.3.2. *Endogeneity issue*

Potential endogeneity could alter our analysis of GBR. We believe that there is simultaneity between CBFs and GBR. The potential reasons are discussed as follows. Ngwu *et al.* (2019) contend that cross-border banking improves competition among financial institutes and therefore leads to a change in governance structures in the host nations. Cross-border banking also fosters financial stability as the banks in the host countries can upgrade the quality of supervision and regulation that are required by the foreign banks and their home supervisors with higher standards (Claessens and Van Horen, 2014). As the global lending flows stem from the developed countries, GBRs that are mainly issued and adopted in the advanced nations are transferred to the emerging and developing ones. Hence, host countries that are actively involved in cross-border banking activities are likely to set up GBRs.

Based on our argument, there is potential endogeneity that may make our findings biased. Thus, we use the IVs model to deal with this problem. We employ regime duration (RD) as an IV. Tokunaga (2020) conducted a systematic review and indicated that the regime transformation is positively associated with environmental reform in Central and Eastern Europe. Adams *et al.* (2016) stated that regime types such as democracy and regime durability fostered environmental performance in Ghana.

We collect data on regime durability (RD) from the GovData360 database that is associated with the Center for Systemic Peace. Variable RD is defined as the number of years since the most recent regime changes or the end of a transition period determined by the absence of steady political institutions.

We now apply the IV method to deal with the endogeneity problem. We first employ endogeneity tests for the validity of IVs and provide the results in Table 6. First, the Hausman tests of endogeneity significantly indicate χ^2 in the model with the GBR variables (GCBA). The results reveal that endogeneity of GCBA and cross-border lending may create a problem in our regression sample. Hence, we should consider the potential endogeneity. Second, the

Table 6. Endogeneity test.

	Coefficient	
GCBA (First Stage Model)	**GCBA**$_i$	**GCBA**$_j$
Hausman test of endogeneity (χ^2)	16.899	43.329
	(0.000)	(0.000)
Kleibergen-Paap LM statistic	122.332	36.585
(Under-identification test)	(0.000)	(0.000)
Cragg–Donald Wald F-statistic	72.838	26.783
	(0.000)	(0.000)

Note: We report endogeneity tests of GCBA on CC from the specification using 2SLS. p-values are in brackets.

Table 7. IV regression.

	(1)	(2)	(3)	(4)
	First	**Second**	**First**	**Second**
Variables	**$GCBA_i$**	**LnC**	**$GCBA_j$**	**LnC**
$LnGDP_i$	–0.00	0.71***	0.03***	0.57***
	(0.005)	(0.081)	(0.009)	(0.108)
$LnGDP_j$	–0.09***	0.66***	0.01	0.13
	(0.018)	(0.211)	(0.014)	(0.166)
D	–0.00	–1.35***	–0.00***	–1.32***
	(0.001)	(0.056)	(0.002)	(0.058)
comlang_off	–0.00	0.26**	0.00	0.41***
	(0.002)	(0.102)	(0.003)	(0.106)
comcol	0.02***	–1.36***	0.03	–0.15
	(0.006)	(0.285)	(0.025)	(0.384)
comrelig	–0.00*	0.85***	–0.00	0.78***
	(0.003)	(0.206)	(0.004)	(0.225)
rta	0.00	0.03	–0.02***	0.17*
	(0.003)	(0.085)	(0.004)	(0.101)
$p\_durable_i$	–0.02***			
	(0.001)			
$GCBA_i$		3.57***		
		(1.319)		
$p\_durable_j$			0.00***	
			(0.000)	
$GCBA_j$				5.33**
				(2.348)
Constant	2.43***	9.01***	0.02	6.10***
	(0.092)	(0.924)	(0.045)	(1.324)
Observations	29,995	29,995	28,736	28,736
R-squared	0.446	0.706	0.210	0.668

Note: Robust standard errors in parentheses. $^{***}p < 0.01$, $^{**}p < 0.05$, $^{*}p < 0.1$.

LM statistics of under-identification tests display that χ^2 statistics are significant, suggesting that the IVs are suitable. Lastly, we show the significant Cragg–Donald Wald F-statistic, indicating that our used IVs are convincing enough to diminish the endogeneity problem. These tests show evidence to confirm that our IVs are usable.

We display the IV regression result in Tables 7 and 8. When the endogeneity problem is taken into consideration, the effects of GBR on cross-border lending become more evident.

Table 8. IV regression.

	(1)	(2)	(3)	(4)	(5)	(6)
Variables	**LnC**	**LnC**	**LnC**	**LnC**	**LnC**	**LnC**
$LnGDP_i$	0.75***	–0.71	0.72***	0.98***	0.75***	0.68***
	(0.080)	(1.016)	(0.079)	(0.117)	(0.080)	(0.109)
$LnGDP_j$	0.70***	0.03	0.79***	0.33*	0.67***	0.20
	(0.156)	(0.369)	(0.172)	(0.179)	(0.151)	(0.252)
D	–1.43***	–1.22***	–1.45***	–1.44***	–1.43***	–1.39***
	(0.059)	(0.150)	(0.058)	(0.060)	(0.059)	(0.070)
comlang_off	0.61***	0.60***	0.60***	0.58***	0.60***	0.57***
	(0.115)	(0.136)	(0.115)	(0.114)	(0.115)	(0.119)
comcol	–1.62***	–0.34	–1.68***	0.07	–1.61***	0.14
	(0.314)	(0.675)	(0.312)	(0.406)	(0.312)	(0.471)
comrelig	0.86***	0.81***	0.88***	0.62***	0.85***	0.68***
	(0.223)	(0.257)	(0.226)	(0.230)	(0.223)	(0.237)
rta	0.00	0.49	–0.04	0.26**	–0.00	0.28*
	(0.075)	(0.351)	(0.074)	(0.123)	(0.075)	(0.169)
$TotalGCBA_i$	1.05**					
	(0.452)					
$TotalGCBA_j$		4.87				
		(3.308)				
$DejureGCBA_i$			2.54**			
			(1.092)			
$DejureGCBA_j$				9.04***		
				(3.121)		
$DejureTotalGCBA_i$					0.99**	
					(0.426)	
$DejureTotalGCBA_j$						4.09**
						(1.948)
Constant	11.15***	9.04***	10.84***	11.44***	11.34***	11.07***
	(0.848)	(2.506)	(0.924)	(0.852)	(0.804)	(1.111)
Observations	29,995	28,736	29,995	28,736	29,995	28,736
Number of pair	2,674	2,518	2,674	2,518	2,674	2,518
Pair FE	Yes	Yes	Yes	Yes	Yes	Yes
Country FE	Yes	Yes	Yes	Yes	Yes	Yes
Year FE	Yes	Yes	Yes	Yes	Yes	Yes
R^2-squared	0.722	0.493	0.715	0.618	0.723	0.604

Note: Robust standard errors in parentheses. $^{***}p < 0.01$, $^{**}p < 0.05$, $^{*}p < 0.1$.

5. Conclusion

This chapter is the first attempt to uncover the influences of green bank regulation on cross-border lending by using dyad panel data of 2,814 country pairs during the 1995–2019 period. We distinguish the *de jure* (formally enshrined in the law) and *de facto* (manifesting in practice) green bank regulations. Our findings reveal that *de jure* regulation acts as a brake, while *de facto* regulation fosters CBFs. When both genres of regulation are matched, the joint effects are positive. Furthermore, these effects are transferred through the environmental risk channel to the extent that the GBR attenuates the consequences of environmental risks on the likelihood of joining the global banking network. The results are robust for alternative measures of green finance regulation and when the endogeneity is controlled.

On the policy front, our findings suggest several critical implications for the central banks and other financial institutions to deal with the environmental degradations that have become a common issue in many countries and promote the safety and soundness of the global banking network. The empirical results suggest not only a novel driver of a country's likelihood to participate in the international banking network but also a novel approach to mitigate the potential occurrences due to a weak ecological system and detrimental consequences of environmental risks that have an effect on the economy in general and the financial market in particular. We show that there is a current transformation trend towards a low-carbon and resilient climate economy. The flow of financial resources has been redirected from environmentally damaging activities to environmentally friendly ones. To avoid falling behind the current trend, countries must make appropriate policy design and implementation changes. Under such circumstances, the role of central banks and other relevant financial regulatory agencies becomes increasingly vital. They should integrate environmental considerations into their operation in a step-by-step manner and review the public financial governance policies more carefully. It is also essential to orient the financial system with sustainable development so that the decisions on investments and lending are based on environmental risk assessment to comply with sustainability standards. Furthermore, a detailed and appropriate guide that helps commercial banks follow and comply with sustainability standards should be quickly constructed and widely published to scale up green finance.

Declaration of Interests

The authors declare that they have no known competing financial interests or personal relationships that could have appeared to influence the work reported in this chapter.

Ethics approval and consent to participate: Not applicable

Consent for publication: Not applicable

Compliance with ethical standards:

- Disclosure of potential conflicts of interest.
- Research involving human participants and/or animals.
- Informed consent.

Data availability statement: Data available on request due to privacy/ethical restrictions.

Appendix

Table A.1. List of countries.

No.	Reporter	%	No.	Reporter	%
1	AUS	5.27	14	IRL	5.12
2	AUT	3.86	15	ITA	1.44
3	BEL	9.12	16	KOR	3.81
4	BRA	1.19	17	LUX	8.69
5	CAN	1.28	18	MAC	0.88
6	CHE	10.37	19	MEX	1.10
7	CHL	1.75	20	NLD	3.16
8	DNK	5.70	21	PHL	0.44
9	ESP	1.93	22	SWE	6.08
10	FIN	3.40	23	TWN	5.11
11	FRA	10.29	24	USA	5.09
12	GRC	0.38	25	ZAF	1.87
13	HKG	1.68			

Table A.2. Detailed description of listed countries in our sample.

No.	Partner	%	No.	Partner	%	No.	Partner	%	No.	Partner	%	No.	Partner	%	No.	Partner	%
1	ABW	0.20	32	CHE	1.00	63	GAB	0.35	94	KGZ	0.21	125	NER	0.29	156	SVK	0.65
2	AFG	0.24	33	CHL	0.86	64	GBR	1.08	95	KHM	0.43	126	NGA	0.63	157	SVN	0.58
3	AGO	0.53	34	CHN	1.03	65	GEO	0.42	96	KIR	0.05	127	NIC	0.44	158	SWE	1.01
4	ALB	0.32	35	CIV	0.44	66	GHA	0.66	97	KOR	0.97	128	NLD	1.00	159	SWZ	0.29
5	AND	0.38	36	CMR	0.43	67	GIN	0.34	98	KWT	0.63	129	NOR	1.00	160	SYC	0.47
6	ARE	0.84	37	COD	0.30	68	GMB	0.30	99	LAO	0.29	130	NPL	0.34	161	SYR	0.20
7	ARG	0.89	38	COG	0.38	69	GNB	0.15	100	LBN	0.71	131	NZL	0.84	162	TCD	0.20
8	ARM	0.32	39	COL	0.71	70	GNQ	0.20	101	LBR	0.57	132	OMN	0.64	163	TGO	0.32
9	AUS	0.96	40	COM	0.12	71	GRC	0.88	102	LBY	0.35	133	PAK	0.75	164	THA	0.89
10	AUT	0.95	41	CPV	0.25	72	GRD	0.24	103	LCA	0.17	134	PAN	0.86	165	TJK	0.12
11	AZE	0.36	42	CRI	0.55	73	GRL	0.13	104	LKA	0.62	135	PER	0.71	166	TKM	0.23
12	BDI	0.24	43	CUB	0.36	74	GTM	0.57	105	LSO	0.14	136	PHL	0.80	167	TON	0.07
13	BEL	0.96	44	CYM	0.18	75	GUY	0.16	106	LUX	0.90	137	PNG	0.24	168	TTO	0.41
14	BEN	0.32	45	CYP	0.84	76	HKG	1.03	107	LVA	0.59	138	POL	0.84	169	TUN	0.58
15	BFA	0.33	46	CZE	0.78	77	HND	0.45	108	MAC	0.50	139	PRT	0.96	170	TUR	0.92
16	BGD	0.61	47	DEU	1.07	78	HRV	0.61	109	MAR	0.70	140	PRY	0.54	171	TWN	0.88
17	BGR	0.74	48	DJI	0.21	79	HTI	0.27	110	MDA	0.27	141	PYF	0.04	172	TZA	0.52
18	BHR	0.77	49	DMA	0.30	80	HUN	0.84	111	MDG	0.36	142	QAT	0.66	173	UGA	0.48
19	BHS	0.85	50	DNK	0.96	81	IDN	0.71	112	MDV	0.25	143	ROU	0.62	174	UKR	0.65
20	BIH	0.41	51	DOM	0.56	82	IND	0.98	113	MEX	0.89	144	RUS	0.86	175	URY	0.71
21	BLR	0.45	52	DZA	0.56	83	IRL	0.92	114	MKD	0.44	145	RWA	0.37	176	USA	0.98
22	BLZ	0.52	53	ECU	0.61	84	IRN	0.69	115	MLI	0.29	146	SAU	0.84	177	UZB	0.38
23	BMU	0.70	54	EGY	0.77	85	IRQ	0.34	116	MLT	0.74	147	SDN	0.21	178	VCT	0.34
24	BOL	0.47	55	ESP	1.02	86	ISL	0.62	117	MMR	0.28	148	SEN	0.50	179	VEN	0.50
25	BRA	0.97	56	EST	0.58	87	ISR	0.85	118	MNG	0.30	149	SGP	0.97	180	VNM	0.67
26	BRB	0.52	57	ETH	0.41	88	ITA	1.01	119	MOZ	0.44	150	SLB	0.13	181	VUT	0.32
27	BRN	0.38	58	FIN	0.91	89	JAM	0.43	120	MRT	0.29	151	SLE	0.24	182	WSM	0.28
28	BTN	0.09	59	FJI	0.27	90	JOR	0.66	121	MUS	0.63	152	SLV	0.43	183	YEM	0.40
29	BWA	0.36	60	FRA	1.01	91	JPN	1.07	122	MWI	0.29	153	SOM	0.03	184	ZAF	0.90
30	CAF	0.24	61	FRO	0.10	92	KAZ	0.54	123	MYS	0.85	154	STP	0.08	185	ZMB	0.43
31	CAN	1.09	62	FSM	0.07	93	KEN	0.66	124	NCL	0.03	155	SUR	0.23	186	ZWE	0.51

Table A.3. Variable description.

Variables	Description	Source
LnC	Natural logarithm of cross-border banking claims.	BIS
Dejure	The dummy taking a value of 1 if a country has explicit or implicit sustainability objectives.	ICBLD
DirectDejure	The dummy taking value of 1 if a country has explicit sustainability goals.	ICBLD
GCBA	The dummy taking a value of 1 if country i's central bank takes green activity in year t.	ICBLD
TotalGCBA	The sum of $GCBA_{it}$ up to year t.	ICBLD
GDP	Log value of GDP in country i(home country) in year t.	The World Bank database
contig	The dummy taking a value of 1 if there is a contiguity between two countries.	CEPII
comlang_off	The dummy taking a value of 1 if two countries have the same official language.	CEPII
colony	The dummy taking a value of 1 if two countries have the colonial relationship.	CEPII
comcol	The dummy taking a value of 1 if a country is a common coloniser post 1945.	CEPII
rta	The dummy taking a value of 1 if a country has a regional trade agreement.	CEPII
D	Log value of the distance between country i and j, and 0 otherwise.	CEPII
comrelig	The dummy taking a value of 1 if two countries have the same region.	WTO

Note: BIS: Bank for International Settlements Locational Banking Statistics; ICBLD: the IMF's Central Bank Legislation Database; CEPII: The Centre d'Etudes Prospectives et d'Informations Internationales.

References

Adams, S., Adom, P. K., and Klobodu, E. K. M. (2016). Urbanisation, regime type and durability, and environmental degradation in Ghana, *Environmental Science and Pollution Research*, 23(23), pp. 23825–23839.

Akomea-Frimpong, I., Adeabah, D., Ofosu, D., and Tenakwah, E. J. (2021). A review of studies on green finance of banks, research gaps and future directions. *Journal of Sustainable Finance and Investment*, 12(4), pp. 1–24.

Austin, J. (1885). *Lectures on Jurisprudence, or, the Philosophy of Positive Law*. Lawbook Exchange.

Bank of England (2015). The impact of climate change on the UK insurance sector. *A Climate Change Adaptation Report.*

Barth, J. R., Caprio, G., and Levine, R. (2004). Bank regulation and supervision: What works best? *Journal of Financial Intermediation*, 13(2), pp. 205–248. doi.org/10.1016/j.jfi.2003.06.002.

Batten, S., Sowerbutts, R., and Tanaka, M. (2016). Let's talk about the weather: The impact of climate change on central banks. Bank of England Working Paper No. 603. Available at: https://econpapers.repec.org/paper/boeboeewp/0603.htm.

Blackstone (1979). Commentaries on the laws of England, *Britannica.* Available at: https://www.britannica.com/topic/Commentaries-on-the-Laws-of-England, accessed 27/05/21.

Bremus, F. and Fratzscher, M. (2015). Drivers of structural change in cross-border banking since the global financial crisis, *Journal of International Money and Finance*, 52, pp. 32–59. doi.org/10.1016/j.jimonfin.2014.11.012.

Busch, P.-O., Heinzel, M., Kempken, M., and Liese, A. (2020). Mind the Gap? Comparing *de facto* and *de jure* expert authority of international public administrations in financial and agricultural policy, *Journal of Comparative Policy Analysis: Research and Practice*, 0(0), pp, 1–24. doi.org/10.1080/13876988.2020.1820866.

Campiglio, E., Dafermos, Y., Monnin, P., Ryan-Collins, J., Schotten, G., and Tanaka, M. (2018). Climate change challenges for central banks and financial regulators, *Nature Climate Change*, 8(6), pp. 462–468. doi.org/10.1038/s41558-018-0175-0.

Carney, M. (2015). Breaking the tragedy of the horizon–climate change and financial stability, *Speech given at Lloyd's of London*, 29, pp. 220–230.

Cassotta, S. and Mazza, M. (2014). Balancing *de jure* and *de facto* arctic environmental law applied to the oil and gas industry: Linking indigenous rights, social impact assessment and business in Greenland, *The Yearbook of Polar Law Online*, 6(1), pp. 63–119. doi.org/10.1163/1876-8814_004.

Chappell, J., German, L., McKay, S. K., and Pringle, C. (2020). Evaluating mismatches between legislation and practice in maintaining environmental flows, *Water,* 12(8), p. 2135.

Choi, S. and Furceri, D. (2019). Uncertainty and cross-border banking flows, *Journal of International Money and Finance*, 93, pp. 260–274.

Claessens, S., and Van Horen, N. (2014). Foreign banks: Trends and impact, *Journal of Money, Credit and Banking*, 46(s1), pp. 295–326.

Cox, D. G. and Drury, A. C. (2006). Democratic sanctions: Connecting the democratic peace and economic sanctions, *Journal of Peace Research*, 43(6), pp. 709–722.

Dafe, F. and Volz, U. (2015). Financing global development: The role of Central Banks, SSRN Scholarly Paper ID: 2797226. *Social Science Research Network*. doi.org/10.2139/ssrn.2797226.

Dell'Ariccia, G., Detragiache, E., and Rajan, R. (2008). The real effect of banking crises, *Journal of Financial Intermediation*, 17(1), pp. 89–112. doi.org/10.1016/j.jfi.2007.06.001.

Dikau, S. and Volz, U. (2018). Central banking, climate change and green finance.

Dikau, S. and Volz, U. (2019). Central banking, climate change, and green finance, in Sachs, J. D., Woo, W. T., Yoshino, N., and Taghizadeh-Hesary, F. (eds.), *Handbook of Green Finance: Energy Security and Sustainable Development* (Springer), pp. 81–102. doi.org/10.1007/978-981-13-0227-5_17.

Dikau, S. and Volz, U. (2021). Central bank mandates, sustainability objectives and the promotion of green finance. *Ecological Economics, 184*, 107022.

Doan, N. T., Le, T. H., To, T. T., Truong, T. N. T., and Nguyen, T. T. H. (2021). Cultural distance and cross-border bank linkages, *Economic Systems*, 45(1), art. no. 100854. doi.org/10.1016/j.ecosys.2021.100854

Fehr, E. and Gaechter, S. (2011). Do incentive contracts crowd out voluntary cooperation? IEW — Working Papers No. 034, Institute for Empirical Research in Economics — University of Zurich. Available at: https://econpapers.repec.org/paper/zuriewwpx/034.htm, last accessed: 27/05/21.

Frame, W. S., Mihov, A., and Sanz, L. (2020). Foreign investment, regulatory arbitrage, and the risk of U.S. banking organizations, *Journal of Financial and Quantitative Analysis*, 55(3), pp. 955–988. doi.org/10.1017/S0022109019000267.

Frey, B. S. and Oberholzer-Gee, F. (1997). The cost of price incentives: An empirical analysis of motivation crowding-out, *The American Economic Review*, 87(4), pp. 746–755.

Fukuyama, F. (2011). Is there a proper sequence in democratic transitions? *Current History*, 110, pp. 308–310. doi.org/10.1525/curh.2011.110.739.308.

Gao, J. and Jang, Y. (2021). What drives global lending syndication? Effects of cross-country capital regulation gaps, *Review of Finance*, 25(2), pp. 519–559. doi.org/10.1093/rof/rfaa019.

Gonzalez, F. (2005). Bank regulation and risk-taking incentives: An international comparison of bank risk, *Journal of Banking and Finance*, 29(5), pp. 1153–1184.

Green, J. F. (2014). *Rethinking Private Authority: Agents and Entrepreneurs in Global Environmental Governance* (Princeton University Press). Available at: https://www.jstor.org/stable/j.ctt5hhqdr.

Hanretty, C. and Koop, C. (2013). Shall the law set them free? The formal and actual independence of regulatory agencies, *Regulation and Governance*, 7(2), pp. 195–214. doi.org/10.1111/j.1748-5991.2012.01156.x.

Henisz, W. J. (2000). The institutional environment for multinational investment, *Journal of Law, Economics, and Organization*, 16(2), pp. 334–364.

Houston, J. F., Lin, C., and Ma, Y. (2012a). Regulatory arbitrage and international bank flows, *The Journal of Finance*, 67(5), pp. 1845–1895. doi.org/10.1111/j.1540-6261.2012.01774.x.

Houston, J. F., Lin, C., and Ma, Y. (2012b). Regulatory arbitrage and international bank flows, *The Journal of Finance*, 67(5), pp. 1845–1895.

IFC (2017). *Green Finance: A Bottom-up Approach to Track Existing Flows.* The World Bank. Available at: https://documents.worldbank.org/en/publication/documents-reports/documentdetail/788041573021878350/Full-Report.

Karolyi, G. A. and Taboada, A. G. (2015). Regulatory arbitrage and cross-border bank acquisitions, *The Journal of Finance*, 70(6), pp. 2395–2450. doi.org/10.1111/jofi.12262.

Katznelson, I. and Weingast, B. R. (eds.) (2005). *Preferences and Situations: Points of Intersection Between Historical and Rational Choice In* (Russell Sage Foundation). Available at: https://www.jstor.org/stable/10.7758/9781610443333.

Khwaja, A. I. and Mian, A. (2008). Tracing the impact of bank liquidity shocks: Evidence from an emerging market, *American Economic Review*, 98(4), pp. 1413–1442. doi.org/10.1257/aer.98.4.1413.

Kling, G., Lo, Y. C., Murinde, V., and Volz, U. (2018). Climate vulnerability and the cost of debt. Available at: SSRN 3198093.

Kose, M. A., Prasad, E. S., and Taylor, A. D. (2011). Thresholds in the process of international financial integration, *Journal of International Money and Finance*, 30(1), pp. 147–179. doi.org/10.1016/j.jimonfin.2010.08.005.

Lewkowicz, J., and Metelska-Szaniawska, K. (2020). De jure/de facto institutions, in Marciano, A., and Ramello, G. B. (eds.), *Encyclopedia of Law and Economics* (Springer), pp. 1–5. Available at: https://doi.org/10.1007/978-1-4614-7883-6_661-3.

McKibbin, W., Morris, A., Panton, A. J., and Wilcoxen, P. J. (2017). Climate change and monetary policy: Dealing with disruption (*CAMA Working Papers No. 2017-77*). Centre for Applied Macroeconomic Analysis, Crawford School of Public Policy, The Australian National University. Available at: https://ideas.repec.org/p/een/camaaa/2017-77.html.

Mechkova, V., Lührmann, A., and Lindberg, S. I. (2019). The accountability sequence: From de-jure to de-facto constraints on governments, *Studies in Comparative International Development*, 54(1). pp. 40–70. doi.org/10.1007/s12116-018-9262-5.

Melton, J. and Ginsburg, T. (2014). Does de jure judicial independence really matter?: A reevaluation of explanations for judicial independence, *Journal of Law and Courts*, 2(2), pp. 187–217. doi.org/10.1086/676999.

Morgan, T. C. and Palmer, G. (2003). To protect and to serve: Alliances and foreign policy portfolios, *Journal of Conflict Resolution*, 47(2), pp. 180–203.

Ngwu, F. N., Ogbechie, C., and Ojah, K. (2019). Growing cross-border banking in Sub-Saharan Africa and the need for a regional centralised regulatory authority, *Journal of Banking Regulation*, 20(3), pp. 274–285.

Ongena, S., Popov, A., and Udell, G. F. (2013). "When the cat's away the mice will play": Does regulation at home affect bank risk-taking abroad? *Journal of Financial Economics*, 108(3), pp. 727–750. doi.org/10.1016/j.jfineco.2013.01.006.

Palmer, G., Wohlander, S. B., and Morgan, T. C. (2002). Give or take: Foreign aid and foreign policy substitutability, *Journal of Peace Research*, 39(1), pp. 5–26.

Posner, R. A. (1997). Social norms and the law: An economic approach, *The American Economic Review*, 87(2), pp. 365–369.

Rothstein, B. and Teorell, J. (2008). What is quality of government? A theory of impartial government institutions. *Governance*, 21(2), pp. 165–190. doi.org/10.1111/j.1468-0491.2008.00391.x.

Sarma, P. and Roy, A. (2021). A scientometric analysis of literature on green banking (1995-March 2019), *Journal of Sustainable Finance and Investment*, 11(2), pp. 143–162. doi.org/10.1080/20430795.2020.1711500.

Semieniuk, G., Campiglio, E., Mercure, J.-F., Volz, U. and Edwards, N. R. (2021). Low-carbon transition risks for finance, *Wiley Interdisciplinary Reviews: Climate Change*, 12(1), p. e678.

Thakor, A. V. (1996). Capital requirements, monetary policy, and aggregate bank lending: Theory and empirical evidence, *The Journal of Finance*, 51(1), pp. 279–324. doi.org/10.1111/j.1540-6261.1996.tb05210.x.

Tokunaga, M. (2020). Regime change and environmental reform: A systematic review of research on Central and Eastern Europe.

Urban, M. A. and Wójcik, D. (2019). Dirty banking: Probing the gap in sustainable finance, *Sustainability*, 11(6), p. 1745. doi.org/10.3390/su11061745.

Voigt, S., Gutmann, J., and Feld, L. P. (2015). Economic growth and judicial independence, a dozen years on: Cross-country evidence using an updated Set of indicators, *European Journal of Political Economy*, 38, pp. 197–211. doi.org/10.1016/j.ejpoleco.2015.01.004.

Volz, U. (2017). *On the Role of Central Banks in Enhancing Green Finance*. Inquiry Working Paper 17/01. Knowledge Repository — UNEP. https://wedocs.unep.org/20.500.11822/16803.

Volz, U., Beirne, J., Ambrosio Preudhomme, N., Fenton, A., Mazzacurati, E., Renzhi, N., and Stampe, J. (2020). *Climate Change and Sovereign Risk*. London, Tokyo, Singapore, and Berkeley, CA: SOAS University of London, Asian Development Bank Institute, World Wide Fund for Nature Singapore, and Four Twenty Seven.

Volz, U., Böhnke, J., Knierim, L., Richert, K., Röber, G.-M., and Eidt, V. (2015). *Financing the Green Transformation — How to Make Green Finance Work in Indonesia* (Houndmills, Basingstoke, UK: Palgrave Macmillan). Available at: https://doi.org/10.1057/9781137486127.

Weber, O. and ElAlfy, A. (2019). The development of green finance by sector, in Migliorelli, M., and Dessertine, P. (eds.), *The Rise of Green Finance in Europe: Opportunities and Challenges for Issuers, Investors and Marketplaces* (Springer International), pp. 53–78. doi.org/10.1007/978-3-030-22510-0_3.

Yuan, F. and Gallagher, K. P. (2018). Greening development lending in the Americas: Trends and determinants, *Ecological Economics*, 154, pp. 189–200. doi.org/10.1016/j.ecolecon.2018.07.009.

Zhang, D., Zhang, Z., and Managi, S. (2019). A bibliometric analysis on green finance: Current status, development, and future directions, *Finance Research Letters*, 29, pp. 425–430. doi.org/10.1016/j.frl.2019.02.003.

https://doi.org/10.1142/9781800614604_0009

Chapter 9

Women and Digital Green Finance

Nimisha Tailor
E-nomics, Singapore
Economic Society of Singapore,
Department of Economics,
National University of Singapore, Singapore
nimisha@e-nomics.com

The pandemic has triggered economies to rethink, rebuild, and transform into inclusive, environmentally friendly digital societies and businesses. A key enabler for the vision is technology, and women are driving the adoption of digital and green financial solutions to achieve economic and social goals. This chapter highlights how women are playing a greater role in protecting the environment, fighting climate change, and addressing financial inclusivity, all through digital finance. However, women are still under-represented, despite being more adversely affected by environmental issues and having less access to digital finance than men. This chapter provides recommendations for using digital financial technology to tackle environmental sustainability and gender equality at the same time.

Keywords: Gender equality; digital finance; financial inclusion; women; climate change; environment

1. Introduction

The COVID-19 pandemic has given economies the opportunity to rethink, rebuild, and transform towards inclusive, environmentally friendly, digital societies and businesses. As the pandemic changes the way people live and work, technology is a key enabler for environmental sustainability and gender financial inclusion. Women are a powerful force that can unlock the benefits of digitalisation and achieve an inclusive and greener future, particularly as the pandemic has widened the gender gap. Through the use of digital finance, women as fintech entrepreneurs, business leaders, investors, and policymakers can support and empower women affected by climate change, by prioritising environmental issues and designing digital green financial products.

Artificial intelligence (AI), Internet of Things (IoT), distributed ledger technologies (DLT), and the growing scale and scope of data, have led to an explosion of innovative fintech products and businesses. These digital solutions are providing women with convenient and affordable financial products and services. Governments, central banks, and international organisations are implementing policies and strategies to ensure more women gain access to digital finance. Internationally, the G20 is committed to inclusive digital finance for women and has developed high-level principles for countries to follow (GPFI, 2022). Thus, over the past decade, more women are using digital financial services like digital payments and mobile money (Demirgüç-Kunt *et al.*, 2022). At the same time, female fintech entrepreneurs have emerged, with some focusing on providing financial services to female consumers. However, despite the progress, access and the use of digital finance by women remain unequal across countries.

This is not the only challenge that women are facing. Women in rural areas are affected by climate change more than men, yet they tend to have less access to digital finance. Improving the availability and use of digital finance is a key solution in mitigating and adapting to the financial risks of extreme weather changes and transitioning to a low-carbon economy. Having more women in senior positions in the financial sector, as advocates for green solutions, will help tailor digital green financial products for women, benefitting society and the economy. Senior women as policymakers in the financial and environmental sector can boost investment and regulatory support for vulnerable women. In fact, more women in the green economy could increase global annual GDP by roughly US$1.5 trillion (Sqalli *et al.*, 2021).

Given the interdependencies of climate change, the environment, and gender equality, governments and central banks should rethink and reshape policies to encourage the adoption of technology that meets women's needs and their desire to care for the environment.

In this chapter, Section 2 describes the landscape for women in digital finance, namely, the benefits, the different types of digital financial services used, and examples of inspiring female-founded fintech start-ups. Section 3 presents the environmental and digital challenges for women, as well as the lack of women in decision-making roles, "the representation challenge" to drive further change. Section 4 discusses the opportunities for women in digital green finance and Section 5 explains how government can rethink digital finance and environmental policies with a holistic approach.

2. The Landscape for Women and Digital Finance

2.1. *Enabling financial inclusion*

Digital technology has transformed financial services by creating innovative fintech companies, providing products and services like payments, credit, and insurance, accessed and delivered through digital channels. Digital financial products and services are providing women with significant benefits but they can be further maximised by understanding the types of products and services women use and how women are disrupting the fintech industry to better serve female consumers.

2.1.1. *Benefits*

Women account for 85% of consumer spending (Yankelovich Monitor and Greenfield Online, 2020). Around the world, there are 252 million female entrepreneurs, and another 153 million women operate well-established businesses (Elam *et al.*, 2019). With women making a number of different financial decisions every day, digital finance can provide faster and safer transactions, saving time and money. A study in Kenya shows that mobile money services enabled women-headed households to increase their savings by more than a fifth (Better Than Cash Alliance, 2020). In Liberia, when salaries were digitalised, teachers saved an average of 13.5 hours, every 2 weeks, and reduced the cost of collecting their income by 90% (Hendricks, 2019).

Key user benefits for women include greater control over their money; lower transaction costs; increased savings; ease of borrowing money; less time spent travelling to a traditional branch; faster transfer of social benefits; greater opportunities to invest, particularly for their own business; and less exposure to crime from cash transactions. These benefits can have social and economic multiplier effects, as more women use digital financial solutions when they see other women doing so.

2.1.2. *Female users*

More women are gaining access to digital financial services compared to a decade ago. In 2014, it was estimated that 41% of females around the world made or received a digital payment. By 2021, this rose to 60% (see Fig. 1). Digital government payments have boosted adoption. In 2017, globally, 80 million women opened their first accounts to receive digital government payments, such as safety net subsidies, public pension funds, or public sector wage payments (Demirgüç-Kunt *et al.*, 2018). During the pandemic, the government rushed to provide financial assistance and used digital payments, so by 2021 around 423 million women in developing economies had opened their first account to receive money from the government (Demirgüç-Kunt *et al.*, 2022). However, there continues to be a gender gap in digital finance, especially in developing economies.

2.1.3. *Adoption of products and services*

Women are benefitting from different types of digital financial products and services. Popular forms include digital payments (see Fig. 1) which increased in a number of regions during 2014–2021 (Demirgüç-Kunt *et al.*, 2022) and mobile money which grew twice as fast as had been forecast for 2020 (GSMA, 2021). Mobile money accounts can be used to carry out different types of transactions, providing a gateway to a wider range of digital financial products and services (Demirgüç-Kunt *et al.*, 2022).

The type of financial product or service used depends on a woman's needs. These needs vary for women living in urban or

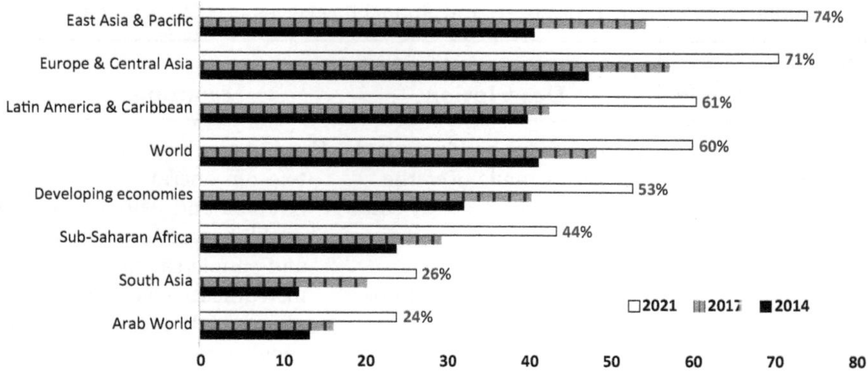

Fig. 1. Percentage of digital payments made by women during 2014–2021. *Source*: The Global Findex Database 2021 survey data (Demirgüç-Kunt *et al.*, 2022).

remote rural regions, as well as for women in developed and devloping economies (see Table 1). It also depends on the countries' stage of digital transformation, which starts with basic access to transaction accounts (Tanzania, Vietnam, and Pakistan), to intensive use of transaction accounts for digital payments (Brazil and India), followed by widespread adoption by women (China and Sweden) (Pazarbasioglu *et al.*, 2020).

Many fintech companies are specifically targeting women. In India, Upwards offers a personal loan exclusively for professional working women. In the US, Nav.it is a financial app helping women pay for loans, automate savings, and track spending. Women are also using a new generation of digital financial services such as Buy-Now Pay-Later (BPNL) services, cryptocurrency, robo-advisory investment platforms, as well as crowdfunding platforms (Brolos and Taylor, 2020). In Australia, a 2019 survey found that the number of female respondents using BPNL payments was over double compared to men (Granwal, 2022).

2.1.4. *Women in fintech*

In addition to being users of digital finance, women are taking a greater role in developing and implementing digital finance, as fintech entrepreneurs. Since 2010, female-founded and co-founded fintechs have grown to 369 in 2019, which is an eight-fold growth, while

Table 1. Different types of digital financial services used by women.

Type of Product/Service	Description	Example
Digital payments	Payments for products and services made over the Internet, e.g., credit cards and mobile payments at point of sale via smartphone applications.	E-commerce platforms or telecom operators (Go-Jek and Alibaba) are enabling digital payments and simple savings instruments using mobile phones, QR codes, and agent networks.
Cross-border remittances	Transfers can be made by connecting to local payment infrastructures and banks or e-money providers.	New fintechs such as Transferwise and MFS Africa.
Digital lending	Digital lending can be tailored to user needs and facilitated using machine learning models without human intervention.	Ant Financial's loans require three minutes to apply, one second to approve, and zero bank staff.
Digital insurance	Digital insurance products, including vehicle, travel, and health insurance, tailored to user needs and delivered through apps or marketplaces.	Some fintech start-ups are using satellite data and machine learning to offer digital insurance and loans to farmers.
Digital investment	Allows online investment in instruments such as bonds, mutual funds, or money market funds.	Kenya's M-Akiba government bond was issued to small savers who invested via their mobile wallet.

Notes: Adapted from Pazarbasioglu *et al.* (2020).

male-founded start-ups grew seven-fold (Eckenrode, 2020). In Latin America, there are five times as many female-founded fintechs as the global average (Acuña Rivera and Mitchell, 2020).

Some women-owned fintechs are catering to women, especially those that are underserved and underbanked (See Box 1). Female fintech communities have also been established. The Women in Fintech Network is a global platform for women to share knowledge and industry experience. In Singapore, the strong fintech community has a large industry association with an active Women in Fintech subcommittee.

Box 1: Women-owned fintech companies

Ellevest was founded in 2014 to assist women to start investing (Cashen, 2021). The US company developed an investment algorithm, taking into account specific issues that may affect its female user base, such as career breaks, longer average life spans, and pay gaps. In 2021, the company achieved US$1 billion in assets under management.

Lucy is a Singapore-based fintech launched in 2021 (FinEquity, 2022). The company focuses on female migrant workers and allows them to receive online salary payments and send money online to banks and mobile wallets. In 2020, it raised US$365,787 in an all-women pre-seed round with female investors from the UK, the US, Singapore, Somalia, Mexico, India, Indonesia, Hong Kong, the Netherlands, Australia, New Zealand, Vietnam, and Germany (Yu, 2020).

2.2. *Enabling environmental sustainability*

Digital finance is increasingly being used by the public and private financial sector to address the number of environmental issues that pose financial risks. With the rapid pace of digitalisation, companies, central banks, investors, and entrepreneurs are using technology to create new financial services, products, strategies, and commercial models that meet sustainable development priorities. For example, AI and Environmental, Social, and Governance (ESG) data are being used to design green financial solutions and assist with investment decision-making. Blockchain is improving the transparency and traceability of critical information to measure and monitor climate impact.

In light of this trend, a growing number of studies are researching how big data, AI, blockchain, cryptocurrency, tokenisation, and IoT can provide a means of mitigating and adapting to climate change (Puschmann *et al.*, 2020). Some studies, most notably from the

Alliance of Financial Inclusion (AFI), highlight how fintech can make green finance more inclusive of vulnerable groups (Volz *et al.*, 2020). Fintech companies have wide distribution channels and low customer acquisition costs, making green finance more accessible to small business and individual users (Stockholm Green Digital Finance, 2017). Indeed, many fintechs are going green (Muhn, 2021). Offerings include digital banking; savings accounts that use client deposits to finance climate-positive projects; a credit card that rewards consumer purchases by using merchant-paid fees to buy carbon offsets; tracking services that connect to users' payment cards to analyse their carbon footprint; and crowdfunding services to fund solar energy products.

However, few studies take an in-depth look at climate change and digital finance for women. Applying a gender lens is vital as women are more financially impacted by climate change and do not always have the necessary tools and support to manage their financial risks.

2.2.1. *Women leading environmental action*

Studies show that women are proactive when it comes to environmental issues in both their professional and personal lives (OECD, 2014). At a personal level, women are more likely to recycle, minimise waste, buy organic food and eco-labelled products, and engage in water and energy savings initiatives at the household level (Yaccato and Jaeger, 2003). Professionally, women on corporate boards consistently prioritise ESG issues, including climate and sustainability (OECD, 2022 and McElhaney and Mobasseri 2012), and research suggests that they are delivering positive results as companies with a higher percentage of female managers are likely to have lower levels of carbon emission (Altunbas, 2022).

Women are also more likely to pursue careers in sustainability than men. In the US, the percentage of females with the position of Chief Sustainability Officer nearly doubled, from 28% in 2011 to 54% in 2021 (Weinreb Group, 2021). Further, 58% of sustainability executives in large companies are female (GreenBiz, 2020).

Women are interested in investing in green finance and their investment portfolio tends to perform better than men because of their less speculative approach (Yiu, 2022).

Finally, women are becoming green entrepreneurs (See Box 2). An Australian green entrepreneurship training programme found that women were more engaged in greening their businesses (Braun, 2010). In Singapore, the Women in Sustainability and Environment (WISE) network, launched in response to COP26 Glasgow, supports green investment opportunities for women-led businesses.[a]

Box 2: Women as green entrepreneurs

A female finance manager in Indonesia established a start-up called Sumba Sustainable Solutions (3S), to provide schools, villages, and community health centres with access to solar power. 3S also provides solar systems for people's homes and solar-powered productivity centres, which are energy hubs for the community. These solutions are improving the quality of life for many women in Sumba (New Energy Nexus, 2021).

In Greece, a female civil and environmental engineer, volunteering in Nigeria to provide green energy, co-founded Dataphoria, which provides a data-driven solution (Analytics-as-a-Service) for organisations to measure, optimise, and report their sustainability transition.[b]

3. Environmental and Digital Challenges for Women

3.1. *The "environmental" challenge*

Even though women are more likely to tackle climate change and protect the environment, gender equality continues to be a pressing issue as women continue to be disproportionately affected by local and environmental change. Women as caregivers and providers of food suffer more from severe weather changes. Natural disasters like flooding and drought, exacerbated by climate change, affect women and their families and businesses, as their incomes are exposed to environmental risks (AFI, 2021). Studies have found that 80% of people displaced by climate change are women (WEN, 2010 UNDP, 2017).

[a]Women in Sustainability and Environment website: https://www.wise.org.sg/about-us/wise/.

[b]Dataphoria website: https://www.dataphoria.gr/.

Women in rural areas are affected by climate change for the following reasons (Osman-Elasha, 2012):

- Many of the women in rural areas work in the agricultural sector;
- Rural women have limited access to and control of land or environmental goods and services;
- Rural women have less access to education and information to manage climate-related risks to agriculture and livestock (WHO, 2011);
- Rural women have less access to funds or loans to cover weather-related losses or adaptation technologies (UNDP, 2017).

Women in developed economies are also likely to be at risk, although to a lesser extent (BIS, 2021). They too are being impacted by a growing number of extreme climate disasters (e.g., extensive wildfires in Canada and the US; severe floods affecting Belgium, Germany, the Netherlands, and Switzerland) and suffering financial losses.

Better access to digital finance can empower women to overcome some of these challenges, build resilience, and adapt and mitigate their exposure to climate change. However, this approach comes with its own digital challenges for women, particularly in developing economies.

> *Women, in particular, often bear the brunt of poverty and limited access to economic opportunity, including unfavourable financial access ... Inequality is not just a moral issue — it is a macroeconomic issue ... Growth has to be more inclusive, and for this, finance has to be more inclusive ... to close the gender and inequality gap.*
>
> Christine Lagarde, Managing Director,
> International Monetary Fund (IMF, 2014)

3.2. *The "digital" challenge*

Despite some progress, women still lag behind men as digital users. Women make up 55% of the world's unbanked population (WEF, 2021). Around 1 billion women have no access to savings or checking accounts, or financial products like insurance, credit facilities, and loans. In fact, many women do not even have access to a mobile phone. The GSMA Gender Gap Report 2020 shows that the gender gap in mobile phone ownership averages 8% in low- and middle-income countries, ranging from 1% in Latin America and the Caribbean to 23% in South Asia (GSMA, 2021). The pandemic has not improved the situation.

Even when women have access to digital finance, their usage is lower than men. On average, in developing economies, 67% of women with an account report making or receiving digital payments, compared with 72% of men with an account (GPFI, 2022). In Mexico and China, nearly one-third of women with mobile phones do not use mobile internet because of lack of digital skills (OECD, 2019). Women also have lower financial literacy and many female entrepreneurs do not even apply for loans for this very reason (Morsy, 2020). Women also tend to worry about their privacy when dealing with online companies and are less willing to share their data with fintechs (Chen *et al.*, 2021).

3.3. *The "representation" challenge*

Despite the financial industry being digitally transformed, the number of women in decision-making roles has not kept pace. Senior women working in finance all over the world continue to be under-represented. In Greece, Japan, and South Korea, only 4% of women are on executive committees (Clempner, 2020).

Globally, only 5.6% of all fintech CEOs are women (Fintech Diversity Radar, 2021), less than 2% of banks' CEOs are women, and less than 20% of board seats at banks are held by women (IMF, 2017). In 2021, the proportion of women in leadership roles within financial service firms was 24% and is projected to only grow to 28% by 2030 (Rogish, *et al.*, 2021). The OMFIF Gender Balance Index 2021 found that out of 540 institutions surveyed only 71 were headed by women and 56 had no women in their executive teams or on their boards (OMFIF, 2021).

The public sector also suffers from a lack of senior female representation. One-fifth of central banks have no women in senior positions and there are only 14 central banks in the world that have a woman in the top job as Governor (OMFIF, 2020).

Women are also under-represented as policymakers in the environmental sector. In 2015, the International Union for Conservation of Nature (IUCN) Environment and Gender Information data showed that only 12% of 881 national environmental ministries across 193 countries were led by women (IUCN, 2015). Five years later, in 2020, there continued to be insufficient women, as only 15% of the ministries had women in the top job.

4. Opportunities for Women in Digital Green Finance

4.1. *Linking financial inclusion and environmental sustainability*

To overcome the environmental challenges and maximise the benefits of digitalisation, there is an opportunity to tackle the connected issues by increasing female participation as business leaders, investors, board members, policymakers and even consumers (see Fig. 2). An AFI study shows that there is a link between green finance and financial inclusion, and inclusive digital green finance can help women adapt to global environmental change and strengthen their resilience (Volz *et al.*, 2020). The OECD has advocated for good practice examples on aligning green financing and green investment with gender equality and women's economic empowerment goals (OECD, 2022). For banks, climate change (87%), gender equality (80%), and financial inclusion (76%) are their most prominent sustainability goals (Statista, 2022).

When women access digital financial services, they are better positioned to start and invest in businesses and provide for their families and be less exposed to environmental shocks and transition to a low-carbon economy. Such access would contribute to climate change, gender equality, and poverty alleviation, which are three of the United Nations' 2030 Sustainable Development Goals (SDG 13, 5, 1, respectively).[c] These SDG goals are interdependent and financial inclusion is a key enabler (UNSGA, 2018 and UNCDF, 2022). Increasing the role of women has the potential to drive compliance with the Paris Agreement on Climate Change which acknowledges the need for gender considerations.[d] Targeting green fintech solutions

[c]United Nations Sustainable Development Goals (SDGs). Available at: https://sdgs.un.org/2030agenda.

[d]There are also references to gender-responsive adaptation action (Art. 7) and capacity-building (Art. 11).

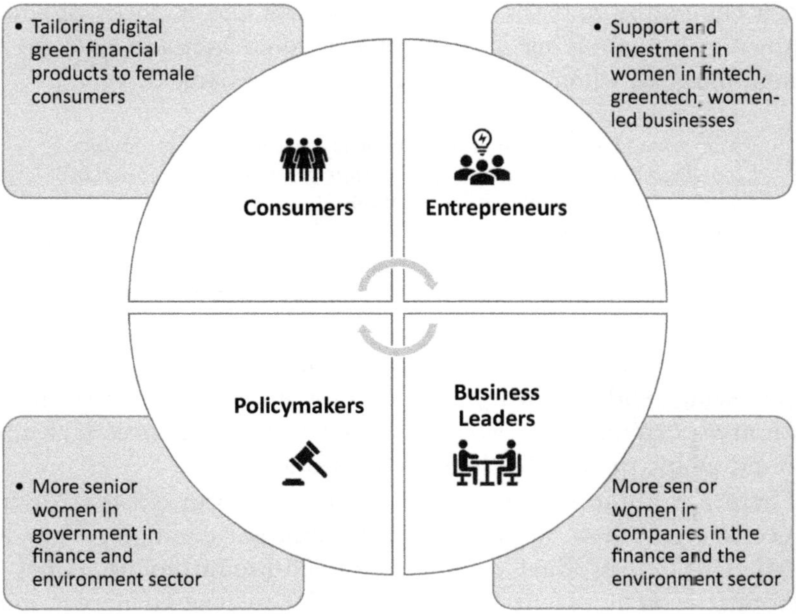

Fig. 2. Increasing the role of women in digital green finance.

to women, increasing gender lens investing, and raising senior female participation are key solutions, all of which are discussed further in detail in the following sections.

> *Climate change is a common concern of humankind. Parties should, when taking action to address climate change, respect, promote and consider their respective obligations on human rights, the right to health, the rights of indigenous peoples, local communities, migrants, children, persons with disabilities and people in vulnerable situations and the right to development, as well as gender equality, empowerment of women and intergenerational equity.*
>
> Paris Agreement on Climate Change

4.1.1. *Tailoring green fintech for women*

Developing current and future digital green finance innovations to suit women can deliver economic and social benefits. It is estimated that financial service firms are missing out on at least US$700 billion, in revenue, each year, by not fully meeting the needs of female customers (Clempner, 2020). At the same time, the number of green fintech companies and the types of products and services provided is growing, but applying a gender focus could increase take up by women, many of whom are underserved and unbanked.

> *The product you are selling to men is probably a good product for them. But the product you design for women is going to work better for everybody. Unfortunately, it does not work the other way around.*
>
> Mary Ellen Iskenderian, President and CEO,
> Women's World Banking

Redesigning green fintech offerings like green credit cards and online savings and borrowing accounts for women in both rural and urban areas can empower women to control their finances and mitigate and adapt to climate change (see Table 2).

There are untapped opportunities to transform existing digital finance to reach more women in rural areas. For example, a pay-as-you-go (PAYGo) product has increased the use of mobile money in developing economies but has the potential to benefit more women if the digital challenges are addressed (see Box 3).

4.1.2. *Increasing female representation*

Given that women are taking the lead on environmental issues, there is scope to draw on their expertise and increase the representation of women in senior positions in relation to digital green finance. Greater female representation can drive innovation, and increase productivity and profitability, leading to better environmental outcomes. A company with 30% or more women on its corporate board produces superior climate governance and innovation (BloombergNEF, 2020). Other studies show that boosting female entrepreneurs in green tech would add US$500 billion to US$600 billion to global GDP annually by 2030 (Lambert, 2020), and more women in green sectors would translate into more small business formation and innovations. Within government, studies have found that countries with higher female parliamentary representation are more likely to adopt policies that combat climate change (Strumskyte *et al.*, 2022). In Sweden, women in government have been empowered to protect the environment and have committed to increase women's participation in policy debates on climate change (Government of Sweden, 2015).

Table 2. Tailoring green fintech for women.

Digital Green Finance	Description	Example	Potential Target Group of Women
Digital payment and account solutions	Payment solutions with green features.	**Paygreen** offers a payment system where the consumer can measure the carbon footprint of the online shop from which they make a purchase.	Women as green consumers, entrepreneurs, and business owners.
Digital green investment solutions	Platforms that provide automated, algorithm-driven green financial planning and investment services with little to no human supervision.	**Inyova** is a mobile application that guides individuals and businesses to make sustainable investments.	Women as green investors.
Digital ESG data and analytics	Solutions for automated green data collection and analytics for finance, including automated green asset rating and indexing.	**Satelligence** provides highly detailed, semi-automated, satellite-based insights and actionable results over large areas, for financial service institutions to monitor deforestation risks.	Women on corporate boards with ESG focus.
Digital green crowdfunding and syndication platforms	Platforms for raising capital from individuals or from institutional investors to finance new green business.	**Bettervest** enables people to jointly invest individual sums of money in renewable energy and energy- and resource-efficiency projects.	Women as entrepreneurs.

(*Continued*)

Table 2. (*Continued*)

Digital Green Finance	Description	Example	Potential Target Group of Women
Digital risk analysis and InsureTech	Software and platforms that optimise green insurance products and services as well as solutions to minimise climate risks.	**Jupiter** provides climate analytics to organisations impacted by climate change. Produces hyper-local hazard estimates based on projected changes in climate, using forward-looking risk analysis.	Women in agriculture.
Digital green deposits and lending	Digital savings options used to finance environmental projects. Digital loans to finance projects or loans linked to green behaviours.	**Pensumo** offers a pension programme to users who adopt greener consumption behaviours by buying from retailers committed to sustainability.	Women as consumers and business owners.
Digital green asset solutions	Tokens and cryptocurrencies with green properties and blockchain capital market infrastructure built for green use cases.	**Treecoin** managed by Global TREE Project (GTP) sells asset tokens that are tied to actual eucalyptus trees.	Women as investors.

Table 2. (*Continued*)

Digital Green Finance	Description	Example	Potential Target Group of Women
Green Regtech solutions	Applications used for compliance by a regulated institution or a financial supervisory authority.	**Central Bank of Spain** is leveraging Natural Language Processing (NLP) capabilities of AI for a Task Force on Climate-Related Financial Disclosure (TCFD) tracking.	Women as policymakers.

Source: Adapted from Green Digital Finance Alliance and the Swiss Green Fintech Network. (2021), Green Fintech Classification.

Box 3: Leveraging PAYGo

In Kenya, a pay-as-you-go (PAYGo) product, M-Kopa, uses mobile money transaction data to allow individuals and business owners to lease and eventually own solar panels to power their households and shops. Credit assessment, disbursement, and payments are made electronically and the scheme allows households to rely on their own solar power (Costa and Ehrbeck 2015, Omwansa *et al.*, 2013).

Over the years, PAYGo devices have expanded to larger household appliances like solar home systems, cookstoves, refrigerators, and solar water pumps. These appliances can free up women's time for income-generating activities, such as charging people to watch TV or charge their phones at their homes, selling home-cooked food, or making textiles (Kumaraswamy, 2021). However, these services could be tailored to women, and greater research and the collection of sex-disaggregated data on impact would help customise the services for women (Kumaraswamy, 2021).

To increase female representation in the finance sector, companies have implemented initiatives like gender equity policies to hire, retain, and promote women, as well as policies to attract women returning to work after a career break (Rogish *et al.*, 2021). This includes mentoring to grow and develop female talent.

In the UK, policymakers introduced the "Women in Finance Charter" where 351 institutions, including the Bank of England and the Financial Conduct Authority, pledged to close the gender gap (HM Treasury, 2019). In 2021, France passed a new bill that requires a quota of at least 30% women among senior management by 2027 and 40% by 2030 for the largest companies. The Netherlands requires large companies to set gender diversity targets, not only within their boards but also within their senior management (Caby *et al.*, 2022).

The representation of women can also be enhanced though industry groups and professional associations linked to promoting and mentoring women in green finance. Examples include networks like Women in Sustainable Finance, the Gender Lens Initiative for Switzerland (GLIS),[e] the GenderSmart Gender & Climate Investment Working Group, and the AFI. Other organisations like Green Digital Finance Alliance could focus on initiatives for women.

4.1.3. *Increase gender lens investing*

Gender lens investing involves taking gender-based factors into consideration across the investment process to advance gender equality. Examples include investing in women-owned or women-led enterprises or investing in enterprises that offer products or services that improve the lives of women and girls.

Combining gender lens investing with climate change can align investments with the goals of the Paris Agreement and boost women's economic and social well-being. The United Nations Climate Change Council (UNFCCC) is already calling for public and private entities to take gender into consideration when financing climate projects. One example is the SheInvest initiative, supported by the European Investment Bank (EIB), which targets gender-responsive climate

[e]The Gender Lens Initiative for Switzerland (GLIS) is a working group set up by Sustainable Finance Geneva in March 2021, at the initiative of the AlphaMundi Group Ltd and with the support of Gender Smart.

financing, which includes projects like enhancing female farmers' ability to respond to climate change, and women's access to water, clean energy, and safe public transport (EIB, 2020).

Recent studies show that not enough attention is being paid to investing in women and providing practical guidance to investors on how to incorporate gender into their strategies (Moran, 2018). In that regard, the Gender-Smart Climate Finance Guide is a useful toolkit that enables investors to identify opportunities and mitigate risks in gender and climate finance (2X Climate Finance Taskforce 2021).[f] This toolkit could help direct investments towards creating more green digital financial products that target women. Some current examples can be found in Box 4.

Box 4: Examples of gender climate investing

Kinnevik is a Swedish company with investments in digital technology in healthcare, food, and consumer and financial services (Kinnevik, 2021). In 2021, the company issued sustainability-linked bonds in response to environmental and social concerns. The bond framework includes a key performance indicator to allocate at least 10% of new capital invested by Kinnevik into female-founded or -led companies.

Agence Française de Développement (AFD) developed an SDG Bond Framework for green, social, and sustainability bond issues in October 2020 (AFD, 2020). The framework requires new projects and loans to receive a neutral or positive grade in six sustainable development dimensions, which include gender equality and climate objectives.

5. Recommendations for Rethinking Policies

There are many government actions, whether they are policies or programmes, to increase women's access to digital financial services. Over 60% of jurisdictions, mainly in middle-income countries, have

[f]Developed by CDC Group, the European Bank for Reconstruction and Development (EBRD) and the European Investment Bank (EIB) joined forces under the framework of the 2X Climate Finance Task Force.

incorporated fintech in a National Financial Inclusion Strategy (IMF-The World Bank Global Fintech Survey, 2019). Many central banks are implementing green fintech policies and initiatives. Switzerland's government launched a Green Fintech Network in 2020 (Hall, 2022). However, green finance and financial inclusion policies are being considered as separate issues when they are interlinked. There is scope for governments to rethink policies and adopt a holistic approach in the following key areas:

- **Design digital financial literacy programmes that educate on climate change and encourage the use of digital green finance.** In 2022, UN Member States agreed upon actions to combat climate change and gender inequality which incorporate measures to include digital and financial literacy for women (CSW66, 2022). These measures could be further enhanced to include green fintech products and services.

- **Develop gender-inclusive policies and regulations that support digital green finance.** Effective consumer protection and data privacy laws can protect women who are at higher risk from online fraud and help increase adoption of digital green finance products. In addition, policies to implement digital identities can help women open bank accounts in a safe and secure manner. In India and Pakistan, the governments successfully rolled out a national digital identity programme and women can now use their national ID number to open digital financial accounts and be linked directly to government services (Hendriks, 2019).

- **Combine national financial inclusion strategies with climate change strategies.** Some countries have included climate change and financial inclusion into their national financial sector strategies (AFI, 2020), with Argentina, Fiji, Jordan, and Rwanda making the link explicit. The AFI is leading this initiative with guidelines and toolkits for its members which span over 90 developing economies (AFI, 2022). Such strategies could be more widely shared with the private sector to seek their expertise and knowledge in achieving each nation's goals.

- **Design regulatory sandboxes for digital green finance solutions for women.** In 2018, the Reserve Bank of Fiji introduced a regulatory sandbox, which included identifying barriers to sustainable finance and introducing digital financial services solutions (AFI, 2020.) In some countries including Bahrain, Malaysia, Sierra Leone, and India, the sandboxes have a specific mandate to advance financial inclusion (UNSGSA, 2019). These regulatory sandboxes could be tailored to digital green financial products and services for women.

- **Track gender-disaggregated data in relation to climate change and access and use of digital finance at the same time.** There is already pressure for regulators and organisations to collect gender data in relation to climate change and digital financial services but as separate datasets. For instance, the Central Bank of Egypt has a policy for strengthening sex-disaggregated data for financial inclusion (AFI, 2019). The IMF disaggregates data by sex (Hendriks, 2019) in its annual Financial Access Survey. There is scope for these data and even company data to be combined with ESG data and/or other climate change-related data, through multi-stakeholder data committees to better understand the measures required to support women.

- **Focus on the role of women and the impact of climate change and digital finance at an international level.** While the G20 Financial Inclusion Action Plan seeks to address the challenges that women face in accessing digital finance, the G20 Sustainable Finance Roadmap and the EU Sustainable Finance Strategy (European Commission, 2021) make very little reference to the role of women. The G20 could tackle these interlinked issues together, through a combined action plan.

- **Public–private partnerships to support women in digital green finance and create economic opportunities for them.** The Singapore–France Digital and Green Economy Partnership (MTI, MCI and IMDA, 2022) aims to support public–private partnerships and private sector-led approaches that harness digital and green technologies. The Joint Working Group that will be established could apply a gender lens to their cooperation on financial innovation to support gender equality in both countries by leveraging public and private sector expertise.

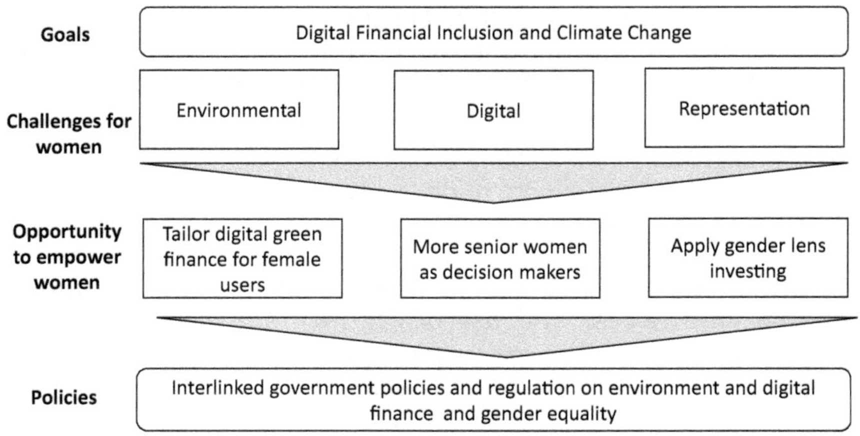

Fig. 3. Transforming challenges for women into opportunities.

By reshaping government policies, there is an opportunity to enhance digital financial inclusion and mitigate and adapt to climate change, through transforming the environmental, digital, and representation challenges that women face into opportunities to use digital green finance solutions that invest, support, and protect future generations of women (see Fig. 3).

References

Acuña Rivera, E. and Mitchell, G. (2020). Women are leading Latin America's Fintech revolution, *Crunchbase News*. Available at: https://news.crunchbase.com/diversity/women-are-leading-latin-americas-fintech-revolution/.

AFD (2020). SDG bond framework, Agence Française de Dévelopement (AFD). Available at: https://www.afd.fr/sites/afd/files/2020-10-07-38-47/sdg-bond-framework-afd.pdf.

AFI (2019). Integrating gender and women's financial inclusion into the Central Bank of Egypt's (CBE) framework, Case Study, Alliance for Financial Inclusion.

AFI (2020). *Inclusive Green Finance: A Survey of the Policy Landscape*, 2nd edition.

AFI (2022). Integrating digital financial services into a national financial inclusion strategy, Guideline note no. 5.

Altunbas, Y., Gambacorta, L., Reghezza, A., and Velliscig, G. (2022). Does gender diversity in the workplace mitigate climate change? European Central Bank Working Paper Series No. 2650.

Better Than Cash Alliance (2020). Women's World Banking, and the World Bank Group. Advancing women's digital financial inclusion. Available at: https://www.gpfi.org/sites/gpfi/files/sites/default/files/saudig20_women.pdf.

BIS (2021). A vision for technology-driven green finance, Project Genesis — Report 1. Bank of International Settlements Innovation Hub.

BloombergNEF (2020). Gender diversity and climate innovation.

Braun, P. (2010). Going green: Women entrepreneurs and the environment, *International Journal of Gender and Entrepreneurship*, 2/3, pp. 245–259.

Broløs, A. and Taylor, E. B. (2020). Female finance, European Women Payments Network (EWPN) and Keen Innovation.

Caby, J., Coron, C., and Ziane, Y. (2022). The effect of top management team gender diversity on climate change management: An international study, *Sustainability*, 14, p. 1032. doi.org/10.3390/su14021032.

Cashen, E. (2021). Top 5 female-fronted fintech firms. *World Finance*.

Chen, S., Doerr, S., Frost, J., Gambacorta. L., and Song Shin, H. (2021). The fintech gender gap (*Bank of International Settlement (BIS) Working Papers 931*). Available at: https://www.bis.org/publ/work931.htm.

Clempner, J. (2020). Women in financial services 2020, *Oliver Wyman*. Available at: https://www.oliverwyman.com/our-expertise/hubs/gender-diversity-in-financial-services.html.

Costa, A. and Ehrbeck.T. (2015). A market-building approach to financial inclusion. innovations: Technology, governance, *Globalization*, 10(1–2), 53–59.

CSW66 (2022). Agreed conclusions. Achieving gender equality and the empowerment of all women and girls in the context of climate change, environmental and disaster risk reduction policies and programmes, 66th United Nations Commission on the Status of Women.

Demirgüç-Kunt, A., Klapper, L., Singer, D., and Ansar, S. (2022). *The Global Findex Database 2021: Financial Inclusion, Digital Payments, and Resilience in the Age of COVID-19* (Washington, DC: The World Bank).

Demirgüç-Kunt, A., Klapper, L., Singer, D., Ansar, S., and Hess, J. (2018). *The Global Findex Database 2017: Measuring Financial Inclusion and the Fintech Revolution* (Washington, DC: The World Bank).

EC (2021). Strategy for financing the transition to a sustainable economy, *European Commission*. Available at: https://finance.ec.europa.eu/publications/strategy-financing-transition-sustainable-economy_en.

Eckenrode, J. (2020). Achieving gender equity in the fintech community, *Deloitte Insights*. Available at: https://www2.deloitte.com/content/dam/insights/us/articles/6918_Within-Reach-Women-in-Fintech/DI_Within-reach-women-in-fintech.pdf.

EIB (2020). Development solutions: How to fight climate change with gender equality, *European Investment Bank.*

Elam, A., Brush, C., Greene, P., Baumer, B., Dean, M., and Heavlow, R. (2019). Babson College, Smith College, and the Global Entrepreneurship Research Association (GERA) Global Entrepreneurship Monitor 2019 Women's Entre- preneurship Report.

FinEquity (2022). Informed Design: A Case Study Series, Insights from Lucy.

Gerard, G. and Schillebeeckx, S. (April 2021). Digital sustainability and its implications for finance and climate change. MAS special feature A, *Macroeconomic Review.*

Government of Sweden (2015). Gender Equality in Sweden.

GPFI (2022). G20 High-level principles for digital financial inclusion global partnership for financial inclusion. Global Partnership for Financial Inclusion.

Granwal, L. (2022). Women who used digital payment services in Australia in 2019, Statista. Available at: https://www.statista.com/statistics/1059365/australia-women-who-used-digital-payment-services-by-type/.

Green Digital Finance Alliance and the Swiss Green Fintech Network (2021). Green Fintech Classification.

GreenBiz. (2020). Women in sustainability: Moving from beginner to Badass.

GSMA (2021). State of the industry report on mobile money: 2021.

Hall, I. (2022). Going green: Governments look to fintech to help combat climate crisis, *Global Government Forum.*

Hendriks, S. (2019). Banking on the future of women, digital financial services are cutting out the middleman to equalise opportunity, Finance and Development, International Monetary Fund.

HM Treasury (2019). Women in finance charter. Available at: https://assets.publishing.service.gov.uk/government/uploads/system/uploads/attachment_data/file/818398/Women_in_Finance_Charter_List_of_Signatories_July_2019.pdf.

IMF (2014). Empowerment through financial inclusion, address to the international forum for financial inclusion by Christine Lagarde, Managing Director, International Monetary Fund.

IMF (2017). Banking on women — A case for more. Available at: https://blogs.imf.org/2017/09/19/chart-of-the-week-banking-on-women-a-case-for-more/.

IMF (2019). The World Bank Global Fintech Survey.

IUCN (2015). Women's participation in global environmental decision making, International Union for Conservation of Nature. Available at: https://portals.iucn.org/union/sites/union/files/doc/egi_factsheet_desicion_making_web_sept2015.pdf.

Kinnevik (2021). Kinnevik has issued SEK 2.0 billion in new sustainability-linked bonds.

Kumaraswamy, S. (2021). Does PAYGo solar improve women's lives? A look at the evidence, Consultative Group to Assist the Poor (CGAP). Available at: https://www.cgap.org/blog/does-paygo-solar-improve-womens-lives-look-evidence.

Lambert, L. (2020). The green economy is poised to create an immense amount of prosperity — But will everyone benefit? *Fortune*. Available at: https://fortune.com/2021/11/19/the-green-economy-is-poised-to-create-an-immense-amount-of-prosperity-women/.

Liu, H., Yao, P., Latif, S., Asalm, S., and Iqbal, N. (2022). Impact of Green financing, FinTech, and financial inclusion on energy efficiency, *Environmental and Science Pollution Research*, 29, pp. 18955–18966. doi.org/10.1007/s11356-021-16949-x.

McElhaney, K. A. and Mobasseri, S. (2012). Women create a sustainable future, *UC Berkeley Haas School of Business*.

Moran, L. (2018). Just good investing: Why gender matters to your portfolio and what you can do about it, *Calvert Impact Capital*.

Morsy, H. (2020). Access to finance — Mind the gender gap, *The Quarterly Review of Economics and Finance*, 78(C), pp. 12–21.

MTI, MCI and IMDA (2022). Singapore and France sign partnership on digital and green economy cooperation. Ministry of Trade and Industry, Ministry of Communications and Information and Infocomm Media Development Authority. Available at: https://www.mci.gov.sg/media-centre/press-releases/singapore-and-france-sign-partnership-on-digital-and-green-economy/.

Muhn, J. (2021). 25 Fintechs going green, *Finovate*. Available at: https://finovate.com/20-fintechs-going-green/.

New Energy Nexus (2021). Empowering women with renewable energy in Indonesia. Available at: https://www.newenergynexus.com/news/empowering-women-with-renewable-energy-in-indonesia/.

OECD (2008). Household behaviour and the environment, reviewing the evidence. Organisation for Economic Co-operation and Development.

OECD (2014). *Greening Household Behavior: Overview from the 2011 Survey*, revised edition. OECD Studies on Environmental Policy and Household Behaviour. Available at: https://www.oecd.org/env/consumption-innovation/greening-household-behaviour-2014.htm.

OECD (2016). International survey of adult financial literacy. Available at: https://www.oecd.org/finance/oecd-infe-survey-adult-financial-literacy-competencies.htm.

OECD (2019). The role of education and skills in bridging the digital gender divide. Evidence from APEC Economies. Available at: https://www.oecd.org/sti/education-and-skills-in-bridging-the-digital-gender-divide-evidence-from-apec.pdf.

OECD (2022). Making climate finance work for women: Overview of bilateral ODA to gender and climate change.

OMFIF (2020). OMFIF gender balance index 2020, Official Monetary and Financial Institutions Forum (OMFIF). Available at: https://www.omfif.org/gbi2020-1/.

Omwansa, T., Maree, J., Piontak, R., Shinyekwa, I., and Njenga, K. (2013). Developmental uses of mobile phones in Kenya and Uganda, *SSRN Electronic Journal.*

Osman-Elasha, B. (2012). *UN Chronicle*, 46(4). Available at: https://doi.org/10.18356/5d941c92-en.

Pazarbasioglu, C., Mora, A. G., Uttamchandani, M., Natarajan, H., Feyen, E., and Saal, M. (2020). Digital financial services, *The World Bank Group.*

Puschmann, T., Hoffmann, C., and Khmarskyi, V. (2020). How green FinTech can alleviate the impact of climate change — The case of Switzerland, *Sustainability*, 12(24), p. 10691. Available at: https://doi.org/10.3390/su122410691.

Rogish, A., Shemluck, N., and D'Souza, D. (2021). Leadership, representation, and gender equity in financial services, *Deloitte Insights*, November.

Statista (2022). Main sustainability goals included in banks' strategy worldwide 2021.

Stockholm Green Digital Finance. (2017). Unlocking the potential of Green Fintech.

Strumskyte, S., Ramos Magaña S., and Bendig. H. (2022). Women's leadership in environmental action, OECD Environment Working Papers No. 193. Available at: https://doi.org/10.1787/f0038d22-en.

Sqalli, Z., Unnikrishnan, S., Mejri, N., Dupoux, P., George, R., and Zrikem, Y. (2021). Why climate action needs a gender focus, *Boston Consulting Group.* Available at: https://www.bcg.com/publications/2021/climate-action-impact-on-gender-equality.

2X Climate Finance Taskforce (2021). The gender-smart climate finance guide 2021. Available at: https://www.2xglobal.org/climate-toolkit-home.

UNCDF (2022). Financial inclusion and the SDGs, United Nations Capital Development Fund.

UNDP (2017). Gender and climate change. Overview of linkages between gender and climate change, *Policy Brief.*

UNSGSA (2018). Igniting SDG progress through digital financial inclusion, UN Secretary-General's Special Advocate for Inclusive Finance for Development, Better than Cash Alliance, UNCDF, The World Bank.

UNSGSA (2019). FinTech Working Group and CCAF. Early lessons on regulatory innovations to enable inclusive FinTech: Innovation Offices, Regulatory Sandboxes, and RegTech, Office of the UNSGSA and CCAF: New York, NY and Cambridge, UK.

Volz, U., Knaack, P., Ramos, L., and Moling, J. (2020). *Inclusive Green Finance: From Concept to Practice* (Kuala Lumpur and London: Alliance for Financial Inclusion and SOAS, University of London).

WEF (2021). Tech can reach the world's unbanked women — But only if they tell us how it should work, *World Economic Forum.*

Weinreb Group (2021). The chief sustainability officer 10 years later.

WEN (2010). Gender and the climate change agenda. The impacts of climate change on women and public policy, *Women's Environmental Network.*

Yaccato, J., and Jaeger, J. (2003). The 80% minority: Reaching the real world of women consumers, *Viking Canada.*

Yankelovich Monitor, *M2W Conference*, and Greenfield Online for Arnold's Women's Insight Team (2020).

Yiu, E. (2022). Women are more likely to invest in green finance and have better-performing portfolios, *South China Morning Post.*

Yu, D. (2020). Women-focused fintech startup Lucy bags $360k in pre-seed round, *TechinAsia.*

https://doi.org/10.1142/9781800614604_0010

Chapter 10

Towards "Sustainable Democracy" and Common Prosperity Territories: The Legal Aspects of Central Bank Digital Currency and Its Roles in Economic Inequality Elimination

Ge (Luna) Zhang
Washington University School of Law, St. Louis, USA
ge.zhang@wustl.edu

The world is marked by an extreme disparity of economic inequality, and the widening gulf of income and wealth distribution between the "rich" and the "poor" is one of the defining challenges of our time (Dabla-Norris *et al.*, 2015). This chapter, set under the contemporary context of cascading disparities within social hierarchies and progressive innovations in financial sectors, outlines the roles of Central Bank Digital Currencies (CBDCs) in the elimination of economic inequality and probes three potential legal obstacles likely to be encountered during the implementation of CBDCs, by studying the correlations between the issuance of a CBDC and the reduction of economic inequality. This chapter, based on the welfare analyses on the socioeconomic manifestations of economic inequality and the roles of CBDC in the elimination of economic inequality, aims to promote common prosperity from the poorest to the people in high places, in order to construct a justified and legitimate economic system and to establish a free market welfare state, departing from poverty and inequality towards sustainable democratic states and common prosperity territories.

Keywords: Inequality and poverty; central bank digital currency (CBDC); common prosperity; sustainable democracy; economic inequality elimination; fintech and green investment; COVID-19; legal aspects and economic perspectives; interdisciplinary study; empirical study

1. Introduction

The world is marked by a widening disparity between the "rich" and the "poor" (Dabla-Norris *et al.*, 2015). Inequality persists over time (Mendes, 2014), while poverty is self-perpetuating (Ravallion, 2013). The existence of inequality is a snapshot that captures the living conditions of people of lower socioeconomic strata (Augustyn, n.d.) and omits the transitional dynamics between multifold social hierarchies. Power and affluence are increasingly concentrated at the top, coexisting with pockets of severe discrimination, deprivation, marginalisation, as well as the lack of human dignities and equal access to opportunities, often side by side (United Nations, n.d.).

This chapter studies the correlations between the reduction of economic inequality and the introduction of a central bank-issued digital currency. The author hypothesises that the issuance of a CBDC will impose socioeconomic consequences on the widespread phenomenon of economic inequality in today's society. The chapter poses the question on the design of a CBDC not merely as an economic question, a monetary question, but also as a political question, a regulatory question (Bjerg, 2017). By studying the connection between the issuance of the CBDC and the reduction of economic inequality, this research aims to provide welfare analyses on the legal aspects of the CBDC in order to construct a justified and legitimate economic system and to establish a free market welfare state, departing from poverty and inequality towards sustainable democratic states and common prosperity territories.

The phenomenon of economic inequality can be epitomised by the following three real-life examples. The first instance demonstrates that economic inequality between different races prevails in labour markets and has been highlighted by the COVID-19 pandemic (Siripurapu, 2022). An inequity in the US called "colour of COVID" reveals that people of colour, especially poor ones, including Black,

Hispanic, Indigenous, and Latin Americans, were more likely to get hospitalised with and die from COVID-19 than White Americans (Siripurapu, 2022). The main reason behind the scenes is that people of colours are more likely to be marginalised, and therefore more likely to be allocated as essential workers (Siripurapu, 2022) who typically have greater exposure to the coronavirus (Siripurapu, 2022).

The second example exhibits the existence of racial discrimination in other fields of the labour market (20 Facts About US Inequality That Everyone Should Know, 2011). From 2001 to 2002, an experiment conducted in the Chicago and Boston areas surveyed the interview callback rates for applicants with "White- or Black-sounding" names (20 Facts About US Inequality That Everyone Should Know, 2011). This scientific research found that applicants with "White-sounding" names, regardless of their gender, were much more likely to receive callback interviews than those with "Black-sounding" names, even though their submitted resumes were entirely identical (20 Facts About US Inequality That Everyone Should Know, 2011).

The third case shows that, in today's society, in addition to the racial segregation, the widening gap between individuals' income and wealth distribution can be tremendous as well (Fontinelle, 2021). Forbes counted that the number of billionaires around the world hit a record high of 2,755 in 2021 within all of its total rankings so far (Fontinelle, 2021). Meanwhile, The World Bank Group estimated that in 2021, by contrast, more than 711 million people across the globe were living on a sum of money less than US$1.90 per day (Fontinelle, 2021).

Examples like these are accumulating (Fontinelle, 2021) — the legacies of self-reinforcing behaviours that constitute the endless, vicious cycle of inequality (Boardman, 1991). These three cases exemplify several occasions when economic inequalities can emerge (Fontinelle, 2021), which, though, oversimplify the actual patterns of socioeconomic distance within the caste system in our society (20 Facts About US Inequality That Everyone Should Know, 2011). When inequality happens, life consequences are substantial (Fontinelle, 2021). Disparities like these — and others many people witness in their everyday lives — have created a "moral crisis"

(Taylor, 2017) and have given rise to questions on inequality — What is it? Why and how does it happen? How to relieve the issues of inequality? (Fontinelle, 2021).

The issuance of CBDCs can be one of the solutions that mitigate the effects of economic inequalities which are manifested by the three real-life examples described previously at the beginning of the Introduction. Existing analyses of economic inequality typically cover the topics of the distribution of income and wealth, education, and healthcare (Andreas and Nico, n.d.). Such academic research has been made by different scholarly strands across disciplines, including economics, sociology, and legal studies (Andreas and Nico, n.d.). Classic references on inequality and economic inequality include *Discourse on the Origin and Basis of Inequality Among Men in 1755, The Wealth of Nations in 1776, Capital: Critique of Political Economy 1867*, and *Capital in the Twenty-First Century in 2013* (Bjerg, n.d.).

As a new financial invention, the design of CBDC has aroused extensive interest from *Academia.*[a] The author acknowledges the contribution of previous studies. This research is among the preliminary legal observations on the CBDC project. Its role is to assist in eliminating economic inequality and promoting common prosperity around the world. This chapter distinguishes itself from previous research by transiting broader perspectives of economic inequality into a narrower focus on how the impacts of CBDC as a financial innovation will alleviate the phenomenon of economic inequality in today's society. The contribution of this chapter is that it initially probes the legal aspects, both the benefits and obstacles, of a CBDC and its roles in economic activities by playing the nexus between the issuance of a CBDC and the elimination of economic inequality. It approaches the research question with a multi-theoretical approach (Christopher, 2010), including an interdisciplinary study, empirical study, and comparative study.

[a]Current analyses on the introduction of a CBDC include *Designing New Money — The Policy Trilemma of Central Bank Digital Currency, The Macroeconomics of Central Bank Issued Digital Currencies, Central Bank Money: Liability, Asset, or Equity of the Nation*, and *Central Bank Digital Currencies: Preliminary Legal Observations.*

This chapter proceeds as follows: Section 1 presents a vista of the phenomenon of economic inequality in today's society. Section 2 defines the core concepts for an understanding of the following passages. Section 3 counts the advantages of a CBDC in economic inequality reduction, Section 4 analyses the legal obstacles that are likely to be encountered. Section 5 resumes the arguments and concludes the chapter.

2. Defining Fundamental Concepts: Economic Inequality and CBDCs in a Broader Context

2.1. *Inequality and economic inequality*

"Poverty is a denial of choices and opportunities",[b] a "pronounced deprivation"(Haughton and Khandker, 2009), of human dignity (Poverty - Statistics & Facts, 2022). Poverty exists when people lack the necessities to satisfy the basic needs indispensable to sustain their survival (Augustyn, n.d.). The "basic needs" may be defined as narrowly as "those necessary for survival" or as broadly as "those reflecting the prevailing standard of living in the community" (Augustyn, n.d.), depending on how "basic needs" are understood (Rohwerder, 2016). However, fundamentally, "basic needs" constitute insecurity, susceptibility to violence, powerlessness, the exclusion of individuals, households, and communities, and livelihood in marginal or fragile environments (Gordon, 2005). How do we measure poverty? (Ravallion, 2013). The World Bank defines "absolute poverty" as US$1.08 a day on such a purchasing power (Ravallion, Chen and Sangraula, 2008), and the "dollar-a-day" poverty baseline was first introduced in 1990 as a threshold to meet such standards of living (Ravallion *et al.*, 2008).

Inequality is a broader concept than poverty.[c] As for poverty, there are various ways to measure inequality.[d] A certain level of

[b] Statement of Commitment for Action to Eradicate Poverty Adopted by Administrative Committee on Coordination (1998). *United Nations*. Available at: https://press.un.org/en/1998/19980520.eco5759.html.

[c] Poverty and inequality. *The World Bank*. Available at: https://datatopics.worldbank.org/world-development-indicators/themes/poverty-and-in-equality.html.

[d] *Ibid.*

inequality may be natural. In advanced economies, especially in Western imperialism, the gap between the rich and the poor has reached an intolerable peak in decades.[e] By contrast, the trends of inequality are more mixed in developing countries and emerging markets — some countries are experiencing declining inequality (Dabla-Norris *et al.*, 2015), but persistent inequality in access to education, healthcare, and sanitation in others still remains.[f] Inequality in access to opportunity can lead to the limitation of upward mobility; however, most people tend to believe in meritocracy, the mentality that people advance in possessions and social status through diligence, not by privileges (Fontinelle *et al.*, 2021).

Economic inequality is one facet of inequality. The essence of economic equality is how various sources of economic interests are allocated in a society (Fontinelle *et al.*, 2021). The definition of economic inequality basically refers to "the disparities in incomes and wealth in a society" (Fontinelle *et al.*, 2021). The national Gini coefficient, the most well-known econometric measure widely used to gauge a country's economic inequality (Gini Coefficient, 2021), is a number that ranges from 0 to 100, where 0 corresponds with perfect equality and 100 corresponds with absolute inequality (Cingano, 2014).

2.2. *Money, currencies, and the modern banking system*

The evolution of the banking system is closely related to the progress of money and currencies. The history of money stems from trading of goods (McIntosh, 2022). Since the birth of economic systems precedes written history, the true origin of money is mostly based on conjecture and logical inference (McIntosh, 2022). Money, whether it is in form of "a seashell, a metal coin, a piece of paper, or a string of code electronically mined by computer" (Beattie and Kelly, 2022), is deemed as "a medium of exchange, a unit of measurement, and a storehouse for wealth" (Shorrocks *et al.*, 2021). Nowadays, global

---

[e]The 2022 World Inequality Report (2022). Available at: https://wir2022.wid.world/.

[f]Inequality Bridging the Divide. *United Nations.* Available at: https://www.un.org/en/un75/inequality-bridging-divide.

total assets are estimated to be around US$420 trillion (Ross *et al.*, 2021).

Compared to money, currency is a relatively narrower concept (Boar, n.d.). Currency is considered to be a tangible form of money, which contains an intangible system of value (Frankenfield *et al.*, 2022). A currency is defined by governments as "money in any form when in use or circulation as a medium of exchange" (Bernstein, 2008).[g] Most countries and regimes have their own currencies. As recognised by the United Nations, there are 180 currently circulating currencies around the world, such as the US dollar, Euro, Chinese Renminbi, Pound Sterling, and Japanese Yen.[h] The value of a currency constantly fluctuates in relation to others (Frankenfield *et al.*, 2022). For example, a Snickers bar costs roughly 14,000 rupiahs in Indonesia but might cost a dollar in the US, after the value of the rupiah is shifted to the US dollar.[i]

The history of currency is fascinating (Ritchie, 2022). Currency may take physical form as a banknote or coin, or may exist as a written or virtual account (Frankenfield *et al.*, 2022). Some of the earliest currencies were creatures chosen from nature (Tikkanen, n.d.). A renowned example is cowrie shells, which were found in the coastal areas of the Indian and Pacific oceans and were first used as currency around 1200 BCE (Tikkanen, n.d.). The adoption of metal for money can be traced back to Babylon before 2000 BCE (Tikkanen, n.d.). Throughout history, precious metals like gold and silver have been used as the most common coinage materials (McIntosh, 2022).

Today, with the popularity of modern information technology, physical cash has gradually fallen out of favour (Frankenfield *et al.*, 2022). In the 21st century, a new type of currency has entered the realm and vocabulary of monetary system: virtual currency (Frankenfield *et al.*, 2022). Virtual currencies are usually traded and

---

[g]Currency. The Free Dictionary. Currency [...] 1. Money in any form when in actual use as a medium of exchange, especially circulating paper money.

[h]Current world currencies, *Travelex*. Available at: https://www.travelex.com/currency/current-world-currencies.

[i]Understanding currencies and exchange rates, *World101*. Available at: https://world101.cfr.org/global-era-issues/monetary-policy-and-currencies/understanding-currencies-and-exchange-rates.

stored electronically (Frankenfield *et al.*, 2022). The bulk of virtual currency, such as Bitcoin and Ethereum, is digital and created by decentralised commercial banks, albeit regulated ones, known as CBDCs, which have highly centralised architecture backed up by sovereign monetary authorities (Frankenfield *et al.*, 2022).

The progress of money and currencies gave rise to the birth of the modern banking system. A bank is defined as a financial institution with the economic function of accepting deposits while making loans (Barone *et al.*, 2022). A continuation of ideas and thoughts of crediting and debiting was generated in the 14th century, while banking in its modern sense took root in the prosperous cities of Renaissance Italy (Trivellato, 2020). As early as 2750 BCE, ancient Egyptians began to manage funds with government control (Mark, 2017).

In modern society, central banks perform not only as a dynamic, robust, and resilient payment infrastructure (Hansen and Delak, 2022) but also as a legal monopoly on increasing the monetary base over coins and banknotes (Henry, 2004). Traditionally, a central bank primarily operates by conducting monetary policies, managing economic fluctuations, and maintaining financial stability (Monetary Policy and Central Banking, 2022). Nowadays, in the modern banking system, most central banks have regulatory and supervisory power to ensure the stability of member institutions, to prevent the risks of bank runs, and to curb reckless or fraudulent behaviour conducted by member institutions (Wijnholds, 2020).

2.3. *Digital currencies and central bank digital currencies (CBDCs)*

The advent of information technologies has become a new entrant reshaping the traditional financial ecosystem. Some economists view the "electronic money standard"[j] as a transitional system (Rogoff and Rogoff, 2017) and deem a cashless economy as a likely ultimate outcome of monetary evolution (Agarwal and Kimball, 2022).

[j]By "electronic money", we include the use of checks, credit cards, and debit cards in commercial transactions. Given this definition of electronic money, "electronic money standard" can act as the alternative to the "paper standard" (Agarwal and Kimball, 2015).

The history of the "kreditivsedlar"[k] and Stockholms Banco tells us a story about the way that the modern banking system responded to the invention of digital currency (Bjerg, 2017).

With the rise of information technology, digital currency was born as an electronic form of money towards cashless regimes (Seth *et al.*, 2022). By redistributing power away from the government, digital currency will democratise finance (Nova, 2021). CBDC, a high-security digital currency backed by a sovereign monetary authority, is regarded as "a means of payment, a unit of account, and a store of value" (Riksbank, 2016). As defined by Bank of England, a CBDC refers to "a universally accessible and interest-bearing central bank liability, implemented via distributed ledgers, that competes with bank deposits as medium of exchange" (Barrdear and Kumhof, 2016).

The history of CBDCs is relatively short. Most central banks across the world have started to explore their own stable central bank-issued digital currencies (Bode *et al.*, 2021). According to Atlantic Council's CBDC tracker, currently 105 countries around the world are researching or developing their own stable CBDCs, representing over 95% of global GDP (Young and Price, 2022). According to PwC's CBDC Global Index, over 60 central banks worldwide are at different stages of research or development of their own CBDCs (Courbe *et al.*, 2021). By April 2021, more than 80% of central banks worldwide are looking at fully convertible central bank money that is analogous to a digital form of a paper banknote (Areddy, 2021).

The tide of financial innovation like the birth of CBDCs is surging ahead. China's digital Renminbi is the first digital currency to be issued by a major economy (Popper and Li, 2021). Since 2014, China's central bank, the People's Bank of China, has been working on a project called Digital Currency Electronic Payment, also referred to as the "digital yuan" as it would be bolstered by the yuan (Kristie, 2020). China's trial of its digital currency, e-cny, has expanded to more than 260m wallets (*The Economist*, 2022). The European Central Bank (abbreviated as "ECB") recently announced that it was proceeding with its "digital euro" as a guarantor of a strong euro (National Bank of Belgium, n.d.) and as a viable,

[k]The "kreditivsedlar" is Europe's first banknote issued by Sweden in 1661.

mainstream payments vehicle (Bode *et al.*, 2021) into a more concrete investing phase (Bode *et al.*, 2021). The US Federal Reserve is also considering the potential benefits and risks of issuing a "Fed digital dollar" (Ackerman, 2022). An official of the US Federal Reserve noted that America would prefer to "get it right than to be first" (*The Economist*, 2021). The Bank of England initiated the One Bank Research Agenda to introduce its CBDC available to all households and business payments in central bank electronic money.[l]

Singapore's central bank is initiating a project — "Project Orchid" — on the technical aspects of launching a CBDC of its own (Look and Pohjanpalo, 2021). The Bahamian sand dollar, the East Caribbean dCash, and the Nigerian e-naira are already circulating (*The Economist*, 2022).

3. The Roles of Central Bank Digital Currencies in Economic Inequality Elimination: A Socioeconomic Outlook

The motivations cited by central banks around the world for pursuing CBDCs include more control over the monetary policy, reduced financial crimes, as well as stronger financial inclusion (Courbe *et al.*, 2021). By researching and developing CBDCs, central banks around the world can use CBDCs to eliminate economic inequalities in the following three ways.

3.1. *Reduce the dominance of political activities over economic behaviours*

Governmental behaviours — such as financial integration, fiscal redistributive policies, and the liberalisation and deregulation of labour markets — are playing an increasingly important role in causing economic inequality within nations.[m] Analyses on the impacts of political mastery on economic activities have been made extensively

[l]UK central bank digital currency. Available at: https://www.bankofengland.co.uk/research/digital-currencies.

[m]The IMF and income inequality introduction to inequality. *International Monetary Fund.* Available at: https://www.imf.org/en/Topics/Inequality/introduction-to-inequality.

by different strands of scholars in academia, including legal and economic literature (Peichl and Pestel, 2015). These bodies of literature discuss how economic inequality affects and is affected by politics (Nolan *et al.*, 2011).

In *The Wealth of Nations*, Adam Smith uses the famous "invisible hand" metaphor to describe any individual performance that has unplanned or unintended outcomes, particularly those that stem from actions not orchestrated by a central authority and that impose observable and patterned effects on the community (Joyce, 2001). Adam Smith was trying to present how an individual, exchanging benefits for his own self-interest, in an unplanned or unintentional manner, impacts the economy as a whole (Smith, 2002). According to Joseph Stiglitz, the "rent-seeking" theory explains another way political power can interfere with economic activities in our society. The process of "rent-seeking" brings excess profits to the rule-makers not from the creation of wealth but from "grabbing a larger share of the wealth that would otherwise have been produced without their effort" (Stiglitz, 2012).

The process of how political activities interfere with economic behaviours was observed by David Hume in the 18th century (Henderson, n.d.). Deflationists regard that the overprinting of paper money would often lead to inflationary bubbles (Kenton *et al.*, 2022). However, there was nothing to stop any sovereign monetary authority from issuing more notes than necessary, since a note has no intrinsic value (Ali *et al.*, n.d.). As a result, the unrestricted overprinting of paper money can often lead to a collapse of the monetary system.[n] This phenomenon increasingly cascaded since the abandonment of the gold standard in the 1930s (Eichengreen, 2019). For example, between 2008 and 2009, Zimbabwe experienced hyperinflation after the government overprinted money trying to stave off a domestic food shortage (see footnote i). This conduct led to soaring domestic prices and inflation rates of over 100 billion percent (see footnote i).

The circulation of CBDCs can reduce the impacts of political dominance on interdependent economic activities, say, quantitative easing, tax collection, or military spending, and therefore circumvent the disadvantages of paper notes as a currency with fragile political

[n]Currency over view. *Collectors Hive*. Available at: https://collectorshive.com/about/knowledgebase/currency-over-view/.

legitimacy under political mastery. Although most central banks are institutionally independent from political interference, control by executive and legislative branches still exists (David, 2016).

The most notable trait of a CBDC is its potential for interest rates no longer restricted by the zero lower bound, under the assumption that a CBDC could pay negative interest and all physical currencies were eliminated (Mackintosh, 2021). If the era of digital payments arrives and people want to demand physical money, it will be much easier for central banks to cut interest rates below zero (Mackintosh, 2021). Consequently, central banks can reduce interest rates as far as needed by adopting deeply negative interest rates if a deflationary spiral happens (Nelson, 2021). Moreover, the introduction of a CBDC can reduce the impacts of political mastery on other kinds of economic activities, such as employment policies, government spendings, as well as army maintenance and financing of wars (Fontinelle *et al.*, 2021).

3.2. *Prevent new forms of financial crimes that can lead to economic inequalities*

The history of currency is littered with swindles (*The Economist*, 2022). Financial crimes happen every day around the world and can occur in diverse forms when the criminals develop new tactics.[o] The changing faces of financial crimes stem from a growing landscape of high technologies and innovative financial institutions (see footnote o). Nowadays, the spectrum of financial crimes ranges from theft or fraud committed by a single individual or institution to large-scale, worldwide schemes masterminded by organised criminal syndicates.[p] New types of financial crimes commonly include cross-border money laundering, international tax evasion and avoidance, as well as global bribery and corruption (Rebovich, 2021).

According to the United Nations Office on Drugs and Crime, it is estimated that up to US$2 trillion in illegal funds are laundered

[o]What is financial crime? *Sanction Scanner*. Available at: https://sanctionscanner.com/blog/what-is-financial-crime-9.

[p]What is financial crime? *Dow Jones*. Available at: https://www.dowjones.com/professional/risk/glossary/financial-crime/.

through the global financial network each year, swinging between 2% and 5% of the global GDP (see footnote p). Taking the global tax crimes in Southern Africa as another example, around 60% of illicit capital flight from Africa is for cross-border tax evasion purposes, and an estimated 30% of sub-Saharan Africa's GDP has been transferred to global tax havens at an artificially low price.[q]

The release of CBDCs can tackle the complexities entangled in new forms of financial crimes that can exacerbate the phenomenon of economic inequality. Firstly, the CBDC can enhance the traceability and transparency of transactions (Courbe *et al.*, 2021) by tracking the transfer of CBDCs with cryptographic techniques (Nelson, 2021), so that these new forms of financial crimes will become more difficult to enact.

Moreover, another motivation behind the creation of a CBDC is the suppression of currency counterfeiting.[r] Cashless transactions make payments less susceptible to counterfeiting, fraud, or double spending (*The Economist*, 2021). Either producing or utilising counterfeit money constitutes a form of fraud or forgery, and is deemed illegal (Finlay and Francis, 2019). The capability of counterfeits to cause significant economic consequences has been extended as a political weapon, especially during war times (Finlay and Francis, 2019). One example of this occurred during the American War of Independence (1775–1783) when the British manufactured counterfeits of Continental banknotes on a vessel anchored in the New York harbour (Finlay and Francis, 2019). These forged currencies were later distributed throughout the colonies by British people, which resulted in the devaluation of banknotes and inflation (Finlay and Francis, 2019), ultimately giving rise to the timely coinage of the phrase "not worth a Continental" (Finlay and Francis, 2019). During World War II, Britain was attacked by the German Government with two secret counterfeiting operations, and pounds sterling were dropped on the British Isles to create hyperinflation (Finlay and Francis, 2019).

[q]Africa Could Gain US$89 Billion Annually by Curbing Illicit Financial Flows. *UNCTAD*, 28 September 2020. Available at: https://unctad.org/news/africa-could-gain-89-billion-annually-curbing-illicit-financial-flows.

[r]Counterfeit currency. *INTERPOL*. Available at: https://www.interpol.int/en/Crimes/Counterfeit-currency-and-security-documents/Counterfeit-currency.

These two examples reflect the importance of eradicating counterfeit currency since it will reduce the value of genuine currency and will potentially destabilise our economic system (see footnote r). A CBDC can be one of the solutions that reduce this type of financial crime and thus alleviate economic inequality in our society.

Furthermore, the issuance of CBDCs can also facilitate government agencies to monitor the digital token, making it harder for highly sophisticated criminal rings to sponsor criminal activities for illegal enterprises or terrorism.[s]

3.3. *Constitute a broader infrastructure of financial inclusion*

"Financial inclusion is the bridge between economic opportunity and outcomes" according to an IMF official (Florant *et al.*, 2020). Financial inclusion means that individuals or institutions have full access to financial products or services that satisfy their needs, delivered in an affordable and sustainable manner (The World Bank, 2022). According to The World Bank, 1.7 billion adults across the globe are estimated as unbanked, with no access to the products or services from the formal financial system (Carstens and Queen Máxima, 2022).

Yet, building a bridge between economic opportunity and outcomes has not been easy (Florant *et al.*, 2020). The first step to fix the system is to understand the causes of social exclusion (Florant *et al.*, 2020). One notable factor is that economic inequality is more easily transmitted from one generation to another as a result of unequal access to education, inherited wealth, and poverty relief (Systematic Inequality, 2018). This phenomenon is compounded in effects and makes escaping this vicious, systematic cycle increasingly difficult (Ravallion, 2013). Additionally, the communities that experience harsh disadvantages are often minorities, and therefore are often segregated either by the central authority or social stratification (Florant *et al.*, 2020). Public policies by no means impact people uniformly (United Nations, n.d.). Those policies that

[s]Financial crime. *Office of the Comptroller of the Currency.* Available at: https://www.occ.treas.gov/topics/supervision-and-examination/bank-operations/financial-crime/index-financial-crime.html.

help the underprivileged can also underpin their long-term prospects to flee from poverty (Ravallion, 2013). Biases against the poor always exist (Ravallion, 2013).

The access to a payment account is the first step towards wider financial inclusion since a bank account allows people to store money and manage payments (The World Bank, n.d.). As indicated by the case in Black communities, in 2016, nearly half of Black families in the US were unbanked or underbanked — a disparity that, over the spectrum of a financial lifetime, can cost nearly US$40,000 in excessive fees. This survey shows that if Black Americans had the same access to financial sector as White Americans did, financial institutions could realise approximately 2 billion US dollars in incremental, additional annual revenue (Florant, 2020).

Nowadays, with the advancement in digital technologies, the landscape of payment systems is changing (Carstens and Queen Máxima, 2022). Cash transactions are declining and shifting towards digital payments (Carstens and Queen Máxima, 2022). Virtual money has been touted for its potential to simplify the financial infrastructure and to usher in a new era of digital financial inclusion (Bode *et al.*, 2021). The issuance of central bank money offers an opportunity to overcome barriers facing the unbanked and the underbanked (Carstens and Queen Máxima, 2022). The CBDC can play an infrastructural role in the monetary system in the interest of public welfare in a capitalist economy (Kumhof *et al.*, 2020). Firstly, CBDCs help to combat social exclusion in the low-income population by drawing people without bank accounts into financial infrastructure with free or low transaction fees (Auer *et al.*, 2022). Secondly, they create opportunities for countries with limited financial facilities to leapfrog directly to a more inclusive, affordable, and efficient payment system (Carstens and Queen Máxima, 2022).

4. The CBDC Paradoxes Through the Lens of Law: The Legal Obstacles of Central Bank Digital Currencies in Economic Inequality Elimination

The major motivation for central banks to launch CBDC projects is to limit the risks inherent in the transition to a new and untested monetary mechanism (Barrdear and Kumhof, 2016). Despite the potential economic benefits, there are also numerous legal obstacles associated with the introduction of CBDCs. Some are identical or similar to those faced by the traditional payment method, while others exhibit unique traits and characteristics. The legal obstacles of CBDCs relating to their functions to reduce economic inequality are threefold:

4.1. *Risks of CBDCs to be accepted as legal tenders and manipulated by politics*

Economic inequality can have adverse social and political consequences (see footnote m). With the aim to reduce economic inequality, an important question should be asked: Should a CBDC be legal tender? (Vogel, 2022) Legal tender is commonly defined as "a form of money that courts of law are required to recognise as satisfactory payment for any monetary debt" (The Royal Mint, n.d.). For the sake of further clarity, the US Federal Reserve defines legal tender as follows: "US law specifically designates US coins and currency (including Federal Reserve notes) as legal tender, 'for all debts, public charges, taxes, and dues'."[t]

The CBDC issued by the central bank that forces the public to accept it as the mainstream payment can probably become a legal tender in its jurisdiction over other payment methods planned by decentralised financial institutions (Look and Pohjanpalo, 2021). Some currencies have already functioned as legal tenders in certain political jurisdictions (Legal Tender, 2021). For example, Jamaica's central bank has authorised the issuance of its CBDC, known as the Jamaica Digital Exchange, and legalised its use as a legal tender circulated by the central government (Young and Price, 2022). As one of the major digital economies, China's plans for the "digital yuan" are forecasted by the outset as its legal tender (Young and Price, 2022). The possibility for a digital euro to be legal tender is "likely" in the Eurozone, as indicated by an ECB Executive Board member in a panel on CBDCs in Helsinki (Young and Price, 2022). The Governor of the Central Bank of the Russian Federation, addressing the same event, concurred (Young and Price, 2022). However, the adoption

---

[t]31 U.S.C. 5103.

of CBDCs as legal tender can in turn aggravate the dominance of political activities over economic behaviours. Furthermore, others believe a CBDC will authorise the monopoly of the central monetary authority and surveillance over people's finances (Young and Price, 2022).

4.2. *Data from tracing money routes can lead to privacy leakage*

While there are various underlying benefits for central banks to launch CBDC projects, one essential concern that calls for widespread attention is privacy protection and data security (Hansen, and Delak, 2022). For example, data from tracing money routes can lead to leakage of financial privacy (Exploring Anonymity in Central Bank Digital Currencies, 2022). There are numerous ways in which a user's financial privacy, tracked with cryptography and stored in CBDCs, can be breached during the process of data collection and processing.

The first privacy controversy is that the trans-border flow of personal data across nations is inevitable in order to combat money laundering and money counterfeiting (see footnote r). When designing CBDCs, central banks should also take into serious consideration the users' economic interests and obligations (Hansen and Delak, 2022). When spending CBDCs, the consumers should have control over their payment information and have the option of sharing it with a wider set of financial service providers (Carstens and Queen Máxima, 2022).

Secondly, in a general-purpose CBDC project, central banks and other institutions need to discriminate sensitive personally identifiable information (abbreviated as "PII") from common information to ensure that sensitive PII is particularly protected from any theft, fraud, or unauthorised disclosure (Hansen and Delak, 2022). Consequently, market participants in CBDCs should be cautioned on the privacy issues arising from cryptography and tracing routes, particularly on sensitive PII.

One of the potential technical solutions for the heated debate over CBDCs is distributed ledger technology (abbreviated as "DLT") (Hansen and Delak, 2022). Another technique to address the growing concerns on data privacy is to hardwire personal data protection into the structure of a CBDC (Carstens and Queen Máxima, 2022). Meanwhile, the legal solutions constitute stricter compliance with various privacy and data protection laws and regulations (Carstens and Queen Máxima, 2022). Central banks should research and develop their own CBDCs with design plans that delicately balance the flow of personal data and the protection of information privacy (Hansen and Delak, 2022). More dialogues, research, and experimental trials will be needed before CBDCs can become a new engine of financial inclusion (Carstens and Queen Máxima, 2022).

4.3. *Potential disruption to the established financial regulatory framework*

Since currency is a social and legal contract, the extensive use of central bank money as fiat currency is backed by legal rules in many regimes (Kumhof *et al.*, 2020). An unregulated or underregulated CBDC plan will pose enormous legal hazards to the established financial ecosystem. The inherent potential of a CBDC can only be realised under the conditions when a well-rounded regulatory framework has been constructed and compliance with respect to the legal status and consequences of each market participant has been ensured (Boar, n.d.). To realise potential benefits, a finalised, official version of a CBDC rollout must be accompanied by regulatory reforms to address potential risks and complexities, such as cybersecurity, financial illiteracy, and political polarisation (Bode *et al.*, 2021).

Currently, at the international level, about two-thirds of the regulatory and supervisory agencies support financial inclusion by enacting loose regulations (Divanbeigi and Chen, 2019). Currently existing international agreements that might be applicable include *Basel III on Prevention of Criminal Use of the Banking System for the Purpose of Money-Laundering*, *the United Nations Convention against Transnational Organized Crime of 2000*, *the United Nations Convention against Corruption of 2003*, and *the Terrorist Financing Convention of 1999* (FATF, 2022). Jurisdictions in different regimes are making efforts to ensure their legal frameworks can meet these challenges when their CBDCs are released in the near future (Boar, n.d.). For example, the US Fed's legislation on a retail CBDC plan is currently in a legal grey zone since there are currently three bills in the US Congress; however, the prospect that these bills will eventually become laws remains blurry (Hansen and Delak, 2022).

Obviously, the introduction of CBDCs will disrupt the established regulatory system (Bode *et al.*, 2021). Given the geopolitical climate, it will be wise for the countries that are considering CBDCs to revise current policies to embrace the future (Nuttall, 2021). In addition to careful critical analyses of the promises of a CBDC (Barber II *et al.*, 2021), these laws and regulations should take into account a broader range of the poor and low-income population (Barber II *et al.*, 2021).

5. Conclusion

The British economist Tony Atkinson clearly states that *"Inequality of outcome among today's generation is the source of the unfair advantage received by the next generation. If we are concerned about equality of opportunity tomorrow, we need to be concerned about inequality of outcome today"* (Atkinson, 2015). Furthermore, economist Thomas Piketty indicates that the widening gap between the two polars is an inevitable and permanent phenomenon of free market capitalism (Piketty, 1971), whereas a fair and justified distribution of income and wealth is a fundamental element of the social contract (see footnote m).

The causes of inequality are highly ideologically charged subjects (Boardman, 1991), and inequality hinders economic growth and fosters political dysfunction (Siripurapu, 2022). The extent of economic inequality is not only driven and measured by income and wealth but also determined by other factors — race, ethnicity, gender, age, origin, disability, sexual orientation, class, political leaning, and religion (United Nations, n.d.). Take the growing risk of homelessness in the US as an example: There are 750,000 homeless Americans on any given night, among who one in five is considered "chronically homeless" (20 Facts About US Inequality That Everyone Should Know, 2011). The population that easily becomes homeless includes disproportionate percentage of Blacks, males, middle-aged people (i.e., ages 31–50), veterans, and the disabled (20 Facts About US Inequality That Everyone Should Know, 2011). This fact of inequality feels unfair (Nova, 2021). The socialist traditions trace the roots of inequality to flaws of distribution and call for redistribution of wealth as the primary solution, whereas the neoliberal school of thought reckons the access for profitable private investment is the real solution (Boardman, 1991). So, is it possible to realise a comparatively "fair" contest that will lead to a more equal and equitable distribution between the rich and the poor in our social hierarchies? (Bivens and Shierholz, 2018) Is the free market in a capitalist society intrinsically tilted against the poor, or whether the distributional tug-of-war between the two polars of the society never truly be "fair"? (Bivens and Shierholz, 2018).

On October 19, 2021, China's President, Xi Jinping, addressed the *Speech on Boosting Common Prosperity*, noting that Chinese Government will "allow some people to get rich first, then guide and help others get rich together."[u] Rural famers, food delivery personnel, and factory workers and white-collar lawyers, investment bankers, and public-trading corporation entrepreneurs are at the opposite ends of the life spectrum — some are struggling, while others are thriving (He, 2021). Their concerns vary, but their questions are surprisingly similar: "How to make a living in this world and how to make my life a little bit better?" (He, 2021).

One possible answer is what is known as a central bank-issued digital currency. The root ideas of central bank money can be traced back to the gold standard (Kumhof *et al.*, 2020). The harmonious combinations of financial technologies, autonomy of will, freedom of contract, as well as market fairness and justice have jointly bolstered the development of the modern monetary system. As a rising alternative payment method, CBDCs can fit in the gaps of numerous shortcomings of the traditional banking system, since they cater to the characteristics of diverse types of newly born economic innovations and provide brand-new solutions to eliminate economic inequality.

To restore the *status quo* (Bjerg, 2017), we need a "sustainable democracy", enshrined in law and practiced in reality. As stated in *An Essay on the Principle of Population* (Malthus and Mayhew, (2015), "*the happiness of a country does not depend, absolutely, upon its poverty, or its riches, upon its youth, or its age, upon its being thinly, or fully inhabited, but upon the rapidity with which it*

[u]Xi Jinping, *Speech on Boosting Common Prosperity.*

is increasing, upon the degree in which the yearly increase of food approaches to the yearly increase of an unrestricted population." By redistributing power among the government, the free market, and the public, CBDCs will "democratise" finance (Nova, 2021). With the rise of the high-tech industry and the advancements in digital economy, the prevalence of CBDCs will become an ideal way to create economic and legal order, maintain market fairness, and construct a strong social welfare system that lifts society from bottom to the top, in order to eliminate economic inequality and achieve "sustainable democracy" and common prosperity (Barber II *et al.*, 2021).

To sum up, this chapter's major implications are stated from three perspectives —- economics, legal studies, and academic scholarship: Firstly, the economic implication of this study is to examine the correlations between the issuance of a CBDC and the reduction of economic inequality in order to promote common prosperity and establish a free market democratic state. The author attempts to demonstrate that the implementation of a CBDC will alleviate the phenomenon of economic inequality in today's society. Secondly, the policy implication of this study is to analyse the legal obstacles that will be encountered during the design of a CBDC in order to structure a well-rounded regulatory framework and establish a legitimate monetary system with market fairness and justice. Thirdly, the academic and pedagogical implication of this study is to provide welfare analyses for the legal aspects of a CBDC in order to provoke further discussion on the introduction of CBDCs and to facilitate the healthy development of a CBDC payment system.

The limitations of this study include the absence of quantitative analyses due to the author's lack of knowledge background and the absence of detailed statutory analyses due to the lack of relevant legislation (Kumhof and Barrdear, n.d.). The author hopes that there will be a broader collaborative effort to work on the research questions raised in this study (Kumhof and Barrdear, n.d.).

Acknowledgements

I would like to offer special appreciation to the publisher, editors, and reviewers of this chapter for their insightful, considered, and constructive readings and comments on this submission.

References

20 Facts About US Inequality That Everyone Should Know (2011). *Stanford Center on Poverty and Inequality.* Available at: https://web.stanford.edu/group/scspi/cgi-bin/facts.php.

Ackerman, A. (2022). Fed launches review of possible central bank digital currency. *The Wall Street Journal.* Available at: https://www.wsj.com/articles/fed-launches-review-of-possible-central-bank-digital-currency-11642706158.

Agarwal, R. and Kimball, M. (2015). Breaking through the Zero Lower Bound, IMF Working Paper No. 15/224, International Monetary Fund, Washington, DC. Available at: https://www.imf.org/en/Publications/WP/Issues/2016/12/31/Breaking-Through-the-Zero-Lower-Bound-43358.

Agarwal, R. and Kimball, M. (2022). The electronic money standard and the possibility of a zero inflation target, *International Monetary Fund*, 7 April. Available at: https://www.imf.org/en/Publications/fandd/issues/2022/03/Future-of-inflation-partIII-Agarwal-kimball.

Ali, R., Barrdear, J., Clews, R., and Southgate, J. (n.d.). The economics of digital currencies. Bank of England. Available at: https://www.bankofengland.co.uk/-/media/boe/files/digital-currencies/the-economics-of-digital-currencies.

Andreas, P. and Nico, P. (n.d.). *International Encyclopedia of the Social & Behavioral Sciences.*

Areddy, J. T. (2021). China creates its own digital currency, a first for major economy, *The Wall Street Journal*, 5 April. Available at: https://www.wsj.com/articles/china-creates-its-own-digital-currency-a-first-for-major-economy-11617634118.

Atkinson, A. B. (2015). *Inequality: What Can Be Done*, 1st edition (Harvard University Press).

Auer, R. *et al.* (2022).Central Bank digital currencies: A new tool in the financial inclusion toolkit? *Bank for International Settlements.* Available at: https://www.bis.org/fsi/publ/insights41.htm.

Augustyn, A. (n.d.). Poverty. *Encyclopaedia Britannica.* Available at: https://www.britannica.com/topic/poverty.

Barber II, R., William, J., *et al.* (2021). Moral policy = good economics, *Economic Policy Institute*, 27 October. Available at: https://www.epi.org/publication/moral-policy-good-economics/.

Barone, A. *et al.* (2022). Bank definition. *Investopedia*, May. Available at: https://www.investopedia.com/terms/b/bank.asp.

Barrdear, J. and Kumhof, M. (2016). The macroeconomics of central bank issued digital currencies, Bank of England Working Paper No. 605.

Available at: SSRN: https://ssrn.com/abstract=2811208 or http://dx.doi.org/10.2139/ssrn.2811208.

Beattie, A. and Kelly, R. C. (2022). The history of money: Bartering to banknotes to bitcoin. *Investropedia*, 20 June. Available at: https://www.investopedia.com/articles/07/roots_of_money.asp.

Bernstein, P. (2008). [1965, 4-5]. A *Primer on Money, Banking and Gold*, 3rd edition (Hoboken, NJ: Wiley). OCLC 233484849.

Bivens, J. and Shierholz, H. (2018). What labor market changes have generated inequality and wage suppression?" *Economic Policy Institute*, 12 December. Available at: https://www.epi.org/publication/what-labor-market-changes-have-generated-inequality-and-wage-suppression-employer-power-is-significant-but-largely-constant-whereas-workers-power-has-been-eroded-by-policy-actions/.

Bjerg, O. (2017). Designing new money — The policy trilemma of central bank digital currency, CBS Working Paper. Available at: SSRN: https://ssrn.com/abstract=2985381 or http://dx.doi.org/10.2139/ssrn.2985381.

Bjerg, O. (n.d.). The author learned how to present the literature review, *Designing New Money — The Policy Trilemma of Central Bank Digital Currency*. Available at: SSRN: https://ssrn.com/abstract=2985381 or http://dx.doi.org/10.2139/ssrn.2985381.

Boar, C. (n.d.). Webinar on the legal aspects of digital currencies. Bank for International Settlements.

Boardman, B. (1991). *Fuel Poverty: From Cold Homes to Affordable Warmth*, illustrated edition (UNKNO).

Bode, I., Higginson, M., and Niederkorn, M. (2021). CBDC and stablecoins: Early coexistence on an uncertain road. McKinsey Company. Available at: https://www.mckinsey.com/industries/financial-services/our-insights/cbdc-and-stablecoins-early-coexistence-on-an-uncertain-road.

Carstens, A. and Queen Máxima, H. M. (2022). CBDCs for the people, *Bank for International Settlements*, Project Syndicate, 18 April. Available at: https://www.bis.org/speeches/sp220418.htm.

Christopher, J. (2010). Corporate governance — A multi-theoretical approach to recognizing the wider influencing forces impacting on organizations, *Critical Perspectives on Accounting*, 21, pp. 683–695. doi:10.1016/j.cpa.2010.05.002.

Cingano, F. (2014). Trends in income inequality and its impact on economic growth, *OECD Social, Employment and Migration Working Papers, No. 163* (OECD Publishing). Available at: http://dx.doi.org/10.1787/5jxrjncwxv6j-en.

Courbe, J. *et al.* (2021). The evolution of money: Why financial institutions should start paying attention to CBDCs, *PwC*, PwC's Financial Services Regulatory Practice, May. Available at: https://www.pwc.com/gx/en/ghosts/assets/evolution-of-money-cbdcs.pdf.

Dabla-Norris, E., Kochhar, K., Suphaphiphal, N., Ricka, F., and Tsounta, E. (2015). *Causes and Consequences of Income Inequality: A Global Perspective* (International Monetary Fund).

David, F. (2016). Fiscal and monetary policies in developing countries, in *The New Palgrave Dictionary of Economics* (Springer), p. 405: The current norm in OECD countries is an institutionally independent central bank.

Divanbeigi, R. and Chen, R. (2019). Can regulation promote financial inclusion? *The World Bank Blog.* Available at: https://blogs.worldbank.org/developmenttalk/can-regulation-promote-financial-inclusion.

Eichengreen, B. (2019). *Globalizing Capital: A History of the International Monetary System*, 3rd edition (Princeton University Press), pp. 7–79.

Exploring Anonymity in Central Bank Digital Currencies (2022). Available at: https://www.ecb.europa.eu/paym/intro/publications/pdf/ecb.mipinfocus191217.en.pdf.

FATF (2022). *Partnering in the Fight Against Financial Crime: Data Protection, Technology and Private Sector Information Sharing*, FATF, Paris, France. Available at: https://www.fatf-gafi.org/en/publications/Digitaltransformation/Partnering-in-the-fight-against-financial-crime.html.

Finlay, R. and Francis, A. (2019). A brief history of currency counterfeiting, *Reserve Bank of Australia*, 19 September. Available at: https://www.rba.gov.au/publications/bulletin/2019/sep/a-brief-history-of-currency-counterfeiting.html.

Florant, A. *et al.* (2020). The case for accelerating financial inclusion in black communities, *McKinsey & Company*, 25 February. Available at: https://www.mckinsey.com/industries/public-and-social-sector/our-insights/the-case-for-accelerating-financial-inclusion-in-black-communities.

Fontinelle, A. *et al.* (2021). Economic inequality, *Investopedia*, 19 November. Available at: https://www.investopedia.com/economic-inequality-4845459.

Frankenfield, J. *et al.* (2022). Currency. *Investopedia*, 22 July. Available at: https://www.investopedia.com/terms/c/currency.asp.

Gini Coefficient (2021). Available at: https://corporatefinanceinstitute.com/resources/knowledge/economics/gini-coefficient/.

Gordon, D. (2005). Indicators of poverty & hunger. Available at: https://www.un.org/esa/socdev/unyin/documents/ydiDavidGordon_poverty.pdf.

Hansen, T. and Delak, K. (2022). Security considerations for a central bank digital currency, *FEDS Notes* (Washington: Board of Governors of the Federal Reserve System), 3 February. Available at: https://doi.org/10.17016/2380-7172.2970.

Haughton and Khandker (2009). The World Bank, p. 1.

He, H. (2021). Common prosperity in China: rich or poor, people have questions about Beijing's attempt to spread the wealth. *China Macro Economy*. Available at: https://www.scmp.com/economy/china-economy/article/3148338/common-prosperity-china-rich-or-poor-people-have-questions.

Henderson, D. R. (n.d.). David Hume, *Econlib*. Available at: https://www.econlib.org/library/Enc/bios/Hume.html.

Henry, J. F. (2004). The social origins of money: The case of Egypt. Credit and State Theories of Money: The Contributions of A. Mitchell Innes, pp. 79–98. doi:10.4337/9781843769842.00009.

Joyce, R. (2001). *The Myth of Morality*. Cambridge Studies in Philosophy (Cambridge: Cambridge University Press). doi:10.1017/CBO9780511487101.

Kenton, W. *et al.* (2022). Bubble, *Investopedia*, 3 April. Available at: https://www.investopedia.com/terms/b/bubble.asp.

Kristie, P. (2020). China leads in race for digital currency. Deutsche Welle. Available at: https://www.dw.com/en/china-digital-currency-yuan-bitcoin/a-55134692.

Kumhof, M., Allen, J. G., Bateman, W., Lastra, R. M., Gleeson, S., and Omarova, S. T. (2020). Central Bank money: Liability, asset, or equity of the nation?, Cornell Legal Studies Research Paper 20-46. Available at: SSRN: https://ssrn.com/abstract=3730608 or http://dx.doi.org/10.2139/ssrn.3730608.

Kumhof, M. and Barrdear, J. (n.d.). The author learned how to draft "the limitations of the study", *The Macroeconomics of Central Bank Issued Digital Currencies*. Available at: SSRN: https://ssrn.com/abstract=2811208 or http://dx.doi.org/10.2139/ssrn.2811208.

Legal Tender (2021). Available at: https://www.investopedia.com/terms/l/legal-tender.asp.

Mackintosh, J. (2021). Digital currencies pave way for deeply negative interest rates, *The Wall Street Journal*, 8 September. Available at: https://www.wsj.com/articles/digital-currencies-pave-way-for-deeply-negative-interest-rates-11631091581.

Malthus, T. and Mayhew, R. (2015). *Essay on the Principle of Population and Other Writings* (Penguin Books Ltd.).

Mark, J. J. (2017). Trade in ancient Egypt, *World History Encyclopedia.* Available at: https://www.worldhistory.org/article/1079/trade-in-ancient-egypt/.

McIntosh, M. A. (2022). Currency and money since the prehistoric world, *Brewminate: A Bold Blend of News and Ideas*, 14 April. Available at: https://brewminate.com/currency-and-money-since-the-prehistoric-world/.

Mendes, M. (2014). *Inequality, Democracy, and Growth in Brazil A Country at the Crossroads of Economic Development*, 1st edtion (Academic Press).

Monetary Policy and Central Banking. (2022). Available at: https://www.imf.org/en/About/Factsheets/Sheets/2016/08/01/16/20/Monetary-Policy-and-Central-Banking.

National Bank of Belgium (n.d.). The three stages of monetary union. Available at: https://www.nbb.be/en/notes-and-coins/history/history-euro/three-stages-monetary-union.

Nelson, B. (2021). The benefits and costs of a central bank digital currency for monetary policy, *Bank Policy Institute*, 15 April. Available at: https://bpi.com/the-benefits-and-costs-of-a-central-bank-digital-currency-for-monetary-policy/.

Nolan, B. *et al.* (2011). *The Oxford Handbook of Economic Inequality* (Oxford University Press).

Nova, A. (2021). Cryptocurrencies could lead to financial instability, Author Warns, *CNBC*, 13 October. Available at: https://www.cnbc.com/2021/10/13/cryptocurrencies-could-lead-to-financial-instability-author-warns.html.

Nuttall, M. (2021). Central Bank digital currencies: The solution to money laundering? *Napier*, 3 November. Available at: https://www.napier.ai/post/digital-currencies-money-laundering.

Peichl, A. and Pestel, N. (2015). *International Encyclopedia of the Social & Behavioral Sciences*, 2nd edition (Vol. 6).

Piketty, T. (1971). *Capital in the Twenty-First Century* (Cambridge Massachusetts: The Belknap Press of Harvard University Press).

Popper, N. and Li, C. (2021). China charges ahead with a national digital currency. Available at: https://www.nytimes.com/2021/03/01/technology/china-national-digital-currency.html.

Poverty — Statistics & Facts. (2022). Available at: https://www.statista.com/topics/781/poverty/#topicHeader_wrapper.

Ravallion, M. (2013). Pro-poor growth: A primer (*The World Bank Group Policy Research Working Papers*), 21 June.

Ravallion, M., Chen, S., and Sangraula, P. (2008). Dollar a day revisited.

Rebovich, D. (2021). The changing face of financial crime: New technologies, new offenders, new victims, and new strategies for prevention and control, victims & offenders, 16(3), pp. 283–285. doi:10.1080/15564886.2021.1876196.

Riksbank, S. (2016). Should the Riksbank issue e-krona? Available at: https://www.bis.org/review/r161128a.pdf.

Ritchie, J. (2022). The history of money: How our currency evolved from pelts to money, *Intuit Mintlife*, 17 February. Available at: https://mint.intuit.com/blog/investments/the-history-of-money/.

Rogoff, K. and Rogoff, K. S. (2017). *The Curse of Cash* (Princeton, NJ: Princeton University Press).

Rohwerder, B. (2016). Poverty and inequality. *GSDRC Applied Knowledge Services.* Available at: https://gsdrc.org/topic-guides/poverty-and-inequality/measuring-and-analysing-poverty-and-inequality/defining-poverty-extreme-poverty-and-inequality/.

Ross, S. *et al.* (2021). Financial services: Sizing the sector in the global economy. *Investopedia*, 30 September. Available at: https://www.investopedia.com/ask/answers/030515/what-percentage-global-economy-comprised-financial-services-sector.asp.

Seth, S., Brown, J., and Kvilhaug, S. (2022). Central bank digital currency (CBDC). *Investopedia.* Available at: https://www.investopedia.com/terms/c/central-bank-digital-currency-cbdc.asp.

Shorrocks, A. *et al.* (2021). The global wealth report 2021. *Credit Suisse*, Research Institute, June 2021. Available at: https://www.credit-suisse.com/about-us/en/reports-research/global-wealth-report.html.

Siripurapu, A. (2022). The U.S. inequality debate, *Council on Foreign Relations*, 20 April. Available at: https://www.cfr.org/backgrounder/us-inequality-debate.

Smith, A. (2002). *The Wealth of Nations* (Oxford, England: Bibliomania.com Ltd.).

Stiglitz, J. E. (2012). *The Price of Inequality: How Today's Divided Society Endangers Our Future* (Norton, Kindle Edition), p. 32.

Systematic Inequality (2018). Available at: https://www.americanprogress.org/article/systematic-inequality/.

Taylor, M. (2017). The paradise papers are just a glimpse at the unreal wealth gap, *Vice*, 9 November. Available at: https://www.vice.com/en/article/59yk75/the-paradise-papers-are-just-a-glimpse-at-the-unreal-wealth-gap.

The Economist (2021). What is the fuss over central-bank digital currencies?" *The Economist*, 16 February. Available at: https://www.economist.com/the-economist-explains/2021/02/16/what-is-the-fuss-over-central-bank-digital-currencies.

The Economist (2022). How central banks are moving into e-money, *The Economist*, 20 April. Available at: https://www.economist.com/special-report/2022/04/20/how-central-banks-are-moving-into-e-money.

The Royal Mint (n.d.). Legal tender guidelines. Available at: https://www.royalmint.com/aboutus/policies-and-guidelines/legal-tender-guidelines/.

The World Bank (2022). Financial inclusion overview, *The World Bank*, 29 March. Available at: https://www.worldbank.org/en/topic/financial inclusion/overview.

Tikkanen, A. (n.d.). A brief (and fascinating) history of money, *Britannica*. Available at: https://www.britannica.com/story/a-brief-and-fascina ting-history-of-money.

Trivellato, F. (2020). Renaissance florence and the origins of capitalism: A business history perspective, *Business History Review*, 94(1), pp. 229–251. doi:10.1017/S0007680520000033.

United Nations (n.d.). Inequality bridging the divide, *United Nations*. Available at: https://www.un.org/en/un75/inequality-bridging-divide.

Vogel, P. (2022). The federal reserve wants input about digital currencies, *Foley & Lardner LLP*, Bloomberg Law, 1 March. Available at: https://www.foley.com/en/insights/publications/2022/03/the-federal-reserve-wants-input-digital-currencies.

Wijnholds, O. (2020). The money masters: The progress and power of central banks. doi:10.1007/978-3-030-40041-5.

Young, M. and Price, G. (2022). Jamaica becomes first country to make a CBDC legal tender, *Beincrypto*, 9 June. Available at: https://beincrypto.com/jamaica-becomes-first-country-to-make-a-cbdc-legal-tender/.

Part III

Case Studies in Fintech & Green Investment

https://doi.org/10.1142/9781800614604_0011

Chapter 11

Digital Youth Banking: Facing the Future

Ruilin Zhu*[,§], Smita Paul[†,¶], and Ivan Muck[‡,‖]

**Department of Management Science,*
Lancaster University Management School,
Lancaster, UK
[†]Management Consultant
[‡]ff.next, Budapest, Hungary
[§]ruilin.zhu@lancaster.ac.uk
[¶]smita.paul.nz@gmail.com
[‖]ivan.muck@ffnext.io

Despite the worldwide strides in advancing financial inclusion amongst the youth, a significant percentage of the population is still financially disadvantaged. While traditional banks have long offered basic financial services to the younger generations, a further opportunity has been spotted to provide better and slicker digital banking to tech-savvy kids and teenagers. This chapter summarises the ongoing development of Digital Youth Banking while highlighting its latest trends. It then explores challenges and opportunities relating to digital youth banking from the accessibility, practicability, and sustainability perspectives. This chapter further presents three exemplary cases to highlight the unleashed potential of digital youth banking from the traditional bank, neobank, and fintech points of view before setting out a series of recommendations to ramp up the endeavours towards financial inclusion of young people in society.

Keywords: Digital; youth banking; fintech; unbanked; underbanked; neobank; accessibility; practicability; sustainability; financial inclusion

1. Introduction

Banking is being revolutionised at an unprecedented speed due to the emergence of "fintech", that is, novel digital technologies that have transformed the way banks manage their customers and the underlying technical infrastructure (Sophia, 2021, Wewege *et al.*, 2020). Adopting fintech has afforded a number of advantages, namely, radically decreased transaction costs, greatly expanded product ranges, and a wider scope of services for bank customers (Wewege *et al.*, 2020). Such advantages have disrupted the current banking industry and encouraged financial institutions to focus on meeting changing consumer digital banking needs (Foscht, 2010). Those financial institutions use fintech to maintain and enhance competitiveness to maintain market share in an increasingly sophisticated industry (Sophia, 2021; Toh and Tran, 2020; Wijland *et al.*, 2016). Fintech has enabled the meteoric rise of mobile payment (Agarwal and Zhang, 2020) and the emergence of digital lending and credit (Cornelli *et al.*, 2021). However, despite the increasing use of fintech by institutions and their customers, almost half of the world's young adults (aged 15–24) are financially excluded (OECD, 2020a). Our aim in this chapter is to problematise this phenomenon and examine how youth can be better served via digital banking.

In our examination, we take an inclusive and broad definition in this research of *youth*, referring to any individual under 29 as the discussions on its precise concept is beyond the scope of the chapter. In the extant literature, the definition of *youth* varies according to the context. For instance, the UN defines youth as those aged between 15 and 24 (UN, 2020), whereas the OECD sets the scope from 15 to 29 (OECD, 2020a). While the upper bound of the age band does not reach an agreement, the lower one differs widely too: It has been set from 0 when a child is born to 7, 12, 13, or 14 (OECD, 2020a). Considering the discrepancy, we take youth to refer to anyone under 29 as this encompasses Generation Z[a] and Generation

[a]Those born between 1997 and 2012 — Parker and Igielnik (2020). Available at: https://www.pewresearch.org/social-trends/2020/05/14/on-the-cusp-of-adulthood-and-facing-an-uncertain-future-what-we-know-about-gen-z-so-far-2/.

Alpha,[b] which will reach 1.2 billion (OECD, 2020a) and 2 billion, respectively, by 2025 (Generation Alpha, 2022).

It is problematic that so many under 29 remain financially excluded from banking and its relevant fintech. Generations Z and Alpha are assumed to be digital natives, that is, having grown up with accessible digital technologies (Kesharwani, 2020) — often through the use of mobile technologies. As more youth have access to fintech, there emerges a new medium and opportunity for the banking industry to improve their financial inclusion. Therefore, digital youth banking is significant for both customers and providers. Speaking from the user perspective, being financially included is widely considered an effective enabler for youth, empowering them with improved livelihoods and increased well-being in accordance with their life stages (Panos and Wilson, 2020). Scholars confirm that access to financial services, such as saving accounts and financial education, positively affects their financial behaviours, enables asset accumulation, improves upward economic mobility, and enhances employment in both the short and the long term (Senyo and Osabutey, 2020).

The provision of digital youth banking also refers to the interest of financial institutions. Whitebread and Bingham (2013) conclude in their empirical work that children start to form their financial habits as young as seven years old. Attracting youth at an early age potentially provides banks with lifelong customers as a quarter of people choose to stay with the same bank they had an account with during childhood (Greenhalgh, 2017). Furthermore, Generation Z already possesses significant spending power, amounting to US$44 billion (Mondres, 2019), and when Generation Z and Generation Alpha fully enter the workforce, they will, by sheer numbers, command remarkable purchasing power (Ng *et al.*, 2019), making them attractive to financial service providers (Thomas and Shivani, 2020).

In this chapter, we first categorise the types of youth that have been financially excluded at varying levels within a three-tier framework of digital youth banking status: the unbanked, the underbanked, and the less financially literate youth. For each category,

[b]Those born between the mid-2010s and 2025 — Generation Alpha (2022). Available at: https://generationalpha.com/.

we present the key and outline the challenges and opportunities facing the banking industry when bringing youth into the formal financial sector. We then offer three exemplary cases, ranging from traditional banks to neobanks and fintech infrastructure providers. Each case summarises the initiatives they have undertaken to engage with youth and their relevant challenges with key developmental issues. We lastly offer recommendations on how financial institutions may use fintech to reach and attract the unbanked and underbanked youth.

2. Challenges Faced by Youth

Similar to other banking customers, the financial needs of the youth vary and evolve based on general social factors, personal circumstances, and life stages (Wang and Ford, 2020). However, youth face particular challenges that affect them disproportionately. This is because, in most countries, young individuals below a certain age are not allowed to utilise formal financial services or can only do so with parental or guardian approval (Goyal and Kumar, 2021). As a result, there are different categories of youth in relation to banking. We examine them in this section, specifically regarding digital youth banking.

2.1. *The unbanked youth*

We define unbanked youth as individuals not possessing a commercial transaction account with a bank and not being able to access services from financial institutions (Breitbach and Walstad, 2014). Despite recent developments to reduce unbanked populations, 1.7 billion people still lack access to at least one of the banking services — 600 million of whom are youths (Statista, 2021). As a matter of fact, on a global scale, almost half of young adults are financially excluded, with those living in developing countries suffering the most (OECD, 2020a).

Several causes are attributed to the unbanked issue. Physically, one significant reason is the lack of bank presence in an area. Financial institutions have utilised fintech and digital banking systems as a form of cost control measure. Such measures have led to physical bank branches being closed down, particularly in rural areas (Kearns, 2018). This requires a number of customers to travel significant distances in order to open and access their accounts (Dupas *et al.*, 2018), imposing excessive costs on the customer to have and maintain an available account, a challenge that impacts youth even more so than general bank customers.

Practically, the reasons for unbanked youth can be better understood from the demand-and-supply perspective. The primary reason on the demand side is that the individual lacks a sufficient and/or stable income to make the holding cost of a bank account worthwhile (Babajic *et al.*, 2018). A vast majority of financial institutions require a minimum amount in the account at any given time; otherwise, a monthly fee will be applied. This is particularly challenging for the youth, who are financially characterised as the ones with a small and irregular income from casual work or parents and families (SEEP, 2013), and/or are more likely to be unemployed (Finmark, 2018). When the financial need arises, youngsters are inclined to seek support from informal sources, such as family lending (Babajic *et al.*, 2018). As a result, they are less incentivised to establish and maintain access to banking services. From the supply side, financial institutions historically do not possess a high degree of incentives to tailor the services and products to this specific segmentation of customers because of the hefty cost to maintain small accounts and the high risk of debt default associated with the youth (Fitzpatrick, 2015).

Being unbanked is highly detrimental to a youth's personal development in both the short and the long term. It is widely confirmed that access to banks is essential in order to save, spend, and receive money (The World Bank, 2022). Not possessing a bank account makes it more difficult for unbanked individuals to build savings that can be invested in education, help weather unexpected needs, and reduce mental stress (Barcellos and Zamarro, 2021; Liu, 2018). Aside from being unable to reap the benefits of banking access, the unbanked youth are more likely to turn to alternative and predatory services, such as emergency payday loans whose interest rates are higher than base rates. The use of predatory lenders leads to worsening financial situations (Sinha and Pierda, 2021). In particular, there is increasing concern over the use of cashless services where the unbanked youth will be deprived of the ability to purchase goods in a convenient manner (Osland and Clinch, 2021). Being unbanked further prevents youth from building credit records/scores and developing financial literacy that will benefit them in the long term (OECD, 2020b). Studies suggest that the earlier the youth can access financial services, the higher the likelihood that they will become more financially successful as they will have generally gained a deeper and wider knowledge of financial markets and obtained richer financial experience (Friedline *et al.*, 2016; Grinstein-Weiss *et al.*, 2010).

Given the long-lasting effects of being unbanked, there are significant steady signs of progress enabled by fintech that is being made in reducing the general unbanked population worldwide. The World Bank has witnessed an increase of 1.7 billion individuals opening formal banking accounts from 2011 to 2017 (The World Bank, 2022). In particular, international organisations, such as The World Bank, the United Nations (UN), and the International Monetary Fund (IMF), have partnered with local private and public shareholders to introduce financial inclusion schemes. This has made tremendous gains in banking previously financially excluded populations by leveraging digital transformation, including mobile technologies and open banking. However, more must be done to reduce the number of unbanked youths, with a focus on accessibility. Later in this chapter, we will outline case studies for how this can be done.

2.2. *The underbanked youth*

Even when youth have access to banking services, the possession of a bank account does not ensure that they will be provided with the needed financial services and/or products. We define underbanked youth as banked individuals with at least one formal transaction account but who are unable to fully meet their financial needs with the existing services and products (Breitbach and Walstad, 2014; Northwood and Rhine, 2017). Being underbanked is a prevalent issue in both emerging and developed economies. For instance, while only 5.8% of people are unbanked in the US, 36.3% are underbanked, most of whom are youth (Lee and Hales, 2021).

Unlike being unbanked, reasons for being underbanked are largely complex and nuanced according to systematic and individual issues. An underbanked customer can be categorised as *passive underbanked* as the individual has been affected by systematic and non-personal issues. The key issue that contributes to the passive underbanked state is a lack of customer data for such types of customers (Baidoo, 2020). The underbanked individual is unlikely to be fully represented in the credit datasets utilised by financial institutions for any customer banking service decisions (Di Maggio *et al.*, 2020). The lack of data is caused by credit invisibility, that is, insufficient credit history recorded in both internal and external databases (Aitken, 2017). This issue is further exacerbated by the high cost of acquiring such data from alternative sources, such as credit bureaus in other countries (Baidoo, 2020).

In contrast, user behaviour results in customers being categorised as *active underbanked.* This relates to the user experience with, trust towards, and privacy concerns over financial institutions. To be specific, some individuals choose to bank with a limited variety of necessary banking products as their previous experience was unfavourable, such as unexpected overdraft fees (Dlugosz *et al.*, 2021). This may further lead to the erosion of the trust that the users have in the bank. In particular, many youths already do not have reliable or trusting relationships with banking institutions and are thus unwilling to take any additional financial services which may be better for them (OECD, 2020b). Adding to the lack of trust is the increasing level of privacy concern. Given the fact that data breaches are increasingly common (Wang *et al.*, 2022), some individuals choose to only use basic banking services by limiting the information they will share with financial institutions (Albashrawi and Motiwalla, 2019).

Being either passive or active underbanked suggests that the individual is unable to obtain the financial services needed from the financial institutions and thus has to use alternative financial services, such as rent to own, payday lenders, and refund anticipation loans, which however often incur extortionate rates (Chen and Friedline, 2022). The burden of these fees associated with high rates is not equally shouldered by all users and falls particularly heavily on the financially fragile — the underbanked group (Di Maggio *et al.*, 2020). For instance, 9% of all accounts generate more than 10 overdrafts per year, which account for 79% of all overdraft fees earned by the banks (CFPB, 2021). As a result, a higher amount of fees spent on serving the interest payments results in less available funding for those affected, especially the youth, to spend on education, health, or any other type of investment/consumption (Chen and Friedline, 2022). To this end, tackling the underbanked is essential to foster personal financial well-being, decrease poverty, and reduce inequality across the population (Mori, 2019).

Fintech, empowered by digital transformation, has progressively decreased the blight of being underbanked. Fintech has enabled financial institutions to leverage alternative data from social media platforms, utility payments, asset ownerships, and other user-permissioned data (Croux *et al.*, 2022) to formulate reliable credit modelling. It also has the potential to offer multiple additional services via mobile services at a lower cost, making the services more affordable, stable, and secure. In this regard, the concerns about being passive and active underbanked can be mediated and the youth can in particular benefit from these developments.

2.3. *The less financially literate youth*

Beyond the dichotomy of the unbanked and underbanked youth, we also bring our focus to youth who are not making the best use of financial services (Chen and Friedline, 2022). Moving beyond such a dichotomy allows the inclusion of a relatively large population whose financial needs await further exploration. More importantly, the current dichotomy treats the banking status of being unbanked and underbanked as a static condition (Chen and Friedline, 2022), suggesting that the eradication of the unbanked and underbanked populations is the target of financial inclusion. Empirical research, however, confirms that being banked does not necessarily lead to financial inclusion (OECD, 2020a). Therefore, understanding how financial services and products can be used meaningfully — financial literacy — is pivotal in achieving financial inclusion.

Financial literacy relates to "the combination of awareness, knowledge, skills, attitudes and behaviours needed to make informed financial decisions and ultimately achieve individual financial well-being" (OECD, 2020b). Being financially literate requires an adequate understanding of the key financial topics, including inflation, numeracy, risk diversification, and compound interest (Lusardi and Mitchell, 2014), and entails the necessary mastery of financial capability to make better-informed decisions on managing finances (Çera *et al.*, 2021). In other words, full financial inclusion can only be achieved when the users not only have access to a range of financial services but are able to use them regularly as well (The World Bank, 2022).

Due to the inadequacy of systematic training and/or education on the subject of finance and banking, almost 56% of youth acquire financial knowledge from their parents and/or by teaching themselves (The London Institute of Banking and Finance, 2022). The education deficiency has been further compounded by the increasing complexity of financial products, partly caused by the diversity of savings and investment choices, and partly driven by digital innovation (Lusardi, 2019), such as cryptocurrencies and non-fungible tokens. As digital natives, a number of youth are attracted to newly available investment products that are inherently digital in nature. This can impose adverse impacts on the youths' financial health as most of such products are not covered by consumer protection laws or are inappropriately regulated (Browne, 2021). Access to digital technologies allows youth to not only engage in digital banking but also interact with high-risk trading apps and social media-based platforms. As an increasing number of potentially high-risk and complex financial products become more accessible to youth, financial literacy becomes a significant need (OECD, 2020b).

Financial literacy not only promotes positive financial behaviours in individuals but also has larger societal benefits (Xiao and Porto, 2017). At the individual level, promoting responsible financial practices towards financial literacy leads to effective and efficient financial inclusion (Fabris and Luburić, 2016). This is echoed by observations from other scholars that good financial habits of saving and investment along with solid financial knowledge result in higher-than-average returns on wealth (Lusardi and Mitchell, 2014; OECD, 2020b).

At the societal level, with more youth gaining financial acumen and responsibility as a result of financial literacy, population-level poverty can be gradually reduced, leading to a more equitable economy (Fabris and Luburić, 2016). The financially literate population can help improve the efficiency, transparency, competition, and accessibility of retail financial markets by reducing information asymmetry and loss of information balance of power between providers and users of financial services (Hussain *et al.*, 2018). Ultimately, the financial literacy of youth transforms into overall public confidence and trust in the financial system, making it sustainable and resilient.

Considering the importance of financial literacy for the youth, a two-pronged approach has been adopted by selective financial institutions, which starts from the provision of transparent educational materials in tandem with financial services to assist customers in making better-informed financial decisions. It is further supplemented by tailored customer service that is well embedded in the company's culture, aiming at short- and long-term targets for both individuals and enterprises.

2.4. *The three categories of digital youth banking status*

We identify three primary challenging banking states that youth currently face and that can be fulfilled by youth banking services, that is, the unbanked, underbanked, and less financially literate youth. Although such statuses have different points of concern, they are conceptually interconnected. While the unbanked issue relates to the individual who does not possess any formal financial service or product, the underbanked issue generally surrounds the person whose financial needs cannot be fully met by existing bank accounts. We extend this dichotomy by introducing the less financially literate issue, referring to the adequate knowledge and capability needed to make the most use of available financial services and/or products. In other words, being unbanked refers to the issue of accessibility to financial services or products, being underbanked focuses on the practicability of the financial services and/or products in fulfilling financial needs, and being less financially literate suggests concerns about the sustainability of the youth's ability to manage their short-term and long-term financial benefits and well-being. As a result, we established a three-tiered framework to appreciate the development of digital youth banking towards financial inclusion (Table 1).

3. Case Studies

In light of the unmet financial needs amongst the youth, enabled by digital transformation, several financial institutions have taken the

Table 1. Three categories of digital youth banking status.

#	Tier	Specification	Point of Concern
1	Unbanked	Not possessing financial service or product	Accessibility
2	Underbanked	Not fully meeting financial needs	Practicability
3	Less Financially Literate	Not fully making use of financial provision	Sustainability

lead in introducing and operating digital youth banking in an effort to financially include the young population worldwide. We present exemplary cases from three stakeholders in the financial ecosystem — traditional banks, neobanks, and fintech infrastructure providers — to showcase the latest measures and moves towards financial inclusion through digital youth banking for the youth.

3.1. *Traditional bank*

Amongst the traditional banks in the UK, NatWest, one of the four leading banks with 19 million customers and £782 billion in total assets (Statista, 2022), is sparing no effort to improve youth financial inclusion by launching digital youth banking. It is aimed at eligible young individuals between 11 and 17 year of age, providing them with a dedicated current account with features ranging from a contactless debit card to compatibility with Apple and Google Pay, and a mobile banking app with a parent's or guardian's approval.

NatWest chose to acquire the standalone app Rooster Money in 2021 to diversify its offerings to the youth while strengthening its endeavours in digital youth banking (NatWest, 2021a). In addition to its Child and Teen Bank, NatWest Rooster Money has expanded its customer base by attracting kids aged 3 to 17. Following the typical pricing scheme of internet service, it outlines three plans with core features free (NatWest, 2021b). Specifically, NatWest Rooster Money starts with the free version, allowing for money tracking and savings goals. While Rooster Plus costs £0.99 per month with features such as a reward for chores and a savings pot where parents can decide the interest rates paid for kids' savings, the Rooster Card, charging a monthly fee of £1.99, provides an additional feature of a contactless debit card, which allows kids to spend "real" money in stores or online conveniently and safely. As the introductory financial product to the youth, the Rooster Card comes without overdraft and can be cancelled at any time, so that the parents have the final say while being kept aware of their children's spending via the app.

Apart from the acquisition of an external standalone digital solution to improve the presence and reach of digital youth banking, some traditional banks, such as OTP Bank, developed their own digital provisions. OTP Bank, one of the largest banks in Hungary, was privatised from a state-run enterprise, securing a quarter of the local commercial banking market in both Hungary and across Eastern Europe, such as Romania and Bulgaria. Facing increasing competition in the banking sector, OTP Bank could no longer rely on its de facto monopoly strategy and thus decided to change its value proposition by introducing a new business unit to effectively compete in a rapidly changing market (Sophia, 2021).

One of the most important moves it sought was to innovate its junior account by further digitalising the product. Departing from the previous version with limited features, the radically overhauled junior account is provided in the form of a mobile app, which offers several innovative features to appeal to its youthful and digitally savvy audience. The app integrates the youth's daily financial needs to increase customer stickiness. For instance, it features tailored functions, such as a youth community of student job postings and volunteer recruitment, and a newsfeed offering educational and financial advice, making the app a one-stop place where the user can align his/her financial and educational needs with digital youth banking.

Despite the different scopes of digital innovation that have driven digital youth banking in the focal banks (external innovation for NatWest and internal innovation for OTP Bank), both have taken the digital solution to reimage the value proposition to specifically target the youth through digital youth banking. NatWest has been more focused on providing practical tools for better financial management, whereas OTP Bank is more inclined to establish an online community-based app where the most pertinent educational, financial, and life needs of the youth can be simultaneously met. In this regard, both are aiming to eradicate the unbanked and underbanked population and promote financial literacy amongst the youth.

3.2. *Neobank*

As the new but significant stakeholder in the fintech ecosystem, neobanks have been proactively engaging in digital youth banking. Touted as the first challenger bank in the UK, Starling Bank is no exception. It was established in 2014 and has been operating as a neobank since 2016. From the outset, Starling Bank has been digitally empowered and digitalised, which is evidenced by the fact that it has substantially and consistently invested in its digital infrastructure to cater to the rapid expansion of the customer base even throughout the pandemic (Ralph, 2021). Notwithstanding its phenomenal success in the routine banking business, Starling Bank has been relentlessly seeking new niche markets in which its digital strength and soul can make inroads. Digital youth banking is one of its latest endeavours as it focuses on the youth market by introducing the Starling Kite to people aged 6 to 16, a less competitive market devoid of financial products (GlobalData Financial, 2020).

Starling Kite, launched in 2020, is an inviting app, aimed at onboarding youngsters while promoting their financial literacy. Available on an app with a three-tiered pricing scheme, Starling Kite is generally cheaper than its traditional counterparts, such as NatWest Rooster, and conditioned on the parent's Starling account. Similar to other competitors, it offers a contactless debit card but with a more powerful parent control function in place (Starling, 2020). The app further features financial literacy functions to teach the targeted customers about financial basics, primarily savings goals and tasks, increasing their financial awareness.

Given its digital nature, Starling Kite is relatively more accessible and affordable compared to traditional alternatives such as NatWest Rooster, marking it as a strong force in serving the unbanked and underbanked youth. It may further step up its efforts in providing more financial educational features to make its footprint on financial literacy increasingly visible to the youth and the public.

3.3. *Fintech infrastructure provider*

The fintech infrastructure provider is another indispensable player in the fintech ecosystem that is restlessly contributing to digital youth banking. Previously known as Family Finances, the Hungary-based and global-reaching fintech enterprise ff.next is an award-winning digital infrastructure provider in this area. As a B2B developer specialising in interactive and dynamic UI (user interface) and UX (user experience) design, ff.next provides a wide range of off-the-shelf modules through its interface design, for banking business units, such as the digital youth banking (ff.next, 2021).

Intrigued by the vision of promoting financial literacy for the youth, ff.next has built its fintech business for commercial customers using a growth mindset with a youth perspective. Development starts with current UI and UX design that visually appeal to the youth. The interface attracts youth end users to keep them engaged (Chau and Ngai, 2010; Rolfe, 2015; Family Finances, 2020). ff.next introduced and improved offerings to digital youth banking to enable ease of use (Family Finances, 2020). In addition to the visual upgrade, ff.next also draws on the concept of entertainment education by redesigning the financial products and providing education at the same time in a more accessible and informative manner (ff.next, 2022). In their deliverables to financial institutions, ff.next takes the form of a visualised money management tool with spending insights, in-app rewards, and finance quizzes. This approach mixes banking services and financial literacy to keep youth end users engaged.

ff.next further leverages the social responsibilities that the younger generation is particularly conscious of, such as environmental awareness, to involve the youth. Considering the fact that a vast majority of Generation Z is environmentally sensitive (Petro, 2021), ff.next assembles a module that can efficiently supplement existing mobile banking applications through a handy and user-friendly tool for customers. Such a module, along with a carbon footprint tracker, setting CO_2 limits, peer analysis, etc., proves to be useful in reducing the end users' carbon footprint and maintaining a more sustainable lifestyle.

These practical digital youth banking features have been well-accepted by financial institutions and aid their digital youth banking strategies to continuously onboard the youth and consistently improve related services. In addition, such innovations, and a financial literacy-focussed perspective, have permeated through ff.next's business network. The adoption of this business network has led to ff.next cultivating its business model as a leader within an emerging digital youth banking ecosystem.

3.4. *Summary*

All three cases from across the financial spectrum have leveraged digital solutions to improve the accessibility, practicability, and/or sustainability of digital youth banking. All have aimed at unbanked, underbanked, or less financially literate youths; they, however, have differed in the manner in which digital youth banking is constructed. Traditional banks and neobanks, such as NatWest, OTP bank, and Starling Bank, provided digital youth banking as an add-on to the existing full services. They thus extended the banking services and/or products from the current customers to others, for instance, the youth. In contrast, the fintech infrastructure provider, such as ff.next, has made digital youth banking a primary output with key social responsibilities juxtaposed with other banking services. In this sense, ff.next transformed its business strategy and/or model to meet the specific needs, including both financial and social ones, of certain groups of end users, such as the youth. Serving niches is not equal to aiming at a small market, as serving the specific needs of a certain customer segment has great depth. As young people are looking for personalised solutions and the best possible customer experience, those brands offering solutions that are aligned with the values and beliefs of users are more likely to succeed.

4. Conclusions

Digital youth banking, one of the latest fintech initiatives in achieving financial inclusion, has come under the spotlight. It has been introduced by various fintech stakeholders to overcome the worrying financial challenges facing youngsters, namely, the issues of the unbanked, the underbanked, and the less financially literate. The unbanked issue emphasises the accessibility for the youth in obtaining the necessary financial services or products, whereas the underbanked issue highlights the practicability of the financial services and/or products in meeting the individual's needs. While the efforts to address unbanked and underbanked issues have significantly contributed to youth financial inclusion, we caution that such impacts can be sustained due to the increasingly complex and volatile nature of the financial market.

We, therefore, stress the importance of financial literacy that refers to the sustainability of digital youth banking, which requires financial knowledge and the capability to make informed and nimble financial decisions. A number of financial institutions have taken the initiative to tackle these challenges. While traditional banks and neobanks expanded provisions to the youth by diversifying the services and products, certain fintech infrastructure providers have taken further steps to align the end user's needs with their business strategy for financial literacy. Despite the differences in practices of onboarding the youth, these institutions are all at the forefront of harnessing digital youth banking to promote the financial well-being of the youth. In this sense, digital youth banking has already demonstrated its potential in addressing the issues of the unbanked, underbanked, and less financially literate, and will have an increasingly significant role in the banking sector in the future for the financial inclusion of the youth.

Acknowledgement

We thank Mr. Alex Bonnard for collecting and collating documents from various sources. We would also like to show our gratitude to the staff from ff.next, namely, Ms. Melinda Havas, the Head of Marketing and Business Development, and Mr. Andras Grabits, the Head of Operations and Finance, for sharing their valuable insights and rich experiences with us during the course of this project.

References

Agarwal, S. and Zhang, J. (2020). FinTech, lending and payment innovation: A review, *Asia-Pacific Journal of Financial Studies*, 49(3), pp. 353–367.

Aitken, R. (2017). 'All data is credit data': Constituting the unbanked, *Competition and Change*, 21(4), pp. 274–300.

Albashrawi, M., and Motiwalla, L. (2019). Privacy and personalisation in continued usage intention of mobile banking: An integrative perspective, *Information Systems Frontiers*, 21(5), pp. 1031–1043.

Babajic, A., Okicic, J., and Jukan, M. K. (2018). Identification of barriers to financial inclusion among youth, *International Business Research (Toronto)*, 11(7), p. 120.

Baidoo, E. (2020). A credit analysis of the unbanked and underbanked: An argument for alternative data, PhD dissertation, Analytics and Data Science Institute, Kennesaw State University.

Barcellos, S. H. and Zamarro, G. (2021). Unbanked status and use of alternative financial services among minority populations, *Journal of Pension Economics and Finance*, 20(4), pp. 468–481.

Breitbach, E. and Walstad, W. B., (2014). Financial literacy and banking affiliation: Results for the unbanked, underbanked, and fully banked, *Perspectives on Economic Education Research*, 9(1), pp. 20–35.

Browne, R. (2021). Most young crypto traders don't realise it's not regulated, UK markets watchdog says. *CNBC*. Available at: https://www.cnbc.com/2021/10/19/young-traders-treat-crypto-investing-like-a-competition-fca-says.html?fbclid=IwAR010EFA9Xyz7vxcMxF6CoPKzPNAg9hrcxkPTgdvl_elbPXWG1cXjXYDrz0, accessed 12/07/22.

Çera, G., Khan, K. A., Mlouk, A., and Brabenec, T. (2021). Improving financial capability: The mediating role of financial behaviour, *Economic Research-Ekonomska Istraživanja*, 34(1), pp. 1265–1282.

CFPB (2021). Levelling up through a purpose-led approach to finance. Consumer Financial Protection Bureau. Available at: https://acss.org.uk/levelling-up-through-a-purpose-led-approach-to-finance, accessed 28/06/22.

Chau, V. S. and Ngai, L. W. (2010). The youth market for internet banking services: Perceptions, attitude and behaviour, *Journal of Services Marketing*, 24(1), pp. 42–60.

Chen, Z. and Friedline, T., (2022). Make the invisible underbanked visible: Who are the underbanked? *Financial Counseling and Planning*, 33(2), pp.160–170.

Cornelli, G., Frost, J., Gambacorta, L., Rau, R., Wardrop, R., and Ziegler, T. (2021). Fintech and big tech credit: What explains the rise of digital lending? *CESifo Forum*, 22(2), pp. 30–34.

Croux, C., Jagtiani, J., Korivi, T., and Vulanovic, M. (2020). Important factors determining fintech loan default: Evidence from a lendingclub consumer platform, *Journal of Economic Behavior and Organization*, 173, pp. 270–296.

Di Maggio, M., Ma, A. T., and Williams, E. (2020). In the red: Overdrafts, payday lending and the underbanked (No. w28242). National Bureau of Economic Research.

Dlugosz, J. L., Melzer, B. T., and Morgan, D. P. (2021). Who pays the price? Overdraft fee ceilings and the unbanked, Staff Report, No. 973, Federal Reserve Bank of New York, New York, NY.

Dupas, P. *et al.* (2018). Banking the unbanked? Evidence from three countries, *American Economic Journal: Applied Economics*, 10(2), pp. 257–297.

Fabris, N. and Luburić, R. (2016). Financial education of children and youth, *Journal of Central Banking Theory and Practice*, 5(2), pp. 65–79.

Family Finances (2020). Market Research.

ff.next, (2021). Products. ffnext.io. Available at: https://www.ffnext.io/products, accessed 9/07/22.

ff.next (2022). Intro to ff.next - FinTech powerhouse for financial innovators. Unpublished internal company document.

Finmark (2018). FinScope SA 2018 Fact sheet: How South Africans are leveraging informal and formal financial markets, Finscope. Available at: http://finmark.org.za/wpcontent/uploads/2019/01/FMT_Fsc_Leavebehind_CB4.pdf, accessed 11/06/22.

Fitzpatrick, K. (2015). Does "banking the unbanked" help families to save? Evidence from the United Kingdom, *The Journal of Consumer Affairs*, 49(1), pp. 223–249.

Foscht, T. *et al.* (2010). Banking on the youth: The case for finer segmentation of the youth market, *Young Consumers*, 11(4), pp. 264–276.

Friedline, T., Despard, M., and Chowa, G. A. N. (2016). Preventive policy strategy for banking the unbanked: Savings accounts for teenagers? *Journal of Poverty*, 20(1), pp. 2–33.

Generation Alpha (2022). Generation Alpha — Born 2010–2024. Generationalpha.com. Available at: https://generationalpha.com/, accessed 20/07/22.

GlobalData Financial (2020). Starling's move into teen banking is where incumbents are most vulnerable. Retail Banker International. Available at: https://www.retailbankerinternational.com/comment/starling-enters-teen-banking-market/, accessed 13/07/22.

Goyal, K. and Kumar, S. (2021). Financial literacy: A systematic review and bibliometric analysis, *International Journal of Consumer Studies*, 45(1), 80–105.

Greenhalgh, H. (2017). Children's bank accounts: A potted history. *Financial Times*. Available at: https://www.ft.com/content/7df18140-07f7-11e7-97d1-5e720a26771b, accessed 16/07/22.

Grinstein-Weiss, M., Yeo, Y. H., Despard, M. R., Casalotti, A. M., and Zhan, M. (2010). Does prior banking experience matter? Differences of the banked and unbanked in individual development accounts, *Journal of Family and Economic Issues*, 31(2), pp. 212–227.

Hussain, J., Salia, S., and Karim, A. (2018). Is knowledge that powerful? Financial literacy and access to finance: An analysis of enterprises in the UK, *Journal of Small Business and Enterprise Development*, 25(6), 985–1003.

Kearns, A. (2018). 5 ways fintech is helping the unbanked and underbanked population in 2018. *FinTech Weekly*. Available at: https://medium.com/fintech-weekly-magazine/5-ways-fintech-is-helping-the-unbanked-cand-underbanked-population-in-2018-54f22417d0b1, accessed 11/07/22.

Kesharwani, A. (2020). Do (how) digital natives adopt a new technology differently than digital immigrants? A longitudinal study, *Information and Management*, 57(2), 103170.

Lee, Y. and Hales, E. (2021). The "unbanked" and "underbanked" in the US: Who are they and how are they different? *Consumer Interests Annual*, 67, 1–2.

Liu, F. (2018). Macroeconomic effects of microsavings programs for the unbanked, *Journal of Economic Behavior and Organization*, 154, pp. 75–99.

Lusardi, A. (2019). Financial literacy and the need for financial education: Evidence and implications, *Swiss Journal of Economics and Statistics*, 155(1), pp. 1–8.

Lusardi, A. and Mitchell, O. S. (2014). The economic importance of financial literacy: Theory and evidence, *Journal of Economic Literature*, 52(1), pp. 5–44.

Mondres, T. (2019). How generation Z is changing financial services. *ABA Banking Journal*. Available at: https://bankingjournal.aba.com/2019/01/how-generation-z-is-changing-financial-services/#:~:text=About%20two-thirds%20of%20Gen%20Z%E2%80%99ers%20have%20bank%20accounts%3B,community%20institutions%20and%2019%20percent%20with%20credit%20unions.%29, accessed 08/07/22.

Mori, M. (2019). Banking underserved market segments, *Open Journal of Social Sciences*, 7(3), p. 506.

NatWest (2021a). Child and teen bank account. Kids debit card. NatWest. Natwest.com. Available at: https://www.natwest.com/current-accounts/childrens-accounts/adapt_account.html, accessed 18/07/22.

NatWest (2021b). NatWest picks up kids banking fintech rooster money. NatWest Group. Natwestgroup.com. Available at: https://www.natwestgroup.com/news/2021/10/natwest-picks-up-kids-banking-fintech-roostermoney.html, accessed 19/07/2022.

Ng, S. I., Ho, J. A., Lim, X. J., Chong, K. L., and Latiff, K. (2019). Mirror, mirror on the wall, are we ready for Gen-Z in marketplace? A study of smart retailing technology in Malaysia. Young Consumers.

Northwood, J. M. and Rhine, S. L. (2018). Use of bank and nonbank financial services: Financial decision making by immigrants and native born. Journal of Consumer Affairs, 52(2), 317–348.

OECD (2020a). Advancing the Digital Financial Inclusion of youth. Available at: www.oecd.org/daf/fin/financial-education/advancing-the-digital-financial-inclusion-of-youth.htm, accessed 11/07/22.

OECD (2020b). OECD/INFE 2020 international survey of adult financial literacy. Available at: https://www.oecd.org/financial/education/oecd-infe-2020-international-survey-of-adult-financial-literacy.pdf, accessed 10/07/22.

Osland, A. and Clinch, N. (2021). Cashless economies: Costs and benefits, in *SAGE Business Cases*, SAGE Business Cases Originals (SAGE Publications), California.

Panos, G. A., and Wilson, J. O. (2020). Financial literacy and responsible finance in the FinTech era: Capabilities and challenges, *The European Journal of Finance*, 26(4–5), pp. 297–301.

Parker, K. and Igielnik, R. (2020). On the cusp of adulthood and facing an uncertain future: What we know about Gen Z so far. Pew Research Center's Social and Demographic Trends Project. Available at: https://www.pewresearch.org/social-trends/2020/05/14/on-the-cusp-of-adulthood-and-facing-an-uncertain-future-what-we-know-about-gen-z-so-far-2/, accessed 21/07/22.

Petro, G. (2021). Gen Z is emerging as the sustainability generation. *Forbes*. Available at: https://www.forbes.com/sites/gregpetro/2021/04/30/gen-z-is-emerging-as-the-sustainability-gene-ration/?sh=72e718958699, accessed 25/10/22.

Ralph, O. (2021). Starling Bank matures from digital upstart to mainstream lender. *Financial Times*. Available at: https://www.ft.com/content/787e221f-4698-4640-96ac-8f910030c245, accessed 14/07/22.

Rolfe, A. (2015). Youth attitudes to banking and online banking services. Payments Cards and Mobile. Available at: https://paymentscardsandmobile.com/youth-attitudes-to-banking-and-www.online-banking-services/, accessed 11/07/22.

SEEP (2013). Understanding youth and their financial needs. Arlington, VA: Youth and Financial Services Working Group, SEEP Network. Available at: https://seepnetwork.org/files/galleries/1058_Understanding_Youth_and_their_Financial_Needs_April_2013.pdf, accessed 11/06/22.

Senyo, P. K. and Osabutey, E. L. (2020). Unearthing antecedents to financial inclusion through FinTech innovations, *Technovation*, 98, 102155.

Sinha, G. R. and Piedra, L. M. (2021). Unbanked in India: A qualitative analysis of 24 years of financial inclusion policies, *International Social Work*, 64(4), pp. 578–595.

Sophia, S. (2021). Financial literacy and financial innovation, *FinTech Journal of the International Academy for Case Studies*, 27, p. 1.

Starling (2020). Starling Kite launches as schools reopen to help teach children money management skills. Starling. Available at: https://www.starlingbank.com/news/starling-kite-launches-as-schools-reopen/, accessed 14/07/22.

Statista (2021). Unbanked population by country 2021. Statista. Available at: https://www.statista.com/statistics/1246963/unbanked-population-in-selected-countries/, accessed 12/07/22.

Statista (2022). Total assets of NatWest group from 2007 to 2021. Statista. Available at: https://www.statista.com/statistics/225077/total-assets-of-the-royal-bank-of-scotland/, accessed 15/07/22.

The London Institute of Banking and Finance (2022). Young persons' money index. The London Institute of Banking and Finance. Available at: https://www.libf.ac.uk/study/financial-education/young-persons-money-index, accessed 11/07/22.

The World Bank (2022). Financial inclusion. World Bank. Available at: https://www.worldbank.org/en/topic/financialinclusion/overview, accessed 12/06/22.

Thomas, M. R. and Shivani, M. P. (2020). Customer profiling of alpha: The next generation marketing, *Ushus Journal of Business Management*, 19(1), pp. 75–86.

Toh, Y. L. and Tran, T. (2020). How the COVID-19 Pandemic may reshape the digital payments landscape, *Payments System Research Briefing*, pp. 1–10.

UN (United Nations, Department of Economic and Social Affairs and Youth) (2020). Frequently asked questions — Definitions. Available at: https://www.un.org/development/desa/youth/what-we-do/faq.html, accessed 10/07/22.

UN (2013). Financial inclusion of youth. Un.org. Available at: https://www.un.org/esa/socdev/documents/youth/fact-sheets/youth-financial-inclusion.pdf, accessed 08/07/22.

Wang, X., Wang, X., Liu, Z., Chang, W., Hou, Y., and Zhao, Z. (2022). Too generous to be fair? Experiments on the interplay of what, when, and how in data breach recovery of the hotel industry, *Tourism Management*, 88, art. no. 104420.

Wang, Y. R. and Ford, M. T. (2020). Financial inadequacy and the disadvantageous changes in time perspective and goal-striving strategies throughout life, *Journal of Organizational Behavior*, 41(9), pp. 895–914.

Wewege L., Lee J., and Thomsett, M. C. (2020). Disruptions and digital banking trends, *Journal of Applied Finance and Banking*, 10(6), pp. 15–56.

Whitebread, D. and Bingham, S. (2013). *Habit Formation and Learning in Young Children* (London: Money Advice Service).

Wijland, R., Hansen, P., and Gardezi, F. (2016). Mobile nudging: Youth engagement with banking apps, *Journal of Financial Services Marketing*, 21(1), pp. 51–63.

Xiao, J. J. and Porto, N. (2017). Financial education and financial satisfaction: Financial literacy, behavior, and capability as mediators, *International Journal of Bank Marketing*, 35(5), pp. 805–817.

https://doi.org/10.1142/9781800614604_0012

Chapter 12

The Fintech Revolution Knocks Out the Financial Problems in the Energy Efficiency Sector: The Case of EFFORCE

Ricky Celenta[*,‡] Valentina Cucino[†,§] and Giulio Ferrigno[†,¶]

[*]*Department of Business Sciences Management and Innovation System, University of Salerno, Via Giovanni Paolo II, Fisciano, Italy*

[†]*Institute of Management and Department L'EMBEDS, Scuola Superiore Sant'Anna, Piazza Martiri della Libertà, Pisa, Italy*

[‡]*rcelenta@unisa.it*

[§]*valentina.cucino@santannapisa.it*

[¶]*giulio.ferrigno@santannapisa.it*

In recent years, we have been living through two epochal transformations in business: the new approach to sustainability and digital transformation. In this chapter, we analyse how these two phenomena intersect. To tackle this research question, we first discuss the opportunities and the limits of the energy efficiency sector, specifically referring to the role of green investments and the challenges of Energy Service Companies (ESCos). Thereafter, we introduce the leading technologies of the digital–financial revolution and illustrate the main features that characterise fintech, especially highlighting the role of blockchain and tokenisation in the energy efficiency sector. Through the analysis of the EFFORCE case, we highlight how in practice fintech and blockchain are supporting the crossing of certain limits of the energy efficiency sector and sustaining green investment.

Keywords: Green investment; ESCos; innovation; digital technologies; sustainability; energy sector; fintech; case study; EFFORCE; financial issues

1. Introduction

Digital technologies are reshaping different sectors, affecting everything from customer behaviours in organisational and production systems to business models to markets and, ultimately, to society (Dąbrowska *et al.*, 2022; Cucino and Ferrigno, 2023). Since the end of the last century, many scholars have begun to discuss energy efficiency (Greening *et al.*, 2000; Turner and Hanley, 2011; Tuominen *et al.*, 2013; Koesler *et al.*, 2016; Dąbrowska *et al.*, 2022) as a way to achieve more with less energy usage in an economy (Retallack *et al.*, 2018). At the same time, energy efficiency has been considered a relevant theme on the public policy agenda of most developed countries worldwide (Patterson, 1996). However, today, the importance of energy efficiency has increases as a key component of any 21st-century energy policy and is crucial to achieving climate change goals, particularly those agreed upon at the COP21 summit in Paris in December 2015 (Della Valle and Bertoldi, 2022). The importance of energy efficiency as a policy objective is linked to commercial and industrial competitiveness, and energy security benefits as well as an increase in environmental benefits (Patterson, 1996).

The International Energy Agency estimates that to achieve the goal of staying below the two-degree limit by 2035, investments in energy efficiency must account for at least half of all global energy investments. Many international institutions (OECD, European Commission, and IEA) suggest that energy efficiency is the best tool to keep energy demand under control and transition towards a low-carbon future. Although there is broad consensus that there is good untapped economic and technical potential for energy efficiency, the measures implemented are insufficient to meet the targets and overcome all the barriers to implementing an energy efficiency project (Giraudet, 2020). In this scenario, energy-saving companies (hereafter ESCos) have the potential to play an important role in providing technical and financial expertise for project development. The importance of ESCos is increasing with the diffusion and application of new digital technologies. Blockchain and other technologies of fintech are supporting the redefinition of the business model of ESCos, enabling a new way to invest in the energy efficiency sector. The case study analyses EFFORCE, a company co-founded by Steve Wozniak, a pioneer application of blockchain to the ESCo business model.

2. Energy Efficiency Sector, Green Investments, and ESCos

2.1. *The energy efficiency sector*

Today, it is necessary to pay considerable attention to renewable energy sources to mitigate environmental degeneration because non-renewable energy consumption contributes to CO_2 emissions (Inglesi-Lotz *et al.*, 2018; Dogan *et al.*, 2020).

However, to ensure environmental sustainability, there is a need to take cognisance of energy efficiency which is the most cost-effective way to ensure there is a reduction in energy consumption (Musibau *et al.*, 2021). In this sense, studies have focused on systematically integrating sustainable practices by companies operating in the energy sector into their business strategy and operations (Battaglia *et al.*, 2020; Cucino *et al.*, 2020, 2023b).

The American Council for an Energy-Efficient Economy (ACEEE) defines energy efficiency as using less energy to provide the same or better products, services, or amenities. Increasing efficiency allows more control over energy use, lowers costs, and offers multiple benefits for households, businesses, and the environment. Energy efficiency impacts various sectors including residential, commercial, industrial, and transportation (Molina *et al.*, 2016).

The definition provided by the ACEEE shows how energy efficiency and energy saving are related concepts, yet they have distinct definitions in the energy world. Energy efficiency usually describes the adoption of a particular technology that reduces overall energy consumption without changing consumer behaviour. The key is the specification of the adoption of technological solutions for the production and reduction of energy consumption. The term "energy efficiency" indicates the reduction in energy use necessary to achieve a certain objective without reducing the objective itself using technology. On the other hand, saving energy or conserving energy involves using less energy and changing behaviour patterns. These are two sides of the same coin, both of which are essential to achieve internationally set targets on greenhouse gas emissions (Stoffel, 2015).

As analysed by some authors (Allcott and Greenstone, 2012), efficiency and savings offer a critical "win-win" opportunity for gain. Energy efficiency can significantly reduce energy consumption, lower the cost of energy, improve energy security, and generate economic, environmental, and social benefits for both individuals and the public.

However, as anticipated earlier, to date, for various reasons, households, businesses, manufacturers, and government agencies have failed to take full advantage of energy efficiency opportunities.

For decades, scholars have been interested in the barriers to the adoption of energy efficiency (Hirst and Brown, 1990; Jaffe and Stavins, 1994). However, the topic is as timely as ever, and as revealed in Giraudet's recent study (2022); the main barriers to adoption are inadequate and asymmetric information (Gupta *et al.*, 2017), high initial investment costs (Stede, 2017), energy price volatility (Retallack *et al.*, 2018), and technology risk. These challenges are a complex combination of technical and financial barriers (Retallack *et al.*, 2018). As Giraudet pointed out, energy efficiency can be viewed as a trusted commodity whose performance is never fully disclosed to the buyer, and this is exacerbated by high upfront costs (Giraudet, 2022).

As shown by Row and Mohareb (2014), the power map of actors that influence the adoption of an energy efficiency policy is complex: Government, industry, and consumers play a strategic role (Taghizadeh-Hesary *et al.*, 2016; Retallack *et al.*, 2018).

The government can influence the demand for energy efficiency through the development of new building codes, or it can set standards for household appliances and other consumer products or finance programmes that aim to support investment in energy efficiency.

To create a transition to an energy-efficient approach, it is vital to ensure that private building owners and entrepreneurs are motivated to make energy-efficient decisions. Political strategies and incentives are not enough. Collaboration between builders, suppliers, equipment, and financial institutions, as well as awareness of and attention from citizens and consumers is needed (European Commission, 2016).

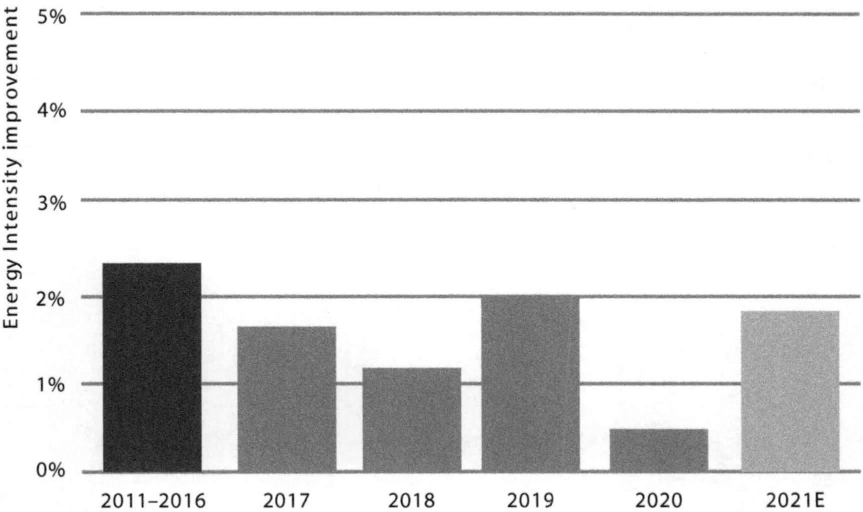

Fig. 1. Primary energy intensity improvement, 2011–2021.
Source: Adapted from International Energy Agency (IEA).

As indicated in Fig. 1, 2020 marked the lowest point in energy efficiency over the past decade.

In 2020, the extraordinary situation created by COVID-19 significantly influenced the behaviour of companies, entrepreneurs, suppliers, and consumers (Chesbrough, 2020; Cucino *et al.*, 2021; Ferrigno and Cucino, 2021). Thus, COVID-19 pushed down total spending on transport efficiency investments, but in the same year, Europe's building efficiency programmes were stronger and offset the transport boost, as shown in Fig. 2.

Additional and more stringent standards increased public spending and incentive structures, while more streamlined planning laws and procedures can help increase investment and make efficient projects more attractive to private financing (Marchi *et al.*, 2018). The International Energy Agency study shows that increased investment and increased public spending on efficiency are linked to the revitalisation plans launched in response to the COVID-19 crisis. New announcements of greater climate ambitions have resulted in energy efficiency trends returning to the 10-year average in 2021, consistent with the forecasts highlighted in Fig. 1.

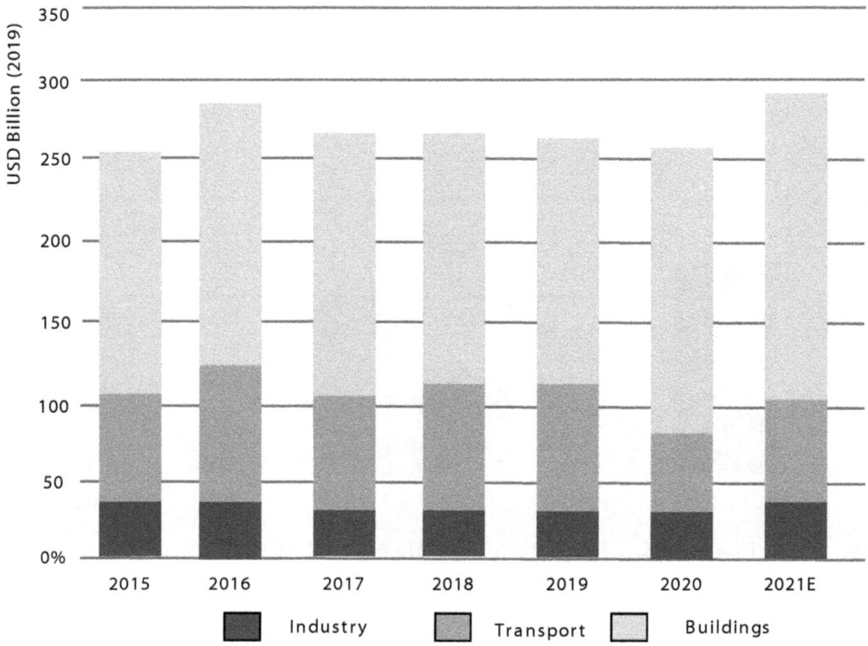

Fig. 2. Energy efficiency investment, 2015–2021.
Source: Adapted from International Energy Agency (IEA).

2.2. *How energy efficiency sector relates to green investment*

From what has been analysed so far, the importance of energy efficiency in terms of environmental protection is clear. Energy efficiency activities, however, require substantial green investments (Liù *et al.*, 2022). Some studies have defined green investment from the perspective of an investment goal coupled with improving the economic system's environmental sustainability (Eyraud *et al.*, 2013), or from the perspective of the direction of investment flow (Mielke and Steudle, 2018). However, the term "green investment" has not received a codified definition in the literature (Magalhaes, 2021). When we talk about green investments in general, we refer to investments that pursue environmental sustainability and circular economy, mitigate and adapt to climate change, or recover the environmental degradation. These are low-carbon and climate-resilient investments, as well as climate change-specific investments, made in companies, projects, and financial instruments that are primarily active in the renewable energy, clean technology, environmental technology, or sustainability markets (Liù *et al.*, 2022).

The literature also identifies energy efficiency investments within green investments. Energy efficiency investments in commercial, institutional, and government buildings typically include lighting, heating, ventilation, and air conditioning (HVAC) and as well as motors, reflective roofs, and a range of other applications. It is possible to divide energy efficiency investments made by industrial companies into two distinct forms. One involves significant changes in technology and production processes, mainly driven by decisions related to technological changes, market demand, and other long-term strategic issues. The other, more frequent than the first, relates to routine or emergency maintenance activities, aimed at marginally improving the energy efficiency of existing production lines and processes. Generally, public finance has a crucial role to play in the field of energy efficiency (see, e.g., Gouldson *et al.*, 2015; Foxon and Bolton, 2016). The energy efficiency markets face challenges across supply chains, from financiers to end users via technology suppliers and consultants. High investment costs and prohibitive calculations of risk and return limit the supply of affordable capital and the demand for such investments (Retallack *et al.*, 2018). Along with the financial barrier, the institutional barrier should also be lifted for energy efficiency investment. The role of government as a market creator and a rule-setter through removing barriers and mobilising necessary capital needs to be emphasised (Lee *et al.*, 2003). Energy Performance Contracting (here-after EPC) implemented by ESCos has been recognised as a mechanism to overcome some of these barriers (Limaye *et al.*, 2011).

2.3. *The challenges for the energy service companies (ESCos)*

ESCos are gaining considerable interest in the energy sector as they include almost all the energy efficiency activities under their umbrella (Fang and Miller, 2013). ESCos are companies that act as intermediaries between financial partners and public or private users that need investments to improve the energy efficiency of their facilities. An ESCo is a business that develops, installs, and finances projects designed to improve energy efficiency and reduce maintenance costs for energy-consuming facilities over certain periods (Lee *et al.*, 2003; Bertoldi *et al.*, 2007).

As highlighted by the European Energy Efficiency Directive (2012/27/EU; EED), the aim of ESCos is to unlock the value of energy savings by facilitating the interaction between financial partners and public or private users. EU Directive No. 2012/27/EU defines the EPC as "a contractual arrangement between the beneficiary and the provider of an energy efficiency improvement measure, where investments in that measure are paid for to a contractually agreed level of energy efficiency improvement". Through Energy Performance Contracts (hereafter EPCs), one can earn positive economic returns on an initial investment in energy system efficiency projects. However, EPCs include the design, installation, and financing of the efficiency project, so ESCos must rely on the revenue stream from cost savings to repay the project costs, receiving full payment for their work only if the project achieves these goals. EPCs allow the savings from reduced energy consumption to be shared between the party that made the investment and carried out the upgrading process and the beneficiary.

Before implementing an energy efficiency project, an energy system owner pays an energy efficiency bill to an electricity and gas supplier. The ESCo directly invests the financial resources, as an intermediate, to implement energy efficiency in the beneficiary's system. Over the contract's life, the beneficiary pays the ESCo and financial partner a portion of the energy savings generated. ESCos use their share of energy savings to earn a return on investment because the savings generated are the actual financial return on the initial investment. ESCos are remunerated only if the project achieves the energy efficiency goals. At the end of the contract, the grantee can take full advantage of the savings and the installed technology. Unfortunately, ESCos have not been able to explore their full potential because they suffer from the same barriers as the broader energy efficiency market. The main challenges for ESCos can be identified as follows:

1. The high upfront costs: access to a complex energy efficiency system requires a minimum investment of 200,000 euros, and meeting financial actors and beneficiaries involves complexities (EFFORCE White Paper, 2018);

2. The needs for technical knowledge of how energy systems work and smart meters to monitor the energy savings achieved;
3. The lack of trust and a meeting point between those who need to invest to improve energy efficiency of their facility and those who want to invest for alternative returns;
4. The inability of either party to make a technical assessment of the actual savings achievable through the efficiency intervention;
5. Uncertainty about the period of return on investment.

Such problems discourage ESCos from supporting small projects. However, increasing global attention towards fintech over the last few years and the recent explosion in the cryptocurrency and non-fungible token markets are revolutionising the financial sector by destroying old barriers and opening new growth horizons (Gomber *et al.*, 2017, 2018; Fosso Wamba, 2020). The fintech revolution can today represent a breakthrough in the scalability of ESCo activities and thus in the financing of energy efficiency investments.

3. Fintech Revolution of the Energy Efficiency Sector

3.1. *Main technologies epitomising the digital–financial revolution*

The use of Information Communication Technologies (ICTs) in the financial sector is not new; at the end of the 20th century, the sector was already characterised by substantial computerisation, as most financial services were dematerialised. However, until recently, certain constraints defined the operating environment. These constraints have been overcome through significant technological advances in two key areas: (1) "increased connectivity" and (2) "low-cost computing and data storage" (Feyen *et al.*, 2021). The Internet and mobile technology have rapidly increased connectivity and thus the ability to transfer information and interact remotely, both between companies and directly with consumers. The spread of the Internet, and related devices and activities, such as social media and e-commerce, has generated vast amounts of new data that are processed at ever lower costs and ever higher speeds. The efficiency of computing has increased exponentially and, simultaneously, the cost of storing data has decreased rapidly. The ability to process data rapidly has increased thanks to advances in artificial intelligence (AI) and deep learning.

In recent years, the development of new digital technologies, such as blockchain, artificial intelligence, big data, mobile services, social media, cloud computing, and Internet of Things, has affected all segments of the financial sector (European Commission, 2017; Gomber *et al.*, 2017). The term "fintech", in fact, generally refers to financial innovation made possible by technological innovation, which can translate into new business models, processes, or products, and the development of new market players (Gomber *et al.*, 2018; Suryono *et al.*, 2020).

Among the various technologies mentioned, it is evident that a particular role is played by blockchain technology (Fosso Wamba *et al.*, 2020) in smart contracts (De Giovanni, 2020), tokens (Chen, 2018; Schletz *et al.*, 2020), and the entire cryptocurrency market (Saman *et al.*, 2018).

3.2. *The potential of blockchain and tokenisation for the energy efficiency sector*

Numerous studies explain blockchain clearly, so one can refer to them for a more in-depth discussion of the technology (Iansiti and Lakhani, 2017; Kamran *et al.*, 2020). Here, we want to highlight the role of blockchain technology in innovation in the energy efficiency sector. The literature suggests that blockchain technology can support energy efficiency processes in three main ways (Schletz *et al.*, 2020). First, blockchain may enable a distributed platform model to support trading for energy efficiency, especially White Certificate Schemes (WCSs) (Khatoon *et al.*, 2019). Second, many scholars advocate that it is possible to use blockchain to facilitate peer-to-peer energy trading systems (Park *et al.*, 2018) by fostering the development of energy markets (Di Silvestre *et al.*, 2020). Third, blockchain could enable decentralised financing mechanisms for ESCos (Schletz, 2020).

Further studies are required, however, to understand how blockchain applications can foster energy efficiency interventions (Treiblmaier, 2018; Schletz, 2020). Therefore, in this chapter, we aim to enrich our comprehension of how blockchain applications can help to solve energy efficiency problems. To achieve this aim, we delve into an in-depth case study. More specifically, we explore EFFORCE, a paradigmatic example of the application of blockchain to innovate in the energy efficiency sector.

4. The EFFORCE Case

4.1. *Theoretical sampling*

As stated earlier, the main aim of this chapter is to analyse how fintech technologies lead to the development of a new business model in the ESCo sector and, thus, the innovation of the energy efficiency sector. To tackle this issue, we choose to adopt a case study methodology (Dagnino and Ferrigno, 2015; Yin, 2018), as it allows in-depth exploration, from multiple perspectives, of the richness and complexity of the topic of interest (Lichtman, 2014). More concretely, we analysed EFFORCE, which, to our knowledge is the first blockchain-based energy-saving trading platform, which allows people to participate and benefit from worldwide energy efficiency projects.

Two important reasons led us to study EFFORCE. First, EFFORCE is a paradigmatic example of an ESCo that acts as an intermediary between financial partners and public or private users that need investments to improve the energy efficiency of their facilities. EFFORCE is a blockchain-based energy-saving trading platform, which allows people to participate and benefit from worldwide energy efficiency projects. The platform brings together those who want to improve the energy efficiency of their buildings or industrial processes and a pool of contributors interested in being repaid in tokens representing the energy savings achieved.

Second, EFFORCE is an exemplary case to analyse because through its platform the energy savings, financed by the contributor, are tokenised (the name of the token is WOZX) and used or sold to energy-intensive consumers, who can thus stop paying their bills to optimise financing and access to capital, i.e., EFFORCE allows the tokenising of energy savings. In fact, through the tokenisation of the energy saved, it will be possible to guarantee liquidity and extend access to capital investment (EFFORCE, 2019).

4.2. *Methodological approach*

This study adopted a historical methodological approach (Di Minin *et al.*, 2019; Ferrigno *et al.*, 2022b; Sood and Tellis, 2005) to explain the application of blockchain to the ESCo business model. In the management literature, the historical methodology is suitable for addressing data narratives (Van Lent and Lerner, 2019) and analysing in-depth phenomena rooted further back in time (Buckley, 2016). Indeed, historical cases can provide the distance needed to observe how an innovation emerges and reshapes its institutional environment (Hargadon and Douglas, 2001). Moreover, the emphasis on context is useful for exploring longitudinal occurrences and changes (Smith and Lux, 1993). These reasons have made the historical approach exceptionally appropriate for investigating trends in levels of innovation. The historical approach is a systematic and structured approach that examines different sources of information, carefully evaluating them, considering their credibility and reliability, and ascertaining how often the same information appears in different sources (Golder, 2000).

4.3. *Data collection*

Most of the historical information is collected from secondary sources. This focus on secondary sources, is a standard historical procedure (Johnston, 2014; Ferrigno *et al.*, 2022b) and its use has been justified by the already large body of literature concerning the history of the company and the ephemeral nature of digital content (Brügger, 2013; Di Minin *et al.*, 2019; Ferrigno *et al.*, 2022a). More concretely, in line with some recent studies (Di Minin *et al.*, 2019; Del Sarto *et al.*, 2022; Ferrigno *et al.*, 2022a), we used the information only after establishing the reliability and credibility of the source and verifying any critical evidence for evaluating an innovation.

Our sources were peer-reviewed articles, magazine articles, YouTube videos, social networks, corporate websites and online archival material, annual reports, and real websites. The variety of sources made it possible to gather further details, through an analysis not only of the event itself but also of the complete context. The data collected helped us understand the evolution of the blockchain sector and analyse the EFFORCE case. Thanks to the documents collected and analysed, we developed a discussion on the application of blockchain to the ESCo business model.

4.4. *Data analysis*

According to Mason *et al.* (1997), we followed five methodical phases of historical investigation. First, the authors determine the domain of investigation (step 1) in applying blockchain technology to the ESCo business model. In particular (step 2), the authors focused on the company's implementation, use, and management of technology in the fintech scenario. Subsequently (step 3), the authors fixed the study in a limited time frame regarding the industrial context, particularly the year 2011. Therefore, the authors collected the evidence for historical research by carrying out research from primary public sources such as articles, books, photographs, and documents, such as annual reports and studies available on trade associations. To give greater validity and reliability to the analysis, we have chosen to use only reliable sources such as the company's website, university libraries, or international journals. We used three databases: Scopus, Google Scholar, and Lexis-Nexis. Subsequently, the information was broken down in chronological order. In step 4, the authors critically examined the existing literature. More concretely, the authors separately counted the number of times the same observation is repeated in the database created in step 2. Subsequently, the authors confronted each occurrence to select the essential information for the analysis. Finally (step 5), the authors interpreted the data first separately and jointly. The goal was to move from the empirical to the theoretical part.

5. Discussion

5.1. *The traditional business model of ESCOs*

AitherCO_2 is an energy services company with offices in Milan, London, Dakar, and San Francisco. With 10 years of experience in energy efficiency, AitherCO_2 has helped over 2,000 clients save more than US$700 million in energy costs. Over the years, AitherCO_2 has worked with a classic ESCo business model, such as the one described in Fig. 3.

As stated by Jacopo Visetti, co-founder of AitherCO_2 and EFFORCE, the classic approach of ESCo is a centralised trust-based model. Indeed, the contractual system of EPC requires parties to be

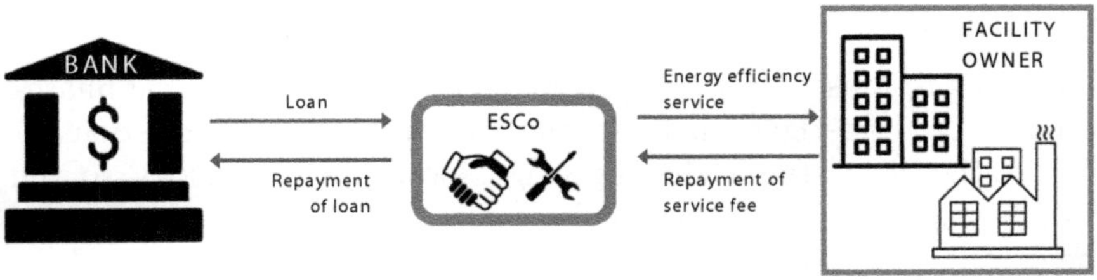

Fig. 3. The traditional model of an ESCo.
Source: Adapted from Schletz *et al.* (2020).

remunerated based on energy savings. However, it is difficult to estimate savings, and the system of tracking and estimation is centrally entrusted to ESCos.

As Visetti pointed out, there are many problems in the classical approach because the parties do not trust each other. The beneficiary company often claims to record lower energy savings than those reported by the ESCo, and at the same time, the lenders claim that the savings are higher than those reported by the ESCo.

To address these obstacles, AitherCO_2, like the other ESCos, had to engage the services of a third-party company to audit the data collected. The cost of the audit service fell on all three actors involved in the chain. The absence of trust between the parties and the centrality of data management thus generate a cost for all actors involved and a disincentive to the development of energy efficiency activities. In this context, EFFORCE was born.

5.2. *The blockchain business model of EFFORCE*

EFFORCE is a blockchain-based energy-saving trading platform, which allows people to participate in and benefit from worldwide energy efficiency projects. The platform brings together those who want to improve the energy efficiency of their buildings or industrial processes with a pool of contributors interested in being repaid in tokens representing the energy savings achieved.

Through its innovative technologies, the EFFORCE platform solves three main problems of the energy efficiency market: (1) the difficulty of connecting contributors and savers; (2) the size of the investments required; and (3) the type of financial return.

Operationally, the EFFORCE model involves the use of smart, Internet-connected meters that enable automatic detection and

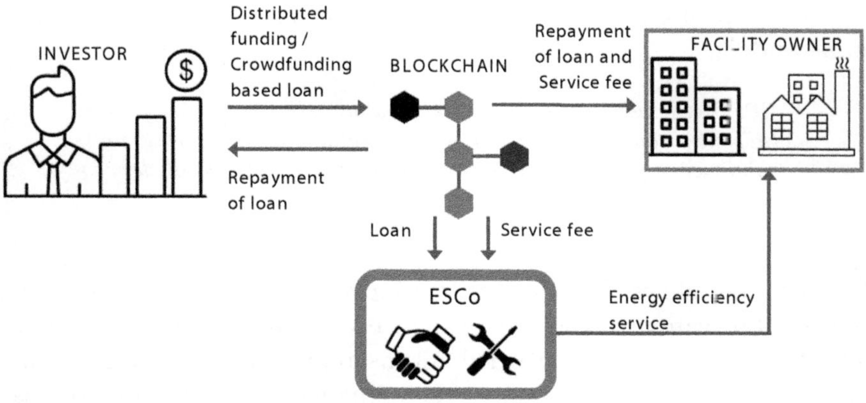

Fig. 4. Blockchain-based mode of operation of an ESCo.
Source: Adapted from Schletz *et al.* (2020).

reporting of energy consumption and, thus, savings. Data are automatically uploaded to a public blockchain so that all stakeholders can see them, and no one can change them independently. Moreover, in the EFFORCE model, EPCs (classic contracts) become smart contracts, called Energy Performance Smart Contracts. This implies that the agreements between the parties are registered on blockchain, so that the profits generated from the saved energy can be redistributed automatically between the parties. In this way, the ESCos' operational process has been revolutionised. From a centralised system, it has moved to a decentralised system as depicted in Fig. 4.

The new system is decentralised, and the absence of trust between parties has been replaced by an automatic data collection and analysis system. This makes it possible to eliminate the cost incurred by audit activity. The underlying technology system of the EFFORCE platform is based on integrating blockchain and the Internet of Things.

Data about beneficiaries' energy savings, validated and certified on blockchain, are thus integral and transparent. These data features mean that each contributor's energy savings can be tokenised and used both to offset energy consumption and to be traded.

EFFORCE's vision goes beyond just the operational benefit but aims to make energy efficiency activities as scalable as possible. Through the blockchain-based energy savings tokenisation system, new financing mechanisms for energy efficiency interventions can be enabled, allowing access to a global investor base, and no longer just large lenders.

> *EFFORCE will enable each Contributors to be an active participant in an E.S.C.o working with qualified counterparties to obtain energy savings to sell or use to reduce the cost of their energy bill.*
>
> EFFORCE, White Paper

Tokenisation allows the aggregation of investments by many medium and small private investors, who can directly finance energy efficiency activities. Investors are awarded tokens representing their share in the ESCo project, which equals their financial contribution to this project in question. In this way, each token holder can access coupon payments that are automatically transferred via smart contracts to token holders (Schletz *et al.*, 2020). EFFORCE tokens are ERC20 Utility Tokens based on the Ethereum blockchain and are named EFFORCE, but the token's symbol is WOZX in honour of Steve Wozniak, the co-founder of Apple, who is one of the co-founders of EFFORCE. There are a total of 1,000,000,000 WOZX tokens, and the new token will never be created.

5.3. *How the combination of new technologies is solving the problems of green investments*

The EFFORCE platform was built to change how energy savings are generated and redistributed globally. The tokenisation of energy savings provides a contractual mechanism between a company that wants to improve the efficiency of its processes and the community of people who want to invest in climate change initiatives. The innovative tokenisation model is organised as reward-based crowdfunding, where contributors are rewarded with free energy savings they can store, sell, or use to offset their energy consumption.

Each EFFORCE token holder will have priority access to energy-saving projects that will be listed on the platform, contributing to the spread of energy efficiency on a global scale. Each project will have a portfolio in which the number of KWh saved by that project will be accumulated. Each token will accumulate the KWh of energy savings achieved in this way. These savings come from efficiency improvement projects with high financial returns carried out by reliable industrial and commercial partners.

Three main actors benefit from the EFFORCE platform. First, through the EFFORCE platform, many **contributors** have access to the auction mechanism to purchase future savings generated by efficiency improvement projects and guaranteed by smart contracts.

Second, the platform enables the **savers** (namely, the owners of industries, transportation systems, buildings, and other energy systems) to benefit from efficiency improvement projects and to use part of the energy savings achieved in their business activities, thus reducing the need to purchase energy.

Last but not least, EFFORCE **provides** benefits to the consumers. Consumers are those who want to purchase energy savings generated by third parties to offset and eventually eliminate their electricity bills. The EFFORCE solution is based on a contractual mechanism between companies that want to improve the efficiency of their processes and energy consumers. So, through EFFORCE, energy end consumers can participate in tokenised energy savings, allowing energy savings to circulate among the savers and the consumers. In this way, all consumers can purchase energy savings and contribute to the global process of energy efficiency. With regard to those consumers willing to reduce their energy costs, EFFORCE "will implement a marketing campaign to reduce its disbursements and channel the interest of small and large buyers to the market for the purchase of energy savings of others" (EFFORCE, White Paper).

6. Implications and Future Research

After the COVID-19 pandemic, some studies have shown that technology adoption is influenced by the perception of the social, economic, and ecological benefits generated by new technologies (Passarelli *et al.*, 2023). Nowadays, energy efficiency is the main factor in reducing the energy sector's environmental impact Linares and Labandeira (2010). ESCos are gaining considerable interest in the energy sector as they include most energy efficiency activities (Linares *et al.*, 2009; Fang and Miller, 2013). They are companies that act as intermediaries between financial partners and public or private users that need investments to improve the energy efficiency of their facilities. As highlighted by the European Energy Efficiency Directive (2012/27/EU; EED), the value of ESCos is to unlock energy savings in the market by facilitating the interaction between financial partners and public or private users.

Their aim is perfectly in line with green investments. According to OCED, "green investments generally refer to low-carbon and climate-resilient investments made in companies, projects, and financial instruments that operate primarily in renewable energy, clean technology, environmental technology, or sustainability-related markets, as well as those investments that are climate change specific" (Inderst *et al.*, 2012).

However, the energy efficiency market is a complex financial system, and the main limitations related to the financial aspect concern the difficulty of connecting contributors and savers, the size of the required investments, and the type and time of financial return. These problems discourage ESCos from supporting small projects (Wellinghoff *et al.*, 2000).

Despite this, given the rising global attention towards fintech over the last few years, the recent explosion in the cryptocurrency and non-fungible token markets is revolutionising the financial sector by destroying old barriers and opening new growth horizons (Gomber *et al.*, 2017, 2018; Goldstein *et al.*, 2019; Chang *et al.*, 2020; Fosso Wamba, 2020). The adoption of blockchain technology and tokens can today represent a breakthrough in the scalability of ESCo activities, and, thus, in the financing of energy efficiency investments. In this chapter, we aimed to analyse how the combined adoption of some fintech technologies allows one to overcome financial barriers in energy efficiency investments.

The EFFORCE case study provides many implications, some representing opportunities for further research in the fintech industry. From the analysis of the EFFORCE case study, we learned that the investments allowing one to pursue energy efficiency are today epitomised by different magnitudes and scopes. Numerous actors are involved, each with their own set of interests that need to be addressed. The EFFORCE case study allows us to understand how using blockchain can satisfy the interests of a multitude of different actors. Moreover, it also suggests that some new takeaways — and future research — could guide investments in energy efficiency.

First, financing energy efficiency measures can be a complex set of financial and regulatory challenges, limiting the rate of growth. Innovative platforms, such as EFFORCE, create a seamless system to boost global energy efficiency, but global process regulation is required. Future research could investigate the role of governments in monitoring and addressing blockchain technologies related to energy efficiency. Second, EFFORCE is an example of an innovation broker that brings together ESCos, projects, and contributors through its multi-party ecosystem. However, this connection could create management problems if openness to innovation is not controlled (Ferrigno *et al.*, 2022a). Future research could investigate the role of individual stakeholders within the EFFORCE ecosystem to analyse barriers to and opportunities for innovation.

Third, through technologies like those developed by EFFORCE, the energy efficiency market becomes accessible to large and small investors, regardless of boundaries, who can then monetise transferable energy savings. However, for small investors, embracing these technologies may not be straightforward, leading to potential disincentives for their adoption due to the complexity involved (Cucino *et al.*, 2023a). Some studies show that the lack of experience and knowledge is a factor that discourages the adoption of new technologies (Passarelli *et al.*, 2023). Therefore, future research could investigate the adoption of the technology and the barriers to investment in the technology.

References

Allcott, H. and Greenstone. M. (2012). Is there an energy efficiency gap? *The Journal of Economic Perspectives*, 26(1), pp. 3–28.

Battaglia, M., Annesi, N., Calabrese, M., and Frey, M. (2020). Do agenda 2030 and Sustainable Development Goals act at local and operational levels? Evidence from a case study in a large energy company in Italy, *Business Strategy & Development*, 3(4), pp. 603–614.

Bertoldi, P. (2007). Latest development of energy service companies across Europe — A European ESCO Update.

Chen, Y. (2018). Blockchain tokens and the potential democratization of entrepreneurship and innovation, *Business Horizons*, 61(4), pp. 567–575.

Chesbrough, H. (2020). To recover faster from Covid-19, open up: Managerial implications from an open innovation perspective, *Industrial Marketing Management*, 88, pp. 410–413. doi.org/10.1016/j.indmarman.2020.04.010.

Cucino, V. and Ferrigno, G. (2023). AI technologies and hospital blood delivery in peripheral regions: Insights from Zipline International. In La Torre D., Appio F., Masri H., Lazzeri F., and Schiavone F. (Eds.), *Impact of AI in Business and Society: Opportunities and Challenges.* ISBN: 9781003304616.

Cucino, V., Ferrigno, G., and Piccaluga, A. (2021). Recognising opportunities during the crisis: A longitudinal analysis of Italian SMEs during COVID-19 crisis. In Castaldo S., Mocciaro Li Destri A., Penco L., and Ugolini M. (Eds.), *Electronic Conference Proceedings of Sinergie — Sima Management Conference Leveraging Intersections in Management Theory and Practice*, Palermo, 10–11 June 2021, University of Palermo, Fondazione CUEIM, pp. 37–41.

Cucino, V., Lungu, D., De Rosis, S., and Piccaluga, A. (2023a). Creating value from purpose-based innovation: Starting from frailty. *Journal of Social Entrepreneurship*, https://doi.org/10.1080/19420676.2023.2263768.

Cucino, V., Marullo, C., Annunziata, E., and Piccaluga, A. (2020). The "humane side" of entrepreneurship. An empirical investigation of startup with a social mission in Italy. In Castaldo S., Giuliani E., Frey M., and Ugolini M. (Eds.), Electronic Conference Proceedings of *Sinergie — SIMA 2020 Conference Grand Challenges: Companies and Universities Working for a Better Society*, Pisa, 7–8 September 2020, University of Pisa, Fondazione CUEIM, pp. 229–233. DOI 10.7433/SRECP.EA.2020.01.

Cucino, V., Marullo, C., Annunziata, E., and Piccaluga, A., (2023b). The human side of entrepreneurship: An empirical investigation on relationally embedded ties with stakeholders. *Management Research Review* https://doi.org/10.1108/MRR-08-2022-0593.

Dąbrowska, J., Almpanopoulou, A., Brem, A., Chesbrough, H., Cucino, V., Di Minin, A., Giones F., Hakala, H., Marullo, C., Mention, A., Mortara, L., Norskov, S., Oddo, C., and Ritala, P. (2022). Digital transformation, for better or worse: A critical multi-level research agenda, *R&D Management*, 52(5), pp. 930–954.

Dagnino, G. B. and Ferrigno, G. (2015). The strategic management of multipartner alliances: Uncovering the triadic alliance problem, in Das T. K. (ed.), *Managing Multipartner Strategic Alliances* (Charlotte, NC: Information Age Publishing), pp. 135–169.

De Giovanni, P. (2020). Blockchain and smart contracts in supply chain management: A game theoretic model, *International Journal of Production Economics*, 228(C), pp. 1–18.

Del Sarto, N., Ferrigno, G., Parida, V., and Di Minin, A. (2022). Do startups benefit from coworking spaces? An empirical analysis of accelerators' programs, *Review of Managerial Science*, 17, pp. 2471–2502.

Della Valle, N. and Bertoldi, P. (2022). Promoting energy efficiency: Barriers, societal needs and policies, *Frontiers in Energy Research*, 9(804091).

Di Minin, A., Ferrigno, G., and Zordan, A. (2019). Technological discontinuities and dominant designs: The case of ford, 1896–1914. In *Academy of Management Proceedings* (Vol. 2019, No. 1) (Briarcliff Manor, NY 10510: Academy of Management), p. 14659.

Di Silvestre, M. L., Gallo, P., Guerrero, J. M., Musca, R., Riva Sanseverino, E., Sciumè, G., Vásquez, J. C., and Zizzo, G. (2020). Blockchain for power systems: Current trends and future applications. *Renewable Sustainable Energy Review*, 119, 109585.

Dogan, T., Yang, Y., and Samaranayake, S. (2020) Urbano: A tool to promote active mobility modeling and amenity analysis in urban design, *Technology Architecture + Design*, 4(1), pp. 92–105.

EFFORCE (2018). White Paper. Available at: www.efforce.io/WP_ENG_V1.pdf?v=3.

European Commission (2016). A study on energy efficiency in enterprises: Energy audits and energy management systems. Available at: https://ec.europa.eu/energy/sites/ener/files/documents/EED-Art8-Implementation-Study_Task12_Report_FINAL-approved.pdf.

European Commission (2017). Digital transformation scoreboard 2017. Available at. https://ec.europa.eu/growth/tools-databases/dem/monitor/scoreboard.

Eyraud, L., Clements, B., and Wane, A. (2013). Green investment: Trends and determinants, *Energy Policy*, 60, pp. 852–865.

Fang, W. S. and Miller, S. M. (2013). The effect of ESCOs on carbon dioxide emissions, *Applied Economics*, 45(34), pp. 4796–4804.

Ferrigno, G. and Cucino, V. (2021). Innovating and transforming during COVID-19: Insights from Italian firms, *R&D Management*, 51(4), pp. 325–338.

Ferrigno, G., Del Sarto, N., Cucino, V., and Piccaluga, A. (2022a). Connecting organisational learning and open innovation research: An integrative framework and insights from case studies of strategic alliances, *The Learning Organization.* doi.org/10.1108/TLO-03-2021-0030.

Ferrigno, G., Zordan, A., and Di Minin, A. (2022b). The emergence of dominant design in the early automotive industry: An historical analysis of Ford's technological experimentation from 1896 to 1906, *Technology Analysis & Strategic Management*, pp. 1–12.

Feyen, E., Frost, J., Gambacorta, L., Natarajan, H., and Saal, M. (2021). Fintech and the digital transformation of financial services: Implications for market structure and public policy. BIS Papers, Bank for International Settlements, 117.

Fosso Wamba, S., Kamdjoug, J. R., Bawack, R. E., and Keogh J. G. (2020). Bitcoin, Blockchain and Fintech: A systematic review and case studies in the supply chain, *Production Planning & Control*, 31(2), pp. 115–142.

Foxon, T. J. and Bolton, R. (2016). Financing the civic energy sector: How financial institutions affect ownership models in germany and the United Kingdom. *Energy Research & Social Science*, 12, pp. 5–15.

Giraudet, L. G. (2020). Energy efficiency as a credence good: A review of informational barriers to energy savings in the building sector, *Energy Economics*, 87 (104698).

Goldstein, I., Jiang, W., and Karolyi, G. A. (2019). To FinTech and beyond. *The Review of Financial Studies*, 32(5), pp. 1647–1661.

Gomber, P., Koch, J. A., and Siering, M. (2017). Digital finance and FinTech: current research and future research directions, *Journal of Business Economy*, 87, pp. 537–580.

Gomber, P., Kauffman, R. J., Parker, C., and Weber, B. W. (2018) On the fintech revolution: Interpreting the forces of innovation, disruption, and transformation in financial services, *Journal of Management Information System*, 35, pp. 220–265.

Gouldson, A. N., Kerr, J., Millward-Hopkins, M. C., Freeman, C., Topi, and Sullivan, R. (2015). Innovative financing models for low carbon transitions: Exploring the case for revolving funds for domestic energy efficiency programmes, *Energy Policy*, 86, pp. 739–748.

Greening, L. A., Greene, D. L., and Difiglio, C. (2000). Energy efficiency and consumption — the rebound effect — A survey, *Energy Policy*, 28(6), pp. 389–401.

Gupta, P., Anand, S., and Gupta, H. (2017). Developing a roadmap to overcome barriers to energy efficiency in buildings using best worst method, *Sustainable Cities Society*, 31, pp. 244–259.

Hirst, E. and Brown, M. (1990). Closing the efficiency gap: Barriers to the efficient use of energy, *Resources, Conservation and Recycling*, 3(4).

Iansiti, M. and Lakhani, K. (2017). The truth about blockchain, *Harvard Business Review*, 95(1), pp. 118–127.

IEA (2021). Global energy review 2021. IEA, Paris. Available at: https://www.iea.org/reports/global-energy-review-2021.

Inderst, G., Kaminker, C., and Stewart, F. (2012). Defining and measuring green investments. Available at: https://ssrn.com/abstract=2742085, accessed on 17 june 2022.

Inglesi-Lotz, R. and Dogan, E. (2018). The role of renewable versus non-renewable energy to the level of CO_2 emissions a panel analysis of sub-Saharan Africa's Big 10 electricity generators, *Renewable Energy*, 123, pp. 36–43.

Jaffe, A. B. and Stavins, R. N. (1994). The energy-efficiency gap what does it mean? *Energy Policy, Markets for Energy Efficiency*, 22(10), pp. 804–810.

Kamran, R., Khan, N., and Sundarakani, B. (2021). Blockchain technology development and implementation for global logistics operations: A reference model perspective, *Journal of Global Operations and Strategic Sourcing*, 14(2), pp. 360–382.

Khatoon, A., Verma, P., Southernwood, J., Massey, B., and Corcoran, P. (2019). Blockchain in energy efficiency: Potential applications and benefits, *Energies*, 12(17), 3317.

Koesler, S., Swales, K., and Turner, K. (2016). International spillover and rebound effects from increased energy efficiency in Germany, *Energy Economics*, 54(C), pp. 444–452.

Lee, M. K., Painuly, J., Park, H., and Noh, J. (2003). Promoting energy efficiency financing and ESCOs in developing countries: Mechanisms and barriers, *Journal of Cleaner Production*, 11, pp. 659–665.

Lichtman, M. (2014). *Qualitative Research for the Social Sciences* (Thousand Oaks, CA: Sage).

Limaye, D. R. and Limaye, E. S. (2011). Scaling up energy efficiency: The case for a super ESCO, *Energy Efficiency*, 4, pp. 133–144.

Linares, P. and Labandeira, X. (2010). Energy efficency: Economics and policy, *Journal of Economic Surveys*, 24(3), pp. 573–592.

Linares, P., Santos, F. J., and Pérez-Arriaga, I. J. (2008). Scenarios for the evolution of the Spanish electricity sector: Is it on the right path towards sustainability? *Energy Policy*, 36(11), pp. 4057–4068.

Liù, L., Zhao, Z., Zhang, M., and Zhou, D. (2022). Green investment efficiency in the Chinese energy sector: Overinvestment or underinvestment? *Energy Policy*, 160, 112694.

Magalhaes, N. (2021). The green investment paradigm: another headlong rush, *Ecological Economics*, 190, 107209.

Marchi, B., Zanoni, S., Ferretti, I., and Zavanella, L. E. (2018). Stimulating investments in energy efficiency through supply chain integration, *Energies*, 11(4), 858.

Mielke, J. and Steudle, G. A. (2018). Green investment and coordination failure: An investors perspective, *Ecological Economics*, 150, pp. 88–95.

Molina, M., Kiker, P., and Nowak, S. (2016). The greatest energy story you haven't heard: How investing in energy efficiency changed the US power sector and gave us a tool to tackle climate change. ACEEE. Available at: https://www.aceee.org/sites/default/files/publications/researchreports/u1604.pdf.

Musibau, H. O., Adedoyin, F. F., and Shittu, W. O. (2021). A quantile analysis of energy efficiency, green investment, and energy innovation in most industrialised nations, *Environmental Science and Pollution Research*, 28, pp. 19473–19484.

Park, L., Lee, S., and Chang, H. A. (2018). Sustainable home energy prosumer-chain methodology with energy tags over the blockchain, *Sustainability*, 10, 658.

Passarelli M., Bongiorno G., Cucino V., and Cariola A., (2023). Adopting new technologies during the crisis: An empirical analysis of agricultural sector, *Technology Forecasting and Social Change*, 186 (Part A), p. 122106. doi.org/10.1016/j.techfore.2022.122106.

Patterson, M. G. (1996). What is energy efficiency? Concepts, indicators, and methodological issues, *Energy Policy*, 24, pp. 377–390.

Retallack, S., Johnson, A., Brunert, J., Rasoulinezhad, E., and Hesary, F. (2018). Energy efficiency finance programs: Best practices to leverage private green finance, ADBI Working Paper Series No. 877.

Row, J. and Moharab, E. (2014). Improving energy efficiency in Alberta's buildings: Best practices, key actors, and the role of sustainable energy organisations, Technical Report (Calgary: Pembina Institute).

Schletz, M., Cardoso, A., Prata Dias, G., and Salomo, S. (2020). How Can blockchain technology accelerate energy efficiency interventions? A use case comparison, *Energies*, 13(22), p. 5869.

Stede, J. (2017). Bridging the industrial energy efficiency gap. Assessing the evidence from the Italian white certificate scheme, *Energy Policy*, 104, pp. 112–123.

Stoffel, B. (2015). The concept of the energy efficiency index (EEI) for circulators and pump units, in Stoffel, B. (ed.), *Assessing the Energy Efficiency of Pumps and Pump Units* (Chapter 8) (Elsevier, Waltham, USA), pp. 95–127.

Suryono, R. R., Indra B., and Purwandari, B. (2020). Challenges and trends of financial technology (Fintech): A systematic literature review, *Information*, 11, p. 590.

Taghizadeh-Hesary, F., Yoshino, H., Abadi, M., Mohammadi, and Farboudmanesh, R. (2016). Response of macro variables of emerging and developed oil importers to oil price movements, *Journal of the Asia Pacific Economy*, 21(1), pp. 91–102.

Treiblmaier, H. (2018). The impact of the blockchain on the supply chain: A theory-based research framework and a call for action, *Supply Chain Management International Journal*, 23, pp. 545–559.

Tuominen, P., Forsström, J., and Honkatukia, J. (2013). Economic effects of energy efficiency improvements in the Finnish building stock, *Energy Policy*, 52(C), pp. 181–189.

Turner, K. and Hanley, N. (2011). Energy efficiency, rebound effects and the environmental Kuznets curve, *Energy Economics*, 33(5), pp. 709–720.

Yin, R. K. (2018). *Case Study Research and Applications: Design and Methods*, 6th edition. (Thousand Oaks, CA: Sage).

https://doi.org/10.1142/9781800614604_0013

Chapter 13

Banco Platform^{TM} by RABC Group and Its Green Fintech Innovations

Gao Phoebe (Fei)[*,‡], Annie Koh[†,§], and Kevin Ow Yong[*,¶]

[*]*Singapore Institute of Technology, Singapore*
[†]*Singapore Management University, Singapore*
[‡]*phoebe.gao@singaporetech.edu.sg*
[§]*anniekoh@smu.edu.sg*
[¶]*kevin.owyong@singaporetech.edu.sg*

Banco platform, which was launched by RABC Group, is a digital banking platform with a mission to align the transformation efforts of enterprises and financial institutions with innovative digital financing products. The company has recently collaborated with Savills (Singapore) Pte Ltd to digitise financing solutions in the property industry and provide more competitive financing options to suppliers and service providers, as well as enhance sustainability practices through accredited green financing options. This partnership is aligned with the initiatives of the Monetary Authority of Singapore (MAS) under the Green Finance Action Plan that was launched in 2019.

Keywords: Green finance; fintech; supply chain financing; sustainability

1. An Introduction to Banco Platform[a] and RABC Group

The Fourth Industrial Revolution ushered in a wave of innovation spanning changes to technology, industries, and societal patterns.

These innovations have been driven by increasing connectivity and smart automation, leading to new ways of doing things. For example, in the area of finance, heightened technological connectivity enables increasing seamless connectivity between banks, lenders, depositors, and customers.

Headquartered in Singapore with subsidiaries in China, Japan, and Indonesia, RABC Group was founded in 2018, which launched a neobank named "banco platform". Neobanks, sometimes referred to as "challenger banks", are fintech firms that offer apps, software, and other technologies to streamline mobile and online banking. They tend to be nimbler and more transparent than their mega-bank counterparts and aim to revolutionise various aspects of the banking experience.

Banco platform is a digital banking platform with a mission to align the transformation efforts of enterprises and financial institutions with innovative financing products. It aims to make financing simple, connected, and inclusive. As the world turns increasingly digital, it is imperative that successful companies stay relevant by being more agile, data driven, sustainable, and adopt an ecosystem-thinking mindset. Banco platform helps companies better manage their cash and working capital through new financing products and new technologies, and in the process, unlocking value and empowering the enterprises and financial institutions of the future. It recently raised US$6.7 million in a Series A funding, led by Japan-based leading financial group SBI Group, alongside investors Sumitomo Mitsui Banking Corporation (SMBC), R3, Savills, KZM & Company, and others.[b]

Banco platform provides digital financing solutions to micro, small, and medium enterprises (MSMEs). It increases accessibility to financing for MSMEs by creating new sector-based financing products in supply chain finance and green finance. It integrates alternative data from enterprise systems, customs, logistics providers, and government databases, and combined with AI and blockchain

[a] "Banco platform" is a registered trademark in Singapore by RABC Group.

[b] More details of banco's Series A funding can be found here: https://www.businessnewsasia.com/2022083052353777-singapore-fintech-startup-banco-raises-6-7m-in-series-a-funding/.

technologies, improves transparency, traceability, and enhanced risk management for fraud protection. Specifically, banco platform has two distinct offerings. That is, the company works with anchor corporates to offer relevant financing products to companies throughout its value chain. The platform also creates a way for MSMEs to get faster approval for financing based on a particular industry sector by utilising big data and credit analysis. Banco platform makes enterprise and financing more accessible and easier for all, by connecting companies, financial institutions, and stakeholders on a single platform. The platform delivers its solutions through the following modular approaches.

Firstly, there is the *banco manage* module, which serves to resolve payment delays by enabling a more efficient and digital process using a accounts payable/accounts receivable (AP/AR) automation and vendor management tool. This smart automation tool uses a four-step process. Initially, invoices are received from various vendors, with little or no manual entry required, to start the payment process. Approval workflows are customised based on existing company policies. The syncing process ensures that data from suppliers (e.g., invoices, purchase orders, delivery confirmation) are simultaneously synchronised between banco platform and the company's accounting software system. Finally, all activities including approvals are tracked and logged digitally on banco platform for easy referencing in relation to audit and compliance.

Secondly, there is the *banco finance* module. It serves to unlock cash for entire value chains with deep-tier supply chain finance, thereby providing suppliers with the flexibility to move towards another financing avenue. A traditional finance approach is 1-tier reverse factoring, which frees up cash flow by allowing enterprises to extend their payment terms to their suppliers while providing the option for their suppliers to get paid early. However, many MSMEs in the long-tail value chain do not have access to the same financing programmes as tier-one suppliers. But the direct suppliers of the anchor corporates are dependent on these smaller sub-suppliers that have been priced out of traditional trade financing.

Deep-tier supply chain finance goes one step beyond that. It allows MSMEs to leverage the higher credit standing of the larger corporate buyers for favourable financing terms. Utilising blockchain technology, Internet of Things (IoT) sensors, and smart application programming interfaces (APIs) allows financiers to lend to upstream suppliers with greater confidence, thereby keeping their supply chains connected. Deep-tier financing means that financiers and fintechs can fund not only the direct suppliers of the anchor corporate but also the entire supply chain. On banco platform, the financing arrangement can be funded by single or multiple financiers (syndicate).

Thirdly, the *banco green* module introduces green and sustainable finance to supply chain management. Incorporating supply chain finance with tailored sustainability assessment allows financial institutions to easily categorise companies based on an accredited sustainability index, to extend favourable green financing rates to companies that are eligible and score higher on the sustainability index. The solution provides real-time supply chain insights on sustainability based on GRI Reporting Standards. Incorporating sustainability elements into the supply chain also provides visibility and transparency for suppliers down the chain. It thus allows anchor corporates to account for sustainability in their evaluation of suppliers. Consequently, this will encourage and reward suppliers, especially MSMEs to adopt more sustainable activities or source for alternative sustainable materials.

2. An Introduction to Savills and Its Role in the Property Sector

Savills plc is a British real estate services company based in London. It is listed on the London Stock Exchange and is a constituent of the FTSE 250 Index. Founded in the UK in 1855, Savills is one of the world's leading property agents. It has extensive global connections, with more than 600 offices across the Americas, Europe, the Asia-Pacific, Africa, and the Middle East. Its scale has given it tremendous specialist and local knowledge, and it has provided best-in-class advice to individuals, businesses, and institutions to make better property decisions for over 160 years, from country cottages to city centre offices, agricultural land to new-build developments.

Savills (Singapore) Pte Ltd's headquarters is located at Raffles Place, the core financial and commercial hub in Singapore. It is a leading real estate advisor and provides the full spectrum of services including agency, planning, development, and consultancy, covering all aspects of residential and commercial markets. In terms of buying/selling and leasing/renting decisions, the company aims to build a trusted relationship with the client by providing relevant information using in-house sector-leading research to enable active participation in the negotiations, leading to the successful signing of property transactions.

Apart from property transactions, the company also engages in occupier services, to advise clients who occupy properties but are not in the property business. Hence, it is possible that a client can fully outsource its real estate functions to Savills. Alternatively, it can also perform the role of a coordinator of single or multiple service lines for occupier clients.

In terms of facility management, the company provides a wide range of specialised facility management and consulting services for property asset owners. Its facility management specialist services and solutions include the following types of work: addition and alteration (A&A) works; building and civil works; building defects and conditional survey; building management compliance; building operations management; car park operations and management; cleaning and janitorial services; energy, waste, and event management; facility management consulting; horticulture and landscaping; mechanical and electrical (M&E) systems; pest control management; security guard services; sustainability management; and tenancy, lease, and vendor contract administrations.

Its property management teams are able to cover all areas and asset types from large-scale shopping centres to residential to industrial portfolios, and a range of services from strata management to asset management.

Savills also provides project management services. It can serve as a project development and construction management specialist, providing a diverse range of allied services that are tailored to suit clients' particular project requirements. For each project, it endeavours to provide an end-to-end service to clients, covering every aspect of property development. Its specialist division of project managers is involved in the planning and implementation of large-scale property ventures, placing special emphasis on timely and budget-conscious solutions to its clients' needs.

Finally, Savills is also involved in providing valuation and advisory services. Its valuation specialists can undertake valuations either on a one-off or repeat basis. Its valuation services look across a number of sectors, including residential, commercial, leisure, retail, healthcare and hotels. To ensure that its valuations are current and market-facing, the valuation team works closely with the market research team. The teams also receive ancillary advice from their colleagues in the investment, planning, and development departments.

3. Literature Review

The objectives of the Paris Agreement and the United Nations Sustainable Development Goals (SDGs) include supply chain transparency, identity and financial inclusion, property rights, expansion of renewable energy, decentralisation of electrical power systems, carbon credit trading, and improved access to climate finance. Different parties are playing important roles to achieve the objective. The primary parties driving this effort include financial institutions, central banks, and other government regulators. Economically, the roles of financial institutions include allocating resources in the market. When there is growth and demand, financial institutions would invest resources into green finance, which will also naturally improve the fintech innovations that have the support of governments.

With the attention and resources on fintech, growth is substantial, with the first acceleration seen in 2015. Figure 1 shows the Google trends record for the keyword "Fintech". The Y-axis is the search interest relative to the highest point on the chart for the given region and time. The maximum value of the search interest is 100, which represents the peak popularity of the term. A minimum value of the search interest is 0, which implies that there was not enough data for this term. If the value of the interest is 50, it means that the interest is half compared to its peak popularity time point. The Google trend data we obtained are at a monthly frequency from January 2004 to May 2022.

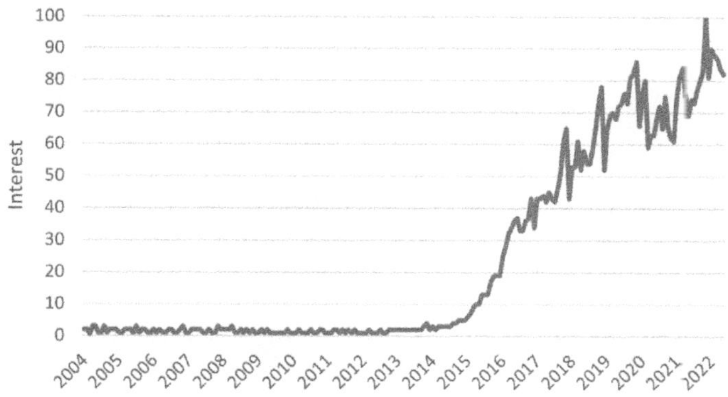

Fig. 1. Worldwide interest in "Fintech" since 2004.

With the increasing attention, a natural question for investors and stakeholders is how to value innovations, as one of the most important factors for investors is the value being created from these investments. In that aspect, researchers have collected data and run empirical tests to try to value these innovations.

3.1. *Fintech innovation value*

Chen *et al.* (2019) find that most fintech innovations yield substantial value to innovators, with blockchain being particularly valuable. In the financial sector, IoT, robo-advising, and blockchain are the most valuable innovation types. They found that innovations affect financial industries more negatively when they involve disruptive technologies from non-financial start-ups, but market leaders that invest heavily in their own innovation can avoid much of the negative value effect.

Lee *et al.* (2021) examine how the development of the fintech industry affects cost efficiency and the technology adopted for China's banking industry. They showed that state-owned commercial banks have the lowest cost efficiency and operate using inferior technology. There is a double beneficial effect as fintech innovations not only improve the cost efficiency of banks but also enhance the technology used by banks. Besides the financial benefits, fintech innovations could contribute to the environmental value of the society

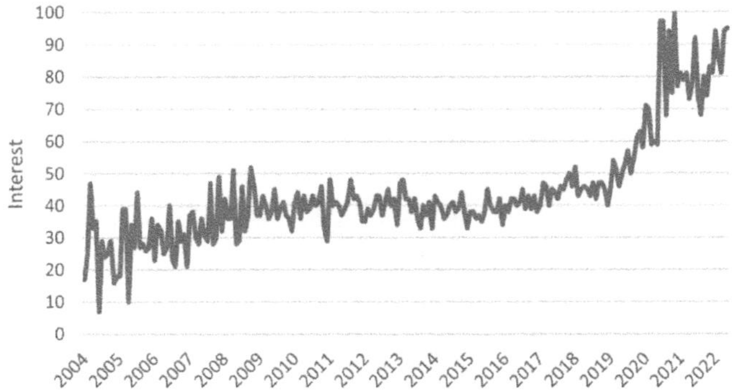

Fig. 2. Worldwide interest in "green finance" since 2004.

and thus lead to a new industry, i.e., green finance. Figure 2 shows the Google trends record for the keyword "green finance". Although the growth is not as dramatic as "fintech", we observe a significant increase in the interests of "green finance" in June 2020.

3.2. *Green finance*

Sachs *et al.* (2019) find that financial institutions show more interest in fossil fuel projects rather than in green projects, mainly due to risks associated with these new technologies and their relatively low rate of return. They propose to open a new file for green projects that provide environmental benefits through new financial instruments and new policies, such as green bonds, green banks, carbon market instruments, fiscal policy, green central banking, fintech, and community-based green funds, which are known as "green finance".

Volz (2017) examines the role of central banks in "greening" financial systems. The chapter suggests that central banks should have an impact on investment decisions and the creation and allocation of credit, including disclosure requirements, climate-related stress testing, and differentiation of reserve or capital requirements according to environmental impact. The chapter also discusses the risks of overstretching central banks' mandates and vesting too much power in unaccountable institutions as well as the division of labour between central banks and other institutions.

3.3. *Development of digital transformation in the fintech sector and green financing*

Nassiry (2018) discusses the development of fintech and the blockchain sectors from the point of view of the policymakers potential impact. At the early stage, fintech and blockchain have rapidly evolved to contribute to green finance and sustainable development. Schletz *et al.* (2020) evaluate the application of blockchain technology for energy efficiency use cases, including peer-to-peer energy trading, white certificate schemes, and energy service companies (ESCOs). When comparing the three cases, the application of blockchain technology requires different governance and system designs and the barriers could be overcome by timely policy action. The development of digital transformation not only depends on the nature of the business and project but also on the different policies by city and effective window.

He *et al.* (2020) document the effect evaluation of the degree of green development in smart cities based on economic transformation from 2013 to 2019. They find that green finance promotes the construction of smart cities and is effective, with an expected influence occurring nine months later. Financial technology has an opposite impact on the construction of smart cities, because the research and marketisation of financial technology are greater, and the cost is also higher, with an expected influence occurring in the next 14 months. While there could be a long wait, the effectiveness of the technology is expected to be positive in environmental protection and beneficial to society in the longer term.

Muganyi *et al.* (2021) show a significant reduction in industrial gas emissions from the evidence in China due to green finance data from 290 cities between 2011 and 2018. They encourage fintech companies to actively participate in environmental protection initiatives that promote green consumption with support from government policies. Vergara and Agudo (2021) argue that the achievement of the SDGs and implementation of the Paris Agreement will require significant new investments, from both financial institutions and regulatory bodies.

4. What is the Singapore Green Plan 2030?

The Singapore government launched the Singapore Green Plan 2030 on February 10, 2021, as a "whole-of-nation" movement to advance the national agenda on sustainable development. The plan, which is spearheaded by the Ministry of Education (MOE), the Ministry of National Development (MND), the Ministry of Sustainability and the Environment (MSE), the Ministry of Trade and Industry (MTI), and the Ministry of Transport (MOT), defines Singapore's green targets over the next 10 years.

The Green Plan also strengthens Singapore's commitments under the United Nation's 2030 Sustainable Development Agenda and the Paris Agreement. As depicted in the Infographic extracted from the https://www.greenplan.gov.sg website, the multi-agency effort has five pillars: City in Nature, Sustainable Living, Energy Reset, Green Economy, and Resilient Future. The Green Plan will influence all aspects of Singaporeans' lives, from the way we live to how we work and play.

Therefore, against the backdrop of the Green Plan, the key considerations for businesses are as follows:

- Serves as a catalyst for economy-wide action with pressure on businesses to be "green" and sustainable.
- Conscious integration of sustainability into the core of business practices across all sectors.
- Have a clear climate action plan and targets.
- Increase staff knowledge and understanding of the sustainability landscape.
- Tapping on government grants and incentives to transition into being greener.

As such, fintech companies like RABC will have an important role to play to help both SMEs and larger companies work together to achieve the targets set in accordance with the Singapore Green Plan 2030.

5. A Green Framework and a Strategic Partnership to Provide Digital Financing Solutions in the Property Sector

On March 29 2022, Savills (Singapore) Pte Ltd announced a strategic partnership with banco platform with the aim of digitising financing solutions in the property industry by focusing on improving accessibility and providing more financing options to suppliers and service providers, as well as enhancing sustainability practices through accredited green financing options.

By transforming payments through a digital process, banco platform simplifies issuance and payments between strata management, such as Management Corporation Strata Title (MCST) stakeholders, creating greater transparency, compliance, and governance for all parties. At the same time, banco platform and Savills will provide easy access to supply chain financing and early payment solutions to the many MSMEs in the sector, making cash and working capital management solutions more readily available at a lower cost, to a group which historically has found access to such solutions expensive and difficult to manage.

This partnership is also aligned with the Monetary Authority of Singapore's (MAS's) initiatives under the Green Finance Action Plan that was launched in 2019. Specifically, the Green Finance Action Plan encompasses Project Greenprint, which is a collection of initiatives that aim to harness technology and data to enable a more transparent, trusted, and efficient ecosystem to support green and sustainable finance.

Under Project Greenprint, MAS will partner with the industry to pilot four common utility platforms to address the financial sector's sustainability data needs. There will be a common disclosure portal for financial institutions and corporates to make reliable ESG disclosures. The portal will also enable conversion and comparability across different reporting frameworks as required under different jurisdictions and purposes. Companies can also use the portal as an internal ESG monitoring and management tool.

There will be a data orchestrator platform which serves to aggregate sustainability data from multiple data sources: major ESG data providers, utilities providers, the common disclosure portal, and other sectoral platforms. The platform will enable new data insights to be generated through data analytics to better support investment and financing decisions, and provide consent-based access to these sources.

There will also be an ESG registry that records and maintains the provenance of ESG certifications and data verified by certification bodies in different sectors. The aim of this portal is to facilitate trusted data flows between the financial sector and real economy sectors. Finally, there is a Greenprint Marketplace. This portal serves to connect green technology providers to investors, financial institutions, and companies to facilitate partnerships and investments. Together, these interoperable data platforms will aggregate new and existing sustainability data across multiple sectoral platforms and industry players, and enable the sharing of data across different stakeholders.

Given Singapore's aspirational "Green Plan 2030" and Deloitte's estimate that the property sector is responsible for 40% of global carbon emissions, there is a need for every aspect of the property management supply chain to work on reducing its carbon footprint. In creating a payment and financing gateway, this partnership will help create an ecosystem around "green financing" which will ultimately power the access of local businesses to supply chain financing to assist in reducing their carbon footprint. Sustainability can be introduced through the value chain where increasingly customers or investors are asking for assurance that their supply chain is going green. The use of digital approaches to supply chain finance is not just about providing immediate liquidity to MSMEs; it may also incentivise the suppliers to be more sustainable as it enables reporting on emissions and other sustainable practices to come further down the supply chain.

6. An Interview with Lincoln Yin, Co-Founder and CEO of Banco Platform, RABC Group

Question: Could you tell us more about yourself?

Lincoln Yin: I love finance and technology, making an impact and creating value in real industrial sectors. I started my first company at the age of 19. It was founded in 2011, a logistics and warehouse

Lincoln Yin, co-founder and CEO of banco platform, RABC Group.

software development company. I entered into the fintech sector in 2013, working with security brokers and exchanges. In 2018, we founded RABC Group in Singapore, which operates as a neobank that connects financial institutions and enterprises with inclusive and sustainable financing products — such as deep-tier supply chain financing and green finance — that were previously not widely adopted.

In 2017, I was one of the Chinese delegates of the G20 Young Entrepreneurs' Alliance. In addition, as a global shaper, part of the Global Shapers Community, an initiative of WEF, we look at how we can create more value for society. Due to business trips, I have opportunities to go to countries such as Israel and Bangladesh. I saw how technology can be used to solve problems and improve social welfare. It was also a great opportunity to meet many global leaders at the Davos summit, and they make me feel that I need to do something to create impact.

I believe strongly in the Japanese concept of ikigai. It is a concept that combines the terms iki, meaning "alive" or "life", and gai, meaning "benefit" or "worth". When combined, these terms mean that which gives your life worth, meaning, or purpose. It gives a person a sense of purpose and a reason for living. I like the fact that the work I do at RABC Group is meaningful and makes an impact.

Question: Could you tell us more about your company?

Lincoln Yin: Our company's mission is to make finance inclusive and green. Inclusive finance means that we are able to reach out to companies that have difficulties in securing loans and trade credit from traditional banks. We also like to develop products for green finance as it is sustainable and good for society. It also helps that there is a huge demand from the government for green and sustainable finance.

In 2018, with the belief that there would be huge demand in Southeast Asia for financing, keeping in mind the regional financing gap for underbanked or underfinanced SMEs, we decided to start the journey of RABC and headquartered in Singapore.

RABC Capital is the finance arm of RABC Group. It creates new financial products and solutions. Banco platform is the digital platform developed and operated by RABC Group. Banco actually means "bank" in Spanish. Under banco platform, we hope to transform different sectors with our innovative green fintech solutions.

Question: Why do you want to collaborate with Savills?

Lincoln Yin: Our company's strategy is to utilise a sector-by-sector approach. We have a financing solution for cleaning and security guard companies in Singapore that have difficulties in securing loans from traditional banks. We adopt this strategy because we believe that a sector-specific product will lead to better risk management for financiers like us and lower financing cost for the SMEs.

When we look at the property sector, I think it makes sense to partner with Savills because it is a major and established player in this sector and the company has been around for more than a century. Since my expertise is in the fintech and digital technology fields, I believe there are a lot of synergies, and both companies can leverage on each other's strengths and contribute to "greening of the sector".

Question: What are your future plans for the company?

Lincoln Yin: Since 2018, we have raised three rounds of funding from leading investors such as SBI Holdings, Marketnode (a joint venture between Singapore Exchange and Temasek), and Linear Capital, amounting to nearly US$10 million funding.

Our mission is to serve more underserved MSMEs with better digital financing products. We have a clear plan to break even and become self-profitable in the next 3 years, with a target to IPO in 3–5 years by creating real impact to benefit the MSMEs regionally.

Currently, our product is available in seven markets, including Singapore, Mainland China, and Hong Kong SAR. We hope to further expand our business presence into the rest of Southeast Asia.

7. The Green Pathway Ahead

The path towards being green and sustainable is no longer driven from top down through regulations, nor dictated just by the board. As consumers, society, and shareholders are increasingly demanding change, these environmental, social, and governance (ESG) mega trends are set to shape the business landscape. In addition, strong ESG performance creates a variety of competitive advantages. With rising expectations from different stakeholders, companies are integrating ESG into their business practices. Singapore has taken active steps to strengthen its commitment towards a sustainable future (e.g., Green Plan 2030 and Budget, 2022).[c]

Therefore, businesses are integrating sustainability strategies across their whole value chains. At some point, businesses will face the challenges of integrating sustainability into their operations. Key performance indicators (KPIs) and commitment are needed to ensure success. Both core operations and support services will play an important role. So, having a fintech start-up like RABC Group is both timely and a good opportunity to help companies, big and small, transform the different parts of their operations. The more a company digitalises its operations, the more transparent the processes are and the usage of paper is minimised. This ensures environmental sustainability, data governance, and electronic payments, with fraud prevention systems in place.

What Savills (Singapore) has done in partnership with banco platform is socially responsible as security and cleaning companies can now pay their workers at weekly frequencies and are no longer tied to just month-end payrolls. It is indeed an amazing case of collaborating for the greater good, and in many ways that is what the literature had emphasised in the value creation of fintech innovations. Indeed, the way forward to build back better for society and the economy in the post-COVID recovery period is through being digital, being inclusive, and being green and sustainable. Let us go out there and forge a green pathway forward across companies, countries, and communities.

[c]Details of the Budget 2022 can be found here: https://www.gov.sg/article/budget-2022.

References

Chen, M. A., Wu, Q., and Yang, B. (2019). How valuable is FinTech innovation? *The Review of Financial Studies*, 32(5), pp. 2062–2106.

He, Z., Liu, Z., Wu, H., Gu, X., Zhao, Y., and Yue, X. (2020). Research on the impact of green finance and fintech in smart city. *Complexity*, 2020.

Lee, C. C., Li, X., Yu, C. H., and Zhao, J. (2021). Does fintech innovation improve bank efficiency? Evidence from China's banking industry, *International Review of Economics & Finance*, 74, pp. 468–483.

Muganyi, T., Yan, L., and Sun, H. P. (2021). Green finance, fintech and environmental protection: Evidence from China, *Environmental Science and Ecotechnology*, 7, p. 100107.

Nassiry, D. (2019). The role of fintech in unlocking green finance, in *Handbook of Green Finance* (Singapore: Springer), pp. 315–336.

Sachs, J. D., Woo, W. T., Yoshino, N., and Taghizadeh-Hesary, F. (2019). Importance of green finance for achieving sustainable development goals and energy security, in *Handbook of Green Finance* (Singapore: Springer), pp. 3–12.

Sangwan, V., Prakash, P., and Singh, S. (2020). Financial technology: A review of extant literature, *Studies in Economics and Finance*, 37(1), pp. 71–88.

Schletz, M., Cardoso, A., Prata Dias, G., and Salomo, S. (2020). How can blockchain technology accelerate energy efficiency interventions? A use case comparison. *Energies*, 13(22), p. 5869.

Vergara, C. C. and Agudo, L. F. (2021). Fintech and sustainability: Do they affect each other? *Sustainability*, 13(13), pp. 1–19.

Volz, U. (2017). On the role of central banks in enhancing green finance, UN Environment Inquiry Working Paper 17/01.

https://doi.org/10.1142/9781800614604_bmatter

Index

D

Milton Keynes UK
Ingram Content Group UK Ltd.
UKHW051934270624
444726UK00029B/57

9 781800 614598